Fighting Stars

GLOBAL EAST ASIAN SCREEN CULTURES

Global East Asian Screen Cultures showcases cutting-edge scholarship on East Asian screen practices and cultures in local, regional and global contexts. Titles in the series take 'East Asia' as a focus, a nodal point interlinked with other regional screen cultures, and a method to reorient the global screen-culture cartography. The series embraces screen studies focused on geographic East Asia as well as work exploring mobility, migration and hybridity as mediated through screen media production, textuality and reception that traverse East Asia and its diasporas.

We welcome proposals that intersect with these areas of investigation. Please direct initial enquiries to series editors Mark Gallagher and Yiman Wang at doctorgalaga@gmail.com and yw3@ucsc.edu.

Fighting Stars

Stardom and Reception
in Hong Kong
Martial Arts Cinema

Edited by
Kyle Barrowman

BLOOMSBURY ACADEMIC
LONDON • NEW YORK • OXFORD • NEW DELHI • SYDNEY

BLOOMSBURY ACADEMIC
Bloomsbury Publishing Plc
50 Bedford Square, London, WC1B 3DP, UK
1385 Broadway, New York, NY 10018, USA
29 Earlsfort Terrace, Dublin 2, Ireland

BLOOMSBURY, BLOOMSBURY ACADEMIC and the Diana logo are trademarks
of Bloomsbury Publishing Plc

First published in Great Britain 2024

Copyright © Kyle Barrowman, 2024

Kyle Barrowman has asserted his right under the Copyright, Designs and
Patents Act, 1988, to be identified as Editor of this work.

Cover images: The One (2001) Directed by James Wong, Shown: Jet Li (© Columbia
Pictures / Photofest); The Big Brawl (1980) Directed by Robert Clouse, Shown: Jackie Chan
(© Warner Bros. / Photofest); Crouching Tiger, Hidden Dragon (2000) Directed by Ang Lee,
Shown: Michelle Yeoh (© Columbia Pictures / Mary Evans); Ip Man (2008) Directed by
Wilson Yip, Shown: Donnie Yen (© Golden Harvest / Mary Evans)

Bloomsbury Publishing Plc does not have any control over, or responsibility for,
any third-party websites referred to or in this book. All internet addresses given
in this book were correct at the time of going to press. The author and publisher
regret any inconvenience caused if addresses have changed or sites have ceased
to exist, but can accept no responsibility for any such changes.

A catalogue record for this book is available from the British Library.

Library of Congress Cataloging-in-Publication Data

ISBN: HB: 978-1-3503-6575-9
        PB: 978-1-3503-6574-2
        ePDF: 978-1-3503-6577-3
        eBook: 978-1-3503-6576-6

Series: Global East Asian Screen Cultures

Typeset by RefineCatch Limited, Bungay, Suffolk
Printed and bound in Great Britain

To find out more about our authors and books visit www.bloomsbury.com
and sign up for our newsletters.

Contents

List of Figures vii

Notes on Contributors xi

Introduction: Fighting (for) Star Studies 1
Kyle Barrowman

1 Kwan Tak-hing: Pioneer of Kung Fu Cinema 19
Wayne Wong

2 Bruce Lee: Effective and Affective Action Techniques 41
Paul Bowman

3 Angela Mao: Lady Kung Fu in Search of International Markets 61
Man-Fung Yip

4 Kara Hui: From Young Auntie to Mother Figure 77
Leung Wing-Fai

5 Gordon Liu: Shaolin Hero 93
Eric Pellerin

6 Sammo Hung: The Kung Fu Comic's Sublime Body 109
Luke White

7 Jackie Chan: A Stunting Star's Industrial Legacy 127
Lauren Steimer

8 Michelle Yeoh: Combating Gender 143
   Kyle Barrowman

9 Cynthia Rothrock: Fame, Style, and the Video Star 163
   Meaghan Morris

10 Jet Li: A Career in Three Acts 187
   Andy Willis

11 Zhang Ziyi: An Alternative Female Action Stardom and
   the Logic of Indeterminacy 201
   Dorothy Wai Sim Lau

12 Donnie Yen: Authenticity, Nationalism, and the Bruce Lee
   Legacy 219
   Leon Hunt

Index 235

Figures

1   The first global fighting star: Bruce Lee's star on the Hollywood
    Walk of Fame. © Alamy.   1
2   Rare promotional photo showcasing Kwan Tak-hing's physique
    in the late 1940s. © Kwan Tak-Hing (KTH) Estate.
    All rights reserved.   19
3   Kwan Tak-hing's demonstration of Chinese martial arts
    forms in the late 1940s. © Kwan Tak-Hing (KTH) Estate.
    All rights reserved.   25
4   A promotional shot of Kwan Tak-hing demonstrating
    Shaolin tiger form in the late 1960s. © Kwan Tak-Hing (KTH)
    Estate. All rights reserved.   32
5   Bruce Lee in his iconic sidekick pose. *Enter the Dragon* directed
    by Robert Clouse. © Warner Bros. 1973. All rights reserved.   41
6   Bruce Lee (Mike Moh) throwing a flying sidekick at
    Cliff Booth (Brad Pitt). *Once Upon a Time . . . in Hollywood*
    directed by Quentin Tarantino. © Columbia Pictures 2019.
    All rights reserved.   45
7   Bruce Lee landing his famous sidekick on Bob Wall.
    Enter the Dragon directed by Robert Clouse. © Warner Bros.
    1973. All rights reserved.   48
8   A powerful high kick from Angela Mao. *Hapkido* directed by
    Huang Feng. © Golden Harvest 1972. All rights reserved.   61
9   Angela Mao using a pigtail knocker as a weapon. *Hapkido*
    directed by Huang Feng. © Golden Harvest 1972.
    All rights reserved.   66
10 Angela Mao with George Lazenby. *The Shrine of Ultimate
    Bliss* directed by Huang Feng. © Golden Harvest 1974.
    All rights reserved.   68
11 Kara Hui in the midst of battle. *My Young Auntie* directed
    by Lau Kar-leung. © Shaw Brothers Studio 1981.
    All rights reserved.   77

12   The stoic and protective mother. *At the End of Daybreak*
      directed by Ho Yuhang. © Paperheart Limited 2009.
      All rights reserved.   88
13   The menacing 13th Madam. *Dragon* directed by
      Peter Chan. © We Pictures 2011. All rights reserved.   89
14   Gordon Liu in fighting form. *The 36th Chamber of Shaolin*
      directed by Lau Kar-leung. © Shaw Brothers Studio 1978.
      All rights reserved.   93
15   Sammo Hung as the "Fat Dragon." *Enter the Fat Dragon*
      directed by Sammo Hung. © Fung Ming Motion
      Picture Co. 1978. All rights reserved.   109
16   Ah Lung (Sammo Hung) tries on a pair of sunglasses
      in hopes of looking like Bruce Lee. *Enter the Fat Dragon*
      directed by Sammo Hung. © Fung Ming Motion
      Picture Co. 1978. All rights reserved.   117
17   Dragon vs Dragon: Ah Lung squares up to Tseng Siu-lung
      (Tony Leung Siu-hung) for a battle of the Bruce Lee clones.
      Enter the Fat Dragon directed by Sammo Hung.
      © Fung Ming Motion Picture Co. 1978. All rights reserved.   119
18   Jackie Chan hanging out in Hollywood. *Rush Hour* directed
      by Brett Ratner. © New Line Cinema 1998. All rights reserved. 127
19   Yim Wing Chun (Michelle Yeoh) invents a new martial art
      and a new model of womanhood. *Wing Chun* directed
      by Yuen Woo-ping. © Century Pacific 1994. All rights reserved. 143
20   Despite being officers of the law, Senior Inspectors Ng
      (Michelle Yeoh) and Morris (Cynthia Rothrock) learn the
      painful lesson that some men are above the law.
      Yes, Madam! directed by Corey Yuen. © D&B Films 1985.
      All rights reserved.   149
21   Wing Chun (Michelle Yeoh), Pok-to (Donnie Yen), and the
      persistence of gender trouble. *Wing Chun* directed by
      Yuen Woo-ping. © Century Pacific 1994. All rights reserved.   155
22   Cynthia Rothrock in her fighting stance. *Lady Dragon*
      directed by David Worth. © Rapi Films/Cinematic
      Collection 1992. All rights reserved.   163
23   Cynthia Rothrock in her competition days.
      © Cynthia Rothrock. All rights reserved.   169
24   Cynthia Rothrock showcasing her fighting ferocity.
      Righting Wrongs directed by Corey Yuen.
      © Golden Harvest 1986. All rights reserved.   173
25   Jet Li prepares for battle. *Fist of Legend* directed by
      Gordon Chan. © Golden Harvest 1994. All rights reserved.   187

26   Zhang Ziyi avenging her father. *The Grandmaster* directed
       by Wong Kar-wai. © Annapurna Pictures 2013.
       All rights reserved.   201
27   Ip Man (Donnie Yen) defends the tradition of Chinese
       martial arts from Gunnery Sergeant Barton Geddes
       (Scott Adkins). *Ip Man 4: The Finale* directed by Wilson Yip.
       © Mandarin Motion Pictures 2019. All rights reserved.   219
28   Former martial arts champion Hahou Mo (Donnie Yen)
       outlines his fighting philosophy. *Kung Fu Jungle* directed by
       Teddy Chan. © Emperor Motion Pictures 2014. All rights reserved.   229

Notes on Contributors

Kyle Barrowman is a media and cinema studies lecturer at DePaul University, USA. He received his PhD from Cardiff University. He has published widely in and between film studies and philosophy, on subjects ranging from authorship, genre theory, and camera movement to skepticism, perfectionism, and ordinary language philosophy.

Paul Bowman is professor of cultural studies at Cardiff University, UK. He is author of many books on diverse issues in film, media, and cultural studies, including numerous studies of Bruce Lee, cultural theory, and different aspects of martial arts in media, culture, and everyday life. He is founder and director of the Martial Arts Studies Research Network and founding co-editor of the journal *Martial Arts Studies*.

Leon Hunt is a Senior Lecturer in Film and TV Studies at Brunel University, UK. His books include *British Low Culture: From Safari Suits to Sexploitation* (1998), *Kung Fu Cult Masters: From Bruce Lee to Crouching Tiger* (2003), *Cult British TV Comedy: From Reeves and Mortimer to Psychoville* (2013), and *Mario Bava: The Artisan as Italian Horror Auteur* (2022), and he is the co-editor of *East Asian Cinemas: Exploring Transnational Connections on Film* (2008) and *Screening the Undead: Vampires and Zombies in Film and Television* (2014).

Dorothy Wai Sim Lau is an Associate Professor at the Academy of Film, Hong Kong Baptist University, HK. Her research interests include stardom, celebrity, fandom, Asian cinema, and digital culture. Her publications appear in journals such as *positions: asia critique*, *Continuum*, *Journal of Chinese Cinemas*, and several edited volumes. Lau is the author of *Chinese Stardom in Participatory Cyberculture* (2019), *Reorienting Chinese Stars in Global Polyphonic Networks: Voice, Ethnicity, Power* (2021), and *Celebrity Activism and Philanthropy in Asia: Toward a Cosmopolitical Imaginary* (2024). She is now writing her fourth monograph, *East Asian Auteurs, Cinephilia and the Media Platform Era* (working title, under contract with Edinburgh University Press).

Meaghan Morris is Professor of Gender and Cultural Studies, the University of Sydney, AUS, and former Chair Professor of Cultural Studies in Lingnan University, HK. Her research focuses on popular historiographies and the changing rhetorics of place, locality, and nation in globalizing conditions. Her books include *Too Soon Too Late: History in Popular Culture* (1998) and *Identity Anecdotes: Translation and Media Culture* (2006). She co-edited *Hong Kong Connections: Transnational Imagination in Action Cinema* (2005) with Siu Leung Li and Stephen Chan Ching-kiu, and her essays on martial arts cinema appear in anthologies and journals including *Inter-Asia Cultural Studies*. A Fellow of the Australian Academy of the Humanities and the Hong Kong Academy of the Humanities, Meaghan is currently writing a book on kung fu cinema in Hong Kong since 1997 with Stephen Chan Ching-kiu.

Eric Pellerin is an Assistant Professor and the Electronic Resources Librarian at Medgar Evers College, City University of New York, USA. His research interests include genre theory, authorship in film, and Hong Kong cinema. He is the author of "Kung Fu Fandom: B-Boys and the Grindhouse Distribution of Kung Fu Films" in *The Oxford Handbook of Hip Hop Dance Studies* (2022) edited by Mary Fogarty and Imani Kai Johnson.

Lauren Steimer is Associate Professor of Media Arts and Film and Media Studies at the University of South Carolina, USA, and Director of the Film and Media Studies Program. Her book *Experts in Action: Transnational Hong Kong-style Stunt Work and Performance* (Duke University Press, 2021) traces a distinct, embodied history of transnational exchange by identifying and defining unique forms of expert performance common to contemporary globalized action film and television genres.

Luke White is Senior Lecturer in Fine Art and Visual Culture at Middlesex University, London, UK. His research focuses on Hong Kong cinema and the global visual cultures of the martial arts. He is author of the books *Legacies of the Drunken Master: Politics of the Body in Hong Kong Kung Fu Comedy Films* (2020) and *Fighting without Fighting: Kung Fu Cinema's Journey to the West* (2022).

Andy Willis is Reader in Film Studies at the University of Salford, UK, and Senior Visiting Curator for Film at Home, Manchester, UK. He is a co-author of *The Cinema of Alex de la Iglesia* (2007) and the editor of *Film Stars: Hollywood and Beyond* (2004). He is also the co-editor of *Defining Cult Movies* (2003), *Spanish Popular Cinema* (2004), *East Asian Film Stars* (2014), and *Chinese Cinemas: International Perspectives* (2016).

Leung Wing-Fai is Senior Lecturer in Culture, Media and Creative Industries at King's College London, UK. Her research focuses on East Asian film and media, gender and sexual identities, creative labour, and anti-Asian racism. Her monographs include *Multimedia Stardom in Hong Kong: Image, Performance and Identity* (2014). She has co-edited *East Asian Cinemas* (2008), *East Asian Film Stars* (2014), and a special issue on Chinese film industries for the *Journal of Chinese Cinemas* (2019). Her monograph *Migration and Identity in British East and Southeast Asian Cinema* (Routledge) was published in 2023.

Wayne Wong is a lecturer in East Asian Studies at the University of Sheffield, UK. His research focuses on the politics, aesthetics, and philosophy of global martial arts and action cinema. He has published in peer-reviewed journals and edited volumes such as *Asian Cinema*, *Global Media and China*, *Journal of Contemporary Chinese Art*, *Archiv Orientální*, *Martial Arts Studies*, *Afro-Futurism in Black Panther*, and *The Worlds of John Wick*. He is currently an editor of the *Martial Arts Studies* journal.

Man-Fung Yip is Associate Professor of Film and Media Studies at the University of Oklahoma, USA. He is the author of *Martial Arts Cinema and Hong Kong Modernity: Aesthetics, Representation, Circulation* (Hong Kong University Press, 2017) and co-editor of *The Cold War and Asian Cinema* (Routledge, 2020) and *American and Chinese-Language Cinemas: Examining Cultural Flows* (Routledge, 2014). His publications have also appeared in *Cinema Journal*, *Cinema e Storia*, and various edited volumes.

Introduction
Fighting (for) Star Studies

Kyle Barrowman

Figure 1 The first global fighting star: Bruce Lee's star on the Hollywood Walk of Fame. © Alamy.

At a provocative point in *The World Viewed*, Stanley Cavell takes a detour from his reflections on the ontology of film to reflect on the peculiarity of film stardom. What, exactly, *is* a "star," and what if anything distinguishes performers who are *stars* from performers who are (merely) *actors*? In his attempt to think through the curious phenomenon of film stardom, Cavell postulates the following:

> An exemplary screen performance is one in which, at a time, a star is born. After *The Maltese Falcon* we know [Humphrey Bogart as] a new star . . . His presence in [*The Maltese Falcon*] is who he is, not merely in the sense in which a photograph of an event is that event; but in the sense that if [this film] did not exist, Bogart would not exist, the name "Bogart" would not mean what it does . . . But it is complicated. A full development of all this would require us to place such facts as these: Humphrey Bogart was a man, and he appeared in movies both before and after the ones that created "Bogart." Some of them did not create a new star (say, the stable groom in *Dark Victory*) . . . but [still] are related to that [star] and may enter into our later experience [of his films]. And Humphrey Bogart was both an accomplished actor and a vivid subject for a camera. Some people are, just as some people are both good pitchers and good hitters; but there are so few that it is surprising that the word "actor" keeps on being used in place of the more beautiful and more accurate word "star"; the stars are only to gaze at, after the fact, and their actions divine our projects.[1]

Despite clearly identifying many of the facts that must be placed by scholars interested in film stars, Cavell is seldom mentioned in relation to "star studies." Indeed, in a strange short-circuit of the history of writing on film, and of classical film theory in particular, most monographs and edited collections devoted to stars/stardom date the beginning of the field of star studies to the 1979 publication of Richard Dyer's *Stars*.[2] To be sure, *Stars*—and its "sequel," *Heavenly Bodies*[3]—provided the vast majority of contemporary scholars with the theoretical foundation on which they built their own influential investigations.[4] However, it is worth noting that our fascination with stars/stardom is by no means a recent development. From almost the instant that film became a narrative art— that is, from the moment that films started to tell stories with characters played by recognizable performers who appeared in film after film—viewers and critics alike have found themselves ensorcelled by the stars. Over time, our language may have become more sophisticated, as we began to discuss star "texts" and "images" and "personas," and as we shifted from exploring the textual vicissitudes of stardom to the extratextual aspects of reception, but the fundamental mysteries of stardom and the enduring appeal of stars have been essential elements of the cinema almost since its invention, hence the preponderance of ruminations on stars from the silent era through to the digital age.

For one example of an early engagement with stars/stardom from the classical film theory canon, the Hungarian poet and scholar Béla Balázs wrote insightfully on such early film stars as Charlie Chaplin and Greta Garbo. Beginning from the premise that "the hero, the paragon, the model . . . is an indispensable element in the poetry of all races and peoples, from the ancient epics to the modern film," Balázs contended that this was "a manifestation of the natural selection of the best, of the instinctive urge towards improvement,"[5] and he saw film stars as the new "lyrical poets whose medium" was not the written word, but rather, "the body, the facial expression, and gesture."[6] But even this, Balázs knew, only partly explains the nature of stardom. For, in the case of Charlie Chaplin, Balázs acknowledged that "there are very many interesting and attractive people in the world," so why did he become such an enormous star?[7] Likewise, in the case of Greta Garbo, Balázs acknowledged that "there are so many perfectly beautiful women," so, again, why did she become such an enormous star?[8] Neither Chaplin's ability to "express [his] own personality with complete intensity"[9] nor "the harmony of Garbo's lines"[10] could in and of themselves "have ensured such a unique privileged position" for them as film stars.[11] Rather, it was the strange alchemy of face, body, character, story, time, and medium—that which allowed Chaplin to convey on the screen "something that lived in all of [us] as a secret feeling, urge, or desire, some unconscious thought, something that far transcends the limits of personal charm or artistic performance" and which allowed Garbo to embody "a beauty which is in opposition to the world of today"—that guaranteed these stars a place in the hearts of millions.[12]

For another example of an early consideration of stars/stardom, the renowned French film critic André Bazin keenly articulated the enduring power of such stars as Chaplin[13] and Jean Gabin.[14] In so doing, Bazin not only offered brilliant insights about the stars themselves, identifying aspects of character and performance with respect to Chaplin and Gabin with the same sort of analytical incisiveness and articulating them with the same sort of poetic power as Balázs, but he was moved to broader observations vis-à-vis the sense of "destiny" about Gabin, whose unique screen identity brought Bazin to the realization that "the film star is not just an actor . . . but a hero of legend or tragedy" who embodies "a destiny with which [filmmakers] must comply" or else the "spell" between star and spectator "will be broken."[15] To Bazin's mind, in the case of Gabin, there was one "text" adherence to which was essential to the spell that he cast on viewers: in each and every film, Gabin's character must come to "a violent end that has the appearance, more or less, of suicide,"[16] otherwise the viewer who "swallows many affronts would undoubtedly feel that they were being taken for a ride." Just as Chaplin's iconic Tramp character is always kicked around by life, only to dust himself off and make his way back out into the hostile world with an eager smile on his face, so Gabin's tragic heroes are always thwarted in their ambitions, brought down by their own fatal flaws, yet still worthy of admiration for the way that they raged against the dying of the light. Bazin even combined industry facts with philosophical investigation, noting how, "before the war, it is said, Gabin insisted before signing any film contract that the story include one of those explosive scenes of anger at which he excels" and wondering if this was the "whim of a star," the "ham clinging to his little touch of bravura," or if this was Gabin's astute intuition that "to deprive himself of [such scenes] would betray his character" as much as it would betray his audience.[17] If it is not possible to answer this question—that is, if it is not possible to determine how much of stardom is luck, chance, coincidence, etc., versus how much of it is responsiveness, planning, construction, etc.—Bazin nevertheless thought it essential to determine the contours of a particular star text so as to distinguish between the true and the false, the genuine and the artificial, the extraordinary and the ordinary in each encounter with each star.

For a final example of an important early consideration of stars/stardom, the German journalist and cultural critic Siegfried Kracauer included remarks in his monumental theorization of film on the different "types" of screen performers, distinguishing between "the non-actor," "the professional actor," and "the Hollywood star." On the latter, Kracauer not only identified stars as commodities— he noted the way that Hollywood, "in institutionalizing stars," essentially "found a way of tapping natural attractiveness as if it were oil," and he described the Hollywood star system's primary function as one of "economic expediency"— but he ruminated more philosophically on the nature of stardom, wondering why one actor becomes a star while others do not, ultimately postulating that it is evidently "something about the gait of the star," about their look, their manner of speech, the way that they carry themselves, etc., that "ingratiates itself so deeply with the masses of moviegoers that they want to see [them] again and again." Echoing Bazin, Kracauer described stardom as something magical or mystical (if not dangerously bewitching), observing how "the spell [a star] casts over the audience cannot be explained unless one assumes that [their] screen appearance satisfies widespread desires," while, echoing Balázs, Kracauer commented on how a star "affects the audience not just because of [their] fitness for this or that role but for being, or seeming to be, a particular kind of person," one who "exists independently of any part" and "in a universe outside the cinema which the audience believes to be reality or wishfully substitutes for it."[18]

In sum, the major historical, critical, and philosophical coordinates for such a field as star studies—the vicissitudes of stardom, the mechanics of the Hollywood star system, the nature of spectatorial identification with/desire for stars, etc.— had already been plotted long before the publication of *Stars*, while additional coordinates have been plotted in recent years which have indicated how much work remains to be done in the field. Undoubtedly the most important recent innovation in star studies is the conscious efforts on the part of scholars to conduct investigations beyond the familiar boundaries of Hollywood. This is not to deny the insightfulness of, say, Andrew Britton's analysis of Katharine Hepburn within the context of classical Hollywood cinema,[19] or the assiduousness of Dave Saunders' analysis of Arnold Schwarzenegger against the backdrop of American culture;[20] rather, it is merely to signal the analytical value in conducting similar such investigations of, for promising examples, an Indian star like Aamir Khan within the context of Bollywood cinema, or a Latin American star like Cantinflas against the backdrop of Mexican culture. Star studies scholarship has been moving in this direction rapidly in recent years, as evidenced by such recent publications as Andrea Bandhauer and Michelle Royer's 2015 collection *Stars in World Cinema*, which features chapters on stars from/stardom in such countries as India, Nigeria, Egypt, Brazil, China, Mexico, and Iran;[21] Sabrina Qiong Yu and Guy Austin's 2017 collection *Revisiting Star Studies*,[22] which features chapters in which contributors are intent not on "conforming to the conventional association of the star with glamor and success,"[23] on "reinforcing the binary of the mainstream and the marginalized,"[24] or on "assum[ing] all [international] stardoms are just mimicry or variants of Hollywood stardom, sometimes deviating from but ultimately conforming to the mechanisms of Hollywood stardom,"[25] but rather, on "expand[ing] the notion of stardom to include the less glamorous, more troubling elements such as the ageing star, the 'crip' star, the porn star, and so on,"[26] as well as on "shak[ing] the seemingly unshakeable Hollywood-centric approach to film stardom";[27] and many of the entries in Bloomsbury's "Film Stars" series, including but not limited to those on such international stars as Madhuri Dixit,[28] Hanna Schygulla,[29] Tony Leung,[30] and Carmen Miranda.[31]

Amidst this shift in star studies away from Hollywood-centric investigations, arguably the most popular arena has been that of Asian cinema. Three important recent collections—Mary Farquhar and Yingjin Zhang's 2014 collection *Chinese Film Stars*,[32] Leung Wing-Fai and Andy Willis' 2014 collection *East Asian Film Stars*,[33] and Jonathan Driskell's 2022 collection *Film Stardom in Southeast Asia*[34]—provided scholars with opportunities to write about such stars as Anna May Wong, Brigitte Lin, Chow Yun-fat, Leslie Cheung, Maggie Cheung, Joan Chen, P. Ramlee, Win Oo, and Jeeja Yanin. Strangely, however, even though most such collections allow a chapter or two for action icons like Bruce Lee and Jackie Chan, at no point in the history of star studies—not even in recent years as scholars have started to consciously look beyond Hollywood to international stars and star systems—has anyone sought to explore the popular and influential realm of Hong Kong martial arts cinema. This is curious for a number of reasons. For one thing, the stars of Hong Kong martial arts cinema have not only proven to be among the most popular stars locally, from Kwan Tak-hing and Bruce Lee to Michelle Yeoh and Zhang Ziyi, but also among the most recognizable film stars globally. For another thing, the evolution of Hong Kong martial arts cinema, from the 1960s and the rise of Shaw Brothers and Golden Harvest studios through the 1990s and the pre- and post-handover films of Tsui Hark and Jet Li, highlights similarities to and differences from the Hollywood studio era and its star system which promise fascinating insights into both eras and industries. As star studies has picked up steam within film studies, and as scholars have begun scanning the globe for interesting stars and star systems, the question on my mind has long been: why has Hong Kong martial arts cinema not been an integral part of such scholarship?

Having spent a good amount of time researching and writing on action films generally and martial arts films specifically, a few possible answers spring to my mind.[35] First and foremost, it must be acknowledged that there is still a regrettable streak of snobbery that runs through the discipline of film studies. Scholars would much rather talk about canonized Hollywood stars or seek out hidden gems in international art cinemas than they would the popular stars of an action genre like Hong Kong martial arts cinema. The action film more broadly has long been the black sheep of the film studies family, and while the rare study of action icons like Yvonne Tasker's *Spectacular Bodies*[36] can gain admittance in the disciplinary canon, this is the exception rather than the rule. To wit, in *A Companion to Hong Kong Cinema*, a popular sentiment is expressed by Mirana May Szeto and Yun-chung Chen as they lament the fact that "Hong Kong cinema achieve[d] its extraordinary transnational reach" courtesy of "the kung fu/martial arts genre that Hollywood ha[d] chosen to globalize" and fetishize, alleging that this "triumph is also [a] curse" inasmuch as "Hong Kong cinema achieve[d] global visibility [by] being stigmatized as a kung fu/action cinema."[37] On the one hand, there is a palpable sense of embarrassment at the fact that, of all that Hong Kong cinema has to offer, it is the "stigmatized" kung fu film for which it has become most famous, and, on the other hand, there is also a sense of wanting to put distance between Hong Kong and Hollywood, thus necessitating a disavowal of the Hollywood-sanctioned genre of martial arts cinema. For both aesthetic and nationalist reasons, a large number of scholars (if not the majority) have considered Hong Kong martial arts cinema a bad or ersatz film object, which has not inspired scholars to seek it out as a possible object of academic inquiry.

Fortunately, there has emerged a large group of scholars in recent years who are keen to challenge the biases and the taste hierarchies of academic writing on film and who have made tremendous strides in the serious study of Hong Kong martial arts cinema. In addition to important early work by such figures as Bey Logan,[38] Stephen Teo,[39] and David Bordwell,[40] there have been a number of scholars—most of whom have authored chapters in this volume—who have paved the way for a major intervention in the academic study of stars vis-à-vis Hong Kong martial arts cinema. In the first "wave," there was Leon Hunt, whose *Kung Fu Cult Masters* provided insightful analyses of Bruce Lee, Jackie Chan, Angela Mao, and Jet Li—of their films and of the unique nature of their respective stardom;[41] there was also Mark Gallagher, whose *Action Figures* provided one of the most rigorous explorations of Jackie Chan's star text and which demonstrated the fecundity of studying a Hong Kong star against the backdrops of Chinese culture on the one hand and the martial arts genre on the other;[42] and there was Paul Bowman, whose studies of Bruce Lee showcased the enormous quantity of analytical riches contained in the Bruce Lee star text and whose mining of these riches—with approaches from film studies and cultural studies, and with emphasis placed equally on the textual constructions of Lee's films and on the extratextual reception of Lee past and present, locally and globally—provides a map for subsequent scholars to follow in their own investigations of myriad other stars.[43] Since these groundbreaking efforts, a plethora of scholars have followed suit, from Man-Fung Yip[44] and Luke White,[45] who have provided comprehensive investigations of Hong Kong martial arts cinema and its stars, to Lauren Steimer[46] and Dorothy Wai Sim Lau,[47] who have followed Hong Kong martial arts cinema stars from off the screen through industries and fan cultures.

Given the long overdue—and encouragingly robust—interest at present in Hong Kong martial arts cinema, it seemed high time for there to be a volume such as this which could contribute to the fields of film studies, cultural studies, and of course star studies. The first of its kind, *Fighting Stars: Stardom and Reception in Hong Kong Martial Arts Cinema* gives pride of place to the genre of martial arts cinema as not merely the most popular and most financially successful, but also the richest and the most historically, culturally, and cinematically fascinating realm of Chinese cinema, which realm has produced the most complex, challenging, and inspiring stars in the history of Asian cinema. From the first Cantonese kung fu films in the 1940s and 1950s which chronicled the exploits of Wong Fei-hung and which starred the legendary Kwan Tak-hing, through the explosive films of the 1960s–80s which introduced the world to such enduring stars as Bruce Lee, Angela Mao, Kara Hui, Gordon Liu, Sammo Hung, and Jackie Chan and which precipitated the global Kung Fu Craze, and up to the contemporary martial arts actioners that have featured the likes of such innovative icons as Michelle Yeoh, Cynthia Rothrock, Jet Li, Zhang Ziyi, and Donnie Yen, *Fighting Stars* brings together the leading scholars of action and martial arts cinema in order to conduct the first comprehensive study of the stars of Hong Kong martial arts cinema. Ordered chronologically in an effort to trace the evolution of art, industry, and culture, the chapters in this volume are each devoted to a single star, and they each provide at once a historical sketch of the star's emergence as well as a critical analysis of their place in film history and their impact on the industries and cultures of Hong Kong and beyond. While many of the chapters do cast their scholarly gaze beyond the strict confines of Hong Kong cinema and culture, as many of the stars included in this volume have had careers that have taken them beyond Hong Kong to other Asian industries/markets and even in some cases to international industries/markets from France and the UK to the US, the focus is on Hong Kong as the primary site of emergence for the genre and its stars.

In Chapter 1, "Kwan Tak-hing: Pioneer of Kung Fu Cinema," Wayne Wong opens the volume with an in-depth analysis of the first martial arts cinema star, Kwan Tak-hing. Wong argues that the early Wong Fei-hung films in which Kwan starred, with the series beginning in 1949 with *The Story of Wong Fei-hung: Part I* and continuing for three decades with nearly a hundred installments featuring Kwan, were not only the films that introduced the world to kung fu on film but were also the films that "gave birth" to the genre and "set its basic conventions." It is Wong's contention that Kwan's stardom, and in particular the ease with which he was able to take on the mythical role of Wong Fei-hung, is understandable with reference to his "dual-track career in Cantonese opera and cinema." While the kung fu comedians of the 1970s and 1980s like Sammo Hung, Jackie Chan, and Yuen Biao brought attention and prestige to Chinese opera training, it was Kwan who showcased in his work as Wong Fei-hung the importance of synthesizing combative skill and genuine acting ability. However, Wong demonstrates that the key ingredient in Kwan's stardom, which was also his own interpretation of Wong Fei-hung as a cinematic icon, was his embodiment of the virtues of the "Confucian gentleman" and his positioning as a "guardian of traditional Chinese culture."

In Chapter 2, "Bruce Lee: Effective and Affective Action Techniques," Paul Bowman investigates the various strands—textual, intertextual, and extratextual—that contribute to people's reception of Bruce Lee not just as a martial arts star but more importantly as a "real" fighter. Pushing on discourses of "reality" in and around martial arts cinema, Bowman approaches Lee obliquely, from the perspective of Quentin Tarantino's recent—and controversial—fictional depiction of Lee in his *Once Upon a Time . . . in Hollywood* (2019). On the one hand, Bowman is interested in understanding one of the most complex facets of the Bruce Lee persona, namely, his status as a legitimate martial artist with skills that extended beyond fight choreography to actual combat. Thus, he considers the ways (and the reasons why) "film is often distinguished from reality" while at the same time insisting that "it cannot ultimately be divorced from it." On the other hand, Bowman is interested in understanding not merely Lee's stardom, but more specifically the way that he has been received by fans, scholars, and martial artists over the years. Thus, he considers the "effective and affective" use throughout Lee's career of the sidekick, one of the quintessential martial arts techniques and one which has been almost as thoroughly identified with Bruce Lee as have his fighting cries and his use of nunchaku. In following these different avenues, Bowman has occasion to think through people's investments in certain "images" of Bruce Lee, controversies surrounding (real-world versus cinematic) violence, and the differences (if any) between Bruce Lee as captured in home movie footage training and Bruce Lee as captured in fiction films fighting in an effort to appreciate the revolutionary, paradigm-shifting "sense event" that was Bruce Lee's arrival on the world cinema stage.

In Chapter 3, "Angela Mao: Lady Kung Fu in Search of International Markets," Man-Fung Yip provides a snapshot of the career of the first female kung fu star, Angela Mao, and the way that she and her films were marketed and exhibited by Golden Harvest. Acknowledging the fact that scholars who have shown an interest in Hong Kong martial arts cinema's women warriors "have typically focused on the cultural politics of gender representation," Yip sets his analytical sights on "the ways in which Mao's films and her star image are intertwined with the larger context of Golden Harvest's concerted efforts toward internationalization." In addition to being cast as Bruce Lee's sister in his Hollywood-Hong Kong co-production *Enter the Dragon* (1973), Mao was often positioned as "the female Bruce Lee." As such, with Lee's untimely death, Golden Harvest saw in Mao the perfect star to continue their push into other markets. On the one hand, Mao took Lee's place in *The Shrine of Ultimate Bliss* (1974), a film which was "originally envisioned as Lee's follow-up" to *Enter the Dragon* and in which he was meant to join forces with "Japanese martial arts star Sonny Chiba" and "one-time James Bond George Lazenby." On the other hand, Mao's training in Korean martial arts put her in a strong position to appeal to other Asian markets, hence her appearances in such films as *Hapkido* (1972) and *When Taekwondo Strikes* (1973) as well as her appearances in films shot on-location in places like Thailand (*The Tournament* [1974]) and Nepal (*The Himalayan* [1976]). For as often as scholars have focused exclusively on the Hollywood-Hong Kong connection, Yip's analysis of Mao's marketing showcases the scope of Golden Harvest's plans for their stars and films and also encourages a reorientation of scholarly focus not just on English-Chinese connections but also on the various Asian connections from Hong Kong to other Asian markets.

In Chapter 4, "Kara Hui: From Young Auntie to Mother Figure," Leung Wing-Fai shines a scholarly light on one of the lesser known but enormously popular martial arts stars of the Shaw Brothers era, Kara Hui. Beginning her career at Shaw Brothers in 1977 and then winning her first Hong Kong Film Award a few years later for her work in *My Young Auntie* (1981), Hui is a fascinating case study as an action icon who earned her acting stripes and received both popular and critical acclaim for her film work. Added to which, unlike the seemingly "forever young" stars like Bruce Lee and Angela Mao, Hui has continued to make her marks on Hong Kong cinema playing older women and mother figures, many of which roles have earned her additional acting honors. Through well-researched and insightful analysis, Leung identifies key markers of Hong Kong action stardom—for instance, the myriad injuries that Hui has sustained throughout her career, marking her as an "authentic" martial arts star despite starting her career with dance training—while also broadening our understanding of Hong Kong cinema stardom to encompass an appreciation of the way that "stardom in Hong

Kong reflects the changing identity and consciousness of the city." As Leung maintains, to the extent that the "distinctive careers of the 1970s and 1980s generations of stars" were predicated on the stars' "skills training and endurance," it is precisely their status as martial arts stars that has "contributed to their revered status." In his consideration of warrior women in Hong Kong martial arts cinema, Bey Logan observed that "nearly every fighting female [had] been cast in a non-action role at one time or another," citing as examples Michelle Yeoh in *Easy Money* (1987), Moon Lee in *Mr. Vampire* (1985), Yukari Ôshima in *Lover's Tear* (1992), and Cynthia Khan in *The Gods Must Be Funny in China* (1992), the latter also featuring Cheng Pei-pei.[48] Kara Hui is unique insofar as she quickly established credibility as an action heroine and a character actor, and far from representing deviations from or failures compared to her martial arts roles, her longevity and versatility as an actress can be attributed, Leung demonstrates, to her emergence as a martial arts star and her equal dedication to martial arts and to the craft of acting.

In Chapter 5, "Gordon Liu: Shaolin Hero," Eric Pellerin analyzes the powerful currency of Gordon Liu's star image as the quintessential cinematic Shaolin martial artist. Orienting his study with reference to the original Hong Kong poster for Liu's most famous film, *The 36th Chamber of Shaolin* (1978), in which Liu can be seen in a Hung Gar kung fu pose, Pellerin argues that there are two related components—that of Liu's "orthodox kung fu lineage," which lineage connects him not merely to his "godbrother" Lau Kar-leung, director of *The 36th Chamber of Shaolin* and many of Liu's other Shaw Brothers classics, but also to the historical Wong Fei-hung, and that of the frequency with which he played specifically Shaolin heroes—that contribute to the creation of Liu's star text. With respect to the first component, that of Liu's genuine kung fu skill, Pellerin assiduously chronicles Liu's early days being a fan of Kwan Tak-hing's Wong Fei-hung films and dreaming of learning martial arts and being a hero like him to his later days as an aspiring film actor training to fulfill his quasi-Bazinian destiny and one day play Wong Fei-hung himself. With respect to the second component, that of Liu's image as a specifically Shaolin hero, Pellerin explores the connections between Lau's films, with Lau himself having worked with Kwan on the original Wong Fei-hung films, and his reimagined films with Liu taking the mantle of the famous folk hero. It is in Lau's reimagining of Wong Fei-hung, and by extension his preoccupation with historical kung fu sagas, that the "established style and motifs" of Liu's star text would coalesce, positioning him as one of the most recognizable and successful stars in the immediate post-Bruce Lee era.

In Chapter 6, "Sammo Hung: The Kung Fu Comic's Sublime Body," Luke White provides a distinctive look at one of the most successful and enduring martial arts cinema icons in Hong Kong's illustrious history, Sammo Hung. Though Hung was an accomplished director and an important producer throughout his career, it is his starring roles that White focuses on in his chapter, and he undertakes in particular to establish the uniqueness of Hung's star image given that, "rather than a youthfully athletic, built body such as that of Bruce Lee or Jackie Chan, what made Hung an iconic figure was the seeming contrast between his rotund frame and his prodigious speed, agility, flexibility, and strength." Juxtaposing Bruce Lee's image as "the little dragon" with his own image as "the fat dragon," Hung's persona is knowingly playful and sagacious. Alongside audience and market concerns, however, White charts Hung's rise through the Hong Kong cinema ranks as he worked in different capacities on films in different genres, from choreographing such classic King Hu *wuxia* films as *The Fate of Lee Khan* (1973) and *The Valiant Ones* (1975) to creating slapstick sequences in such comedies as the Hui brothers film *Private Eyes* (1976), on the one hand, and from playing imposing antagonists opposite the heroic figures played by Angela Mao in *Hapkido* and Bruce Lee in *Enter the Dragon* to playing lovable heroes in his own films *Iron-Fisted Monk* (1977) and *Enter the Fat Dragon* (1978), on the other. Most provocatively, White demonstrates the way that "Hung developed a comic world of dog-eat-dog competition" which was "borrowed from the modern-day Hui Brothers comedies" but transposed by Hung "back into a southern-Chinese rural past located somewhere towards the end of the nineteenth and the start of the twentieth centuries," and he argues that "the cynicism with which Hung's characters seek to get one over" on others can be interpreted as a reflection of "the economic reality of laissez-faire capitalism in 1970s Hong Kong." In such a context, then, Hung can be said to have "developed for himself a comic persona in equal part hapless everyman and cunning trickster," at once a Chaplinian tramp who always takes it on the chin and a Cantinflas-esque rascal who can give as good as he gets provided he gets the opportunity, but with a physicality that anchors his persona in a body indicative, White persuasively argues, of a Bakhtinian "non-ideal carnival aesthetic" which embraces a certain "corporeal excess" very much at the heart of kung fu comedies thanks to the enduring influence of Sammo Hung.

In Chapter 7, "Jackie Chan: A Stunting Star's Industrial Legacy," Lauren Steimer takes a fresh look at the career of Jackie Chan. Rather than focus on his image on the screen or his persona in the press, Steimer provides new insights by going behind-the-scenes and analyzing Chan's legacy as a stunt worker. Starting out in the Hong Kong film industry, Chan's ability to work between Hong Kong and Hollywood not only helped him to grow his own star, but, as Steimer insightfully chronicles, it also initiated a paradigm shift in Hollywood stunt work. Steimer begins with the provocative argument that, while star studies often emphasize "the unique character or discursive formations that define individual stars," it is nevertheless the case that a star's "identity and reception are also defined by the divisions of labor and regulatory structures underpinning the transnational media industries in which they work." Given this, Steimer does not allow Chan's star image on the screen to cast a spell over her. Instead, she soberly breaks down the labor involved in the production of the image of Jackie Chan as the supreme screen daredevil, specifically the working conditions and habits to which Chan became accustomed in the Hong Kong film industry and how his Hollywood work compared. At once a fascinating portrait of the two stunt working industries and a novel approach to one of the most beloved Hong Kong martial arts stars, Steimer positions Jackie Chan between two national cinemas and two eras of stunt work, convincingly arguing for Chan's importance in the emphasis that Hollywood has placed on stunt work and fight coordinators and the importance of his Hollywood and Hong Kong films like *Battle Creek Brawl* (1980) and *Police Story* (1985) to such contemporary films as *The Matrix* (1999) and *Birds of Prey* (2020).

In Chapter 8, "Michelle Yeoh: Combating Gender," I strive to contextualize the international superstardom of Michelle Yeoh—whose star has never shined brighter than it is shining today, thanks to such massive hits as *Crazy Rich Asians* (2018), *Shang-Chi and the Legend of the Ten Rings* (2021), and *Everything Everywhere All at Once* (2022)—with respect to her early work in such Hong Kong martial arts films as *Yes, Madam!* (1985) and *Wing Chun* (1994). Inspired by Andrew Britton's study of Katharine Hepburn, in which Britton admirably refused to reduce Hepburn to one character type or to force her career into one clear teleology, preferring instead to segment Hepburn's career in order to better understand and appreciate the historical specificity of her work at distinct points in her career, I distinguish between distinct *phases* or *periods* in Yeoh's career, and I focus in particular on the first phase of her career from *Yes, Madam!* to *The Stunt Woman* (1996). It is my contention in this chapter that the Michelle Yeoh star text can best be understood "with reference to a conception of *combating gender*." As I argue, "Yeoh's characters represent challenges to conventional notions of what a woman is/should be" and "the frequency with which she played such characters in her films created a star persona that was so *femininely* powerful that she challenged the conventions of action cinema and effectively redefined the woman warrior archetype." Moreover, in an effort to understand the connective threads between her first starring vehicle, *Yes, Madam!*, and her most recent starring vehicle, *Everything Everywhere All at Once*, I strive to indicate the ways in which the latter film can be understood as responsive to her four decades as an international action icon, effectively synthesizing the various strands that have fed into her star text between phases, between industries, between cultures, and between time periods.

In Chapter 9, "Cynthia Rothrock: Fame, Style, and the Video Star," Meaghan Morris offers a remarkably nuanced and innovative analysis of the long and varied career of American martial arts champion and Hong Kong film star Cynthia Rothrock. As Morris points out early in her chapter, "if Western critics tend to exaggerate the freedom that women enjoyed to play action leads in Hong Kong after the late 1960s 'masculinization' of its martial arts cinema," what is perhaps even more problematic is the tendency to "under-estimate the force of racial exclusiveness in [Hong Kong] cinema's social imaginaries." It is no small feat the way that Rothrock emerged as the only white martial artist to shift from playing villains to heroes; as Morris explains, Rothrock was not only the first white woman to co-star in a Hong Kong feature—alongside Michelle Yeoh in *Yes, Madam!* as a Scotland Yard investigator—nor was she merely the first white person to headline a Hong Kong film—as an American FBI agent in *The Blonde Fury* (1989)—she also impressively enjoyed "relative longevity as a pan-Asian film personality," starring in fourteen films between 1985 and 2000. But more than just her on-screen presence, Morris interrogates the mechanisms of stardom which allowed her to initially achieve film stardom as "Law Fu Lok" in Hong Kong in the 1980s, which saw her shift to the American direct-to-video market as Cynthia Rothrock in the 1990s, and which in more recent years has included yet another shift to a "cyber-based phase of stardom" resultant from her "exuberant participation in social media platforms and on-line sites." Starting her career in an era of theatrical release followed by VHS release and continuing her career all the way up to the present age of Facebook pages and podcasts, Rothrock is anomalous in more ways than one, and Morris' chapter enumerates several of the key components that have come together to shape Rothrock's multifaceted star text.

In Chapter 10, "Jet Li: A Career in Three Acts," Andy Willis continues the methodological trend of segmenting stars' careers. Willis begins his chapter by making the crucial point that, because stars' images are not fixed, "those who are able to sustain a career as a star across a number of decades often have certain phases that reflect their popularity, their geographical transitions, and, as that career progresses, their aging," on the basis of which he proceeds to analyze the career of Jet Li through the "three major phases" of his career: first, his initial rise to stardom in Hong Kong martial arts cinema in the 1990s; second, his transition to international productions in the US and France in the late 1990s and 2000s; and third, his return to East Asia and his popularity in mainland China blockbusters of the twenty-first century. By following Li's career so closely, and always attuned to the shifting industries and cultures, Willis captures both the trajectory of Li's career, which is unique among Hong Kong martial arts stars for its flexibility and resilience given the sheer number of industrial, national, and genre boundaries it crossed, and the evolutions of Hollywood and Hong Kong cinema. From Li's centrality to pre-handover Hong Kong martial arts cinema as the inheritor of the Wong Fei-hung mantle in *Once Upon a Time in China* (1991), through his arrival in Hollywood and his importance to the "hip hop kung fu" cycle of films including *Romeo Must Die* (2000) and *Cradle 2 the Grave* (2003), up to his roles in such mainland blockbusters as *Hero* (2005) and *Fearless* (2006), Willis situates Li against the shifting backdrops of the American and Chinese film industries and cultures while also historically contextualizing his film roles with respect to the evolutions of Hollywood and Hong Kong action films.

In Chapter 11, "Zhang Ziyi: An Alternative Female Action Stardom and the Logic of Indeterminacy," Dorothy Wai Sim Lau charts the intriguing journey of Zhang Ziyi through the genres of romantic melodrama and *wuxia* and the industries of Hong Kong cinema and Hollywood. To begin, Lau contextualizes Zhang's ascent to martial arts superstardom on the strength of her performances in such contemporary classics as *Crouching Tiger, Hidden Dragon* and *The Grandmaster*, but she quickly makes the provocative claim that, despite her martial arts star "credentials," which are traded on even in her non-combat roles in such films as *2046* (2004) and *Sophie's Revenge* (2009), Zhang's stardom cannot be "categorized and appraised under the rubrics of martial arts stardom in any conventional sense." First, as Lau argues, the extent to which Zhang's martial artistry in her films is technologically mediated thanks to wirework and CGI makes it difficult to sustain a reading of her film work on the basis of "body-focused choreography and the physical prowess of representing and interpreting the female fighter identity." Second, Lau maintains that the way that Zhang is positioned in her martial arts roles is distinct from such earlier women warriors as Cheng Pei-pei, Angela Mao, and Michelle Yeoh. For, in the cases of the latter women warriors, they are "acclaimed for their hard-fighting image and knight-errantry," which "highlight[s] their capacity to compete with their male counterparts" and which by extension creates the image of a warrior, whereas, in the case of Zhang Ziyi, filmmakers like Ang Lee and Wong Kar-wai have used her differently to where her "martial arts presence" is both "romanticized and virtualized" in a manner unprecedented in the genre.

Lastly, in Chapter 12, "Donnie Yen: Authenticity, Nationalism, and the Bruce Lee Legacy," Leon Hunt brings this volume to a close with a consideration of the career of Donnie Yen, the most recent major Hong Kong martial arts star to emerge and whose star is still shining very brightly over the film world. In a way that nicely connects the present to the past and joins together the many cinematic and cultural threads weaved throughout the previous chapters, Hunt analyzes Yen's films against the shifting backdrops of Hong Kong cinema and culture on the one hand and Chinese politics on the other, arguing that Yen is a "controversial figure" who can shift from Hong Kong and Hollywood but whose position as a major Chinese star is precarious given the tensions between Hong Kong and mainland China. Tracing Yen's rise to stardom after years of playing supporting characters and villains, Hunt demonstrates the key ways that Yen established his stardom on a foundation of "authenticity" related to the influential films of Bruce Lee, whose realistic style of choreography would come to inform Yen's own fight sequences in such films as *Kill Zone* (2005) and *Flashpoint* (2006), before pivoting to a more "nationalistic" position upon "re-embedding" himself in Chinese culture, first by playing the newly minted folk hero Ip Man in a series of films that harken back to Kwan Tak-hing's patriotic turn as Wong Fei-hung and Jet Li's revival of the famous figure in an explicitly pre-handover context, and then by renouncing his American citizenship and proclaiming his undying commitment to, as expressed in a title dedication in *Kung Fu Jungle* (2014), "the fine tradition of Hong Kong action cinema." Despite consciously positioning himself in these ways and striving to create a legacy in line with those of such predecessors as Bruce Lee, Jackie Chan, and Jet Li, Yen's reception has shifted so significantly over the years that his is a fascinating case study in both stardom and reception, thus making his case a fitting final chapter to close out this volume.

Taken together, it is my hope that the chapters in this volume highlight the incredible richness of this fine tradition of Hong Kong cinema while at the same time doing justice to the endlessly fascinating careers of its brightest stars. In one of the earliest efforts at what would come to be called film theory, the German-American psychologist Hugo Münsterberg found the art of film to be a profoundly *emotional* art. For him, more even than in theatrical drama, the stars of the screen are "subjects of emotional experiences. Their joy and pain, their hope and fear, their love and hate, their gratitude and envy, their sympathy and malice, give meaning and value to" our experiences of them on the screen.[49] But all the same, he was quick to point out that no analysis of film could focus entirely on the screen. "This," he astutely averred, "cannot be sufficient." For, in addition to the stars on the screen, there is also the spectator watching them, the "mental activities and excitement" in whom are "projected into the moving pictures."[50] This is as true of movie-going today as it was when Münsterberg was writing in 1916. Film is an emotionally overwhelming art form, and our ability not just to *imagine* abstract characters in our minds but actually to *see* flesh-and-blood human beings on the screen goes a long way toward explaining the powerful connections that we form to our favorite stars. But martial arts stars are unique even among film stars. Former US Army explosive ordinance specialist and internationally certified stage fight director Aaron Anderson, in describing his experience of watching Bruce Lee in *Enter the Dragon* with his US Army company the night before the final physical training test of their basic training, described how the senior drill instructor instructed them to watch Bruce Lee on the screen so that they could *be* Bruce Lee the next day and pass their test. Sure enough, Anderson reported that, after the film, they were all so "intoxicated" that they "stayed up all night long 'kungfu-ing' each other."[51] Similarly, the film scholar David Bordwell has acknowledged the way that Hong Kong martial arts cinema, which he describes as an "ecstatic cinema" in line with the theoretical postulations of Sergei Eisenstein, can "infect even film professors, heavy with middle age and polemics if not baked brie, with the delusion that they can vault calmly over the cars parked outside the movie theater."[52]

Whether an intensely physical soldier-to-be or a sedentary academic, whether a child full of wonder or a cynical adult, whether man or woman, Asian or

American—there is no border that cannot be chopped through or leapt over in pursuit of the pleasures and insights that are afforded by Hong Kong martial arts cinema, and just as early audiences were captivated by Chaplin's indefatigable waddle and Garbo's alluring beauty, so later audiences have been thrilled and even moved to physical action by the awe-inspiring martial artistry of fighting stars from Kwan Tak-hing and Bruce Lee up to Michelle Yeoh and Donnie Yen. In *Fighting Stars*, readers will be treated to attempts by experts in the fields of film and cultural studies and leading scholars of action and martial arts cinema to sketch the contours of the stars who helped to shape Hong Kong martial arts cinema in its earlier years and who are continuing to reshape it today. Perhaps the chapters contained herein will not inspire readers to take to ecstatically "kungfu-ing" their colleagues or classmates, but I hope that, at the very least, they inspire readers to (re)turn to the realm of Hong Kong martial arts cinema to explore, for the first time or once again, one of the crown jewels of world cinema.

Notes

1   Stanley Cavell, *The World Viewed: Reflections on the Ontology of Film* (Cambridge, MA: Harvard University Press, [1971] 1979), 28–9.

2   Richard Dyer, *Stars* (London: BFI, [1979] 1998).

3   Richard Dyer, *Heavenly Bodies: Film Stars and Society* (London: Routledge, [1986] 2004).

4   In the words of Karen Hollinger, Dyer's work "precipitate[d] a seismic shift" in film studies and cultural studies vis-à-vis stardom (see her *The Actress: Hollywood Acting and the Female Star* [London: Routledge, 2006], 35), while, in the words of Martin Shingler, "Dyer's combination of semiotics and sociology . . . stimulated considerable interest in star images across films, publicity, and promotional materials," thereby "demonstrating that star studies had become a legitimate area of academic inquiry" (see his *Star Studies: A Critical Guide* [London: BFI, 2012]).

5   Béla Balázs, *Theory of the Film: Character and Growth of a New Art* (London: Dennis Dobson, [1948] 1952), 283.

6   Ibid., 285.

7   Ibid.

8   Ibid., 285–6.

9   Ibid., 285.

10 Ibid., 286.

11 Ibid.

12 Ibid., 286–7.

13 André Bazin, "Charlie Chaplin," in *What is Cinema? Volume 1*, ed. and trans. Hugh Gray (Berkeley, CA: University of California Press, [1948] 2005).

14 Bazin, "The Destiny of Jean Gabin," in *What is Cinema? Volume 2*, ed. and trans. Hugh Gray (Berkeley, CA: University of California Press, [1950] 2005).

15 Ibid., 176.

16 Ibid.

17 Ibid., 177.

18 Siegfried Kracauer, *Theory of Film: The Redemption of Physical Reality* (Princeton, NJ: Princeton University Press, [1960] 1997), 99–100.

19 Andrew Britton, *Katharine Hepburn: Star as Feminist* (New York: Columbia University Press, [1984] 2003).

20 Dave Saunders, *Arnold: Schwarzenegger and the Movies* (London: I.B. Tauris, 2009).

21 Andrea Bandhauer and Michelle Royer (eds.), *Stars in World Cinema: Screen Icons and Star Systems Across Cultures* (London: I.B. Tauris, 2015).

22 Sabrina Qiong Yu and Guy Austin (eds.), *Revisiting Star Studies: Cultures, Themes, and Methods* (Edinburgh: Edinburgh University Press, 2017).

23 Sabrina Qiong Yu, "Introduction: Performing Stardom: Star Studies in Transformation and Expansion," in *Revisiting Star Studies*, 3.

24 Ibid.

25 Ibid., 16.

26 Ibid., 3.

27 Ibid., 16.

28 Nananda Bose, *Madhuri Dixit* (London: BFI, 2019).

29 Ulrike Sieglohr, *Hanna Schygulla* (London: BFI, 2019).

30 Mark Gallagher, *Tony Leung Chiu-Wai* (London: BFI, 2019).

31 Lisa Shaw, *Carmen Miranda* (London: BFI, 2019).

32 Mary Farquhar and Yingjin Zhang (eds.), *Chinese Films Stars* (London: Routledge, 2014).

33 Leung Wing-Fai and Andy Willis (eds.), *East Asian Film Stars* (London: Palgrave, 2014).

34 Jonathan Driskell (ed.), *Film Stardom in Southeast Asia* (Edinburgh: Edinburgh University Press, 2022).

35 For more in-depth rehearsals of the low esteem in which action and martial arts films have been held in both popular and academic discourses, and arguments against such misguided condescension, see Kyle Barrowman, "Bruce Lee: Authorship, Ideology, and Film Studies," *Off-screen* 16, no. 6 (2012), https://offscreen.com/view/bruce_lee_authorship_part_1; "Blockbuster Ideology: Steven Seagal and the Legacy of Action Cinema," *Off-screen* 17, no. 4 (2013), https://offscreen.com/view/blockbuster_ideology_part_1; "History in the Making: Martial Arts between Planet Hollywood and Planet Hong Kong," *Martial Arts Studies* 1 (2015): 72–82, https://mas.cardiffuniversitypress.org/articles/10.18573/j.2015.10020; and "Origins of the Action Film: Types, Tropes, and Techniques in Early Film History," in *A Companion to the Action Film*, ed. James Kendrick (Malden, MA: Wiley-Blackwell, 2019), 11–34.

36 Yvonne Tasker, *Spectacular Bodies: Gender, Genre, and the Action Cinema* (London: Routledge, 1993).

37 Mirana May Szeto and Yun-chung Chen, "Hong Kong Cinema in the Age of Neoliberalization and Mainlandization: Hong Kong SAR New Wave as a Cinema of Anxiety," in *A Companion to Hong Kong Cinema*, eds. Esther M.K. Cheung, Gina Marchetti, and Esther C.M. Yau (Malden, MA: Wiley-Blackwell, 2015), 92.

38 Bey Logan, *Hong Kong Action Cinema* (London: Titan Books, 1995).

39 Stephen Teo, *Hong Kong Cinema: The Extra Dimensions* (London: BFI, 1997).

40 David Bordwell, *Planet Hong Kong: Popular Cinema and the Art of Entertainment* (Madison, WI: Irvington Way Institute Press, [2000] 2010).

41 Leon Hunt, *Kung Fu Cult Masters: From Bruce Lee to Crouching Tiger* (London: Wallflower, 2003).

42 Mark Gallagher, *Action Figures: Men, Action Films, and Contemporary Adventure Narratives* (London: Palgrave, 2006).

43 Paul Bowman, *Theorizing Bruce Lee: Film-Fantasy-Fighting-Philosophy* (Amsterdam: Rodopi, 2010) and *Beyond Bruce Lee: Chasing the Dragon through Film, Philosophy, and Popular Culture* (London: Wallflower, 2013).

44 Man-Fung Yip, *Martial Arts Cinema and Hong Kong Modernity: Aesthetics, Representation, Circulation* (Hong Kong: Hong Kong University Press, 2017).

45 Luke White, *Legacies of the Drunken Master: Politics of the Body in Hong Kong Kung Fu Comedy Films* (Honolulu: University of Hawai'i Press, 2020) and *Fighting without Fighting: Kung Fu Cinema's Journey to the West* (London: Reaktion Books, 2022).

46 Lauren Steimer, *Experts in Action: Transnational Hong Kong-Style Stunt Work and Performance* (Durham, NC: Duke University Press, 2021).

47 Dorothy Wai Sim Lau, *Chinese Stardom in Participatory Cyberculture* (Edinburgh: Edinburgh University Press, 2018) and *Reorienting Chinese Stars in Global Polyphonic Networks: Voice, Ethnicity, Power* (London: Palgrave, 2021).

48 Logan, *Hong Kong Action Cinema*, 158.

49 Hugo Münsterberg, *The Photoplay: A Psychological Study and Other Writings*, ed. Allan Langdale (London: Routledge, [1916] 2002), 99.

50 Ibid., 104.

51 Aaron Anderson, "Action in Motion: Kinesthesia in Martial Arts Films," *Jump Cut* 42 (1998), https://www.ejumpcut.org/archive/onlinessays/JC42folder/anderson2/index.html.

52 David Bordwell, "Aesthetics in Action: Kung-Fu, Gunplay, and Cinematic Expression," in *Poetics of Cinema* (London: Routledge, [1997] 2008), 411.

Chapter 1

Kwan Tak-hing: Pioneer of Kung Fu Cinema

Wayne Wong

Figure 2 Rare promotional photo showcasing Kwan Tak-hing's physique in the late 1940s. © Kwan Tak-Hing (KTH) Estate. All rights reserved.

Introduction

The notion of "kung fu stars" is commonly associated with renowned figures such as Bruce Lee, Jackie Chan, and Jet Li. Undoubtedly, the kung fu genre experienced its heyday in the 1970s, primarily fueled by Bruce Lee's remarkable ascent and the proliferation of martial arts films and television shows.[1] However, preceding this era, kung fu films as a genre had their roots firmly established in the collective consciousness of older Hong Kong and Chinese viewers. These viewers recognized the aforementioned stars as successors to a cinematic tradition of hand-to-hand combat, with Kwan Tak-hing (1905–96) serving as a pivotal pioneer in this regard.[2]

Kwan Tak-hing was the first actor to portray the iconic role of Wong Fei-hung (fl. 1847–1924), a kung fu master from the late Qing and early Republican periods renowned for his proficiency in Hung Gar techniques. The original Wong Fei-hung film series commenced in 1949, and the legend of this esteemed master has since been depicted in over a hundred films. Kwan Tak-hing featured in an impressive seventy-seven of these productions before his passing in 1996.[3] The longevity and popularity of the Wong Fei-hung films were instrumental in spawning the kung fu cinema genre and establishing its fundamental conventions. Thus, not only did Kwan Tak-hing play a critical role in shaping the perception of a kung fu star, but his portrayal also left a permanent mark on the on-screen persona of the kung fu master. To date, scholars have acknowledged the significance of Kwan's portrayal of Wong Fei-hung in this long-standing film series.[4] However, there remains a notable gap in understanding Kwan's personal journey and how his concurrent careers in Cantonese opera and cinema during the 1930s and 1940s contributed to his emergence as the first kung fu star.

Consequently, the existing body of scholarly work has predominantly overlooked Kwan Tak-hing's star image beyond his involvement in the Wong Fei-hung film series. This omission leads to a void in the literature, particularly concerning the crucial question of why, in 1949, a forty-four-year-old Kwan was uniquely suited for the role of Wong Fei-hung. The lack of comprehensive analysis into Kwan's earlier years as a trailblazing Cantonese opera star, a highly skilled martial artist, and a patriotic individual prevents a thorough understanding of Kwan's personal connection to and influence on the history and evolution of kung fu cinema over the subsequent seven decades. By closely examining Kwan's background, upbringing, and early career both before and during the Second World War, I argue that the opera star was an ideal fit for the portrayal of Wong Fei-hung, and that the conventions of kung fu cinema were significantly shaped by Kwan's distinct on-screen and off-screen persona, just as much as by the film series itself.

Kwan Tak-hing's impact on kung fu cinema will be examined from three distinct perspectives. Firstly, his exceptional martial arts ability established a benchmark for the genre. Subsequent martial arts stars were expected to demonstrate a certain level of "corporeal authenticity" in their martial arts displays, emphasizing genuine martial arts skills and performances without the use of stunt doubles.[5] Secondly, Kwan's often overlooked background in opera unveiled a crucial aspect of his success as the inaugural kung fu star: his ability to seamlessly integrate acting and combat skills. Striking a delicate balance between these two disciplines, Kwan exemplified a versatile fighting star who continually introduced innovative elements to his operatic and cinematic performances. Lastly, Kwan's personal interpretation significantly contributed to the prevailing image of the kung fu master as a Confucian gentleman and guardian of traditional Chinese culture. It is largely through

Kwan's portrayal that this depiction has become ingrained in popular consciousness.

This chapter delves into the relationship between Kwan Tak-hing and his lasting influence on kung fu cinema. Rather than reiterating the significance of the original Wong Fei-hung films within the genre, the focus shifts toward Kwan's pivotal role in shaping the character and thus the films. Several key questions arise: what sets Kwan apart as a distinctive fighting star? Why was he an apt choice for the portrayal of Wong Fei-hung in 1949? To what extent did he shape the conventions of kung fu cinema? By pursuing answers to these questions, we gain insight into Kwan's profound inspiration of subsequent generations of Hong Kong kung fu stars and filmmakers, who continually revitalized and transformed the kung fu genre over the span of seven decades. To facilitate comprehensive analysis, this chapter is divided into three sections, each critically engaging with Kwan's martial skills, his amalgamation of acting and martial skills, and his interpretation of Wong Fei-hung as both a Confucian gentleman and a custodian of Chinese cultural values.

"Real Kung Fu"

During the late 1940s, the prevalence of fighting stars possessing genuine martial arts capabilities was not as commonplace as it is in contemporary times. At that time, the martial arts genre was predominantly influenced by the *shenguai wuxia* tradition, rooted in 1920s Shanghai, which emphasized extravagant and supernatural martial arts performances.[6] Concurrently, martial arts displays were intimately associated with operatic customs, where the aim was not necessarily to showcase "real" kung fu, but rather to employ stylized techniques to enhance expressiveness on the theatrical stage.[7] It was within this context that Kwan Tak-hing emerged as the first and most indelible star to undertake the portrayal of Wong Fei-hung.

Kwan Tak-hing was renowned for his mastery of White Crane, a southern school (*nanpai*) martial arts style, as well as his exceptional lion dance performances.[8] During his early years, he studied Hung Gar, the southern style closely associated with the historical figure of Wong Fei-hung, which subsequently became prominently featured in the film series. Kwan's proficiency in lion dancing, an art in which the real Wong Fei-hung himself excelled, was frequently highlighted in the films. An illustrative example of this can be found in the opening scene of the inaugural Wong Fei-hung film, *The Story of Wong Fei-hung: Part I* (1949), where Kwan is introduced as the lead performer in a lion dancing sequence. A decade later, in *How Wong Fei-hung Defeated the Tiger on the Opera Stage* (1959), Kwan continues to captivate audiences with his accomplished lion dancing skills. This association between Kwan's lion dance skills and the character of Wong Fei-hung quickly established a strong correlation between the two during the 1950s.

A noteworthy but often overlooked source of Kwan Tak-hing's martial arts competence stems from his early career as a Cantonese opera star, during which he portrayed martial arts roles known as *xiaowu* (or *wusheng* in Peking Opera). His repertoire included historical and fictional *xia* (martial chivalry) heroes from Chinese literary classics. Among these roles, he gained renown for his portrayals of Guan Yu, a famous general of the late Eastern Han dynasty revered as a military deity in *Romance of the Three Kingdoms*, and Wu Song, the legendary tiger-slayer in *Water Margin*.[9] Kwan commenced his operatic training for these roles at the age of fifteen and subsequently rose to prominence as the lead actor in bringing these heroic characters to life throughout the 1930s and 1940s. Importantly, many of these stage performances were later adapted into films, such as *Daxia Gan Fengchi* (*The Knight*, 1939), *Sheng Wu Song* (*A Living Hero*, 1940), and *Guangong Yuexia Shi Diaochan* (*General Kwan Seduced by Diaochan Under Moonlight*, 1956). These operatic portrayals not only provided Kwan with physical preparation for his portrayal of Wong Fei-hung in 1949, but they also played a vital role in shaping his interpretation of Wong as a chivalrous kung fu master within his cinematic performances.

In 1949, it became evident that Kwan Tak-hing's presentation of "real kung fu" (*zhengongfu*) served as a deliberate strategy to differentiate the Wong Fei-hung film series from the fantastical *shenguai wuxia* films and the stylized "false kung fu" found in operatic performances. Kwan himself acknowledged this distinction in an interview, stating, "Before, everything was swordplay and magic! Our audience wanted something different, a new kind of hero, and that was what we gave them."[10] Departing from the mythical past often inhabited by fictional *wuxia* heroes, the central character, Wong Fei-hung, was portrayed as a genuine hero from the Guangdong region during the late Qing and early Republican era.[11] Cinematically, particularly in the first four installments released in 1949 and 1950, the Wong Fei-hung films emphasized what Leon Hunt identifies as "archival," "cinematic," and "corporeal" authenticities.[12] These categories refer to the practice of featuring actual martial arts practitioners executing genuine martial arts styles, minimizing editing or visual effects. Considering these parameters, it became apparent that, despite the presence of younger and more renowned Cantonese opera stars in the late 1940s, the forty-four-year-old Kwan emerged as the most suitable candidate for the role of Wong Fei-hung.[13]

However, it is imperative to subject the notion of "real kung fu" to careful examination, as it gives rise to epistemological inquiries regarding the genre. Stephen Teo emphasizes that cinematic martial arts performances ought to be regarded as "representations of the real," involving various forms of resemblance, performance, and meticulous choreography.[14] From this perspective, the term "real kung fu" is employed by filmmakers and performers themselves to describe the constructed reality presented on-screen, with fans of the genre actively participating in their expectations that what they witness is genuine.[15] While the initial four Wong Fei-hung films released in 1949 and 1950 gained recognition for their direct capturing of martial arts performances through extended takes, such as the showcase of Hung Gar's tiger-crane fist (*huhe shuangxing*) and the pole fighting of Wulang and Bagua (wulang bagua gun) at the outset of *The Story of Wong Fei-hung: Part I*, this practice gradually diminished in subsequent films. Thus, the concept of "real kung fu" should be perceived as "edited fragments of real-time kung fu performance."[16]

Indeed, Kwan Tak-hing's martial abilities have encountered scrutiny on two fronts. The first pertains to his background in Cantonese opera, while the second concerns the archival authenticity of his martial arts performance in the Wong Fei-hung films. Critics argue that despite Kwan receiving some martial arts training, his primary expertise lay in opera rather than martial arts.[17] Lau Kar-leung, in discussing Kwan's Hung Fist, remarked, "[Kwan] was, in fact, my pupil. The guy [Kwan] was an opera actor, and he didn't know anything about Tiger's Claws or Crane's Beak. But he could strike beautiful poses, and that made him look like the real Wong Fei-hung."[18] Critics argue that operatic martial arts differ from authentic martial arts practice, as they possess a sense of staginess and prioritize theatrical elements such as acrobatic somersaults.[19] This staginess and theatricality are associated with martial artist-acrobats known as *longhu wushi* (dragon-tiger masters), often associated with *beipai* (the northern school) and Peking opera.[20] Also, it is important to note that the martial arts performance in Cantonese opera should be distinguished from that of Peking opera, as the former incorporates moves and routines derived from the Southern school *nanpai*.[21] However, according to Lau Kar-leung, martial arts performers in Cantonese opera can also be categorized as *longhu wushi*, thereby inheriting the theatrical characteristics of the northern school.[22] As a result, questions have been raised regarding Kwan's combat abilities due to his connection to opera.

The second challenge concerning Kwan Tak-hing's martial abilities is closely intertwined with the first, as it relates to his inability to present authentic martial arts, particularly regarding the Hung Gar style, in the Wong Fei-hung films. Notably, the martial arts demonstrations and weapon displays in the early Wong Fei-hung films were performed by local masters rather than Kwan himself.[23] In *The Story of Wong Fei-hung: Part II* (1949), for instance, Kwan's character, Wong Fei-hung, showcases the shadowless kick (*wuying jiao*), a signature technique within Hung Gar's tiger-crane fist, to his students. However, according to Hung Gar masters who have reviewed the film and analyzed the authenticity of the performance, Kwan's demonstration bears little resemblance to authentic Hung Gar techniques.[24] In the sequence, Kwan assumes an operatic stance, extending his arms widely and anticipating the attack of imaginary adversaries. This stance, as they recall, was Kwan's preferred pose during his portrayal of Guan Yu in Cantonese operatic plays. In this light, Kwan's martial arts skills and performances in the Wong Fei-hung films can be best characterized as a synthesis of the authentic and the theatrical.[25]

While it is reasonable to raise inquiries regarding Kwan Tak-hing's martial arts capabilities as an opera star with some martial arts training in 1949, it would be problematic to dismiss him as a martial artist subsequent to his involvement in the Wong Fei-hung films. It is worth noting that the existing scholarship has perhaps overlooked the significance of the Wong Fei-hung film series, which stands as the lengthiest cinematic series centering on a single character in film history. I argue that the seventy-seven films featuring Kwan served as an ideal training ground for him, considering the time and repetition required for martial arts practice. Through this extensive film series, southern and northern martial arts talents were brought together, providing them with motivation, resources, and the confidence to perform, exchange ideas, and experiment with diverse styles. Within this innovative process, Kwan found himself in his prime years, learning from authentic martial artists and actively participating in the fight choreography of the films. Through synthesis and innovation, Kwan was able to develop into a bona fide martial artist, thereby paving the way for the global phenomenon of kung fu in the 1970s.

First, Kwan Tak-hing's affiliation with the southern school was significantly strengthened by his collaboration with martial arts practitioners who maintained a direct connection to the historical figure of Wong Fei-hung. The choreography of the first Wong Fei-hung film was undertaken by Leung Wing-heng, one of Wong's second-generation disciples.[26] Another disciple was Lau Cham, the father of Lau Kar-leung, who choreographed and performed in numerous Wong Fei-hung films since 1949.[27] Both Leung and Lau were disciples of Lam Sai-Wing, a highly renowned disciple of Wong. Lam's stories served as inspiration for many film adaptations, such as *The Magnificent Butcher* (1979). Additionally, Wong's wife, Mok Gui Lan, served as an advisor for the third and fourth films.[28] Through these valuable connections, Kwan was afforded the opportunity to refine his Hung Gar style further. Lau Kar-leung recalls that Kwan sought his assistance in mastering Hung Gar's tiger and crane forms.[29] Thus, despite Kwan's operatic background, which drew influence from northern martial arts traditions, his collaboration with numerous southern masters allowed him to deepen his understanding of southern martial arts practices.

Second, Kwan Tak-hing reaped the benefits of the exchange between the southern school and the northern school as he assumed the role of choreographer following the first Wong Fei-hung film.[30] Specifically, Kwan collaborated extensively with Shek Kin, who frequently portrayed Wong's adversary and possessed expertise in praying mantis, a northern martial arts style.[31] Reflecting on their collaboration, Shek remarked, "It wasn't like today, where you have a

Figure 3 Kwan Tak-hing's demonstration of Chinese martial arts forms in the late 1940s. © Kwan Tak-Hing (KTH) Estate. All rights reserved.

fight director telling you what to do. Kwan Tak-hing and I would decide which techniques went well together. The main problem was finding a new way for me to get defeated every time!"[32] The constant pursuit of innovation played a pivotal role in the evolution of kung fu cinema, with one crucial catalyst for this progress being the exchange of the northern and southern styles. Kwan's partnership with Yuen Siu-tin, the father of Yuen Woo-ping and another significant choreographer for the Wong Fei-hung films, facilitated this exchange.[33] The Yuen family played a vital role in harmonizing practicality and theatricality, thereby achieving an aesthetic balance in the martial arts performances depicted in the films.[34] In other words, Kwan had the opportunity to learn from the exceptional talents of both the Lau and Yuen families, enabling him to draw from the finest aspects of both worlds.

The primary focus of my argument does not revolve around the debate regarding whether Kwan Tak-hing was primarily an opera star or a martial artist at the inception of his career. Instead, I argue that the enduring legacy of the Wong Fei-hung film series spanning over half a century constitutes a decisive factor that warrants consideration when evaluating Kwan's martial arts capabilities. Given his background as an opera star with martial arts training, renowned for his martial arts roles in operatic plays, it would not be surprising if Kwan displayed a rapid learning curve and adeptly mastered both southern and northern styles through collaborations with authentic martial artists. However, an aporia lies in the ingrained bias within martial arts cinema, which assumes that acting and fighting styles are distinct qualities. In Kwan's case, it is often assumed that an opera star, if skilled in acting, may not possess comparable proficiency in combat, and vice versa. Nevertheless, Kwan defied this assumption, emerging as a prototype that challenged the dichotomy between acting and fighting in the martial arts genre. His example serves to demonstrate the possibility—and indeed, the necessity—of integrating acting and fighting, thereby inspiring subsequent luminaries such as Bruce Lee, Jackie Chan, and Jet Li.

Versatile Operatic Star

In martial arts cinema, acting and fighting skills are commonly perceived as incompatible. It is often assumed that proficient fighting stars have limited acting abilities, and that acting through facial expressions holds greater intellectual value than physical movements. However, it is imperative to recognize that acting and martial arts should not be regarded as mutually exclusive. As Sabrina Yu argues, the Chinese audience places greater emphasis on the overall performance rather than solely on martial arts or acting skills. Within the *wuxia* genre, filmmakers such as King Hu and Chang Cheh in the 1960s prioritized actors and actresses with distinguished acting abilities over exceptional fighting skills.[35] Figures such as David Chiang, Ti Lung, Cheng Pei-pei, and Hsu Feng were selected based on their screen image and how well it aligned with the *wuxia* characters they portrayed. In kung fu cinema, Bruce Lee exemplified the command of both facial expressions and physical movements in his martial arts performances. An unforgettable scene in *Fist of Fury* (1972) showcases Chen Zhen (Bruce Lee) restraining his fury at his master's funeral despite enduring public humiliation by a treacherous Japanese translator (Paul Wei Ping-ao). In this scene, Wei presents a large framed piece of calligraphy which reads "Sick Man of Asia." Torn between responding to the challenge and upholding the solemnity of the funeral, Chen suppresses his anger while enduring a slap to the face in a medium-close-up shot. The audience can discern the subtle movements of Lee's facial muscles and the intricacies of his acting. The success of these stars stemmed not solely from their martial capabilities but also from their adeptness in acting. It is my contention that the concept of synthesizing fighting and acting skills, which has become a prominent aspect of martial arts cinema, can be attributed to Kwan Tak-hing, the first Hong Kong fighting star to embody such a fusion.

Kwan's uniqueness lies in his mastery of two distinct acting modes: impersonation and personification.[36] Impersonation is "produced by the actor who transforms his or her body and voice in ways that signify the differences between the characters he or she plays," while personification is "the continuity of the star's image over and above different characters." Actors proficient in impersonation can adapt their screen persona to suit various characterizations, whereas personification entails performers consistently embodying the same screen persona regardless of different characters.[37] When applied to martial arts cinema, impersonation refers to action stars assuming diverse roles and adopting varying fighting styles based on the requirements of each character. Conversely, personification applies to actors or actresses who consistently portray similar (or identical) roles and maintain a consistent fighting style across different characters.

An apt illustration of the aforementioned concepts can be found in the career of Jet Li, exemplifying the impersonation mode. Li has demonstrated his versatility by portraying a wide range of martial arts roles throughout his filmography, encompassing a Shaolin monk in *Shaolin Temple* (1982), the young Wong Fei-hung in *Once Upon a Time in China* (1991), and Chen Zhen in *Fist of Legend* (1994). These diverse roles not only encompass varying martial arts capabilities but also demand exceptional acting skills from the performer. For instance, Li's portrayal of Wong Fei-hung in *Once Upon a Time in China* depicted a character torn between the encroaching influence of Western modernity, epitomized by the advent of firearms, and the perceived futility of traditional Chinese kung fu. This internal struggle is poignantly depicted in a scene where Wong Fei-hung (Jet Li) mournfully cradles the lifeless body of a kung fu master who has succumbed to gunshot wounds. In contrast, Kwan Tak-hing was widely regarded as an actor who personified Wong Fei-hung, attaining such an indelible association with the character that he encountered difficulty in portraying other roles thereafter. Kwan even declined offers for cameo appearances that conflicted with the revered master persona he had cultivated. For example, he rejected a cameo role in *Millionaires Express* (1986) where Wong Fei-hung was to be portrayed as a kidnapped figure in need of rescue.[38]

The decision of Kwan Tak-hing to personify Wong Fei-hung might lead one to assume that he lacked versatility as an actor, limited by his purportedly constrained acting abilities. However, a closer examination of his early career reveals Kwan to be a well-rounded performer who excelled in both personification and impersonation across a wide spectrum of genres in both opera and cinema. During the 1930s and 1940s, Kwan undertook a diverse array of roles in opera plays and films, spanning genres ranging from romance to American Western, prior to assuming the iconic role of Wong Fei-hung in 1949. These formative experiences not only facilitated the amalgamation of his acting and martial arts skills but also stimulated his inclination to incorporate elements from various genres into martial arts cinema at a later stage. In other words, the focus is on how Kwan's operatic background and multifaceted experience endowed him with the capacity to impersonate diverse roles adeptly while also instigating innovative conventions within martial arts cinema.

While contemporary stars often view acting and martial skills as distinct domains, Kwan Tak-hing's exposure to both disciplines commenced at a remarkably young age. Within Cantonese opera, young male performers typically assume either scholarly (*xiaosheng*) or martial (*xiaowu*) roles. The former focuses on honing acting and vocal abilities, while the latter centers on proficiency with a diverse array of weaponry (*bazigong*) and acrobatic movements (*tanzigong*). In Kwan's case, his early opera training encompassed engagement with both types of roles. At the age of fifteen, in 1920, Kwan embarked on a journey of artistic development under the tutelage of Xin Bei, a highly regarded Cantonese opera luminary recognized for his scholarly portrayals.[39] Subsequently, Kwan became a disciple of Jing Yuanheng, a renowned opera star known for his martial roles, a year later. With the guidance of these esteemed figures from the opera realm, Kwan concurrently acquired proficiency in acting and martial arts skills. In the span of seven years, he ascended to the position of a martial arts lead within one of the premier opera troupes and eventually established his own troupe while actively participating in the creation of opera plays.[40]

To a certain extent, Kwan Tak-hing's challenging upbringing contributed to his physical and mental resilience, facilitating his rapid acquisition of acting and martial skills. Kwan's father passed away when he was merely seven years old, compelling him to abandon formal education at the age of nine and assume the role of a cowherd to provide for his mother. Reflecting upon this period, Kwan recounts the hardships endured by his family, "When we were living in the ancestral temple, my mother fed us by washing clothes and she would scrub on the washing board, until, her fingertips went rotten. I was a cowherd for four dollars a year. That was enough to feed myself. At that time, you could buy a son for 20 dollars, but if you lost a head of cow, you had to pay 50 dollars to compensate. Humans were worthless."[41] At the age of thirteen, Kwan transitioned to working as a coolie for a year before embarking on a journey to Singapore at the age of fourteen in search of alternative employment prospects.[42] These early experiences effectively primed Kwan for his subsequent initiation into formal opera training, which commenced a year later.

Kwan Tak-hing's amalgamation of acting and martial skills was further enriched during his tour in the United States. This period afforded him the opportunity to embark upon a film career and engage with diverse genres. In 1932, at the age of twenty-seven, Kwan received an invitation from the Mandarin Theater in San Francisco to showcase his renowned Cantonese plays.[43] Over the course of his two-year tenure in the United States, he assumed the leading male role in *Gelü Qingchao* (*Romance of the Songsters*, 1933), one of the early Cantonese sound films produced overseas.[44] Diverging from

Kwan's customary repertoire of operatic productions centered around Chinese military heroes, this particular film represented a contemporary, lighthearted song and dance production (*gewu pian*) that revolved around a couple within a Cantonese opera troupe, interspersed with elements of comic relief.[45] Particularly, the film's self-reflexivity facilitated Kwan's forays into the intersection between operatic and cinematic realms, as well as the juxtaposition of traditional and modern elements.

Following the favorable reception of *Romance of the Songsters* within the Chinese communities in the United States, Kwan established his own opera troupe in 1934, aligning with the prevailing trend of incorporating contemporary attire (*xizhuangxi*) into Cantonese opera during the 1930s.[46] However, unlike his contemporaries who primarily sought to innovate within the operatic domain, Kwan displayed a remarkable capacity for career development and ongoing innovation across both opera and cinema. Upon his return to Hong Kong, Kwan secured roles in two additional song and dance films, namely *Zuori Zhige* (*Yesterday's Song*, 1935) and *Cange* (*Song of Sadness*, 1935). Similar to *Romance of the Songsters*, these films explored the integration of Cantonese opera singing within the cinematic medium, with promotional materials highlighting the utilization of "soft lighting" to enhance the performances.[47] These cumulative experiences enabled Kwan to emerge as one of the few artists who successfully traversed the realms of Cantonese opera and cinema, endowing him with exceptional versatility and adaptability as an actor.

During his tour in the United States, Kwan underwent significant growth in his martial abilities and skillfully incorporated them into Cantonese opera and cinema. In addition to his involvement in song and dance films, Kwan ventured into swashbuckling roles after being inspired by Douglas Fairbanks, renowned for his performance in *The Thief of Bagdad* (1924). Drawing inspiration from Fairbanks, Kwan acquired bullwhip and lasso skills, which he subsequently integrated into his performances in Cantonese opera plays and films upon his return to Hong Kong. One of these productions was *Shenbianxia* (*The Knight of the Whip*), which was adapted into a film in 1936. In promotional materials, Kwan was referred to as the "Eastern Fairbanks," illustrating his aspirations to revolutionize traditional opera.[48] Within the context of *The Knight of the Whip*, Kwan skillfully showcased his newly acquired whip and lasso techniques while infusing elements reminiscent of American Westerns, such as the rescue of a damsel in distress (*yingxiong jiumei*), which he juxtaposed with recurring themes in traditional opera, including enduring contempt and insults (*renru fuzhong*).[49] At the same time, Kwan continuously experimented with diverse song and dance elements. Specifically, he demonstrated his versatility by assuming a cross-dressing role and engaging in tap dance accompanied by Mexican tunes within *The Knight of the Whip*.[50] These examples underscore Kwan's remarkable versatility in acting and his ability to innovate within Cantonese opera.

In this light, Kwan's tour in the United States during the 1930s sparked his inspiration to amalgamate his acting and martial skills, resulting in the introduction of fresh elements into his performances. This spirit of innovation played a pivotal role in his later portrayal in the Wong Fei-hung films and the overall development of kung fu cinema. The significance of Kwan's versatile acting background in his early career became evident in the inaugural Wong Fei-hung film, *The Story of Wong Fei-hung: Part I*, which showcased a remarkable level of novelty. The film's Chinese title, "*bianfeng miezhu*" (snuffs the candle flame with whiplash), provided a glimpse of Kwan's whip techniques, prominently featured in the climactic fight scene of the film. In this sequence, Kwan adeptly extinguished the candle lights on two sets, each containing approximately ten candles, with a flick of his whip. In this light, the very first kung fu film exhibited the genre's ingenuity, adaptability, and hybridity, with the enduring Wong Fei-hung films continually pushing the boundaries of creativity.[51]

In brief, Kwan stands as a pioneer in introducing a non-Chinese weapon, the bullwhip, to kung fu cinema. Just as Bruce Lee claimed the nunchaku as his signature weapon, Kwan asserted the bullwhip as his own. Rather than perceiving Kwan as an unyielding kung fu master resistant to change, he should be acknowledged as an innovator who fearlessly challenged established norms and conventions. His inclination to synthesize acting and martial arts skills, as well as his incorporation of diverse generic elements, paved the way for future multidisciplinary martial arts performances by figures such as Bruce Lee and the kung fu comedy genre epitomized by Jackie Chan three decades later.

Wen-Wu Synthesis and Patriotism

Kwan's integration of martial and acting skills holds significant implications for the portrayal of the traditional kung fu master. Existing scholarly discourse has underscored the influential role played by the Wong Fei-hung films in shaping this image, evident through two distinct manifestations. Firstly, the association of the kung fu master with the Confucian archetype of the superior gentleman (*junzi*), exemplifying martial virtues (*wude*) and martial chivalry (*wuxia*) by embodying moral ideals such as humaneness (*ren*) and righteousness (*yi*).[52] Secondly, the alignment of the kung fu master with "cultural nationalism," rendering the genre susceptible to the propagation of nationalist sentiments.[53] While the intimate connection between Wong Fei-hung and these personas is well-documented, closer examination of Kwan's personal association with this construction is necessary. In relation to the Confucian link, I argue that Kwan's proficiency in calligraphy and knowledge of Chinese medicine are pivotal in cultivating his literati persona, which further enhances his synthesis of the literary (*wen*) and the martial (*wu*) in his later portrayal of Wong Fei-hung. Regarding the connection to cultural nationalism, particular attention will be directed toward Kwan's early career experiences before and during the Second World War, potentially illuminating the reasons behind his interpretation of Wong Fei-hung as a guardian of traditional Chinese culture.

In comparison to subsequent actors who portrayed Wong Fei-hung, such as Jackie Chan and Jet Li, Kwan Tak-hing enjoyed greater artistic freedom in shaping the character. It is widely acknowledged that the early Wong Fei-hung films from the late 1940s to the 1950s operated under tight production schedules, often working with incomplete scripts.[54] Thus, Kwan's significant contribution to shaping the image of Wong Fei-hung becomes evident. This is particularly noteworthy when considering the portrayal of Wong in the original serialized novels authored by Zhu Yuzhai during the 1930s, which served as the basis for the Wong Fei-hung film adaptations. In the novels, Wong is depicted as a more unruly character, unable to tolerate provocation. He exhibits aggression and is unafraid to create scenes in order to achieve greater and greater renown.[55] Additionally, he frequents brothels and even engages in robberies alongside his disciples. In 1949, Kwan's interpretation of Wong Fei-hung presented a reimagined portrayal of the "original" Wong to the audience. Specifically, he transformed the character from a rebellious figure into a Confucian scholar-martial artist, skillfully synthesizing the masculine qualities of *wen* and *wu*.

Wen refers to "genteel, refined qualities that were associated with the literary and artistic pursuits of classical scholars," whereas *wu* is "a concept which embodies the power of military strength."[56] Kwan Tak-hing's early career in Cantonese opera exposed him to both these ideals, as he underwent training in both the scholarly (*xiaosheng*) and martial (*wusheng*) roles. Kwan's renowned portrayal of Guan Yu in Cantonese opera plays further exemplifies this synthesis. While Guan Yu is commonly recognized for his martial valor, his literary image is often overlooked. In fact, Guan Yu is imagined as a military general who embodies the connection between the literary and martial worlds. A persistent portrayal of Guan Yu involves him leisurely reading Confucian classics, such as *The Spring and Autumn Annals* (*Chunqiu*).[57] Thus, Kwan's stage persona as Guan Yu not only associates him with martial dexterity but also aligns him with literary endeavors.

In his later career as Wong Fei-hung, Kwan further reinforced this synthesis. While critics have acknowledged Kwan's martial abilities in the Wong Fei-hung film series, his literati persona often goes unnoticed. One aspect that highlights Kwan's *wen* image is his attire. In contrast to the overt display of kung fu prowess exemplified by his successors, such as Bruce Lee and Jackie Chan, Kwan's portrayal of Wong Fei-hung is characterized by composure and reserve.[58] Throughout the Wong Fei-hung films, Kwan consistently buttons up his tang suit, directing the audience's attention to his pedagogical exchanges

Figure 4 A promotional shot of Kwan Tak-hing demonstrating Shaolin tiger form in the late 1960s.

with disciples and villains before showcasing his martial skills. As noted by Hector Rodriguez:

> The protagonist's primary aim was not to force citizens to do what is right, but to bring them to desire it in a spontaneous way. Social harmony invariably depended on [Wong Fei-hung's] capacity to thus educate those around him through the sheer exemplary force of his upright behavior. By illustrating the power of virtue, the plots reaffirmed Confucian conceptions of harmony, civility, and self-containment that marked the protagonist as a civic-minded guardian of the Chinese nation's moral stature and an instrument of social reform.[59]

The focus lies not on Kwan's muscular physique, but rather on his words and wisdom. In contrast, his disciples and villains in the films display less discipline in their attire, often leaving their tang suits unbuttoned to reveal their undershirts. This deliberate contrast has inspired Kwan's successors to emphasize further the literati's modesty and humility by donning the *changshan* (long gown), as seen in Jet Li's portrayal of Wong Fei-hung in *Once Upon a Time in China* and Donnie Yen's portrayal of Ip Man in *Ip Man* (2008).[60]

Kwan Tak-hing's literary persona is further exemplified through his personal interest in calligraphy. Renowned for his calligraphy skills, Kwan organized a fundraising exhibition of his work in 1961.[61] Since his portrayal of Wong Fei-hung in *The Story of Wong Fei-hung: Part I*, Kwan's characterization of Wong Fei-hung frequently depicted the master engaged in reading or writing within his study, rather than focusing solely on martial training with his disciples. The film *The Magnificent Butcher* accentuates this literati persona in a memorable scene where Wong's knowledge of Confucian teachings is showcased through calligraphy. In this particular scene, Wong is confronted in his study by Master Ko from a rival school, who disrupts Wong's calligraphy practice. Ko scornfully questions Wong's proficiency in calligraphy, to which Wong humbly and patiently responds, "A pen can put one's family affairs in order, run a country well, and achieve world peace." This reply demonstrates Wong's literary erudition, as it originates from a well-known line in the *Daxue* (The Great Learning) chapter of *Liji* (The Book of Rites), a canonical text of Confucianism, outlining the hierarchical priorities for a virtuous ruler. Following an impressive duel employing calligraphy brushes, Wong inscribes the phrase "*renzhewudi*" (the humane is invincible), derived from the *Mencius*, another significant Confucian text. In short, Kwan's off-screen reputation as a man of letters serves to enhance his on-screen portrayal of Wong Fei-hung, depicted as a Confucian sage who promotes *ren* (humaneness) and *yi* (righteousness) through the embodiment of martial virtue.

In order to augment his off-screen literary persona further, Kwan Tak-hing established Bo Chi Lam, a Chinese apothecary located in North Point, Hong Kong, in 1952.[62] The establishment's name directly associates with the apothecary run by the historical figure of Wong Fei-hung, as portrayed in the Wong Fei-hung film series. Kwan's depiction of Wong Fei-hung extends beyond that of a martial artist solely relying on physical ability, as he simultaneously embodies the role of a medical practitioner who tends to the injured and imparts knowledge of Chinese medical practices to his students and acquaintances. Demonstrating his benevolent and compassionate character (*ren*), Wong Fei-hung attends to the wounds of both his students and adversaries after their conflicts. This fusion of medical expertise with martial competency further enhances the synthesis of *wen* and *wu* ideals, as it illustrates that Confucian values are not confined to theoretical concepts but can be practically applied, even when such actions may be inconvenient or unappreciated. As Kwan expressed in an interview, "If he [Wong Fei-hung] hurts somebody in a fight, he tends to his wounds, and as to the bad guys, he gives them a chance to live. That's why Wong Fei-hung won the respect of people."[63] In effect, Kwan's reputation as a calligrapher and proprietor of an apothecary contributed to his on-screen embodiment of the *wen-wu* ideals through the character of Wong Fei-hung.

In addition to linking the persona of the kung fu master with Confucian ideals, Kwan Tak-hing also played a pivotal role in associating it with nationalism or patriotism. However, the nationalist or patriotic sentiments conveyed through Kwan's portrayal of Wong Fei-hung differ from those depicted by later kung fu heroes such as Bruce Lee's Chen Zhen in *Fist of Fury* or Donnie Yen's Ip Man in *Ip Man*. Rather than emphasizing the notion of Chineseness and establishing a binary opposition between Chinese kung fu and foreign/imperialist martial arts (such as Western boxing and Japanese karate), the Wong Fei-hung films emanate a sense of cultural or abstract nationalism.[64] This form of nationalism, on one hand, focuses on "the dissemination and preservation of Confucian morality as a foundation for the cultural unification and political stability of China."[65] On the other hand, it is associated with localism and regionalism, as it highlights Cantonese folk culture, music, landmarks, festive activities, and religious practices in the early Wong Fei-hung films. Examples of such representations include lion-dancing, visits to tea houses, dragon boat competitions, and the incorporation of southern tunes (*nanyin*).[66] These cinematic portrayals serve to reinforce the solidarity of diasporic Chinese communities in Hong Kong and Southeast Asia, providing a source of comfort amid the political turbulence of the 1940s and 1950s.[67] As Feng Pu aptly notes, the Wong Fei-hung films were crafted by and for Guangdong emigrants, allowing them to express their nostalgia for their lost homeland and maintain a sense of identity while residing in an unfamiliar environment.[68]

In fact, Kwan Tak-hing was an emigrant himself as he started his operatic career in the Guangdong province and then moved to Hong Kong in the 1940s. However, his commitment to Chinese nationalism or patriotism began a decade earlier. His affiliation with the Kuomintang (KMT) party in 1935 and subsequent recognition as a "patriotic artist" (*aiguo yiran*) by the KMT government were the outcomes of his charitable endeavors during the Second World War.[69] Following the outbreak of the Marco Polo Bridge Incident in 1937, Kwan halted his operatic tour in San Francisco and commenced offering free operatic performances within various diasporic Chinese communities.[70] The Chinese People's Political Consultative Conference (CPPCC) historical archive reveals that Kwan managed to raise approximately USD 300,000 for the KMT government, contributing to the procurement of fighter jets at a cost of approximately USD 12,000 each in 1937.[71] Kwan's remarkable success and influence were such that the Japanese authorities even placed a bounty on his head.[72]

Upon his return to Hong Kong in 1938, Kwan Tak-hing embarked on the formation of a Cantonese operatic troupe with a primary focus on organizing fund-raising performances, which entailed extensive tours throughout Guangdong, Guangxi, and Hunan. Simultaneously, Kwan made significant contributions to the cinema industry by starring in a variety of patriotic films across diverse genres, including *Song of Sadness*, *Xuejian Erliu Zhuang* (*Bloodshed at the Twin-Willow Manor*, 1936), and *The Knight*. In *Song of Sadness*, Kwan portrays a patriotic youth imbued with a revolutionary vision, with the film's promotional material emphasizing its employment of song and dance to "awaken the soul of Chinese people" amidst foreign oppression. *Bloodshed at the Twin-Willow Manor* and *The Knight*, on the other hand, showcase heroes who safeguard the nation from adversaries, offering a reinvention of popular chivalric (*xia*) narratives in Cantonese opera with a patriotic undertone.[73] In essence, Kwan's experiences during the war played a pivotal role in shaping the image of the kung fu master as a heroic figure entrusted with the responsibility of safeguarding the nation from external threats and invasions. While Kwan's portrayal of Wong Fei-hung may not overtly express such nationalistic sentiments, the character's alignment with Confucian values and traditional Chinese culture provided a solid foundation for subsequent kung fu cinema icons such as Chen Zhen and Ip Man.

Conclusion

When compared to globally renowned kung fu stars such as Bruce Lee and Jackie Chan, Kwan Tak-hing may be relatively unfamiliar to international audiences, as he did not attain the same level of widespread recognition as his successors. Nevertheless, Kwan remains an integral figure in the history of Hong Kong kung fu cinema and, to a certain extent, action cinema as a whole. Firstly, his martial arts ability established a benchmark for the genre's emphasis on realism and authenticity since 1949, laying the groundwork for Bruce Lee's transformative impact in the early 1970s. Kwan's background in operatic martial arts training also facilitated the exchange of southern and northern kung fu within the Wong Fei-hung film series, thus enabling accomplished choreographers like Yuen Woo-ping and Lau Kar-leung to merge these two styles through kung fu comedies in the late 1970s. Secondly, Kwan's fusion of acting and martial skills underscores the significance of both aspects in kung fu cinema, as successful action stars must not solely focus on one dimension. The achievements of Bruce Lee, Jackie Chan, and Jet Li hinge upon their genuine martial skills as well as their charismatic acting performances, exemplified in their portrayals of characters like Chen Zhen and Wong Fei-hung in films like *Fist of Fury, Fist of Legend, Drunken Master*, and *Once Upon a Time in China*. Lastly, Kwan played a pivotal role in shaping the archetype of the kung fu master. More than just a legendary fighting star, Kwan emerged as a true auteur, or "starteur"; as one of the dominant creative forces in the shaping of Wong Fei-hung across so many films, Kwan exerted a greater influence on the conventions of the kung fu genre than even the directors of the Wong Fei-hung films.[74] On one hand, Kwan synthesized the ideals of Chinese masculinity encompassing the literary and the martial, both on-screen and off. On the other hand, his patriotic image and charitable endeavors during the war contributed to his interpretation of the kung fu master as a guardian of the nation, thereby sowing the seeds for the prevalence of cultural and abstract nationalism in kung fu cinema, evident in films ranging from *Fist of Fury* to *Ip Man*. Accordingly, Kwan was one of the few performers "whose acting capabilities and screen personas are so potent that they embody and define the very essence of their films."[75] Above all, Kwan not only exemplified a unique fighting star who traversed the worlds of opera and cinema but also exemplified how a genuine kung fu master could stand steadfast and embody martial virtues amidst the global conflicts of the twentieth century. Therefore, Kwan should no longer be regarded solely as the actor who portrayed the legendary Wong Fei-hung, but rather as the legendary artist who introduced Wong and kung fu cinema to the world.

Notes

1   During the early 1950s, the term "kung fu films" (*gongfupian*) was not commonly employed. Instead, these films were referred to as "fist and kick wuxia films" (*quanjiao wuxia pian*). It was not until the emergence of Bruce Lee in the early 1970s that the term "kung fu films" gained popularity, distinguishing the hand-to-hand combat tradition from the more fantastical swordplay prevalent in the 1960s. (See Shing-hon Lau, "Introduction," in *A Study of the Hong Kong Martial Arts Film*, eds. Shing-hon Lau and Tony Rayns [Hong Kong: Urban Council of Hong Kong, 1980], 3–8). For the purpose of argument and clarity, the term "kung fu films" will be used in this chapter.

2   Throughout this chapter, I have predominantly employed the *pinyin* system to transcribe Chinese names, words, and phrases. Nevertheless, in the case of Cantonese names, I have maintained their customary spelling with the surname preceding the given name, hyphenated when necessary, such as "Kwan Tak-hing" rather than "Guan Dexing."

3   Hong Kong Film Archive, *The Making of Martial Arts Films: As Told by Filmmakers and Stars* (Hong Kong: Provisional Urban Council, 1999). See also Siu-Leung Li, "Kung Fu: Negotiating Nationalism and Modernity," *Cultural Studies* 15, nos. 3–4 (2001), 540.

4   Bey Logan, *Hong Kong Action Cinema* (New York: Overlook Books, 1996); Hector Rodriguez, "Hong Kong Popular Culture as an Interpretive Arena: The Huang Feihong Film Series," *Screen* 38, no. 1 (1997): 1–24; Leon Hunt, *Kung Fu Cult Masters: From Bruce Lee to Crouching Tiger* (London: Wallflower, 2003).

5   Hunt, *Kung Fu Cult Masters*, 39.

6   Stephen Teo, *Chinese Martial Arts Cinema: The Wuxia Tradition* (Edinburgh: Edinburgh University Press, [2009] 2016), 71.

7   See Mo Wen Yu, "The Prodigious Cinema of Huang Fei-hong: An Introduction," in *A Study of the Hong Kong Martial Arts Film*, 80, as well as King Sang Mak, "*Huang Feihong icon de bentu zaizao: Yi Liu Jialiang he Xu Ke de dianying weizhongxin* [Local Reinventions of the Wong Fei-hung Icon: Centering on the Films of Lau Lar-leung and Tsui Hark]," in *Xianggang kai guangdong wenhua* [*Cantonese Culture in Hong Kong*], ed. Kit Wah Man (Hong Kong: Shangwuyinshuju, 2014), 91.

8   Yu, "The Prodigious Cinema of Huang Fei-hong," 75; Rodriguez, "Hong Kong Popular Culture as an Interpretive Arena," 10; Gina Marchetti, "Martial Arts North and South: Liu Jialiang's Vision of Hung Gar in Shaw Brothers Films," *EnterText* 6, no. 1 (2006), 89; Feng Pu, "*Hongfei na fuji dongxi: Huang Feihong dianying de zhuanbian licheng* [The Transformation of the Wong Fei-hung Films]," in *Pupuxianggang: yuedu xianggang pujiwenhua 2000–2010* [*Popular Hong Kong: Reading Hong Kong Popular Culture 2000–2010*], eds. Chi Wai, Chun Hung Cheung, and Chung Kin Tsang (Hong Kong: Xianggang jiaoyu tushu gongsi, 2012), 158.

9   Kwan Yuk Ng, "*Cong xinliangjiu dao Huang Feihong: Guan Dexing xiying shengya diandi* [From an Opera Star to Wong Fei-hung: Kwan Tak-hing's Acting Career]," in *Zhushan weishi: Huang feihong dianying yanjiu* [*Mastering Virtue: The Cinematic Legend of a Martial Artist*], eds. Po Fung and Yao Lam (Hong Kong: Hong Kong Film Archive, 2012), 84.

10 Logan, *Hong Kong Action Cinema*, 12.

11 Yu, "The Prodigious Cinema of Huang Fei-hong," 73.

12 Hunt, *Kung Fu Cult Masters*, 39.

13 Ng, "From an Opera Star to Wong Fei-hong," 94.

14 Teo, *Chinese Martial Arts Cinema*, 70.

15 Ibid., 70. The historical authenticity of Wong Fei-hung remains a subject of debate, primarily because the majority of accounts about this martial arts figure originate from *wuxia* novels serialized in Hong Kong newspapers during the 1930s, authored by Zhu Yuzhai. See Yu, "The Prodigious Cinema of Huang Fei-hong," and Mak, "Local Reinventions of the Wong Fei-hung Icon."

16 Ibid.

17 Che Zhang, "Creating the Martial Arts Film and the Hong Kong Cinema Style," in *The Making of Martial Arts Films*, 19; Sabrina Qiong Yu, *Jet Li: Chinese Masculinity and Transnational Film Stardom* (Edinburgh: Edinburgh University Press, 2012), 58; Mak, "Local Reinventions of the Wong Fei-hung Icon," 89.

18 Lau Kar-leung quoted in Cheuk-to Li, "Interviews," in *A Tribute to Action Choreographers: 30th Hong Kong International Film Festival Programme*, ed. Cheuk-to Li (Hong Kong: Hong Kong International Film Festival Society, 2006), 60..

19 Yu, "The Prodigious Cinema of Huang Fei-hong," 80.

20 Zhang, "Creating the Martial Arts Film and the Hong Kong Cinema Style," 19.

21 Ka You Ho, "*Yuejuchuangzao de wuxi—xiaowu* [Martial Arts Performance Created by Cantonese Opera—Martial Roles]," *Opera Preview* (2020), http://www.operapreview.com/index.php/網上雜誌/item/1588-粵劇創造的武戲——小武 (accessed July 15, 2022).

22 Teo, *Chinese Martial Arts Cinema*, 72.

23 Q. Liu, "Hongquan shifu tan Huang Feihong dianying zhong de hongquan [Hung Gar Masters Discussing the Hung Gar Forms in the Wong Fei-hung Films]," in *Mastering Virtue*, 196–7.

24 Ibid., 197–8.

25 Hunt, *Kung Fu Cult Masters*, 17.

26 Yu, "The Prodigious Cinema of Huang Fei-hong," 77.

27 Marchetti, "Martial Arts North and South," 79.

28 Pu, "The Transformation of the Wong Fei-hung Films," 157.

29 Li, "Interviews," 53.

30 Yu, "The Prodigious Cinema of Huang Fei-hong," 77.

31 Pu, "The Transformation of the Wong Fei-hung Films," 158.

32 Logan, *Hong Kong Action Cinema*, 12.

33 Yu, "The Prodigious Cinema of Huang Fei-hong," 77.

34 Liu, "Hung Gar Masters Discussing the Hung Gar Forms in the Wong Fei-hung Films," 204.

35 Yu, *Jet Li*, 60.

36 Barry King, "Articulating Stardom," in *Star Texts: Image and Performance in Film and Television*, ed. Jeremy G. Butler (Detroit: Wayne State University Press, 1991), 125–54; Paul McDonald, "Star Studies," in *Approaches to Popular Film*, eds. Joanne Hollows and Mark Jancovich (Manchester: Manchester University Press, 1995), 79–97.

37 Yu, *Jet Li*, 61–2.

38 Logan, *Hong Kong Action Cinema*, 14.

39 Shaozhang Zhu, *Chen jintang yanyi pingsheng [Chen Jintang's Life in Performing Arts]* (Hong Kong: Sanlianshudian [Xianggang] youxiangongsi, 2018), 9.

40 Ng, "From an Opera Star to Wong Fei-hung," 85.

41 Hong Kong Film Archive, *The Making of Martial Arts Films*, 59.

42 Ng, "From an Opera Star to Wong Fei-hung," 85.

43 Poshek Fu, *Between Shanghai and Hong Kong: The Politics of Chinese Cinemas* (Stanford: Stanford University Press, 2003), 57.

44 Ng, "From an Opera Star to Wong Fei-hung," 86.

45 Kar Law, "The American Connection in Early Hong Kong Cinema," in *The Cinema of Hong Kong: History, Arts, Identity*, eds. Poshek Fu and David Desser (Cambridge: Cambridge University Press, 2000), 51–2.

46 Ng, "From an Opera Star to Wong Fei-hung," 86.

47 Ibid., 89.

48 Ibid., 89.

49 Ibid., 87.

50 Ibid., 86–8.

51 Logan, *Hong Kong Action Cinema*, 12; Rodriguez, "Hong Kong Popular Culture as an Interpretive Arena," 3.

52 Yu, "The Prodigious Cinema of Huang Fei-hong," 75; Pu, "The Transformation of the

Wong Fei-hung Films," 162; Teo, *Chinese Martial Arts Cinema*, 63.

53 Rodriguez, "Hong Kong Popular Culture as an Interpretive Arena," 15; Teo, *Chinese Martial Arts Cinema*, 65.

54 Pu, "The Transformation of the Wong Fei-hung Films," 159.

55 Ibid., 157.

56 Kam Louie and Louise Edwards, "Chinese Masculinity: Theorising Wen and Wu," *East Asian History* 8 (1994), 141–2.

57 Ibid., 144.

58 Kwai-Cheung Lo, "Muscles and Subjectivity: A Short History of the Masculine Body in Hong Kong Popular Culture," *Camera Obscura* 39 (1996): 105–26.

59 Rodriguez, "Hong Kong Popular Culture as an Interpretive Arena," 17.

60 Wayne Wong, "Synthesizing *Zhenshi* (Authenticity) and *Shizhan* (Combativity): Reinventing Chinese Kung Fu in Donnie Yen's Ip Man Series (2008–2015)," *Martial Arts Studies* 3 (2017), 77.

61 Hong Kong Film Archive, *The Making of Martial Arts Films*, 175.

62 Kei Sek, "The Development of 'Martial Arts' in Hong Kong Cinema," in *A Study of the Hong Kong Martial Arts Film*, 12; Logan, *Hong Kong Action Cinema*, 14; Teo, *Chinese Martial Arts Cinema*, 75.

63 Hong Kong Film Archive, *The Making of Martial Arts Films*, 59.

64 Teo, *Chinese Martial Arts Cinema*, 65.

65 Rodriguez, "Hong Kong Popular Culture as an Interpretive Arena," 15.

66 Pu, "The Transformation of the Wong Fei-hung Films," 158; Mak, "Local Reinventions of the Wong Fei-hung Icon," 88; Teo, *Chinese Martial Arts Cinema*, 66.

67 Rodriguez, "Hong Kong Popular Culture as an Interpretive Arena," 5.

68 Pu, "The Transformation of the Wong Fei-hung Films," 158.

69 H.X. Lu, *Xianggang wu lin ming shi ji* [*A Collection of Famous Hong Kong Martial Artists*] (Hong Kong: Hong Kong Wushu & Art Service Centre, 2005), 107.

70 Ng, "From an Opera Star to Wong Fei-hung," 88.

71 Zhou Yuan, "Aiguo yiren guan dexing yanyi guangxi chuanqi [Patriotic Artist: Kwan Tak-hing's Legendary Stories in Guangsi]," The Chinese People's Political Consultative Conference Wuzhou Commitee, 2016, http://www.gxwzzx.gov.cn/themes/content/content_1955.htm..

72 Logan, *Hong Kong Action Cinema*, 14.

73 Ng, "From an Opera Star to Wong Fei-hung," 88–9.

74 Laurence F. Knapp, *Directed by Clint Eastwood* (Jefferson, NC: McFarland, 1996); Dave Saunders, *Arnold: Schwarzenegger and the Movies* (London: I.B. Tauris, 2009); Kyle Barrowman, "Bruce Lee: Authorship, Ideology, and Film Studies," *Off-screen* 16, no. 6, https://offscreen.com/view/bruce_lee_authorship_part_1 (accessed September 23, 2023); Eric Pellerin, "Bruce Lee as Director and the Star as Author," *Global Media and China* 4, no. 3 (2019): 339–47.

75 Patrick McGilligan, *Cagney: The Actor as Auteur* (New York: Da Capo Press, [1975] 1980), 199.

Chapter 2

Bruce Lee: Effective and Affective Action Techniques

Paul Bowman

Figure 5 Bruce Lee in his iconic sidekick pose. *Enter the Dragon* directed by Robert Clouse. © Warner Bros. 1973. All rights reserved.

Introduction

Bruce Lee's film action choreography has long been esteemed by action film aficionados and martial artists alike, not just for its spectacular character, but also because it seems to have a powerful connection to "real fighting." Something about his on-screen performances leads many to conclude that he must also have been able to fight exceptionally in real life.[1] Others, however, have taken issue with his spectacular choreographies and rejected the idea that he could really fight, or fight to an exceptional level in real life.[2] And, of course, there are a range of middle-ground positions, which acknowledge his exceptional choreographic and performance skills, and draw inferences from that about the effects of his obsessive investment in ideas of the ultimate value of reality and realism, but who may hesitate to draw strong conclusions about his "real" fighting abilities.[3] In fact, the public debate about how good a fighter Bruce Lee "really was" has raged since before his untimely death at thirty-two in 1973.[4] At the time of writing in 2022, this debate still shows no sign of abating. In 2019, for instance, a high-profile dispute sprang up (and continues to this day) on both social and mainstream media about Quentin Tarantino's depiction of Bruce Lee in his explicitly revisionist or false history nostalgia film, *Once Upon a Time . . . in Hollywood*. This film inserts fictional characters into historical moments while changing historical events, most notably in relation to the "Manson Family" murders in Los Angeles in 1969. As is to be expected with the reception of any Tarantino film, there was some consternation about the violence within the film. But this debate soon came to be subordinated to a longer-running and more impassioned dispute about the status of the depiction of Bruce Lee.

Controversy arose in relation to a couple of dimensions of the representation of a caricatural "Bruce Lee."[5] One issue was about race. The question arose: was Tarantino's depiction of Bruce Lee racist? The other issue was about Bruce Lee "himself." The question was: was Tarantino's depiction of Bruce Lee accurate or fair? It is worth noting that these controversies were not formulated by film scholars, but by former friends, colleagues, and family. For film scholars, it would be more pertinent to note that *Once Upon a Time . . . in Hollywood* is not merely a Tarantino movie, it is also a movie that is explicitly set in Tarantino's postmodern, hyperreal "cinematic universe." Because of this, then, perhaps the most that can be said is that if the movie is deemed to be "about" anything at all in the real world, then that would principally have to be *other films*.[6]

As such, it is relevant that *Once Upon a Time . . . in Hollywood* is not only a film that is "about" other films on an intertextual level, or on the level of its construction. It is also literally about film stars and the Hollywood film industry of the late 1960s. Moreover, this is a film about film that also seems intent on making a point about films and their relation to reality—specifically film violence and its relation to real violence—perhaps particularly in relation to Tarantino's own body of work. The point about violence might be phrased like this: no matter how violent this (or any) film may appear, it is *nothing* compared to the violence of the living, breathing, moving, non-cinematic "real" world. Phrased differently: the violence in *Once Upon a Time . . . in Hollywood* is *obviously trivial* when compared with the actual violence of the Manson murders of 1969. (This might be interpreted as a kind of performative rebuff to critics who judge Tarantino's violent films to be culturally or socially deleterious). Moreover, the film's historically revisionist ending (as with other historically revisionist Tarantino films) provides a fantasy "happy ever after" that momentarily produces a kind of delight. The sweetness, levity, and optimistic happiness of the ending of *Once Upon a Time . . . in Hollywood* would not have been possible without the intense, fictional but "historically" reparative violence that immediately preceded it.

However, the public debate about the representation of Bruce Lee took place as if this film were a documentary or a work of responsible journalism. This is unsurprising as the main complainants included members of Bruce Lee's family, friends, colleagues, and students—many of whom have a vested interest in promoting a rather different image of Bruce Lee than was seen in *Once Upon a Time . . . in Hollywood*. However, I want to insist on treating the film as a film, and one that is (like all Tarantino films) mainly about other films; and always in more than one way. Specifically, I want to treat the film as *a text that forwards an artistic, performative argument about the relation of film to reality*. The film does this most blatantly in relation to the historically major theme of Sharon Tate and the Manson murders. But I want to contribute to the debate about the relation of film to reality via an exploration of the figure of Bruce Lee, beginning from the treatment of Bruce Lee in *Once Upon a Time . . . in Hollywood*.[7]

Fighting Co-stars and Body Doubles

The controversial scene, from which commentators have raised questions about possible racism and biographical inaccuracy, is a short, six-minute affair, which opens with Bruce Lee lecturing on the theme of combat, and which culminates with him getting into a fight and exchanging techniques with someone who disagreed with him. Before rushing headlong into questions of its treatment of race, history, biography, personality, or anything else, my proposition is that we should begin by approaching it in terms of its literal content: who says what to whom and who does what to whom. The six-minute-long scene is freely available online, so readers might like to view or review it before proceeding, if only to verify that the details I single out to treat as key coordinates in my outline are justifiable. Of course, viewing the scene in isolation won't provide all of the information required for a fully informed interpretation: inevitably, the scene makes a very different kind of sense when viewed in the context of the overarching story. Indeed, in terms of the plot and the explicit themes of the film, the scene serves merely as a light-hearted way to illustrate one theme of the film: the fact that the character Cliff Booth (Brad Pitt) keeps getting fired and is finding it harder to get work as a stunt man and stunt double for the movie actor Rick Dalton (Leonardo DiCaprio). Booth is Dalton's long-time friend and sidekick, and much of the film is concerned with their relationship.

The scene proceeds as follows. Bruce Lee (Mike Moh) struts around on the set of the television show *The Green Hornet* (1966–1967) lecturing a large impromptu audience of miscellaneous cast and crew about how much he admires fighters like Cassius Clay (aka Muhammad Ali). Lee praises such fighters' warrior-like, life-or-death, kill-or-be-killed intensity, and contrasts them with rule-bound sports martial arts competitors who fight for points.[8] Upon being asked whether he thinks he could beat Clay/Ali himself, Lee first states that such a fight would never happen, but then, when pressed on the matter, he says he would "cripple" Ali. Among the audience is stuntman Cliff Booth, who cannot stifle his laughter at this suggestion. When Lee aggressively asks Booth to explain himself, Booth at first tries to excuse himself in order to avoid a confrontation. However, when Lee belligerently insists on an explanation, Booth seems to realize or decide that conflict is now almost inevitable without a loss of face, so he rises to the challenge and says that he believes Lee is "a little man with a big mouth and a big chip," and states that Lee should be "embarrassed" to think that he could beat Ali, as, after a fight, Lee would be "nothing more than a stain on the seat of Cassius Clay's trunks."

Thus, the scene progresses toward conflict. However, both Lee and Booth are working on film or TV productions: Booth is a stunt-double for a movie star, while Lee is dressed in the chauffeur uniform he wore as the character Kato in the 1960s TV series *The Green Hornet*. Hence, neither can jeopardize their visual appearance. So, they agree to a contest with no hitting to the face and no trying to damage each other (thereby making a mockery of Lee's earlier declared contempt for rule-bound contests). The aim is simply to knock the other down. Booth stands and takes off his stunt-double wig and his jacket; Lee takes off his sunglasses and jacket in the frantic/frustrated manner seen in some of the real Bruce Lee's martial arts films; and he squares off wearing a white vest, identical to his attire in *The Way of the Dragon* (1972). He then postures, moves between stances, and makes noises similar to those made famous in his films of the early 1970s. In short, this is a *cinematic* Bruce Lee—a Bruce Lee made up of a mélange of the cinematic and televisual stereotypes about him that grew up in the wake of his film and TV roles. His appearance is first a mishmash (or mismatch) of Lee as Kato in *The Green Hornet* of 1967 combined with the haircut he adopted in the early 1970s. It then changes to include other visual clichés drawn from *The Big Boss* (1971) and *The Way of the Dragon*. His way of speaking is a kind of intensification or hyperbolic parody of famously intense moments of speech delivered in his TV and film career: there are elements taken from his powerful "jeet kune do" lesson-delivery in the TV show *Longstreet* (1971); moments drawn from his famous Pierre Berton TV interview; and aspects echoing the lecture given to his student Lau in *Enter the Dragon* (1973).

Meanwhile, Booth stands stock-still, waiting, with his fists held in a relaxed, low guard. Bruce Lee skips toward him and takes him by surprise with a jumping sidekick to the chest, knocking Booth to the ground. As he quickly returns to his feet, Booth says, "Not bad, Kato. Try that again." Lee does indeed try the exact same move again, but Booth is a fast learner. As the kick arrives, Booth grabs Lee's leg and spins him away, slamming him into a car, which is badly dented. Lee returns to his feet and both men exchange a flurry of blows, with neither showing decisive or definitive dominance. In the midst of this, the contest is

Figure 6 Bruce Lee (Mike Moh) throwing a flying sidekick at Cliff Booth (Brad Pitt). *Once Upon a Time . . . in Hollywood* directed by Quentin Tarantino. © Columbia Pictures 2019. All rights reserved.

interrupted by the appearance of the director's wife, who halts the conflict and sacks Booth—which is the ultimate narrative point of the scene.

Holy Sidekicks, Batman

Within the context of a postmodern film such as this, every aspect of this scene deserves to be appraised in terms that are more complex and subtle than knee-jerk reactions based on feelings about historical, biographical, or personality-focused accuracy. For instance, once we reflect on these textual features in terms of their connections both with the rest of the film and with the textual features of other pertinent film and media, we might actually come to regard the entirety of *Once Upon a Time . . . in Hollywood* as a film that is best characterized as a sidekick movie. It is a film that is all about its sidekicks. Cliff Booth is the sidekick of Rick Dalton. Cliff Booth's own "sidekick"—one who will play a pivotal role in the denouement of the film—is his own well-trained dog. In the real-world historical TV show, *The Green Hornet*, Kato (who was played by Bruce Lee) was the sidekick of "the Green Hornet," Britt Reid (Van Williams). And so on. Hence, one way to evaluate what we see in this scene in *Once Upon a Time . . . in Hollywood* might be to approach it as a contest between two sidekicks, each coming from different shows, or "universes." The contest ends unclearly, in a kind of draw, upon the arrival of an important female character.

Formulated like this, Bruce Lee fans will likely recall a clear textual precedent for the fight between sidekick Booth and sidekick "Kato." This is the fight between The Green Hornet's sidekick, Kato, and Batman's sidekick, Robin, in 1967, when the two TV shows crossed over into each other's realms. The 1967 Robin vs.

Kato fight also ended prematurely, with the entrance of a female character into the scene. If the Kato/Robin fight is the intertextual precedent of the Lee/Booth fight, it is also interesting that both the "original" 1967 fight and the 2019 "remake" are characterized not only by the fact that *metaphorical* sidekicks are fighting, but also by the status of *literal* sidekicks within both. Lots of sidekicks are thrown in the 1967 scene; the same jumping sidekick is thrown twice in the 2019 scene. The sidekick is a very specific combat technique in which the knee is raised and the foot thrust out to the side, to strike an opponent with either the bottom of the heel or the side of the foot. In *Once Upon a Time . . . in Hollywood*, Lee opens with a dramatic "flying" sidekick, a kick that involves a skip-step followed by a jump, so that the heel or side of the foot hits while the other foot is off the ground.

Thanks to his spectacular proficiency at jumping or "flying" sidekicks, and thanks also to the frequency and elegance with which Lee executed both standing and airborne sidekicks, the force of his semiotic association with the sidekick quickly became strong. In fact, arguably, Lee effectively changed the cultural status of the technique. For, although the sidekick has demonstrably existed for centuries, and been trained and used in diverse combative contexts across cultures, Lee's execution of sidekicks on-screen arguably elevated the sidekick to a new aesthetic status. Thanks to the success of the image of Bruce Lee performing the sidekick (whether jumping or standing), it arguably ultimately came metonymically to "stand for" Asian martial arts *tout court*. In other words, despite the sidekick's well-documented existence in, for example, Historical European Martial Arts, or French savate, Bruce Lee made the sidekick his own, made it stand for him, him for it, with both becoming the very symbolic encapsulation of Asian martial arts.

Bruce Lee's Sidekicks

Given all of this, I want to single out and reflect on Bruce Lee's sidekick. I want to do so as a way to think further and more deeply about the impact of the image of Bruce Lee's spectacular sidekick (whether moving or static)—and hence the impact of one specific aspect of "Bruce Lee"—on reality. This is because looking at how one part of one realm intersects with other parts of other realms offers a way to think further about the relationship between "film" and "reality," or (more precisely) about the effects of aspects of film on *other areas* of reality. Of course, because of its specificity, this study will in no way be "comprehensive": it is merely one look at one specific element (sidekicks) associated with one film star (Bruce Lee). But, although we are dealing with only one small feature (both of "film" and of "reality"), the ramifications of this approach are nonetheless far-reaching. This is at least because this style of approach offers some important potential operating principles for film studies, principles that, I argue, could prove useful in organizing the study of film, conceived neither in isolation nor as some isolated medium or realm, but rather as a significant "working part" of culture.

Put differently, although film is often distinguished from reality, it cannot ultimately be divorced from it. Films are real in any number of ways. They are part of the makeup of reality in numerous ways. Nonetheless, it is common (all too common) for film to be *contrasted* with reality. In one sense, this is understandable, perhaps even provisionally justifiable: there is a long history of conceiving of reality principally by contrasting it with fictional representation. Plato, for instance, would expel the creators of fictions, and fiction per se, from his ideal republic. Following Plato, the history of Western philosophy and Western thought more broadly has reserved the status of "real" for that which is verifiably true in ways that fiction can never be.

Along with the distinction between fiction/reality, there exists an equally understandable and equally tenacious phenomenological sense that the "most real"—or most materially present and pressing—form of reality is always going to be that which intersects with our physical bodies. That which enters our senses or impacts on our bodies in "real" ways is part of "reality." Cultural productions such as literature, theater, drama, film, music, and so on are all encountered through our bodily senses, of course, but they are easily regarded as secondary, non-necessary, supplementary add-ons. To reiterate the point made in different ways by both Stuart Hall and Tarantino's *Once Upon a Time . . . in Hollywood*, the dog on the screen can bark but it cannot bite.[9] Nonetheless, it is important to note that Plato disdained fiction and its purveyors for a very precise reason: because of its potential effects on reality. Fiction must be expelled from the republic because of its powers to affect people, in belief and action.

Of course, Bruce Lee's cinematic sidekicks are not simply fake or fictional: they are within the reach of many people, as technically achievable bodily movements. They are not even all that difficult to do. They merely require disciplined training, and regular, repeated practice. But they do appear within fictional narratives and curated, edited choreographies. So, in the terms of the naïve or pre-critical ontology sketched out above, they inhabit two realms at once: reality and unreality. Of course, naïve versions of ontology are ultimately unhelpful here. There are many other understandings of our relationships with images and objects. To evoke just a few different perspectives that have been influential in film studies at different times: to use the terms of Jacques Derrida's textual approach to ontology, for instance, we might say that images of Bruce Lee may become a *supplement* to our reality. Memories and aspirations related to Lee's sidekick might *haunt* our own attempts to emulate him/them.[10] Or, in terms of Lacanian psychoanalysis, we might say that the power of the image of

Lee's sidekick might stoke a desire, related to the desire for full subjective plenitude, or the desire to overcome our own sense of lack by attaining "phallic" mastery.[11] Or, in more Deleuzean terms, one potential "affect" of images of Lee's sidekick would be changing people's relation to their own bodies, the status of their own legs and feet, changing their understandings of and interests in what they do with them. And so on. In short, Lee's sidekicks (along with all of the other potential "parts" or potential effective/affective details about him) radiate *out* from his films and other images and texts, entering into other contexts, arrangements, assemblages, or "machines."

Lee's sidekicks are so good that I am certainly not the first to single them out and analyze them. Very many people have already reflected on and examined Lee's sidekicks—in books and magazines and, most recently, in YouTube and other online analysis videos. Such analyses focus on one or more repository or genre of archival footage: whether final cut film fight footage from Bruce Lee films, outtakes, Lee home video footage, or footage of demonstrations featuring Bruce Lee. In the interests of time and space, and because the issues are uncontroversial, there is no need to dig into the specifics of different online analyses. Instead, it is possible to make some sweeping statements about the conclusions drawn by the vast majority of the online "Bruce Lee breakdown" analyses.

First, the broad consensus is that Bruce Lee's sidekicks, as seen in his films, are powerful kicks delivered with significant force. The most famous sidekick may be the one he delivers to Han's henchman O'Hara (Bob Wall) in *Enter the Dragon*. The critics' view is that this is a real kick. Second, the sidekicks we see Lee thud into punchbags in his home video footage are also powerful. Third, the kicks we see Lee deliver in such public contexts as his sparring demonstrations during the Long Beach martial arts competitions in the 1960s,

Figure 7 Bruce Lee landing his famous sidekick on Bob Wall. *Enter the Dragon* directed by Robert Clouse. © Warner Bros. 1973. All rights reserved.

while being valid (albeit controlled/pulled) in and of themselves, are nonetheless surrounded by some less than perfect movements and less than perfect techniques. As one online commentator put it, the video footage of Lee's sparring demonstrations at Long Beach seems to show that, at that time, he and his students had not done very much free sparring (certainly not when judged by today's standards). In other words, even Bruce Lee's most spectacular cinematic sidekicks tend to be regarded as "real"—as in, technically correct, powerful, and both theoretically and practically valid. However, it is still a huge leap from this observation to the conclusion that "therefore" Lee's ability to "really fight" would overall be as excellent and exceptional as his sidekick (or any of his other cinematically curated techniques). Ultimately, then, it remains unclear whether Bruce Lee in non-choreographed, non-curated, non-controlled action would be greater than (or anywhere near as great as) the sum of his choreographed parts. Hence the interminability of the debate about his "real" abilities.

Real Fighting Action

In actual fact, as with "reality" so with "fighting": the notion of "real fighting" harbors the same ontological or metaphysical problems. For, upon interrogation, the notion of "real fighting" is actually hugely problematic and contains all manner of untenable assumptions and false universals. Most obviously: when people evoke or invoke "real fighting," they tend to be thinking of something akin to a formal duel, such as we see regularly in Bruce Lee's and many other action films. But this is not in any way a universal—or even particularly common—"real form" of interpersonal violence.[12] To elevate the myth of the "fair fight" or duel to the status of exemplar is a kind of romanticization and hypostatization (or essentialism) of fighting—one that owes as much to familiarity with literary, theatrical, and cinematic conventions as it does to sporting institutions such as boxing.[13] In fact, real-world violence, conflict, attacks, and assaults rarely take the form of the cinematically recognizable duel.[14] As such, whenever we are tempted to evoke "real fighting," many more qualifications and clarifications are required, such as where, when, why, with whom, how many, with what objectives, under what conditions, under what legal system, what social and cultural institutions supervene, what is the anthropotechnic environment (or general level or forms of trained skill), and so on. In other words, the question of "real fighting" is just like any other question of the real: namely, mired in uninterrogated generalizations and preconceptions, and based on a cultural fantasy scenario elevated to the status of norm, ideal, or yardstick.[15]

There are many directions that debates about "real" versus "cinematic" fighting can (and do) go. In this discussion, I want to stick to the interlinked themes of

Bruce Lee's "real" fighting ability and of the relations between the real and the cinematic (or between film and reality) that we have been entangled in since the outset.[16] As already noted, even films themselves sometimes seem to comment on their own relations to other aspects of reality. *Once Upon a Time . . . in Hollywood*, for instance, seems to want us to think more clearly about the *difference* between fictional violence on-screen and embodied violence in other locations. Indeed, it seems aligned with Stuart Hall's famous argument in his landmark essay "Encoding/Decoding" that the dog on the screen—Cliff Booth's highly trained dog, in *Once Upon a Time . . . in Hollywood*, perhaps—can't actually bite *you*. In fact, even when not discussing realism, film studies (much like film itself) is arguably structured by investments in questions of the relationships between film and other aspects of reality, whether that be identity or desire, sexuality or ethnicity, justice or politics, the understanding of history, or how to intervene in diverse contexts. This can be seen clearly even if we limit ourselves to a glance at the focus of academic work done on Bruce Lee. For example, studies have connected his film work to new possibilities for masculinity,[17] new versions of Asian and Asian American identity,[18] various nationalist subject-positions,[19] to subaltern, colonized, and postcolonial energies,[20] to post-racial and cosmopolitan dreams,[21] to the ethos of anti-institutional individuality,[22] and other real-world concerns.

All such orientations have value. They often take aspects of films as symbols, images, metaphors, and allegories, or signs of traumas, symptoms, and desires, and so on. However, in what follows, I will focus on one literal (i.e., denotative, not connotative) image of embodied physical reality, one that that is manifestly present in virtually all of Bruce Lee's work. I will not turn it into a symbol or treat it as a symptom. I will treat it as what it is: one *technique*. Admittedly, in focusing on this one detail, I also believe that it "stands for" m/any other possible examples. As such, it can perhaps be taken as a metonym. But I prefer to think of it as a case study. The case study taken is a recurring image that has immediate, non-metaphorical, non-symbolic, non-allegorical—i.e., literally physical—connections with, influences on, effects within, and transformative (affective) capacities in the lived, embodied, physical, "real world," in numerous ways. This technique is Bruce Lee's sidekick.

As mentioned, Lee's sidekick is indelibly wedded to his image. In a way, he stands for it and it stands for him. It is, as they say, "iconic."[23] Furthermore, it can immediately be considered a thing of beauty, something powerful, and hence highly evocative, balletic, in a way also "poetic."[24] It is something that can be romanticized, fantasized about, desired, in the way one might desire to be able to do this or any other impressive thing. But before that, it is merely a *technique*.[25] It is something that can be attempted, learned, and performed, with more or less practiced skill.[26] It can be emulated, performed differently, mimicked, worked on. and "perfected" in numerous different ways.

Affective Techniques

The passage from seeing to doing, from representation to practice, is at least as old as the possibility of the phrase "from reel to real" and as current as the formulation "from digital to physical" or "from virtual to embodied." Marcel Mauss noted many decades ago that French youth had been influenced in their physical behavior (the way they walked) by American movies.[27] Such affectations demonstrate film's affective power, or its power to affect—or (more awkwardly), its power "*of*" affect.[28] The three components of this observation—that *film* can *affect* the *body*—are the key coordinates of the passage from (and deconstruction of) the ostensibly "unreal" realm of film or fiction into the so-called "real world." In reflecting on this route, it becomes possible to discern the weakness of naïve or metaphysical ontologies, which would place "film" (and "fiction") on the side of "unreality" and the body firmly on the side of "reality" (because of its material presence). The capacity of film to affect the living material physical body deconstructs the unreal/real binary. This is precisely what can be seen (and felt) in the impact of Bruce Lee's screen sidekicks on the circulation of ideas about, training practices for, beliefs about, and pragmatic approaches to "real fighting" in the "real world."[29]

Of course, one might still ask whether Bruce Lee's sidekick is a flashy, spectacular, cinematic technique that "escaped" from film and changed the "real" world of bodily practice by affecting the way people thought about superlative fighting. The dissemination of this image certainly seemed to change what people thought superlative fighting *looked like*.[30] Or was Lee's signature sidekick simply brought (or translated) into film from the "real" world of martial arts, self-defense training, and combat sports? The sidekick is well-documented in fighting styles across cultures and throughout history. It is present in Early Modern European "fight books." It is well-known in Asian martial arts. And it is equally present in modern kickboxing styles such as French savate. The jumping or flying sidekick is somewhat rarer. The high kicking style of taekwondo was not created until the early 1950s, and even taekwondo would not start to develop spectacular jumping kicks in earnest until the late 1950s.[31] However, Bruce Lee's kicking abilities had been significantly aided by tuition from the Korean martial artist and kicking expert, Jhoon Rhee. So, there is an obvious sense in which Bruce Lee brought the spectacular sidekick into film from the outside, embodied, physical world.

But something *happened* when Bruce Lee transported or translated the sidekick into cinema. *His* sidekick had a unique affective power. In the terms of traditional Chinese martial arts, Lee's cinematic sidekick demonstrated not merely technical correctness (or *fa*, 法), but power in performance (or *gong*, 功)—and with an almost unique intensity.[32] This intensity constituted what Alain Badiou or Deleuze and Guattari would call an *event*—an affective "sense event" the force of which ripples outwards, into other realms and registers of human life. To my mind, this affective intensity is precisely what Tarantino's Bruce Lee in *Once Upon a Time . . . in Hollywood* strives hardest to capture and convey; but it is perhaps what most evades capture in attempts to represent Bruce Lee, on-screen or off. It is a quality that forever consigns all attempts to emulate Bruce Lee to the status of parody.

Effective Techniques

Similarly, just as *Once Upon a Time . . . in Hollywood* can easily be read as making an argument about one of the relationships between film violence and real-world violence, so Lee has often been read as inserting his own arguments about "real fighting" into his otherwise fictional TV and film appearances. In *Longstreet*, for example, Lee has his character give lectures on the principles of his own self-created martial art of jeet kune do. In *Way of the Dragon*, Lee has his character Tang Lung beat Chuck Norris's Colt by liberating himself from the strictures of classical combat approaches, in line with his argument in his own published article "Liberate Yourself from Classical Karate." In *Enter the Dragon*, Lee gives a philosophical account to his teacher of the ultimate aim of martial arts training, and soon thereafter lectures his own student Lau on the primacy of the proper psychological and emotional attitude needed in both combat training and in conflict. Finally, by all accounts, *The Game of Death* was intended to be an extended parable on the values of transcending the strictures of limited and limiting styles. In other words, it is always possible to "read" Lee's fight scenes as containing lessons or arguments about one or another principle of his own beliefs, theories, and practices of real-world fighting.

Nonetheless, according to his long-time friend and student, Dan Inosanto, Lee himself would often evoke a distinction between flashy cinematic techniques (whose purpose was *entertainment*) and "simple and direct" techniques (whose purpose was *effective* combat use). As Inosanto saw it, for Bruce Lee there was (so to speak) "street" jeet kune do and "screen" jeet kune do. Screen jeet kune do was bigger, flashier, more spectacular. Street jeet kune do was straighter, tighter, more linear.[33] The question is: where, in among all of this, is the sidekick is to be situated—as simple and direct, pragmatic and effective, or flashy and unrealistic? The sidekick is certainly flashy. This remains the case whether it is targeted high or low, whether to knee, belly, chest, or head, whether it is delivered from a stock-still grounded position, or whether it is on the end of a running jump. Moreover, a sidekick is certainly not a "natural" move. It requires training. It cannot be executed without skill acquisition. In my own half-century lifetime so far, I have never once seen someone do a sidekick correctly the first time. Most people need at least some instruction and some correction, and the majority take many lessons to get a sense of how to do it. It is a technique to be learned through training—what Michel Foucault would approach in terms of "discipline," "the means of correct training," and/or "technologies of the self";[34] or what philosopher Peter Sloterdijk calls "anthropotechnics," by which he means exercises that are habitually (indeed, religiously) practiced in order to foster, train, improve, and increase bodily capacities and skills. As Sloterdijk sees it, unlike other animals, humans are "beings who result from repetition," and can produce new versions of themselves by practicing different repetitions.[35]

It is interesting, then, that across all recorded media, from film to book publication, Lee gives prime position to the sidekick. He does so cinematically, in huge jumping sidekicks, and skip-and-step-in sidekicks. He also does so in television, in the jeet kune do episode of *Longstreet*, for example. And he does so in his home training videos. Perhaps this was in part precisely because the sidekick is a technique that needs to be *trained*. If you don't train it, you can't do it. As such, it is the hallmark of a disciplined, self-perfecting, practicing subject.[36] As a large and easily legible technique, the sidekick has a powerful semiotic and affective charge: you see it on-screen, and you can almost feel the impact it has on its target. Bruce Lee's devastating slow-motion sidekick against O'Hara in *Enter the Dragon* is the technique that ultimately destroys both O'Hara's physical body and the last remaining vestiges of any moral or psychological self-control: a vengeful Lee has chipped away at O'Hara from the start of their competition, by felling him numerous times with blindingly fast, technically brilliant, and ultimately humiliating single techniques. Lee has allowed no back-and-forth at all. In the end, the otherwise conclusive sidekick does not lead O'Hara to admit defeat, but rather to reveal his murderous character, hence even further justifying Lee's mortal retribution against a man who caused his sister's death.

While we may want to regard the sidekick—in its sheer largeness, its striking visuality—as a spectacular and therefore cinematic technique, it does not hold this status for Lee. Rather, Lee actually centralizes it in his own avowedly "practical" self-defense publications. The front cover and the entirety of the first chapter of his posthumously published book, *Bruce Lee's Fighting Method: Self-Defense Techniques*, for instance, is saturated with sidekicks. On the front cover, Lee sidekicks an opponent up into the air. On the contents page, he sidekicks an attacker on the street squarely in the chest. On the next page, he sidekicks another in the leg. On the next, he sidekicks to the front of the knee. On the next, he sidekicks to the back of the knee. On the next, he sidekicks a groin. On the next, the chest. And so on. So, it is sidekicks on the cover, the contents page, and through the entire first chapter. This seems to provide evidence that Lee regarded the sidekick as an effective and practical technique of self-defense.

Of course, this book was published posthumously, so Bruce Lee cannot be held personally responsible for its final design. Moreover, publications need to catch the eye and the imagination, so perhaps marketing considerations were involved in promoting the sidekick to the cover and the entirety of chapter one. But the very existence of these step-by-step technical photographs suggest that Lee regarded the sidekick—even the high sidekick—to be not *just* a flashy cinematic display, but *also* an entirely valid self-defense technique, to be used—perhaps even as a primary go-to technique—in real fighting on the street. (I once read that using the sidekick as an opening technique could be effective against both non-martial artists and people unaware that you were a kicking stylist—as it is not a natural technique for the untrained and can therefore easily take people by surprise. Anecdotally, my own personal experience confirms this. However, as Cliff Booth "demonstrates" in *Once Upon a Time . . . in Hollywood*, the sidekick will not remain surprising, effective, and unanswerable for long.)

The key point here is that the sidekick is *both* one of the most spectacular *cinematic* techniques—fast, explosive, devastating, entertaining, beautiful (sublime, even)—and *also* one of Bruce Lee's favorite *practical* techniques—adhering to all of the principles of linearity ("directness"), efficiency, and efficacy that he advocated as a martial artist.[37] It is also a fairly clear illustration of the importance of "anthropotechnics": for the sidekick to come *easy*, to seem *natural*—especially if it is to become a *reflex* response to a *surprise* attack—this requires *training*: lots and lots of training; training in how to execute the movement, and training in how to execute it *automatically*, or *pre-reflexively*, as a rapid response to a fluid situation.

To Train to Train

The question is: what does this teach us about the relations between film and reality? Was Lee's cinematic choreography informed by and infused with his street-level pragmatism? Or was his pragmatic and practical thinking and innovation in and around martial arts unwittingly influenced by cinematic performance? Put differently: when we see Bruce Lee kicking the heavy bag outside his home, we know he is *training*. But what is he training *for*—the street or the screen? Or might he indeed be like a teacher in their classroom, training merely for the delivery of a lesson—perhaps only ever training to train people how to train? The most we can say is that he is training for *performance*. Perhaps "to train" is an intransitive verb.

An insight attributed to Miyamoto Musashi is that one can only fight the way one trains.[38] Your training becomes you. As Sloterdijk puts it, "the subject itself is nothing other than the carrier of its own exercise sequences."[39] Crucially, our training is always infused with and organized by a *theory* of practice—whether explicit or tacit, whether we know it or not. This is why there is no fixed ontological stability to either the form or content of combat. Street combat can easily be informed by the cinematic; cinematic combat can easily be informed by the street. Not to mention many other contingent contexts of life. The human is environmental, ethological, biosemiotic, and always inventive.[40] As Lee famously said, in different ways at different times, humans have at most two hands and two feet. This led him to ask, rhetorically, how many ways of fighting there can really be. His belief was that ultimately such small and equally shared numbers of limbs and digits should tend toward universality; that *styles* were limitations, ossifications, and strictures. What he had not finished thinking through were the full implications of the fact that you can only fight the way you train, and that there are an unknown and unknowable number of ways to train. But where does this leave us vis-à-vis the question of Lee's real fighting abilities?

Conclusion: Happily Ever After in Hollywood

In terms of the crude binary of real (body) versus unreal (image), the question of how good a fighter Bruce Lee really was might never be conclusively answered. However, within the terms of film studies, media studies, and cultural studies, it is eminently possible to offer a very clear, well-supported, and well-evidenced answer. Bruce Lee really was an *amazing* fighter. You can *see* it. You can *feel* it. Bruce Lee choreography was like a wave sweeping up a beach and destroying and reconfiguring all of the sandcastles, footprints, and other indentations and etchings in its path. Bruce Lee conquered and transformed so many things. Put differently, the deconstruction of the supposed borders between "film" and "reality" should not be regarded as a purely theoretical enterprise, or a dead-end process—an academic exercise from which we turn around and leave as soon as we've finished reading or writing, and we look up, and go back "into" the "real world." Rather, deconstruction should produce a reconfigured sense of the relation and the border, and of what it means to be in the real world. After our deconstruction and rethinking of reality, when we return to the question of how good a fighter Bruce Lee really was, we should now be operating with a more expansive understanding of reality, one that is not wedded and welded to a kind of parody of a crude Platonic or Rousseauian myth in which "real reality" is the stuff we experience once we have excluded all of the other experiences that come to us via media, texts, words, images, or institutions. Rather than this, the affective power—that is, the power to change and be changed—of all experiences, mediated as much as unmediated, should be accorded and approached in terms of our retooled and retrained ontological and phenomenological theory.

In an important passage in *Parables for the Virtual*, Brian Massumi tracks the movement of affect outward from a football game, out into the crowd in attendance, and then into televisual media and hence into living rooms and other audience viewing locations, and beyond.[41] The effects are real. Captured by different contexts (stadium, television set), the effects produced are different in each context; but this is precisely what must be borne in mind when discussing reality. Viewed from this vantage point, the cinematic, televisual, magazine, and book publications that have captured, encoded, and disseminated so many images of Bruce Lee performing different techniques (here we have only considered the sidekick) can be seen and shown to have had profound effects in myriad different contexts. Whereas a Lacanian approach might suggest that Bruce Lee's image produced different desires, in the vocabulary of Deleuze and Guattari we might instead say that the image plugged into desires to produce different "machines."

The documented cases of people who saw Bruce Lee films in the 1970s and left the cinema performing their first ever attempts at high kicks, jumping kicks, improvised exotic kung fu stances and sounds can be regarded as the first productions of "Bruce Lee desiring machines," which would culminate in the appearance of countless martial artists in the years and decades that followed. Studying the technique of the sidekick as executed by Bruce Lee was part of this production process. In other words, Lee's techniques affected desires and caused a proliferation of new anthropotechnic practices. His choreographies produced what Deleuze and Guattari might call a superlative sense event. Put differently: Bruce Lee was *so good* an on-screen fighter that he actually changed the understanding of what good fighting looked like.

As such, the film studies answer to the question of how good a fighter Bruce Lee really was is of course absolutely unequivocal: measured by any standards, Bruce Lee was so good that he changed the standards and even the modes of measurement of good fighting. He was instrumental in precipitating a paradigm revolution, both in film action choreography and in martial arts training and practice, the world over.

Notes

1   Davis Miller, *The Tao of Bruce Lee* (London: Vintage, 2000).

2   Robert W. Smith, *Martial Musings: A Portrayal of Martial Arts in the 20th Century* (Erie, PA: Via Media, 1999).

3   Matthew Polly, *Bruce Lee: A Life* (New York: Simon and Schuster, 2018).

4   Daryl Joji Maeda, *Like Water: A Cultural History of Bruce Lee* (New York: New York University Press, 2022).

5   Tarantino himself has stated publicly that his Bruce Lee in this film was a parody, but this point has either been ignored or taken as further evidence of "disrespect."

6   Maybe all films are only ever about other films, at least insofar as they are intelligible, recognizable, familiar, and so on. (Cf. Meaghan Morris, "Learning from Bruce Lee: Pedagogy and Political Correctness in Martial Arts Cinema," in *Keyframes: Popular Cinema and Cultural Studies*, eds. Matthew Tinkcom and Amy Villarejo [London: Routledge, 2001.]) With Tarantino, the connection of his films with other films is always very self-conscious and deliberate. As is well known, in discussing the filmmaker as artist, Tarantino once famously stole a phrase from Picasso, saying that good artists borrow, but great artists steal.

7   In doing this, I will have to marginalize attention to Lee's personal and professional biography. But this is justifiable, as there is now a readily accessible range of different kinds of work that focus on his biography. (See Polly, *Bruce Lee*, and Maeda, *Like Water*). In addition, I myself have written three books on Bruce Lee's martial arts, choreography, and cultural impact. (See Paul Bowman, *Theorizing Bruce Lee: Film-Fantasy-Fighting-Philosophy* [Amsterdam: Rodopi, 2010]; *Beyond Bruce Lee: Chasing the Dragon through Film, Philosophy, and Popular Culture* [New York: Columbia University Press, 2013]; *The Treasures of Bruce Lee: The Official Story of the Legendary Martial Artist* [New York: Applause Theater & Cinema Books, 2013].) It therefore seems appropriate to *build upon* rather than *repeat* what has already been established.

8   This does reflect Lee's actual, published position. See Bruce Lee, "Liberate Yourself from Classical Karate," *Black Belt Magazine* (1971), https://blackbeltmag.com/liberate-yourself-from-classical-karate (accessed September 23, 2023).

9   Stuart Hall, "Encoding/Decoding," in *Culture, Media, Language*, eds. Stuart Hall, Dorothy Hobson, Andrew Lowe, and Paul Willis (London: Routledge, 1980).

10   Jacques Derrida, *Specters of Marx: The State of the Debt, The Work of Mourning, and the New International* (London: Routledge, 1994); Paul Bowman, *Mythologies of Martial Arts* (London: Rowman & Littlefield International, 2017).

11   Kaja Silverman, *The Subject of Semiotics* (Oxford: Oxford University Press, 1983); Slavoj Žižek, *The Sublime Object of Ideology* (London: Verso, 1989).

12   Rory Miller, *Meditations on Violence: A Comparison of Martial Arts Training & Real World Violence* (Boston, YMAA Publication Center, 2008); Randall Collins, "The Micro-sociology of Violence," *British Journal of Sociology* 60, no. 3 (2009): 566–76.

13   Rory Miller, *Violence: A Writer's Guide* (CreateSpace Independent Publishing Platform, 2012).

14   Miller, *Meditations on Violence*; Collins, "The Micro-sociology of Violence" and "Micro and Macro Causes of Violence," *International Journal of Conflict and Violence* 3, no. 1 (2009): 9–22.

15   This may sound obvious to self-defense researchers and teachers. (See Rory Miller and Barry Eisler, *Facing Violence: Preparing for the Unexpected* [Wolfeboro, NH: YMAA Publication Center, 2011.) However, some who debate such topics as "real" fighting remain blind to it, and either intentionally or unintentionally avoid facing up to the complexity, uncertainty, and unpredictable heterogeneity of "reality."

16   There are various ways into this complex field, and many who have studied and theorized films have engaged with the question of the relationships between cinematic representation and reality in diverse ways. Debates about "realism" have an important place in the long history in film studies, with important contributions from such luminaries as Siegfried Kracauer (see his *Theory of Film: The Redemption* *of Physical Reality* [Princeton, NJ: Princeton University Press, {1960} 1997]), André Bazin (see his *What is Cinema? Vols. 1 and 2*, ed. and trans. Hugh Gray [Berkeley, CA: University of California Press, 2005]), and Stanley Cavell (see his *The World Viewed: Reflections on the Ontology of Film* [Cambridge, MA: Harvard University Press, {1971} 1979]). In the more recent history of martial arts cinema studies, scholars who have engaged with questions of realism in relation to Bruce Lee films include Leon Hunt (see his *Kung Fu Cult Masters: From Bruce Lee to Crouching Tiger* [London: Wallflower, 2003]), Kyle Barrowman (see his "Action Aesthetics: Realism and Martial Arts Cinema," *Off-screen* 18, no. 10 [2014], https://offscreen. com/view/action-aesthetics-pt1 [accessed September 23, 2023]), and Wayne Wong (see his "Synthesizing *Zhenshi* [Authenticity] and *Shizhan* [Combativity]: Reinventing Chinese Kung Fu in Donnie Yen's Ip Man Series [2008–2015]," *Martial Arts Studies* 3 [2017]).

17 Jachinson Chan, "Bruce Lee's Fictional Models of Masculinity," *Men and Masculinities* 2, no. 4 (2000): 371–87.

18 Sylvia Shin Huey Chong. *The Oriental Obscene: Violence and Racial Fantasies in the Vietnam Era* (Durham, NC: Duke University Press, 2012).

19 Ackbar Abbas, *Hong Kong: Culture and the Politics of Disappearance* (Minneapolis: University of Minnesota Press, 1997); Stephen Teo, *Hong Kong Cinema: The Extra Dimensions* (London: BFI, 1997).

20 Vijay Prashad, *Everybody Was Kung Fu Fighting: Afro-Asian Connections and the Myth of Cultural Purity* (Boston: Beacon Press, 2002) and "Bruce Lee and the Anti-Imperialism of Kung Fu: A Polycultural Adventure," *Positions* 11, no. 1 (2003): 51–90; M.T. Kato, *From Kung Fu to Hip Hop: Globalization, Revolution, and Popular Culture* (Albany: State University of New York Press, 2012).

21 Bowman, *Beyond Bruce Lee*.

22 Daniele Bolelli, *On the Warrior's Path: Philosophy, Fighting, and Martial Arts Mythology* (Berkeley: Blue Snake Books, 2003).

23 Bowman, *Mythologies of Martial Arts*, 77–81.

24 Barry Allen, *Striking Beauty: A Philosophical Look at the Asian Martial Arts* (New York: Columbia University Press, 2015).

25 Benjamin Spatz, *What A Body Can Do: Technique as Knowledge, Practice as Research* (London: Routledge, 2015).

26 Peter Sloterdijk, *You Must Change Your Life: On Anthropotechnics*, trans. Wieland Hoban (London: Polity, 2013).

27 Marcel Mauss, "Techniques of the Body," in *Incorporations*, eds. Jonathan Crary and Sanford Kwinter (New York: Zone, 1992), 455–77.

28 Melissa Gregg and Gregory J. Seigworth, *The Affect Theory Reader* (Durham, NC: Duke University Press, 2010).

29 Bowman, *Theorizing Bruce Lee*.

30 BBC Radio 4, "Kung Fu, Series 15, In Living Memory—BBC Radio 4," *BBC* (2012), https://www.bbc.co.uk/programmes/b01c7rgs (accessed September 23, 2023); BBC4, "Everybody Was Kung Fu Fighting: The Rise of Martial Arts in Britain, Series 12, Timeshift—BBC Four," *BBC4*, http://www.bbc.co.uk/programmes/b01p2pm6/clips (accessed September 23, 2023).

31 Alex Gillis, *A Killing Art: The Untold History of Tae Kwon Do* (Ontario: ECW Press, 2008); Udo Moenig, *Taekwondo: From a Martial Art to a Martial Sport* (London: Routledge, 2015).

32 Timothy J. Nulty, "*Gong* and *Fa* in Chinese Martial Arts," *Martial Arts Studies* 3 (2017): 50–63.

33 Dan Inosanto, *Jeet Kune Do: The Art and Philosophy of Bruce Lee* (London: Atlantic Books, 1994).

34 Michel Foucault, *Discipline and Punish: The Birth of the Prison* (New York: Pantheon Books, 1977); *Power/Knowledge: Selected Interviews and Other Writing, 1972–1977*, ed. Colin Gordon (New York: Pantheon Books, 1980); *The History of Sexuality, Volume 3: The Care of the Self* (London: Penguin, 1990). Foucault, Michel. 1977.

35 Sloterdijk, *You Must Change Your Life*, 4.

36 Ibid. See also Kyle Barrowman, "Bruce Lee and the Perfection of Martial Arts (Studies): An Exercise in Alterdisciplinarity," *Martial Arts Studies* 8 (2019): 5–28, and "Lessons of the Dragon: Bruce Lee and Perfectionism between East and West," *Global Media and China* 4, no. 3 (2019): 312–24.

37 D.S. Farrer, "Efficacy and Entertainment in Martial Arts Studies: Anthropological Perspectives," *Martial Arts Studies* 1 (2015): 34–45.

38 Despite its popularity in Musashi memes, neither this statement nor anything close to it occurs anywhere in Musashi's writings. (Cf. Miyamoto Musashi, *The Complete Musashi: The Book of Five Rings and Other Works*, trans. Alexander Bennett [Enfield: Tuttle, 2018].) The translator of his complete works, Alexander Bennett, confirmed in a personal email that there is nothing in the original Japanese text that could be directly translated into the words "You can only fight the way you train," although the sentiment is in line with—or amounts to a kind of paraphrase of—many of Musashi's own teachings.

39 Sloterdijk, *You Must Change Your Life*, 242.

40 Judith Wambacq and Sjoerd van Tuinen, "Interiority in Sloterdijk and Deleuze," *Palgrave Communications* 3, no. 1 (2017): 1–7.

41 Brian Massumi, *Parables for the Virtual: Movement, Affect, Sensation* (Durham, NC: Duke University Press, 2008).

Chapter 3

Angela Mao: Lady Kung Fu in Search of International Markets

Man-Fung Yip

Figure 8 A powerful high kick from Angela Mao. *Hapkido* directed by Huang Feng.

Introduction

More than any other film industries, Chinese-language cinema has developed and maintained a vibrant tradition of powerful action heroines, the origin of which can be traced to Shanghai martial arts films of the late 1920s and early 1930s. When the genre was revived in Hong Kong at the end of the 1940s, the woman warrior figure was also given a new lease on life, and the following decades saw a proliferation of actresses—among them Yu Suqiu, Cheng Pei-pei, Hsu Feng, and many others—who captivated viewers with their portrayals of strong, self-determining women marked by exceptional martial arts skills. Even with the growing dominance of the kung fu genre in the early to mid-1970s, whose aggressive, intensely physical fighting style may put women at a disadvantage, there was no lack of powerful female fighters in martial arts films of the period. A good example is Angela Mao Ying; appearing in more than forty films between 1968 and 1992, Mao is best known for her roles as hard-hitting heroines in a string of kung fu movies from the 1970s, notably Huang Feng's *Lady Whirlwind* (*Tie zhang xuanfeng tui*, 1972), *Hapkido* (*Heqi dao*, 1972), and *When Taekwondo Strikes* (*Taiquan zhen jiuzhou*, 1973), as well as Jeong Chang-hwa's *Broken Oath* (*Po jie*, 1977).[1]

Discussions of Mao (and other female action stars) have typically focused on the cultural politics of gender representation. While the issue will be addressed in this chapter, my focus is broader and directs attention to the ways in which Mao's films and her star image are intertwined with the larger context of Golden Harvest's concerted efforts toward internationalization. At the outset, with emphasis given to her arduous training with Korean martial arts experts and to her spinning high kicks, Mao was touted as a "female Bruce Lee" to capitalize on the nascent kung fu craze and the growing status of Lee as a global popular icon. This strategy continued despite—or rather because of—Lee's sudden death in the summer of 1973. For instance, Mao was chosen to take Lee's place in Huang Feng's *The Shrine of Ultimate Bliss* (*Tie jingang da po ziyang guan*, 1974; released in the US as *Stoner*), a film originally envisioned as Lee's follow-up to the Warner Bros. production *Enter the Dragon* (1973) and supposed to bring together Lee, Japanese martial arts star Sonny Chiba, and one-time James Bond George Lazenby. Like *Enter the Dragon*, which sought to reinvent Lee as a quasi-James Bond figure with martial arts, *The Shrine of Ultimate Bliss* played like an action-spy thriller in which Mao appeared as a "Jane Bond" of sorts (much like what Tamara Dobson and others did within the context of blaxploitation movies at the time). Efforts were also made to broaden the market scope of Mao's films through collaborations with South Korea (*Hapkido*; *When Taekwondo Strikes*) and foreign location shooting in Thailand and Nepal (Huang Feng's *The Tournament* [*Zhong tai quantan sheng si zhan*, 1974] and *The Himalayan* [*Mizong sheng shou*, 1976], respectively). While these attempts to turn Mao into an international star did not have the same level of success as the previous campaign with Bruce Lee, they did build a sizable fan base for her in Asia and throughout the globe. The impact of her films was also readily observable, notably in the *Sister Street Fighter* series (1974–6) where Shihomi Etsuko, a protégé of Sonny China, stars as a half-Chinese martial arts champion strongly reminiscent of Mao's hard-nosed heroines (rumors were that Shihomi was a last-minute replacement for Mao). More recently, Quentin Tarantino cited *Lady Whirlwind* and *Broken Oath* as an influence on his *Kill Bill* series (2003–4) and, like an enthusiastic fan, organized an Angela Mao kung fu night at the New Beverly Cinema in Los Angeles.[2]

In the Shadow of Bruce Lee

Born as Mao Ching-ying in 1950, Angela Mao received her first martial arts training at the age of six, in the Peking Opera school founded and run by her father shortly after he moved from China to Taiwan in 1949. By her own admission, this opera background played a crucial role in her success as an action star. Mao was playing *wu dan* (female warrior) roles in a Peking Opera troupe when Huang Feng, who was to become one of her regular directors, discovered her and recommended her to Raymond Chow, the head of the newly founded Golden Harvest. Eventually, she signed a contract with the studio in 1970.

Wasting no time, Golden Harvest quickly put Mao to work, who appeared in a total of ten films during her first three years in the studio. With these efforts, Mao established herself as one of the most prominent female action stars in Hong Kong cinema. Meanwhile, the emerging kung fu craze around the world also gave Mao's films increasing international—and what was most important to Golden Harvest from a commercial perspective, US—exposure. On May 16, 1973, *Lady Whirlwind*, released under the name *Deep Thrust* in the US, was ranked second on *Variety*'s list of the week's top box-office draws; it went on to reach the top spot in the week of May 23 and would stay on the chart for more than a month. Indeed, together with Jeong Chang-hwa's *King Boxer* (*Tianxia diyi quan*, 1972; released in the US as *Five Fingers of Death*) and Lo Wei's *The Big Boss* (*Tangshan daxiong*, 1971; released in the US as *Fists of Fury*), *Lady Whirlwind* was one of the films that initiated the kung fu craze in the United States.[3] This craze continued for much of 1973, and films featuring Mao were some of the most popular among the Hong Kong imports. *Hapkido* (released in the US as *Lady Kung Fu*), for instance, reached number one on *Variety*'s list for the week of September 19 and knocked *Enter the Dragon*, which had been at the top of the chart in the previous two weeks, down to the third spot. *The Opium Trail* (*Hei lu*, 1973; released in the US as *Deadly China Doll*), another Mao vehicle directed by Huang Feng, was the top box-office hit for the week of October 10.[4] Indeed, from late March 1973 until mid-October of the same year, a total of six Hong Kong martial arts films reached the top spot, at least for one week, and of those six films, Mao starred in three of them.

Among both critics and fans, Mao has often been referred to as a "female Bruce Lee." While this makes sense in many ways, some qualifications are needed. Golden Harvest signed a contract with Mao in 1970, one year before it landed a deal with Bruce Lee, and the first films the studio assigned to her—Lo Wei's *The Invincible Eight* (*Tian long ba jiang*) and Huang Feng's *The Angry River* (*Gui nu chuan*)—were both released in the first half of 1971, before Lee's first kung fu film, *The Big Boss*, scored big in the box-office later that year. And the fact that both *The Invincible Eight* and *The Angry River* belong to the *wuxia* or swordplay subgenre (as opposed to the more hard-hitting kung fu film) suggests that Mao's persona in the films are indebted more to the female knight-errant figure in previous martial arts movies of the Shaw Brothers and other companies than to the muscular, fist-fighting hero exemplified by Lee.[5] But following the huge box-office successes of *The Big Boss* and later *Fist of Fury* (*Jing wu men*, 1972; released in the US as *The Chinese Connection*) and *The Way of the Dragon* (*Meng long guo jiang*, 1972; released in the US as *Return of the Dragon*), there was a clear shift in focus, with Golden Harvest making a more concerted effort to refashion Mao as a female counterpart of Lee. *Lady Whirlwind* was released in June 1972, three months after *Fist of Fury*, followed by *Hapkido* in October 1972, *The Opium Trail* in June 1973, and *When Taekwondo Strikes* in September 1973. All these titles show a switch from *wuxia* to kung fu and incorporate many of the features—struggle against Japanese foes or drug-smuggling thugs, the "rival schools" narrative, etc.—characteristic of Lee's films.[6] *Hapkido*, in particular, has often been said to be a clone of *Fist of Fury*, recycling not only the latter's narrative premises (a conflict between Japanese and Chinese martial arts schools; the choice between violence and restraint) and strong anti-Japanese sentiments, but also the ways in which some of the fights unfold (e.g., the protagonist taking on a large group of rival students before finally battling the *sensei* or master).[7]

While the 1970s saw other notable female kung fu stars (such as Shangkuan Lingfeng and Nancy Yen), Mao stood out in that her fight scenes were the most intense, intricate, and believable—in other words, the closest to the unprecedented standard set by Bruce Lee. According to Hsiung Ping Chiao, Lee made popular the trend of using real fighters instead of mere actors in martial arts films. The new rule of the game was proficiency in actual fighting skills, and film studios sought to promote their action stars by emphasizing how they trained in particular martial arts styles.[8] As noted earlier, Mao had received martial arts training in her father's Peking Opera school and was already an accomplished *wu dan* when she became a film actress, but even that was not enough in the new era of martial arts cinema defined by "real kung fu" (*zhen gongfu*). This explains why months before shooting for *Hapkido* started, Mao—along with Zhang Yi and Sammo Hung—was sent to study the eponymous Korean martial art with famed master Ji Han-jae. In an article published in *Golden Harvest News*, the studio's official magazine, Mao recounts in detail the grueling training she had to go through, which involved redirection of *chi* energy (the life force that runs through the individual), jumping with sandbags attached to legs, and repeated practices of leaping kicks. Toward the end, the action star notes with pride that, despite lots of sweats and tears, she was able to overcome all the hardship and obstacles and to pass the first-degree black belt examination.[9] This focus on the off-screen training process was a common promotional tactic of film studios at the time and served to grant an actor or actress an aura of legitimacy and authenticity in terms of their martial arts and physical skills.[10] Not coincidentally, while hapkido is a hybrid martial art that comprises a host of different techniques (including hand strikes, joint-locks, and even use of weapons), the emphasis of Mao's report is on the jump kicks. This comes as no surprise, for Mao's on-screen fighting style is centered to a large extent on her head-kicking ability, which in turn may be seen as an effort to emulate Lee's spectacular high kicks.

The notion of Mao—and other female action stars, for that matter—as a simulation or even copy of Lee points to the complex gender politics pertaining to her star image. On the one hand, the fact that Mao's characters, like the ones played by Lee, are consistently active in the narratives and possess top-notch martial arts skills that allow them to fight men as equals undermines the essentialized connection between codes of masculinity and femininity and their respective sexes, and opens up a space where the traditional gender boundary is increasingly blurry and flexible. On the other hand, an imitation or a copy often connotes a sense of falsehood or inferiority, and the appropriation of qualities— such as hardness and strength—historically associated with men, while empowering in some ways, may also paradoxically bolster the dominant norms of masculinity and turn them into a stable foundation.[11] These contradictory meanings caution us against a facile celebration of the woman warrior figure as an icon of female power and liberation. Yet it is also important to bear in mind the necessary incompleteness of masculinity as a normative foundation and recognize those moments, however brief they may be, that elude the control of regulatory masculine norms. A good case in point can be found, again, in *Hapkido*: in her fight against the Chinese chief instructor of the rival Japanese martial arts school (played by Bai Ying), Mao's character uses her pigtail knockers as a weapon to whip her opponent's face repeatedly. Needless to say, Lee never did something like that in his films, and it is a telling moment that sets Mao apart from her male model and highlights her own identity as a female fighter.

Also complicating the image of Mao as a female Bruce Lee is the propensity, most noticeable in the marketing of her films in the West (especially the US), to view her as a tough and aggressive fighter while invoking at the same time the stereotype of (East) Asian women as a tantalizing sexual object. For instance, *Lady Whirlwind* was released as *Deep Thrust* in the US—a sly reference to *Deep Throat* (1972), an enormously popular American pornographic film directed by Gerard Damiano that launched the so-called "porno chic" trend. This tendency to "sexualize" Mao became even more brazen with the publicity efforts for *Hapkido*. The film's US poster reads: "Here Comes the Unbreakable China Doll Who Gives You the Licking of Your Life!" This line, narrated by a gruff-sounding male voice, was reiterated in the American trailer of the film, which also exploits the pigtail attack discussed earlier with another double entendre: "Watch out for the pigtail that whips you up and wipes you out." All this seems to make little sense, given the asexual nature of the characters Mao played, not just in *Hapkido* but in most of her films. In fact, the actress herself had a rather conservative stance toward on-screen sexuality and was known to be a "prude" among her

Figure 9 Angela Mao using a pigtail knocker as a weapon. *Hapkido* directed by Huang Feng. © Golden Harvest 1972. All rights reserved.

colleagues.[12] It is likely that the US distributors used the made-up erotic appeal of Mao as an additional draw for the young male adults who constituted the primary audiences for the imported martial arts films at the time, but the tactic may also be understood as a means to "soften" the masculine connotations of the actress's star persona. (The regular use of the China Doll trope, manifested not only in the aforementioned tagline of *Hapkido* but also in the title *Deadly China Doll* given to the film *The Opium Trail* in its US release, lends further credence to this view.) It is as though the potential threats posed to hegemonic masculinity by an active, self-assured woman warrior, one possessing a high degree of physical prowess capable of domination, needed to be alleviated by a softer image that foregrounds female sexuality and "conventional" feminine attributes such as delicacy and docility.

This "taming" of the female fighter could also help explain Mao's role—Su Li, the doomed sister of Bruce Lee's character—in *Enter the Dragon*, Golden Harvest's first blockbuster film (co-produced with Warner Bros.) targeted at the global market. While arguably giving the actress the most exposure to US and international audiences (by virtue of the film's massive global box-office success worldwide) and cementing the association of her star persona with that of Lee, the role, in contrast to the ones Mao played in her Hong Kong films, only has limited screen time. More importantly, despite being a skilled fighter who can fight better than most men, the character ultimately takes her own life to rid herself from the terrifying prospect of rape at the hands of a white American assailant. In the words of May Joseph, Mao's character, while personifying "an agent against patriarchy and traditional notions of femininity who dismantles the coordinates of gender role-playing," also illustrates through her death the failure of this feminist vision "by reiterating the reductive ways that gender and sexuality work to subject women's and other minority bodies to violence."[13]

What we see above, then, are the complex and often contradictory gender politics associated with the star identity of Mao (and other cinematic women warriors). These tensions, I should add, can be observed not only in the portrayal of her characters or in how the actress was marketed to the US and international audiences; they were also manifested in the gap separating the screen persona of the actress and her real-life self. The irony here is that, despite the powerful characters Mao impersonated in her films, the actress herself, in real life, had little power vis-à-vis the hard-nosed policies of Golden Harvest and could even be said to be exploited by the studio. For instance, it was widely rumored that Mao was paid a meager salary of US$150 a week even after her rise to stardom. When asked about this, Andre Morgan, a US expatriate who worked as a general director at Golden Harvest during the 1970s, dismissed the question without refuting it outright, noting merely that the actress was "doing all right" by Hong Kong standards.[14] In addition, it was evident that Mao did not have much power in choosing her roles or even getting her opinions heard. Again, Morgan's remarks shed some light on the situation: "[Mao] is allowed to change a line here or there, or even suggest scenes, but . . . the studio has the final say."[15] He went on to note that Hong Kong studios (such as Golden Harvest) were akin to Hollywood of by-gone days, when big studio bosses kept their stars literally under their heels. Mao herself appeared to acknowledge her lack of choices and tried to rationalize it in this way: "As an artist, I know producers must give what the public wants. I may not like the roles, but I know I'm only an instrument of the public demands and a tool for the producer to meet that demand [sic]. And if kung-fu movies are what the public wants, then kung-fu movies are what we'll give them."[16] In a way, Mao's position is diametrically opposite to that of a star such as Katharine Hepburn. According to Andrew Britton, Hepburn's feminist presence, which is always more radical than her films, creates contradictions in a way "that not only resists their resolution in a stable, affirmable ideological coherence, but which also continually threatens to produce an oppositional coherence which is registered by the films as a serious ideological threat."[17] In the case of Mao, the contrary is true: her screen roles offer a significantly more empowering and uncompromising presence that is nonetheless undercut or at least given a reality check by the subservient position that the actress, like many other women at the time, was forced to take in real life.[18]

The James Bond Connection

After the unexpected death of Bruce Lee in the summer of 1973, Golden Harvest was in desperate search of someone who could fill the shoes of its most profitable star and enable the company to continue its ambitious goal toward internationalization. To deal with this challenge, the studio turned to a number of different names, both old and new, including Jimmy Wang Yu, Jhoon Rhee, and Wong Tao, to lead some of its most high-profile projects. Yet these efforts to find a successor to Lee proved to be a difficult task, and none of the names just mentioned were able to capture the charisma, the electrifying energy, and most importantly, the enormous box-office returns that Lee delivered. It was not until 1978, when Jackie Chan broke through with his kung fu comedies, that Golden Harvest was finally able to regain a superstar, even though it would take two more decades before Chan established himself as a popular cultural icon worldwide, rivalling and even exceeding Lee in terms of global popularity.

For Golden Harvest, then, the period between 1973 and 1978 was a time of trial and error when it came to filling the void left by the death of Bruce Lee. Not surprisingly, given the worldwide (including US) success of some of Mao's films and her reputation as a "female Bruce Lee," the studio's executives had high hopes for the actress and sought to propel her into international stardom. As part of this effort, they hired an instructor from the US to teach her English conversation and gave her the name Angela, which was deemed more recognizable to, and thus more easily remembered by, foreign audiences.[19] More substantially, Mao was assigned a lead role in *The Shrine of Ultimate Bliss* (hereafter *The Shrine*), a project originally planned as a co-production with Warner Bros. and intended to star Bruce Lee alongside George Lazenby and Sonny Chiba. Both Chiba and Warner Bros. backed out following Lee's untimely demise, but instead of abandoning the project altogether, Golden Harvest decided to salvage it by pairing up Lazenby with Mao. Without the support of Warner Bros., the film saw millions shaved off its budget, but it was still conceived to be a high-concept international production with the participation of a one-time James Bond (Lazenby) and a

Figure 10 Angela Mao with George Lazenby. *The Shrine of Ultimate Bliss* directed by Huang Feng. © Golden Harvest 1974. All rights reserved.

female duplicate of Bruce Lee (Mao) as well as location shooting in Australia, Taiwan, Thailand, Hong Kong, and the US.[20]

The plot of the film involves an Australian cop (Lazenby), ironically called Stoner, who goes after a Hong Kong drug ring after its powerful aphrodisiac called "happy pill" has caused his sister's death. At the same time, a Taiwanese special agent (Mao) is sent to investigate the same crime organization and eventually teams up with Stoner to fight the drug lords. One cannot help but feel a sense of déjà vu here, for the storyline is in many ways a reprise of *Enter the Dragon*, where Bruce Lee's character, in addition to being also a covert government agent probing an underground operation involved in drug trafficking, has too lost his sister (played, as noted earlier, by Mao) to the criminal group. The specter of Lee haunts other aspects of the film as well. The casting of Ting Pei is a case in point: the actress, who was rumored to be Lee's mistress and was with the kung fu star in her apartment during the final hours of his life, had a "femme fatale" persona that was brazenly exploited in the film. This can be seen not just in her casting as a seductive villainess who seeks to sabotage Stoner's investigation; more overtly, a scene in the film where Ting's character lets an injured Stoner rest on her bed and later has sex with him—all of which is a set-up so that the drug dealers can obtain photographic evidence of the "affair" and use it against him—may be taken as a conscious allusion to the widespread speculation and conspiracy theories surrounding Lee's death in real life.

Judging from both the original Chinese title of *The Shrine* (which frames the film as a James Bond movie of sorts) and its US and international release title (which takes after the name of the film's male protagonist), it would appear that Lazenby was intended to be the spotlight of the production. Yet other aspects of the film seem to tell a different story. In the local Hong Kong as well as international versions, for instance, Mao gets top billing ahead of the ex-Bond actor, which renders her, theoretically at least, the lead star of the film. And while both Mao and Lazenby are given ample screen time and opportunities to showcase their fighting skills, it is Mao's character who stands out and emerges as more important as the film moves toward its end. At one point, trapped inside a cage in the drug dealers' lair, she beats up Stoner, Lazenby's character, pretty badly as the latter, under the influence of the "happy pill," tries to approach her with vile intentions. Later, thanks to her resourcefulness (she finds a way to open her and Stoner's handcuffs with a hairpin), the two characters are able to escape captivity, much to the surprise of their foes. In the final climactic battle that follows, Lazenby is seen fighting only with a bunch of minor henchmen whereas Mao's opponents are the drug bosses played by Takagi Joji and Hwang In-Shik. This arrangement, which can perhaps be explained by Mao's superior martial arts skills on par with those of Takagi and especially Hwang,[21] swings the focus to the actress and underlines Golden Harvest's effort to turn her into an international star.

Around the period when *The Shrine* was made, a growing trend of blaxploitation films featuring tough female action heroines had emerged in the US. In Jack Hill's *Coffy* (1973), for instance, Pam Grier plays a hardened vigilante seeking violent revenge on drug dealers responsible for her sister's addiction to heroin, while *Foxy Brown* (1974), also directed by Hill, sees her in a very similar role—an ordinary woman with no official authority or power taking on a drug gang who murdered her boyfriend. Even more pertinent to my discussion here is the *Cleopatra Jones* series featuring Tamara Dobson. In Jack Starrett's *Cleopatra Jones* (1973), Dobson stars as a secret agent for the US government and is pitted against a female drug kingpin. The sequel, Charles Bail's *Cleopatra Jones and the Casino of Gold* from 1975, was co-produced by Warner Bros. and Shaw Brothers, and much of the film is set in Hong Kong, where Dobson's character is sent to investigate, with the help of a fellow agent from the Hong Kong Police Force, an underground drug empire operated by the so-called "Dragon Lady." The similarities of the films to *The Shrine*, which is also an action thriller with a James Bond-like heroine going after an organized drug ring, are perhaps no mere coincidence. Golden Harvest was keenly aware of the blaxploitation trend and its broad audience appeal—one that cut across racial and ethnic lines—based in part on its contemporary urban themes and eclectic appropriation of genres (martial arts films, James Bond-type spy movies, etc.). Apparently, the studio considered this approach a winning strategy and had incorporated it in *Enter the Dragon* before continuing the effort with *The Shrine*. Compared to the female-led blaxploitation action films, however, *The Shrine* is notably different in one important aspect, viz. its refusal to subject Mao's character to the kind of overt sexualization typically attached to African-American action heroines.[22] This does not mean that the film refrains from sexualizing female bodies, but merely that it focuses its exploitation on the femme fatale character played by Ting Pei and the hapless victims of the "happy pills."

The Shrine represented arguably the most concerted attempt of Golden Harvest to help launch Mao into global stardom.[23] But despite some high expectations, the film did rather poorly in the overseas box offices, and this lack of success is indicative of the difficulties confronting the studio in its push toward internationalization. The kung fu craze of 1973 had given Hong Kong martial arts films temporary access to American and international markets, but this access was tenuous at best as the studio was unable to develop any ongoing production relationship with a major foreign company. The fact that Warner Bros., following the death of Bruce Lee, pulled back from the co-production projects that had been planned is a clear reminder of this challenge. The lack of foreign capital put a lot of constraints on a local company like Golden Harvest, which did not have the financial resources to make their films competitive on a global scale. *The Shrine* is a case in point: the decision of Warner Bros. to withdraw from the project resulted in a greatly reduced budget—three million Hong Kong dollars (approximately US$600,000)—which, while still high by Hong Kong standards, paled into comparison with many Hollywood productions at the time.[24] Distribution was another major hindrance: lacking its own distribution network within the United States, Golden Harvest had to rely on one of the major American studios to handle the distribution of its films. As it turned out, many of their films were not often marketed or released properly, partly because they were considered marginal and not competitive by the distributors.[25]

The Regional Focus

At the same time as Golden Harvest, as part of its larger goal of going international, tried (without much success) to propel Mao into a global stardom, it also set upon using the emerging star to consolidate and expand its regional market. Even before the kung fu craze in the early 1970s, Hong Kong films had already established a strong regional presence—particularly in Taiwan and among the sizable diasporic Chinese population in Southeast Asia. But the international breakthrough of Bruce Lee and the kung fu film led Golden Harvest and other Hong Kong studios to actively expand their market reach in Asia. Japan was no doubt the most sought-after market in the region, but it was also the most difficult one to break into due to its established film industry and the relatively advanced quality of its productions. By comparison, South Korea, also an underdeveloped market for Hong Kong film companies, appeared to offer more accessible opportunities. For one thing, there had already been a "martial arts craze" in South Korea in the 1960s, first triggered by martial arts fiction from Taiwan and then intensified by the Mandarin swordplay films of Shaw Brothers.[26] The popularity of Hong Kong martial arts cinema continued with the shift from swordplay to kung fu, thanks to Bruce Lee but also to the anti-Japanese sentiments of many kung fu films, which tapped into the lingering hostility of Korea to Japan, its past colonizer. Among Mao's films, *Hapkido* and *When Taekwondo Strikes* are the ones most clearly geared toward the South Korean market (while also aiming at and managing to capture a larger international audience thanks to the kung fu craze): the refashioning of Mao in Lee's image, the demonization of Japanese characters, and the inclusion of Korean-style martial arts and Korean martial artists turned actors can all be seen as conscious efforts to appeal to the local viewers in the new and growing market.

This regional focus continued with *The Tournament* (1974). Shot in Thailand and Hong Kong, the film is notable for its mixed use of Chinese kung fu and muay thai (Thai boxing), the latter seldom seen in Hong Kong cinema before.[27] In many ways, the incorporation of muay thai was motivated by a desire to make the film more appealing to Thai moviegoers, but it aimed to draw the interests of a larger group of local, regional, and international audiences as well, for whom the "exotic" martial arts style served as a marker of differentiation, a way to make the film stand out from the many kung fu movies crowding the market at the time. Moreover, the use of muay thai also fitted with the emphasis on authenticity—not only in terms of the fighting style but also as a means to confer legitimacy on the action star—in martial arts movies of the period. A publicity article on the film, for instance, notes the involvement of two well-known Thai boxing champions and stresses the surprise they received in discovering how "well versed" Mao was in the "Siamese kick." It also shows various film stills where Mao, in shorts and gloves, battles with the Thai boxers in a professional boxing ring.[28]

After Thailand, the next destinations were more exotic. In the prologue of *The Himalayan* (1976), it is stated that the production team had to travel to Tibet and Nepal in search of a nearly extinct martial arts style associated with an esoteric Buddhist sect known as *mizong*, so that it can be presented in the film. This turned out to be no more than a gimmick, as there was little, if anything, about the fighting in the film that could be identified as a recognizably *mizong* style, and given that China was still very much closed to the world at the time, it is doubtful that the crew were able to set foot on Tibet. Nepal, on the other hand, was accessible, and a large part of the film was indeed filmed in the Himalayan nation, a fact very much underscored in the trailer and poster of the film. In this case, however, location shooting in a foreign Asian country was not so much about consolidating or opening up a regional market (Nepal's film market was virtually non-existent) as about bringing more "international colors" (*guoji secai*) to the film.[29]

But despite the rhetoric, it needs pointing out that the international scope of *The Himalayan* was rather diminished when compared to Golden Harvest's previous efforts. For one thing, there are no Western actors—not even in a supporting role—in the cast, and while the film showcases some dazzlingly impressive kung fu performances from Mao and from her co-stars Tan Tao-liang and Chan Sing, its story—a good-and-evil struggle over a family fortune in a rural Tibetan village—harks back to traditional martial arts movies and is far removed from the urban-centered, James Bond-style plots of *Enter the Dragon*, *The Shrine*, and other Golden Harvest productions with international aspirations. The lackluster box office of *The Shrine* had no doubt put the brakes on Golden Harvest's global plan for Mao, but what also played a role was the studio's strategy shift from exporting its stars for global consumption to financing and filming its own English-language productions with mainly Western stars and locations.[30] While there were exceptions (e.g., the unsuccessful attempts to popularize Jackie Chan worldwide), the general trend was to keep local and regional production separate from global production, which explained to a large extent the return to "tradition" in *The Himalayan* and, for that matter, *Broken Oath*, the final film Mao made with Golden Harvest in 1977.[31]

Conclusion

In this chapter, I situated Mao's career within the context of the kung fu craze and the subsequent attempts of Golden Harvest to expand into the international (and especially American) market. This offers a larger context for understanding Mao's star persona as a female Bruce Lee and the James Bond connections in *The Shrine*, which was meant to be an international "breakout" film for the actress following the death of Lee. These efforts to turn Mao into a global star, while not without brief moments of success, ultimately failed, but the intense screen presence of the actress as a female fighter with exceptional physical power and agility, and the versatility and flexibility she showed in her ability to perform hapkido, muay thai, and Chinese kung fu, endeared her to many viewers and helped her establish a devoted fan base.

Compared to Cheng Pei-pei, Michelle Yeoh, and Zhang Zhiyi, Mao is arguably less well-known as a female action star. This is true not only with the general audience but also among critics and scholars.[32] Yet her impact cannot be overstated; lauded as the "Queen of Kung Fu," she helped expand the scope of female performers in the martial arts film and paved the way for those—not only Yeoh but also Kara Hui, Cynthia Rothrock, and many others—who followed and extended her trailblazing path.

Notes

1 Aside from some cameo appearances in the early 1990s, Mao effectively concluded her film career in 1983.

2 John Scott Lewinski, "Quentin Tarantino Saves L.A. Theater," *Reuters* (2010), https://www.reuters.com/article/us-tarantino-idINTRE61I17U20100219 (accessed August 30, 2022).

3 David Desser, "The Kung Fu Craze: Hong Kong Cinema's First American Reception," in *The Cinema of Hong Kong: History, Arts, Identity*, eds. Poshek Fu and David Desser (Cambridge: Cambridge University Press, 2000), 20–1, 23.

4 Ibid., 34.

5 For more discussion of the female knight-errant figure before the rise of the kung fu subgenre, see Stephen Teo, "The 'Missing' Female Knight-errant in Hong Kong Action Cinema 1965–1971: Back in Critical Action," *Journal of Chinese Cinemas* 4, no. 2 (2014): 143–54.

6 A couple of exceptions are Lo Chi's *Thunderbolt* (*Wu lei hong ding*), first seen on local screens in October 1973, and King Hu's *The Fate of Lee Khan* (*Yingchunge zhi fengbo*), which was released two months later.

7 Another female-led film closely modeled on *Fist of Fury* is Lo Wei's *Kung Fu Girl* (*Ti wa*, 1973), which stars Cheng Pei-pei as the action heroine. For more discussion of this film, see Man-Fung Yip, *Martial Arts Cinema and Hong Kong Modernity:*

Aesthetics, Representation, Circulation (Hong Kong: Hong Kong University Press, 2017), 127–33.

8 Hsiung-ping Chiao, "Bruce Lee: His Influence on the Evolution of the Kung Fu Genre," *Journal of Popular Film and Television* 9, no. 1 (1981), 33–4.

9 Angela Mao, "Wo yu Heqidao" ["Hapkido and Me"], *Golden Harvest News* 2 (1972): 38–41.

10 Man-Fung Yip, "Yuanzhenxing, chuancheng, ziwo shizian: Xianggang wuxia dianying zhong 'xunlian' de yiyi" ["Authenticity, Succession, Self-Actualization: The Multiple Meanings of Training in Hong Kong Martial Arts Cinema"], in *Shunliu yu niliu*: *Chongxie Xianggang dianyingshi [Currents and Crosscurrents: Rewriting Hong Kong Film History]*, eds. Su Tao and Poshek Fu (Beijing: Beijing University Press, 2020), 222–4.

11 Kwai-cheung Lo, "Fighting Female Masculinity: Women Warriors and Their Foreignness in Hong Kong Action Cinema," in *Masculinities and Hong Kong Cinema*, eds. Laikwan Pang and Day Wong (Hong Kong: Hong Kong University Press, 2005), 138.

12 Sergio Ortiz, "Angela Mao-Ying," *Fighting Stars* (October 1974), 28.

13 May Joseph, *Nomadic Identities: The Performance of Citizenship* (Minneapolis: University of Minnesota Press, 1999), 61–2.

14 Ortiz, "Angela Mao-Ying," 22.

15 Ibid., 28.

16 Ibid.

17 Andrew Britton, *Katharine Hepburn: Star as Feminist* (New York: Columbia University Press, [1984] 2003), 8.

18 For more in this direction vis-à-vis feminism and female fighting stars, see Kyle Barrowman's chapter on Michelle Yeoh in this volume.

19 Fang Fang "Mao Ying yi cheng guoji juxing" ["Mao Ying has Become an International Star"], *Golden Harvest News* 20 (1973): 28–9.

20 Xingkong Ma, "Mao Ying, Huang Feng, Tie Jingang" ["Mao Ying, Huang Feng, James Bond"], *Golden Harvest News* 21 (1973), 39; Ruxu Liu, "Fang Huang Feng tan xinpian: Tie Jingang Da Po Ziyangguan" ["An Interview with Huang Feng on his New Film: *The Shrine of Ultimate Bliss*"], *Golden Harvest News* 22 (1974), 53–4.

21 Known for his many supporting roles in Hong Kong martial arts movies of the 1970s, Hwang was an accomplished hapkido practitioner and awarded a 10th-degree black belt by the World Hapkido Association.

22 Yet, as discussed earlier, the US marketing of some of Mao's earlier films did try to exploit the (imaginary) erotic appeal of the actress, in ways similar to the sexualization of Grier, Dobson, and other African-American actresses in blaxploitation action films.

23 After the box office flop of *The Shrine*, Golden Harvest shifted its tactic in Brian Trenchard-Smith's *The Man from Hong Kong* (*Zhi dao huang long*, 1975), where Lazenby was paired with Jimmy Wang Yu, best known for his roles in *One-Armed Swordsman* (*Du bei dao*, 1967), *The Golden Swallow* (*Jin yanzi*, 1968), and other classic swordplay films directed by Chang Cheh for the Shaw Brothers studio. While not a runaway success, the film performed better than *The Shrine* and swayed the Golden Harvest executives, at least temporarily, into thinking that Wang had the

better potential to become an international star. Mao did make another film—
A Queen's Ransom (*E tan qun ying hui*, 1976), directed by Ting Shan-Hsi—with
Lazenby. However, Mao's character, an exiled Cambodian princess, is a rather small
one and appears tagged on to the main plot about a terrorist from the Ireland
Republican Army (Lazenby) leading a motley group of international mercenaries,
including Wang's Viet Cong guerrilla, to assassinate Queen Elizabeth II during her
visit to Hong Kong.

24 The difference is put into relief when we consider that *The Man with the Golden Gun*,
a James Bond film starring Roger Moore from 1974, was produced at a budget of
US$7 million. Steven Spielberg's *Jaws* (1975) went further, costing almost US$12
million and ushering in a trend of blockbuster productions that would become the
norm in American cinema for years to come.

25 Mike Walsh, "Hong Kong Goes International: The Case of Golden Harvest," in *Hong
Kong Film, Hollywood, and the New Global Cinema*, eds. Gina Marchetti and Tan
See Kam (London: Routledge, 2007), 173.

26 Sangjoon Lee, "Martial Arts Craze in Korea: Cultural Translation of Martial Arts Film
and Literature in the 1960s," in *East Asian Cinema and Cultural Heritage: From
China, Hong Kong, Taiwan to Japan and South Korea*, ed. Yau Shuk-ting Kinnia
(New York: Palgrave Macmillan, 2011), 173–95.

27 Chang Cheh's *Duel of Fists* (*Quan ji*, 1971), also shot on location in Thailand, is one
of the few Hong Kong films with a focus on muay thai.

28 Defu Wen, "Mao Ying li zhan tai quanwang" ["Mao Ying battles Thai Boxer
Champion"], *Golden Harvest News* 30 (1974): 41–3.

29 Sha, "Jiahe yewu de shin fangxiang" ["The New Business Directions of Golden
Harvest"], *Golden Harvest News* 46 (1976), 22.

30 Walsh, "Hong Kong Goes International," 170–3.

31 While Mao continued to make films for other companies until she retired from acting
in the early 1980s, most of them were low-budget productions of inferior quality and
are hardly remembered now.

32 For instance, Mao is noticeably absent in Lisa Funnell's otherwise outstanding book
on Chinese cinematic women warriors, *Warrior Women: Gender, Race, and the
Transnational Chinese Action Star* (Albany: State University of New York Press,
2014).

Chapter 4
Kara Hui: From Young Auntie to Mother Figure

Leung Wing-Fai

Figure 11 Kara Hui in the midst of battle. *My Young Auntie* directed by Lau Kar-leung. © Shaw Brothers Studio 1981. All rights reserved.

Introduction

The Hong Kong actor Kara Hui (b. 1960, also known as Kara Wai and Wai Ying Hung) began dancing in a nightclub at the age of fourteen, followed by a martial arts film career at the Shaw Brothers studio from the age of sixteen where she remained until the mid-1980s. She won her first Hong Kong Film Award in 1982 for the starring role in *My Young Auntie* (1981).[1] Hui steals scenes, often playing the only key female role in the highly androcentric kung fu genre. Like many female martial arts stars, Hui picked up her performance skills through dance first, then martial arts training. She established a style of kung fu action with "big moves and variations,"[2] which, I would argue, is analogous to dance choreography. This combination of dance and martial arts ability was often quintessential in action performance in the Hong Kong film industry, especially for actresses. Lauren Steimer's work on stunt performers, for instance, discusses the invisible labor, precarity, and lengthy wushu (martial arts) and dance training involved in creating Hong Kong-style action as transnational body spectacles.[3] Like other kung fu stars, in particular Jackie Chan, Hui has reported multiple physical injuries, which implies an authentic Hong Kong-ness through hard graft and sacrifice.[4] Describing her acting work and stardom as an escape route from poverty, Hui also exemplifies my assertion (Leung 2015) that stardom in Hong Kong reflects the changing identity and public consciousness of the city—the distinctive careers of the stars of the 1970s and 1980s, whose work entailed incredible on-the-job skills training and endurance which contributed to their revered status, have as much to teach us about Hong Kong itself as they do about the stars.

In recent decades, particularly, Hui has morphed from a martial arts ingénue to become a credible character actor, embodying a range of unusual roles and proving versatility in her dramatic acting ability—not something ordinarily assumed in martial arts stardom. Several Hong Kong Film Awards illustrate this shift: *At the End of Daybreak* (2009) and *Happiness* (2016) for the Best Actress award; *Rigor Mortis* (2013) and *Tracey* (2018) for the Best Supporting Actress Awards. In 2017, she was named Best Actress for her role in the Taiwanese film *The Bold, the Corrupt, and the Beautiful* at the Golden Horse Awards, where the movie also won Best Film. In these later roles, Hui receives accolade through her performance of the older woman and mother figure, acting with minimal or no makeup, and her characterization usually deals with age-appropriate health and family issues. Without formal dramatic acting training, Hui, nonetheless, excels in psychological transformation and the naturalistic portrayal of these tormented female protagonists. Hui's evolution into a versatile character actor in diverse genres foregrounds a viable career trajectory for the aging female star body, a rare occurrence in the beauty and youth-obsessed media sector that usually offers few standout roles to middle-aged actors.[5]

This chapter charts Hui's stardom as a representation of the rags-to-riches ethos at the heart of the Hong Kong dream, foregrounding the decline of the city's film industry alongside the political change since the 1990s. Thus, Hui's career invites nostalgic longing for the golden age of the sector; her stardom is "a form of image-making associated with a distinctive discourse of performance and a symbolic marker in the discursive construction of a collective identity."[6] This chapter analyzes her key film performances from *My Young Auntie* to more recent critical accolades and media interviews. Through a focus on these performances and Hui's changing image—becoming a star persona in flux— contextualized against the backdrop of the film industry and the historical transformation in Hong Kong, this study demonstrates the significance of her stardom in its specific cultural and historical conjunctures.

Stardom in Hong Kong

Richard Dyer's seminal work on stardom includes the key claim that "stars are only of significance because they are in films and therefore are part of the way films signify."[7] Beyond the films, stars engage with sociological issues and are tied to the "dominant ideology in any society."[8] Stars are unique identities; these identities are also unstable and are constantly in flux. Their fame and popularity wax and wane, which is likely to reflect the changing cultural discourse, too. Chris Rojek proposes a typology of different celebrity statuses that includes a type termed *achieved* celebrity, where individuals' fame derives from their perceived accomplishments in competition. Rojek also discusses celebrities who attain an intense burst of fame, such as one-hit wonders, for whom he reserves the term *celetoids*.[9] Christine Geraghty, meanwhile, categorizes stars into three groups: celebrities, professionals, and performers. Professionals are the ones "associated with work and the public element of the star duality rather than the private life of the celebrity."[10] All these elements are present in star texts, which, Dyer asserts, are polysemic—stars are simultaneously ordinary and extraordinary.[11]

Stardom plays a significant part in a community's media discourse, and it is continuously made and remade, and historically situated. The importance of individual stars depends on the mediasphere and public perception of them at various historical junctures. Paul McDonald cautions about the star image approach in which stars are analyzed in isolation, and often those focusing on star texts lose sight of historical and cultural specificities.[12] Even so, it raises questions of "what defines and delimits a 'context,' and what forms of context are to be judged as of social relevance to the study of stardom."[13] In the context of the present collection, one must consider the articulation of stardom in relation to the social and cultural history of Hong Kong, while at the same time challenging the Eurocentrism of the broader field of star studies.

The modernization and industrialization of the former British colony Hong Kong became most pronounced alongside postwar mass migration from mainland China because of the Second World War, the civil war (1945–9), and subsequently the inauguration of the People's Republic of China (PRC) in 1949. Having experienced military conflicts and the resultant atrocities, many of these newcomers to the city focused on the survival of the family and endured poverty, responding to the conveniently advocated "rags-to-riches" Hong Kong dream.[14] Sociologists within Hong Kong Studies such as Benjamin Leung contend that the migrants' motivation to work hard has been prompted by a perceived meritocratic possibility for social mobility, ultimately engendering the city's economic miracle as an Asian Tiger economy in the 1970s and 1980s alongside Taiwan, Singapore, and South Korea. A generation born and brought up in Hong Kong saw themselves as the city's natives with a distinctive culture. During this period of rapid economic and social changes, a highly successful local media sector emerged and produced film, television, and popular music primarily in the Cantonese dialect. Many of these media products, however, were distributed in East and Southeast Asian markets, as well as to the global Chinese diasporas, often in dubbed formats.

Stars are contradictory public figures who possess qualities (extraordinary good looks, recognized performance skills, etc.) that make them special, and yet they are individuals imaginable as ordinary.[15] Stars who became synonymous with a "golden age" (1980s and early 1990s) of Hong Kong media, such as the actor Chow Yun-fat and singer-actress Anita Mui, therefore, reconcile the extraordinary and ordinary qualities of local stardom because "the biographies of stars, a frequent subject of circulation by the media, have become part of the articulatory practices between stardom, local history, and a collective cultural and social identity."[16] In particular, many of the generation of 1970s and 1980s stars present their success as a result of work ethics and hard-earned performance skills, thereby embodying the Hong Kong dream. In other words, these stars have achieved their celebrity status, and they assert themselves as professionals *and* performers. Their diligence and success are often explained by a shared background of childhood hardship and suffering, so that their rise to stardom represents a metaphor for social mobility and material accomplishment. Chow Yun-fat is well-known for his humble beginning, having grown up in one of the fishing villages of an offshore island in Hong Kong. This golden age of local media, alongside its generation of stars, encountered a crisis around the time of the handover in 1997 not so much because of the political changes, but due to economic, cultural, and social development. The highly prolific and commercially successful Hong Kong film industry (producing 200–300 films a year during the 1980s and early 1990s) contracted to making only fifty-two films in 2019.[17] Consumer patterns in Hong Kong and changing export markets, the new generation of young media users, piracy, and perceived inferior quality of local films accounted for this decline. How the previous generations of stars survive in this challenging media sector can illustrate the changing attitudes toward the associated core social values as the city transformed, and this chapter uses Kara Hui as an exemplar of a star who has evolved and adapted along this local cultural and media history.

Young Auntie and Authentic Performance

Kara Hui was born in 1960 in Hong Kong. Her family is of Manchu heritage and originally came from Shandong, Northeast China. One of six children, Hui's family was so poor that she had to beg and sell gum on the street at the age of three, and she continued to do so for ten years.[18] The older siblings, including the actor Austin Wai (1957–2012), were sold to a Beijing opera troupe. This kind of practice appears common at that time for impoverished families. Well-known martial arts actors Jackie Chan (b. 1954) and Sammo Hung (b. 1952), for example, apprenticed in the same Beijing opera troupe (China Drama Academy), which afforded them the vigorous physical training necessary for their subsequent martial arts stardom. Kara Hui began dancing in the Miramar nightclub in Kowloon at the age of fourteen, and later she trained in Northern-style martial arts with master Mark Bow-sim, who would go on to be the mother, and *sifu*, of another star, Donnie Yen.

At sixteen, Hui joined the Shaw Brothers studio, which was founded by Run Run Shaw in 1956. Her entry into film stardom coincided with a period of prolific martial arts genre production at the studio in the 1980s. Shaw Brothers had focused on martial arts film production from the 1960s, typically aimed at the new migrants in Hong Kong and overseas markets in Southeast Asia and Taiwan. The director Chang Cheh's *yanggang* films (depicting normative masculinity and violence) epitomized the mostly androcentric genre productions at Shaw. Cheng Pei-pei (*Come Drink with Me*, 1966; *The Lady Hermit*, 1971) and Shih Szu (also in *The Lady Hermit*) were earlier examples who acted in Shaw *wuxia* productions that featured female warriors.[19] Hui was often the only female protagonist among a regular band of male martial arts performers, so much so that she gained the nickname "Young Lad Hung" among her peers. Chang Cheh also became Hui's godfather, illustrating her firm position in the male-dominated genre. The director and martial arts choreographer Lau Kar-leung first spotted Hui and gave her the breakout role in *The Brave Archer* (1977). Lau would continue to use her in many of his film projects at Shaw, so she became a staple star of the 1970s and 1980s surge of locally produced and exported martial arts and action films at the studio until 1984 when she made her last film there, Lau's *The Eight Diagram Pole Fighter*.

Performance in the martial arts genre in Hong Kong has a distinctive history, hence, the lack of distinction in the use of the terms (dramatic) acting and performance in the current analysis. While American cinema has adopted and revered the Russian Stanislavski system of performance techniques known as method acting, an actor's ability to empathize and express the inner emotions of the character, this is not the only system of film acting. In particular, this kind of expressive dramatic performance usually takes precedence over body movement and physicality and therefore engenders an assumption that action stars cannot act.[20] In fact, action movies as a "cinema of attractions" can problematically be considered primitive and mindless, in spite of the fact that the performance tradition can be traced all the way back to silent comic stars such as Charlie Chaplin and Buster Keaton, whose distinctive forms of performance and stunt work are of a piece with the iconic martial arts performances of Bruce Lee and Jackie Chan.[21] Indeed, physical performance is central in the dominant genres of comedy and action in Hong Kong.[22] The traditional forms of theater in Chinese culture, in particular the importance of opera in a range of dialects, has influenced the discourse of "good performance" in the media industry in Hong Kong. In addition, good performance is often connected to long and arduous training. Among different film genres, martial arts most closely relate to operatic training and the stars' physical ability, since Chinese opera traditions require multiple skills involving facial expression, singing, and physical/kinetic skills. The legendary lead actor Kwan Tak-hing, who played arguably the most well-known Cantonese martial artist Wong Fei-hung in seventy-seven films from 1949 to 1970, was trained in Beijing opera and is widely assumed to be the first "authentic" performer of the genre.[23]

Authenticity is nonetheless an elusive concept to employ in these contexts. Writing on the authenticity in news journalism, John Fiske asserts that it should guarantee the "truth" of what is being mediated and allows, most importantly, what has been interpreted to present itself as objective: "the 'unauthored' voice."[24] In his theorization, disruptive events need to be mediated (clawed back) into the dominant value system in order to preserve this authenticity. In other words, authenticity is about constructing a set of coherent cultural value and explaining what appears to contradict that authenticity. Authenticity arguably comes from two articulations in the Hong Kong martial arts/action genre: authenticity of the performers as martial artists and fighters, and authenticity of their success as stars.

The aforementioned Kwan Tak-hing and Bruce Lee were both credited as pioneers for showcasing authentic martial arts in their films. Following Kwan and Lee and with their Beijing opera training, Jackie Chan and Sammo Hung then established a type of authentic action and martial arts performance represented by Chan's "no fear, no stuntman, no equal"[25] slogan. Chan also reported multiple injuries while filming and the inclusion of bloopers in his films' end credits provides ample evidence. The other well-known martial arts star Jet Li came from wushu championships in China and made his film debut in *Shaolin Temple* (1982); therefore, his stardom was also predicated on authentic martial arts skills. However, martial arts performance on-screen is essentially spliced sequences of choreographed movements and is widely known within the industry and among audiences to have been highly constructed. Usually, the crew break down an extended fight sequence and film it as separate movements. The director Tsui Hark explains how he likes to build such a vignette: "You see somersaults and flips and fights and it's very visual and then at a high point before the climax it stops for tension or suspense and then it goes on and they do a fantastic demonstration."[26]

Many female performers in the martial arts and action genre share a dance background, which provides the physical training, allowing them to follow fight-scene choreography. Prominent examples include Cheng Pei-pei, Michelle Yeoh, and Zhang Ziyi. Kara Hui's dance and martial arts training made her a master of the necessary physical requirements. Indeed, Hui boasts in an interview about her ability to process choreographed movements quickly: "When I'm on set for a film, there might be twenty or so moves that I have to do. Once the director tells me what he wants, I can just do it. I don't need anyone to show me. I can just do it by listening to directions."[27] She describes the fight scenes as a formula: combinations of big moves to which she would adapt and add personal touches. She is rightly proud of her versatility, describing how she would play multiple roles during an action sequence, performing also as a stunt double/replacement if someone was injured or had an accident during filming, before changing costumes quickly and going back to her own role. Hui is therefore known for her agility, grace, and speed. This kind of performance authenticity is often expressed through the physical toll it has on the performer. Like other martial arts stars, she has suffered physical injuries.[28] Contrarily, numerous cinematic techniques can enhance the excitement of these martial arts showpieces: undercranking while filming, which allows for the speeding up of the motion later, and exaggerated sound effects. Even Jet Li, famous for his martial arts credentials, was criticized for the use of cinematic technology (special effects, wirework, and stunts) to create fight scenes in his films, but this kind of practice should not be seen as "inauthentic."[29] From my discussion with actors and creatives in the Hong Kong film industry, martial arts performance relies on what looks good on camera, which diverts from the idea of psychological preparation and expression associated with method acting. Lengthy training of a different kind and physical ability to create these scenes are nonetheless vital for martial arts performance and for the creation of (the appearance of) real fighting, which, when combined with acting ability, makes for a genuine fighting star. What Hui delivers, therefore, is the performative display of choreographed and improvisational fighting ability. This combines with a youthful, gendered image to render her distinctive *and authentic* among her male counterparts at Shaw Brothers.

The Chinese title of *My Young Auntie*, *zhangbei*, means one's elder (a gender-neutral noun). It is a martial arts comedy in which Hui is pitted against the director and action choreographer Lau Kar-leung, as well as Shaw's staple martial arts actors. Hui plays Cheng Tai-nan, a young martial artist who has married an elderly man so that his estate does not fall into the hands of his brother. After her husband's death, Tai-nan travels to Guangdong to stay with her nephew-in-law, Yu Cheng-chuan (Lau) and his son (her great nephew) Yu Tao (Hsiao Ho), who has been studying in Hong Kong. Tai-nan is the eponymous young auntie, a traditional woman from the provinces. Numerous comedic moments ensue when she spars with the "Westernized" Yu Tao. The film follows a Shaw formula that ensures a fight scene every ten to fifteen minutes. Hui's performance elevates this formulaic narrative. In particular, she excels as a country-bumpkin-in-the-modern-city with humor and subtlety. The themes are crudely played out in several sequences: Tao persuades Tai-nan to go to a Western dance party; she goes shopping for cloth materials and ends up in a modern white *qipao* (Chinese dress) and high heels (Figure 11). She still provides energetic fights in whatever attire she is wearing. Tai-nan is a kung fu version of a female warrior who is not afraid to sort out familial problems. Toward the end of the narrative, her late husband's brother manages to steal the deed after all, leading to the finale in which Hui engages in combat using a series of traditional weapons such as the long spear and sword. Lau's choreography for Hui often concludes in a pose not unlike those found in traditional Chinese dance routines. The centrality of Tai-nan's role is reversed, though, when her brother-in-law captures her. Cheng-chuan and Tao, as well as other brothers and uncles, come along to save her. The final fight scenes revert to showcase Lau's various swordplay and fighting styles. This is a shame, given the rarity of female-led martial arts films at the studio in the late 1970s and early 1980s. The fact that Hui received a Hong Kong Film Award can be seen as a recognition of her standout performance, providing a rare example of the official recognition of martial arts acting skills.

Lau Kar-leung also helmed *The Lady is the Boss* (*zhangmen ren*, literally "the person in charge," also gender-neutral; 1983), which capitalized on the success of *My Young Auntie*. This outing transposes *My Young Auntie* to a modern-day Hong Kong where Wang Hsieh Yun (Lau) teaches traditional martial arts at a school, but his outdated values and dogmatism are turning potential students off. The school's master is due to return from the USA to relocate the school, but he is ill and, surprisingly, his Americanized daughter Mei Ling (Hui) turns up. *The Lady is the Boss* offers kung fu comedy built on the cultural clash between traditions and modernity, as the bandana-wearing, gum-chewing Mei Ling intends on modernizing the martial arts school while Wang stubbornly resists change. Many Shaw stars, including Gordon Liu and Xiao Hsiao, once again support Hui in this film. Fight scenes intersperse a narrative in which Mei Ling attempts to recruit younger people for the school, which causes problems with the police and local gangs who run the dance clubs. She has various successes, such as teaching self-defense to young sex workers. Here, the use of props in the various fight sequences shows off Lau's choreography and Hui's physical ability. In one sequence, she leads a small following on BMX bikes and ambushes the gang boss on the street. Mei Ling and her disciples fight on and with the bikes. Just like in *My Young Auntie*, however, the local gang captures Mei Ling toward the end and Wang comes to her rescue in a gymnasium, a setting that seems gratuitous except to provide different pieces of gymnastic equipment (parallel rings, trampoline, the weights, and balance beam) as props in the ensuing fight scenes, showcasing Lau's skills. Hui has a smaller role in this final brawl in which she once again demonstrates elegant dance movements.

Hui continued to steal the scenes in these Shaw-produced and Lau Karleung-directed martial arts films, usually as the only female lead among male action stars: *Dirty Ho* (1979), *Martial Club* (1981), *Legendary Weapons of China* (1982), and *The Eight Diagram Pole Fighter*. In *Martial Club* (*Wuguang*), Hui plays another ingénue, the sister (Chu-Ying) of the young Wong Fei-hung (Gordon Liu)'s good friend. She is loyal to her family and a gallant fighter who is not afraid to avenge her hot-headed brother. Fight scenes are staged to highlight her use of swords and a three-section staff, which once more are employed as dance props. These martial arts performances from the Shaw productions also have one thing in common: while they sometimes involve extreme violence, the employment of comedy eases the significance of actual harm. Often, the ensemble cast resolve grievances, and opponents are quickly back on their feet and become friends again or enemies eventually find ways to smooth their differences. These Shaw films therefore introduced cartoon violence to Hong Kong and Chinese diasporic audiences, contributing to Hui's image as a cocky but likeable young heroine, as well as asserting its influence on the later popularity of Jackie Chan's kung fu comedies.

After leaving Shaw in the mid-1980s, Hui began to perform in contemporary action, but she was often typecast as a self-assured, hot-headed fighter. Produced by Jackie Chan for Golden Harvest, *The Inspector Wears Skirts* (Wellson Chin, 1988) exemplifies Hui's career at this point. The film features an ensemble cast of then popular female stars, including Kara Hui (who plays the character May) and the American martial artist and actress Cynthia Rothrock as Madam Law. In *The Inspector Wears Skirts*, a group of women are getting trained as a special unit of female police officers. May's characterization illustrates her star persona in the plotline, in which she complains to the lead inspector, Madam Hu (Sibelle Hu), that one particular member of the group has let down the team, and she wants that person removed. This foregrounds how May is over-confident in her own ability and does not tolerate weak links in the elite squad. In order to keep her in line, Madam Hu publicly humiliates May to show the importance of teamwork. After learning her lesson, May is admitted back to the team. Hui and Rothrock provide the final fight sequence, using a long axe and nunchaku in addition to hand-to-hand combat.

In these early years of her acting career, Hui achieved stardom at Shaw studio through personification: having a star image over and above different on-screen characters that the actors play in a practice that Yu calls "personification in fighting."[30] Her characterization denotes an ingénue, a confident martial artist despite her young age, and she is able to command respect among male counterparts. Fighting skills are by no means secondary in this early process of personification for Hui's stardom but are instead absolutely integral and authenticated. This analysis of Hui's early star texts demonstrates that her authentic performance involves an iterative process of physical ability and a gendered persona which suited the then young actress.

Mother Figure and Longing for a Collective Identity

Hong Kong stars from the 1970s onwards often assumed role models of social mobility alongside rapid economic transformation and cultural development. A generation of native-born citizens in Hong Kong received better education and experienced relative social and economic stability in the 1980s and early 1990s, although a sense of anxiety regarding the 1997 handover permeated the popular cultural sphere. With the reduction in productivity in the film industry, the rise in cultural and commercial power of television, drama products, and pop music in East Asia (most notably, from South Korea and the PRC), the confidence of the media sector in Hong Kong began to decline in the late 1990s, coinciding with the handover of the British colony to mainland China in 1997. Kara Hui's career waned after her Shaw period, although she acted in action comedies such as the aforementioned *The Inspector Wears Skirts* and its sequels (1988, 1989, 1992). Often these films had large ensemble casts and offered more minor roles to the actress. She also shifted into some television drama acting in the 1990s. In terms of her personal life, Hui has spoken openly about her suicide attempt at the age of forty because of depression, which accounted for the dramatic reduction of her overall output around that time. Her return to active work in film and television was not until the mid-2000s. By this time, the Hong Kong media industry re-focused on CEPA-oriented production,[31] often considered a "re-Sinicization process" in the local media industry.[32] In the subsequent two decades, Hui has participated in many Hong Kong-China co-productions, as well cross-border productions within the East and Southeast Asian region.

Leaving behind the image of a confident fighter on-screen, Kara Hui, now in her forties and fifties, has assumed a prominent position among a group of dramatic actors in Hong Kong, locally known as *jincao yanyuan* (literally, gold leaf actors). These actors are respected for their performance skills and endurance in the industry; frequently, their lack of formal acting training resulted in a performance style that is spontaneous and natural. Hence, in interviews, these actors, such as Lam Suet and Lau Ching Wan, assert the importance of life experience and hard work for their acting skills. The Hong Kong media industry, like most commercial film and television production centers, can be inherently sexist in that female performers mostly rely on youth and beauty, and they often find substantive roles more difficult to come by as they age. However, Hui's return to acting marks a second peak in her career; while she stops personifying in fighting, she has evolved into a versatile character actor in diverse genres, which exemplifies a viable career trajectory for the aging female star.

Many of her acting awards have in fact come from this period, as detailed in the introduction. *At the End of Daybreak* is a tonally dark Hong Kong/Malaysian/Korean co-produced tragi-melodrama, in which Hui plays the mother whose ex-husband had run away with her sister, and she has a drinking problem. Her son Tuck (Tsui Tin-Yau) is a layabout who goes out with a fifteen-year-old schoolgirl Ying (Ng Meng-Hui) and gets into trouble, so his mother has to step in and intervene. Despite her own issues, the mother tries her best. When Ying's parents discover the youngsters' relationship, they want to report Tuck for having sex with an underage minor. The mother foregoes her pride and borrows money from her divorced husband to pay off Ying's family. Later, Tuck and his two friends kill Ying and her friend. A scene symbolizes the difficult mother-son relationship and violence against women, in which Tuck returns from his attempt to conceal the deaths of the two young women as a rape-and-murder by random strangers. He comes home and pushes his mother from behind, provoking a dirty fight between the two, leaving her sprawled on the floor crying. The police subsequently arrests Tuck's two friends/accomplices and put the mother in a white interrogation room in the police station. Left alone to stew, she picks on the clinically white wall. In the following scene, Hui remains resolutely poised in a medium close-up, as an off-screen police officer asks questions about Tuck's whereabouts (Figure 12). She remains silent; tears well up, then she smirks without betraying her son. Her stoic appearance represents a complete dedication to Tuck no matter what he has done. The mother does not have a name in the film but is known simply as Tuck Chai's mother, which is telling. This film set a precedent for a character type Hui would become known for: the middle-aged mother figure who has various social issues and is often enmeshed in highly problematic family relationships and social roles.

Set in a dilapidated apartment block with plenty of vampire hunters and Taoist black magic, *Rigor Mortis* displays disturbing sexual and physical violence. Hui's character Yang Feng is a terrified single mother whose husband had raped one of

Figure 12 The stoic and protective mother. *At the End of Daybreak* directed by Ho Yuhang. © Paperheart Limited 2009. All rights reserved.

two twin sisters, causing his own death as well as the deaths of the sisters who now haunt the tenement building. Yang wages war against the ghosts of the twins and a vampire to protect her son. Her Best Supporting Actress Award was a tribute to how she expressed the trauma of this extremely vulnerable middle-aged woman. By this time, Hui's roles in contemporary drama followed a similar pattern of psychological preparation and impersonation of vulnerable older women. Her next award-winning role in *Happiness* sees her playing yet another aging woman, Yuen-fan, who has a head full of white hair and wanders around the working-class neighborhood in Hong Kong. She is at the onset of an age-related cognitive disorder, resulting in the loss of memory. On top of these health issues, she also battles a drinking problem. By chance, Yuen-fan meets a young man, Kai-yuk (Carlos Chan), who has come from mainland China to Hong Kong to find his father, who had previously abandoned him and his mother. Losing his mother and having been rejected by his father, Kai-yuk settles into life with Yuen-fan as a surrogate mother figure who provides an imperfect but happy home for the young migrant. In an interview, Hui conveyed how she was concerned whether she should take the role because of the character's dowdy physical appearance, but she was persuaded by the excellent script and ended up considering the role a breakthrough.[33] She won another Best Supporting Actress award for *Tracey* at the Hong Kong Film Awards in 2019, which depicts a trans woman, Travis/Tracey (Philip Keung), who has hidden her identity for many years from her family but remains married to wife Anne (played by Hui) despite their estrangement within a loveless marriage.

As Hui aged, she moved away from martial arts filmmaking and shifted to roles of older women represented by a changing body, naturally aged physical appearance, and acute facial expressions. When not playing these characters on-screen, Hui in fact keeps a relatively youthful appearance and is often seen in glamorous dresses at formal ceremonies and film releases. Her rarer martial arts roles are impressive, too. For *Dragon/Wuxia* (2011), Hui plays 13th Madam the 72 Demons' Master's wife and she was once again nominated for the Best Supporting Actress award at the Hong Kong Film Awards.

Surprisingly, Hui only appears in two relatively brief scenes and is largely a silent, menacing presence in the few minutes she is in the movie. In a scene at the compound of the 72 Demons, 13th Madam stands perfectly still and ominous before going to retrieve the Master's son Tang Long/Liu Jinxi (Donnie Yen) (Figure 13). Her nomination is likely for the seven-minute fight sequence between 13th Madam and Tang Long. Hui brings the intimidating 13th Madam to life as she randomly slashes the throat of an innocent villager to provoke Tang Long into revealing himself. She grabs another bystander, her eyes bulging, teeth bared. Armed with two hand blades, her fight in the sequence is fast and furious, punctuated by elegant kicks and a mid-air body-roll. She chases Tang Long on the rooftops (a double is clearly used for a few seconds here). Later, Tang Long forces her into a cowshed and deprives her of the blades, leading to tense hand-to-hand combat, which exposes the character's weakness. Even then, 13th Madam responds with ferocity, before being trampled by the cows. The scene ends with a dramatic fall to her death into a waterfall while still maniacally smiling.

Figure 13 The menacing 13th Madam. *Dragon* directed by Peter Chan. © We Pictures 2011. All rights reserved.

Hui also acted in a couple of outlier films, such as *The Bold, the Corrupt, and the Beautiful.* This is a thriller set in the southern city Kaohsiung, Taiwan, where Hui plays an elegant antique dealer Madam Tang who has two daughters: the older Ning is sexually predatory while the younger sister Chen appears an innocent college student. The film presents a vastly convoluted plot involving political corruption among the county mayor and other local elites. The set, costumes, and makeup are exquisite, and Hui plays a rare role full of intrigue, a ruthless criminal mind orchestrating the murder of Legislator Lin and his wife, while their child Pien Pien is injured and left in a coma. Madam Tang again has highly problematic relationships with both daughters, especially Ning, who appears to use her sexuality to do her mother's dirty bidding. Tang's family secret will be revealed later, but when the mother figure gives advice to the two young women, it is less about the love of a parent for their children and more about a predatory character preparing her children for a life of evil machinations. Both Ning and Chen die in tragic circumstances, directly or indirectly at the hands of Madam Tang, who is left alone to contemplate a lonely future.

If stars in the Anglo-US contexts are about "getting to the top"[34] from humble backgrounds and chasing the American dream, stardom in Hong Kong follows a similar capitalist ethos and a core social myth. Stars are role models in a society that venerates meritocracy, mobility, and the possibility of success for all, engendering a strong work ethic, which justifies their success. Despite her extreme poverty, Hui has endured forty years in a cutthroat industry and achieved many accolades and respect while the sector itself transformed dramatically. She represents a martial arts star who first emerged at the height of the Shaw Bros. command of the genre. In numerous androcentric martial arts and kung fu films, she shines alongside the Shaw stable of male co-stars for her dance-movement infused performances. Her subsequent career trajectory has not been adversely affected by her aging body. In fact, she exploits her own aging by playing middle-aged female characters with little or no makeup who suffer a range of psychological and physical illnesses. In other words, Hui embodies these characters who have to meet the challenges of the "mother figure" with all its complex emotional tensions. It therefore can be argued that she has grown to personify both senses of authenticity: the performance skills that can rival any method actors and stardom that symbolizes survival and social mobility from an impoverished beginning. Hui herself is aware of this association, attributing her own status to a uniquely Hong Kong-based mobility ethos. Repeatedly, she declares that work and stardom were her way to escape from poverty, amplifying stardom as a symbol of the city's changing social and cultural identity in the past forty years.[35] This endurance confirms the importance of the local media sector and the significance of stardom that metaphorizes survival, while the film industry declines and morphs, engendering a nostalgia for the golden age of pre-handover Hong Kong. Though she is not extremely famous outside of Asia and fans of the martial arts genre, Hui is one of the key stars who excel in representing this rags-to-riches Hong Kong dream. Her stardom exemplifies the local discourse of authentic performance and solidifies her status as a role model of social mobility, as she celebrates four decades of an exceptional acting career.

Notes

1 This was the inaugural Hong Kong Film Awards. Sabrina Qiong Yu states that David Chiang was the only *wuxia* actor who has ever won an acting award for *Vengeance!* (Chang Cheh, 1970) at the Asian Film Festival, but this is only correct if *wuxia* and kung fu films are strictly distinguished. See Yu, "Can a Wuxia Star Act? Martial Arts, Acting and Critical Responses to Jet Li's *Once Upon a Time in China*," *EnterText* 6, no. 1, https://www.brunel.ac.uk/creative-writing/research/entertext/documents/entertext061/ET61Wux5YuED.pdf (accessed September 23, 2023).

2 Arthur Tam, "Kara Hui on Humble Beginnings and 40 Years in the Film Industry," *Timeout* (2016), https://www.timeout.com/hong-kong/film/kara-hui-on-humble-beginnings-and-40-years-in-the-film-industry (accessed September 23, 2023).

3 Lauren Steimer, *Experts in Action: Transnational Hong Kong-Style Stunt Work and Performance* (Durham, NC: Duke University Press, 2021).

4 Tam, "Kara Hui on Humble Beginnings and 40 Years in the Film Industry." See also Leung Wing-Fai, "From Wah Dee to CEO: Andy Lau and Performing the Hong Kong Subject," *Film International* 40, no. 7 (2009): 19–28.

5 Chris Holmlund, "Celebrity, Ageing and Jackie Chan: Middle-Aged Asian in Transnational Action," *Celebrity Studies* 1, no. 1 (2010): 96–112.

6 Leung Wing-Fai, *Multimedia Stardom in Hong Kong: Image, Performance and Identity* (London: Routledge, 2015), 129.

7 Richard Dyer, *Stars* (London: BFI, [1979] 1998), 1.

8 Ibid., 2.

9 Chris Rojek, *Celebrity* (London: Reaktion, 2001).

10 Christine Geraghty, "Re-examining Stardom: Questions of Texts, Bodies and Performance," in *Reinventing Film Studies*, eds. Christine Gledhill and Linda Williams (London: Arnold, 2000), 187.

11 Dyer, *Stars*, 3.

12 Paul McDonald, "Reconceptualising Stardom," in Dyer, *Stars*, 200.

13 Ibid., 179.

14 Benjamin K.P. Leung, *Perspectives on Hong Kong Society* (Oxford: Oxford University Press, 1996), 55–60.

15 Leung, *Multimedia Stardom in Hong Kong*, 61.

16 Ibid., 109.

17 https://www.fareastfilm.com/eng/archive/catalogue/2020/un-anno-caotico-il-botteghino-di- hong-kong-nel-2019/?IDLYT=31711#:⬛:text=52%20local%20films%20were%20released,than%202018's%20HK%24250m (accessed September 23, 2023).

18 https://www.todayonline.com/8days/sceneandheard/entertainment/kara-hui-says-she-had-beg-money-streets-age-3-13?fbclid=IwAR20xYI-ndCuhenuCYvLPHnI0Kss5C1UIAWQrEh6jTZI-L5xsGHxdJO269o (accessed September 23, 2023).

19 Scholars have explored the prominence of female performers in martial arts cinema history, but they often refer to different time periods and different stars or films. See Rong Cai, "Gender Imaginations in *Crouching Tiger, Hidden Dragon* and the Wuxia World," *Positions: Asia Critique* 13, no. 2 (2005): 441–71; Man-Fung Yip, "The Difficulty of Difference: Rethinking the Woman Warrior Figure in Hong Kong Martial Arts Cinema," *Chinese Literature Today* 3, nos. 1–2 (2013): 82–7; and Lisa Funnell, *Warrior Women: Gender, Race, and the Transnational Chinese Action Star* (Albany: State University of New York Press, 2014).

20 Yu, "Can a Wuxia Star Act?," 134–5. See also Steimer, *Experts in Action*.

21 For more on the connections between martial arts cinema stars and different traditions of action, see Kyle Barrowman, "Origins of the Action Film: Types, Tropes, and Techniques in Early Film History," in *A Companion to the Action Film*, ed. James Kendrick (Malden, MA: Wiley-Blackwell, 2019).

22 Leung, *Multimedia Stardom in Hong Kong*, 83.

23 For more on Kwan Tak-hing, see Wayne Wong's chapter in this volume.

24 John Fiske, *Television Culture* (London: Routledge, 1987), 289.

25 This was the tagline for *Rumble in the Bronx* (1995).

26 Tsui Hark quoted in Ange Hwang, "The Irresistible: Hong Kong Movie *Once Upon a Time in China* series: An Extensive Interview with Director/Producer Tsui Hark," *Asian Cinema* 10, no. 1 (1998), 18.

27 Tam, "Kara Hui on Humble Beginnings and 40 Years in the Film Industry."

28 Hui herself put the number at fifty-one in her interview with Tam, "Kara Hui on Humble Beginnings and 40 Years in the Film Industry."

29 Talk given by Lauren Steimer with respondent Poshek Fu for the EASC New Book Series: Sinophone Studies, https://www.youtube.com/watch?v=Z2NDRxdRLY0 (accessed September 23, 2023).

30 Yu, "Can a Wuxia Star Act?," 154.

31 The Closer Economic Partnership Agreement (CEPA) was first enacted in 2004 to allow Hong Kong-based companies priority access to the PRC market, which yielded a large number of film and television co-productions.

32 See E.K.W. Ma, *Culture, Politics and Television in Hong Kong* (London: Routledge, 1999). See also Gary Bettinson, "Yesterday Once More: Hong Kong-China Co-production and the Myth of Mainlandization," *Journal of Chinese Cinemas* 14, no. 1 (2020): 16–31.

33 *Happiness* press conference at the Asian American International Film Festival (July 20, 2016), https://www.youtube.com/watch?v=bNRk5fDaxV4 (accessed September 23, 2023).

34 Dyer, *Stars*, 42–3.

35 M.L. Reifschneider, "The Tigress of Shaw Brothers: Top Three Kara Hui Roles," *Celestial Pictures* (n.d.), http://www.shawbrothersuniverse.com/the-tigress-of-shaw-brothers-top-three-kara-hui-roles (accessed September 23, 2023).

Chapter 5

Gordon Liu: Shaolin Hero

Eric Pellerin

Figure 14 Gordon Liu in fighting form. *The 36th Chamber of Shaolin* directed by Lau Kar-leung. © Shaw Brothers Studio 1978. All rights reserved.

Introduction

One poster embodies almost completely Gordon Liu's star image. The original Hong Kong theatrical poster for *The 36th Chamber of Shaolin* (1978) features a large black and white photograph of Liu in the center in a scissors stance Tiger kung fu pose. This pose is from the Hung Gar kung fu that he learned from Lau

Cham's school in Hong Kong, from Lau Cham and his son Lau Kar-leung. This ties him to the historical Wong Fei-hung as a direct disciple. The poster also shows all around him in the form of a color photo collage the subject of the film, the Shaolin Temple and the arduous process of learning kung fu the Shaolin monks had to go through at the temple. These two components–first, the image of a specifically Shaolin hero, and second, the possession of an orthodox kung fu lineage and genuine kung fu skills–are chiefly responsible for the stardom of Gordon Liu in and beyond Hong Kong.

In analyzing Gordon Liu in this chapter, I am using Richard Dyer's approach to studying star images from his book *Heavenly Bodies*.[1] He says that "the Star phenomenon consists of everything that is publicly available about stars. A film star's image is not just his or her films, but the promotion of those films and of the star through pin-ups, public appearances, studio hand outs and so on."[2] Dyer also includes interviews, what has been written about stars, including biographies, and how stars appear in popular culture as crucial to understanding the star image and how it is constructed. For Dyer, the star images are "always extensive, multimedia, and intertextual."[3] He examines the textual and multimedia information about a star in conducting his analysis of specific stars, and in *Heavenly Bodies*, situates this analysis within the historical and cultural context with which each star, such as Marilyn Monroe or Judy Garland, is associated. I am using this method to analyze Gordon Liu within the context of Hong Kong cinema, and its reception to a worldwide audience. In this chapter, I also draw upon concepts Dyer outlined in his first full-length study of stars, the epochal *Stars*.[4] In *Stars*, Dyer set out to develop the study of stars within film studies itself, and it was the first full-length consideration of star studies. It is a much broader study, and covers a lot of ground, including the history of the concept of stars from the theater. He introduces the concept of the "star image," and he analyzes stars from both a semiotic and sociological point of view.

After Bruce Lee and Jackie Chan, Gordon Liu was one of the biggest stars of Hong Kong kung fu films in what I call the golden era from 1971 to 1985. Even more so than Lee or Chan, Liu represented orthodox kung fu, and portrayed these forms and traditions accurately on-screen. Lee was using his own style jeet kune do, a non-traditional amalgam he created, and Chan had learned Chinese Opera as his foundational discipline, which incorporates a lot of tumbling and acrobatics. My argument in this chapter is that Gordon Liu represents on-screen perhaps more than any other star the idea of orthodox kung fu, and that his performance of this tradition is what made him a star in Hong Kong first and later internationally. The poster for *The 36th Chamber of Shaolin* is made up of a collage of stills from the film itself, and features the Shaw Bros. standing sets in the right hand corner. This places Gordon Liu in and part of the self-contained Shaw Bros. factory system of movie making, which over the course of its filmography created an imaginary dream world of ancient China, and it is this reusing of the same sets to represent ancient China that caught the imagination of Hong Kong and international audiences.[5] They also caught the imagination of Quentin Tarantino and led him to cast Gordon Liu in his *Kill Bill* films, which featured an homage to Shaw Bros. films as part of their story. This homage by Tarantino brought Gordon Liu's stardom to a whole new international audience.

Creation of a Hero

Gordon Liu (Liu Chia-hui in Mandarin or Lau Kar-fai in Cantonese) is so identified with the Lau family, through cinema especially, that a lot of people do not realize that he comes from a different family entirely. His real name is Sin Kam-hei and he was born in Hong Kong in 1955.[6] He had an English grammar school education and worked in an office as a clerk before working in films with Lau Kar-leung.[7] He has been described as Lau Kar-leung's "godbrother" in the Shaw Bros. own promotional magazine "Southern Screen" in the February 1980 issue or as an adopted son of Lau's father Lau Cham.[8] Gordon Liu described to author Bey Logan his background this way:

> Actually, I come from a different family (than the other Lau brothers). I attended an English school in Hong Kong. My parents were quite well off. After I finished school I worked as a shipping clerk! Kung fu was just my hobby. I trained at Lau Charn's kwoon and became very close to Lau Kar Leung's mother, and so she "adopted" me.[9]

Gordon Liu's adoption of the Lau family name as his stage name for his films makes sense given his closeness to the Lau family and their kung fu lineage. Stage names play an important part in the creation of film stars in Hollywood and around the world. Richard Dyer in his book *Stars* points out some important examples of stage names as opposed to birth names that helped create a star image in the case of Marilyn Monroe, a.k.a. Norma Jean Baker, and John Wayne, a.k.a. Marion Morrison.[10] Gordon Liu is known throughout the world by his stage name just like John Wayne, and like Wayne, his name brings up his star image as a hero, similar to John Wayne's stage name representing the idea of a male hero of the Western.[11]

Gordon Liu himself was aware of the power of a film star's image as a hero in the case of Kwan Tak-hing portraying Wong Fei-hung in around eighty-five black and white films starting in 1949. Liu was so taken with Kwan Tak-hing's portrayal of Wong Fei-hung that he wanted to learn kung fu because of his admiration of Kwan Tak-hing. Liu related in an interview for *The 36th Chamber* of *Shaolin* DVD extras that "I liked going to the cinema with my uncles. We saw Kwan Tak Hing in Wong Fei Hung. I thought Kwan Tak-Hing was very manly playing Wong Fei

Hung . . . That kind of hero made a deep impression on me."[12] He goes on to relate that he wanted to learn kung fu because of watching Kwan Tak-hing on-screen: "I asked my friend what kung fu style was the best. He said it depended on what I liked. I told him I wanted to learn the most difficult style, which would build character. He told me to take up Hung Fist. Okay, so I chose Hung Gar. I didn't know that Wong Fei Hung was practicing Hung Gar." Gordon Liu ended up going to learn Hung Gar from Lau Kar-leung's father Lau Cham's school in Hong Kong.

Gordon did not know that the real-life Wong Fei-hung practiced Hung Gar, and that by studying Hung Gar at Lau Cham's school he was learning from a direct disciple of the real Wong Fei-hung. He also did not know that the person behind the portrayal of Kwan Tak-hing's Hung Gar was Lau Kar-leung, Lau Cham's son, and eventually Gordon Liu's director of his greatest starring roles. The involvement of real-life Hung Gar masters in the Wong Fei-hung films was discussed by the Hong Kong Film Archive in their study about Wong Fei-hung in cinema *Mastering Virtue: The Cinematic Legend of a Martial Artist*. In discussing these masters, Lau Yam noted: "Amongst them, Sifu Lau Cham, who portrayed his own mentor, Lam Sai-wing, was perhaps the most well-known. His son, Lau Kar-leung, also acted in a number of films and has continued to promote Hung Fist and Wong Fei-hung's legacy since becoming a director in the 1970s."[13] Lam Sai-wing was Wong Fei-hung's favorite disciple, and was an important figure in the history of Hung Gar and its preservation. He wrote and published the first Hung Gar manuals beginning around 1923 that detailed Hung Gar's main three forms, which allowed non-practitioners to see the movements of Hung Gar.[14] The lineage of Lau Kar-leung's kung fu goes right back to the historical Wong Fei-hung. Roger Garcia said that Lau learned Hung Gar formally from his father from the age of nine until he was twenty-eight and that "the legends and practice of martial arts; the lineage and tradition (Liu being, in effect, a third-generation disciple of Huang Fei-Hong) . . . and the relationship of these things to both family and life and involvement in the cinema therefore establish, very early on, a framework for Liu's approach to the martial arts genre."[15] This relationship between martial arts lineage, family, and cinema would come to define Gordon Liu's star image through his roles for Lau Kar-leung when he became a director in 1975.

Lau Kar-leung learned orthodox kung fu in his father's school, and also followed his father into the film business by playing small parts in the Wong Fei-hung films starring Kwan Tak-hing. Lau told the Hong Kong Film Archive that he had been hired as an action choreographer for the Wong Fei-hung films, and that he devised the moves for Kwan Tak-hing. He related: "I knew Hung Fist, and Kwan learned it from me. So he was in fact my pupil. The guy was an opera actor . . . but he could strike beautiful poses, and that made him look like the real Wong Fei-hung."[16] By choosing to learn kung fu from Lau Cham's school, and learning from Lau Cham and Lau Kar-leung, Gordon Liu was in fact learning the same kung fu that his cinema hero Kwan Tak-hing learned for the film as well as the historical character he was portraying. It was a good choice and one that seems destined to have him portray the hero image he so admired on-screen for a new generation of Hong Kong and international audiences.

After working on the early black and white Wong Fei-hung films, Lau Kar-leung worked his way up in the Hong Kong film industry. Lau said he was willing to work without any complaints, and because of this he became a popular choreographer.[17] Lau began working with friend and fellow stuntman Tong Kai as a choreographer, and the two choreographed an important swordplay movie *The Jade Bow* (1966). The film was a success, and this was due largely to its innovative action design. It is considered to be the first "new style" martial arts film, and was the first film shot in Hong Kong to use wires. Because of the success of this film, Lau Kar-leung and Tong Kai were recruited by Shaw Bros. to work as choreographers for their studio, primarily on Chang Cheh films.[18] The Shaw Bros. studio in Hong Kong was based on the old Hollywood dream factory method of filmmaking, a vertically integrated system that had everything on the lot, including the actors and directors, who lived in dormitories located at the studio. The Shaw Bros. studio as we know it from the films made at the Clearwater Bay studio was created by Run Run Shaw to compete with his main rival, MP&GI (Motion Picture and General Investment Co Ltd).[19] Run Run Shaw moved to Hong Kong from Singapore in 1957 to personally oversee the building of the new Shaw Brothers (HK) Ltd Studio. He bought 46 acres of land from the Hong Kong government for a steal, at forty-five cents a square foot, and this eventually included the extensive standing sets that came to represent ancient China around the world.[20] Shaw's goal of building the studio was to standardize production and ensure quality. Run Run Shaw created a vertically integrated movie studio, based on the Classical Hollywood studios like MGM and Warner Bros. Just like those Classical Hollywood studios, Run Run Shaw had every star and director under standard long-term low paying contracts. I have discussed elsewhere how Bruce Lee's decision to sign with Shaw's rival Golden Harvest for a more modern, short-term two picture deal when he returned to Hong Kong in 1971 began to change Hong Kong cinema's method of production away from long-term contracts and vertical integration.[21] For directors like Lau Kar-leung and his star Gordon Liu, working for Shaw Bros. meant stability, but it also meant being under long-term contract and conforming to the studio's factory like production methods.

Gordon Liu began his film career by following Lau Kar-leung at his request into the industry first as a stuntman and then as a co-star on Chang Cheh's film *Shaolin Martial Arts* (1974). Gordon himself explained how he got his start in films through Lau Kar-leung:

In 1974 Lau Kar Leung introduced me to director Chang Cheh. I signed a three
year contract. I was supposed to be in stunts and acting for three years . . . I
stayed in Taiwan about one and a half years. After Lau Kar Leung split from
Chang Cheh, Lau Kar Leung returned to Shaw Brothers and directed his first
movie *The Spiritual Boxer*. *The Spiritual Boxer* made Lau Kar Leung famous.
Lau Kar Leung used his influence and brought me back to Hong Kong . . . My
first movie with Shaw Brothers was *Challenge of the Masters*.

The reason for Lau Kar-leung's promotion from action choreographer to director
was that the Shaw Bros. studio did not want to let him go. Lau told *Cahiers du
Cinéma* in 1984 that after he returned to Hong Kong from Taiwan, he had decided
that he would terminate his contract and go to teach kung fu full time in the United
States.[22] Run Run Shaw told him that Mona Fong wanted to speak to him. Mona
Fong was Shaw's Executive Vice President at the time, and she proposed that
Lau could direct his own movies for the studio. She asked Lau if he could bring
new life to kung fu movies, which at the time had grown formulaic under directors
like Chang Cheh. Lau said he felt he could, and decided to film his directorial
debut as kung fu with comedy, instead of using the excessive bloodshed style of
Chang Cheh. His debut, *The Spiritual Boxer*, can be considered the first film in a
new genre, the kung fu comedy, which would make Jackie Chan a star a few
years later with the films *Snake in the Eagle's Shadow* (1978) and *Drunken Master*
(1978). Lau's first film as a director, *The Spiritual Boxer* is not indicative of his
preoccupation with historical kung fu stories and displays of authentic kung fu
seen in his other films as a director, beginning with *Challenge of the Masters*
(1976). In *The Spiritual Boxer*, the story centers on a young disciple of a "Spiritual
Boxer," a man who cheats people out of their money by pretending to be able to
invoke the spirits or gods, to expel the evil ones. The young disciple is played by
Wong Yu, who puts in a bravura performance as a mischievous kid who gets into
comical situations, and has to use his kung fu to get out of those situations.

It was Lau Kar-leung's second film as a director, *Challenge of the Masters*,
and the first film that Gordon Liu starred in that would set the established style
and motifs that Lau would develop in his films as a director for Shaw Bros. from
1975 until 1985. *Challenge of the Masters* is Lau's update on the Wong Fei-hung
film cycle that had begun with the black and white films starring Kwan Tak-hing
that he had worked on as a choreographer, stuntman, and actor. Lau chose his
adopted brother Gordon Liu to be the star of the film, portraying a young Wong
Fei-hung. Gordon Liu said that he was cast in this role for a reason: "Lau Kar
Leung wanted to make a film. He wanted to show what he taught me. I was
about 20 or 21 years old, I had no objection . . . People started noticing what I
could do, like the Hung Gar style." By choosing his real-life disciple Gordon Liu
to be the star, Lau Kar-leung was able to showcase authentic Hung Gar on the
screen in a way that it had not been seen before in Hong Kong cinema. David

Bordwell has said about Lau Kar-leung's use of Gordon Liu: "Lau's favored player, his bald, scowling brother Lau Kar-fai, serves less as a character than as an abstract exemplar of the single-minded dedication demanded by the martial arts."[23] I see this casting of Gordon Liu by Lau related to Dyer's conception of what he calls the "perfect fit," in which in certain instances, all elements of a star's image line up with the character they are portraying, or more broadly cast by the director because the star's image will represent what they want to communicate on-screen perfectly. This can be seen in stars like John Wayne and his usage by John Ford, or Cary Grant and his usage by Alfred Hitchcock.[24]

Right from the opening credit sequence, Lau Kar-leung uses the unlimited studio resources of Shaw Bros. for a highly stylized cinematic portrayal of authentic Hung Gar techniques. Against an all-white background interior studio wall of over fifteen feet, Gordon Liu enacts segments of Hung Gar forms for the camera and the audience. An enormous couplet has been painted in calligraphy on the white studio wall which the English subtitles translate as "In a duel, gradually merging force with mercy . . . combined with Qi Gong, can the foe be controlled." This phrase is a translation of what are known as the twelve bridge hands in Hung Gar, which in general refers to the forearms. Hung Gar master Lam Chun Fai explains that "the twelve bridge hands of Hung Kuen can be loosely described as keywords for 12 individually unique techniques or methods that encompass some of the core concepts and principles of the system."[25] This includes the use of the combination of hard and soft techniques in Hung Gar, the both of which must be mastered in order to fully maximize the system. To underscore this, Lau has Gordon Liu enact hard techniques in front of a giant Chinese character that reads "hard," and he enacts some soft techniques in front the character for "soft," and keeps going in this fashion for most of the twelve bridge hands. In this sequence, the Chinese characters have now been isolated individually from the couplet against the white backdrop. Hing Chao describes this scene when discussing Lau Kar-leung's choreography: "The martial artist-actors Gordon Liu and Chan Kuan Tai perform Hung Kuen against a plain white background with the lines 'gong, yao, bik, zik, fun, ding, cun; tai, lau, wun, zai, ding, kin, kun' on the sides." Chao goes on to explain the text's meaning this way: "The couplet is a key mnemonic rhyme for Tid Sin Kuen (Iron Wire Boxing), often regarded as the most esoteric boxing set in Hung Kuen."[26] In his manual on Tid Sin Kuen, Lam Chun Fai notes that traditionally, in order to remember the twelve bridge hands, they were learned as a rhyme.[27] Lau Kar-leung uses Gordon Liu's real-life skill in a unique way in this credit sequence. Instead of pausing the film in between the action in the credit scenes like he did in *Spiritual Boxer* and later in *Dirty Ho* (1979), he has Gordon pause his body himself, with the camera still rolling, which can be discerned if watched closely. This is much harder on the performer, and foreshadows the extreme lengths he would push Gordon Liu's real life skill on film in later films, especially in *The 36th Chamber of Shaolin*.

This opening credit sequence showcases Hung Gar's twelve bridge hands, and relays it to the audience. Lau said using his films as a pedagogical tool was a conscious decision on his part; when asked about *The 36th Chamber of Shaolin*, he said, "But the greatest thing was my idea to use this film to 'preach' to the audience. Pretty daring isn't it? I want to put the sense of movement of kung fu in my films, and I always use real kung fu. Kung fu is the driving force in all of my films."[28] *Challenge of the Masters* is about a young Wong Fei-hung learning kung fu from his father's master Lu Acai. It realistically portrays the arduous process of learning kung fu the old way, in which students had to stand in a low horse stance for hours at a time for months or even years before they could learn any techniques.[29] By making a Wong Fei-hung film, Lau was signaling himself as the rightful heir to the kung fu film genre, as well as linking his film to his real life lineage to the historical Wong Fei-hung. Gordon Liu, in starring as Wong Fei-hung, had begun to portray the hero image on-screen that he admired from Kwan Tak-hing, which was the reason he wanted to learn kung fu in the first place. The films he made with Lau Kar-leung would end up inspiring a whole new generation of kung fu fans, and even inspire some to take up kung fu themselves.

Gordon Liu would not star in Lau's next film *Executioners from Shaolin* (1977), but he does have an extended cameo as a Shaolin hero, who stands up to the Manchu villains, and showcases a number of authentic Hung Gar techniques to fight them before his character is killed at the beginning of the film. Gordon was part of Lau Kar-leung's troupe, the Lau Gar Ban, and would be cast in smaller parts in Lau's films that he did not star in. Even though Run Run Shaw had everyone under long-term contract, and wanted a centralized system, Stephanie Chung noted that "in time, cliques began to form under the directors, each with their favourite cast and crew."[30] She notes that under these cliques, the directors were able to make a lot of films in their chosen genre with their favored team. Due to competition between directors, and differences in the types of films they made, it led to an accidental diversity of within the factory system.[31] The Lau Gar Ban was made up of Lau Kar-leung's favorite actors and stuntmen, and worked on every Shaw Bros. film he made as a director.[32] Gordon Liu did not star in every one of Lau's films, but he did work on each one as part of the team. Gordon himself has said that he did not feel that his stardom was due just to himself, but that it was a team effort by the Lau Gar Ban that was led by Lau Kar-leung that enabled him to become a star.

Shaolin Stardom

The next film Gordon Liu starred in for Lau Kar-leung was *The 36th Chamber of Shaolin*. This is the film that solidified Liu's stardom, and defined his star image for the rest of his career. *The 36th Chamber of Shaolin* tells the story of San Te, the Shaolin monk responsible for bringing kung fu to laymen; he is supposedly the first monk to teach non-Buddhist monks kung fu in China by creating the thirty-sixth chamber. This film becomes about San Te's rigorous training regimen at the Shaolin Temple, and how kung fu practitioners obtain their seemingly superhuman skills. As in *Challenge of the Masters*, the training sequences are portrayed realistically, but in much more detail, as each skill has a separate chamber, like the "steady gaze chamber," which sharpens a student's eyes. Roger Garcia and Tony Rayns have both commented on how this film is actually a sort of documentary of the intense physical work that Lau Kar-leung made Gordon Liu go through to make the film. About the training sequences, Garcia notes how "into the system, Liu inserts the body of Liu Chia-hui from whom he derives the pleasure of experiencing History; and his body gradually becomes a diary of the progress made–it is marked and scarred, he limps, he falls into water, he is burnt in his progress through the various chambers."[33] Tony Rayns has a similar view on how the film records the work of Gordon Liu. Rayns observes how "there is an extremely detailed exposition of the precise skills taught in the temple's 35 chambers, and the film is shot in such a way that the actors' real-life capabilities are tested to the utmost. From this point of view, the film is a fictional documentary on the resilience and skill of its lead actor Liu Jiahui."[34] Both Garcia and Rayns are correct to point out that the film records the real-life work that was put into making it. It was not only the hard work of shooting the film that contributed to Gordon Liu's stardom; Liu himself was conscious of constructing his own star image. He related about the making of *The 36th Chamber of Shaolin*: "Everyday, before we started filming at 10 o'clock, I'd arrive at Shaw Brothers at 8:30 to do some exercise. I was hard working and wanted to build a muscular body." Dyer notes the work that stars do to create their own image: "Stars are involved in making themselves into commodities; they are both the labour and the thing that the labour produces." He goes on to cite certain ways which stars shape themselves, including "make-up, coiffure, clothing, dieting and body-building [which] can all make more or less of the body features they start with, and the personality is no less malleable, skills no less learnable."[35]

This hard work paid off, and the film became a hit in Japan and in the West, something Shaw Bros. did not set out to do on purpose. Gordon said that after he shaved his head to play a monk, more people took notice of him. While he was promoting the film in Japan, he said, "A lot of Japanese people told me that I reminded them of someone. I asked 'Who?' They said Yul Brynner . . . I liked this actor too. I was happy that I looked like him." It was due to the success of *The 36th Chamber of Shaolin* that audience members began to conflate his star image with his real life person. Gordon Liu told Bey Logan that on a trip in Paris, a black man approached him, bowed to him, and asked Liu to be his sifu.[36] This is almost the same thing that happened to Gordon's cinematic hero Kwan Tak-hing after portraying Wong Fei-hung in so many films. Kwan Tak-hing's son said that many people would come up to Kwan Tak-hing on the street and address him as Wong Fei-hung.

Lau Kar-leung was known for being one of the most demanding directors, and his background as a choreographer and real-life kung fu master played a part in this. Lau's goal in making films was to aestheticize kung fu, and he achieved this by portraying authentic techniques on the screen in a cinematic way, using the actors' profilmic skill and his inventiveness as a director and choreographer. One of Lau's stuntmen, Tung Wai, told the Hong Kong Film Archive that "as an action stuntman, the toughest job was on a Lau Kar-leung picture. He was very demanding, one shot would have at last 40 moves—it could be man-to-man combat or twelve against one (the male lead)."[37] Tung Wai is describing having to perform at least forty kung fu movements before the camera cuts to the next shot. Lau preferred these long takes, which are very difficult on the actors to perform; if one person makes a mistake, the whole thing must be shot again. Garcia commented on the importance of choreography in Lau's films, especially during the later period from 1979, when he was less concerned with knowledge of historical stories: "Liu's films, when separated from the context which provides this knowledge, become studies of technique and the choreography of movement."[38] Gordon Liu himself noted this aspect of Lau's filmmaking, and that this is what made it appealing to Western audiences particularly:

> People may say it is because he has a lot of experience, but I think he is a genius. He transformed kung fu into a type of body language. Foreigners watch kung fu not for its strength. Instead, Lau used kung fu and movements to communicate some non-verbal ideas.

It was during this second half of Lau Kar-leung's career as a director at Shaw Bros. that Gordon Liu starred in the one film that critics have singled out for its intricate choreography, *Dirty Ho*. In the films that Gordon appeared in after the success of *The 36th Chamber of Shaolin*, whether as a star or in a supporting role, he appeared as a fighting monk, or as a modern Shaolin exponent. In *Dirty Ho*, he has a different look: he is a Ching Dynasty prince traveling incognito and sports a mustache and a wig with a long braid, showing half of his shaved head. This film is a retelling of a legend about the eleventh son of Emperor Kang Xi, Wang Chin-Chin, who travels incognito to appreciate antiques and wine. He is joined by the rascal character Ho Chi, played by Wong Yu, who becomes his disciple after being poisoned by Wang's female accomplice's sword. Wang poisons Ho in order to teach him to leave his criminal ways behind by becoming his disciple in the martial arts, in which he is an expert. Together they defeat an evil general so Wang can make it back to the palace just in time for the Emperor's naming of a successor. This film was named by the Hong Kong International Film

Festival as "the first technically introspective kung fu movie."[39] *Dirty Ho* contains many kung fu set pieces where the choreography was highly inventive and trend setting. In one scene, Hui Ying Hung's character is controlled by Gordon Liu, unbeknownst to Wong Yu's character Ho. Ho thinks that Hung is Gordon Liu's bodyguard and an expert in kung fu. The audience can see that Hung's body is being controlled by Gordon Liu, he is making her execute every strike against Ho, almost like a puppet. Another much-discussed scene in *Dirty Ho* is the wine tasting scene. Gordon Liu and Wang Lung Wei appear to be tasting wine as far as Ho is concerned, but they are in fact fighting each other. Stephen Teo considers *Dirty Ho* to be Lau's masterpiece, and the wine tasting scene as an example of choreography that is "genie-like in wonder and illusion."[40]

Gordon Liu continued to star in Lau Kar-leung's films, but as a contract player at Shaw Bros. he also starred in films by other directors. Almost all of these films, like *Young Vagabond* (1985) and *Crazy Shaolin Disciples* (1985), feature Liu performing kung fu, because that is what his acting and stardom were based on. Two films that he starred in in the late 1970s and early 1980s that were not directed by Lau Kar-leung were very important to Liu's international stardom and a revival later in his career. *Fists of the White Lotus* (1980) was a semi-sequel to Lau's *Executioners from Shaolin* (1976) directed by Lo Lieh, who portrayed the villain Bai Mei in both films. This portrayal of Bai Mei, and Gordon Liu's starring role in this film, was what caught Quentin Tarantino's attention, and led him to cast Gordon Liu in two different roles in *Kill Bill: Volume 1* (2003) and *Kill Bill: Volume 2* (2004). Even though Lo Lieh is credited as the director of *Fists of the White Lotus*, which was a Shaw Bros. film, Lau Kar-leung was the choreographer and most probably helped direct it, since it was Lo Lieh's first film as a director. Gordon Liu plays Hung Wen Ting, the hero who defeated Bai Mei in *Executioners from Shaolin*. In *Executioners from Shaolin*, Hung Wen Ting was played by Wong Yu. In *Fists of the White Lotus*, Gordon Liu defeats the brother of Bai Mei (who looks exactly like Bai Mei), who wants revenge against the Shaolin Temple and Hung Wen Ting, since they killed his brother. *Fists of the White Lotus* has more intricate choreography, being made in 1979, when Lau's choreography was reaching its peak. It also has elements of silly humor, and more of a fantasy feel than *Executioners from Shaolin*. One of the kung fu moves Bai Mei uses is called the seven paces technique. When he hits an opponent with this strike, they will die after taking seven steps. Tarantino took this element and used it in *Kill Bill: Volume 2*, as we shall see.

The other film that Gordon Liu starred in that played an important role in his international stardom was *Shaolin and Wu Tang* (1983), which was directed by himself on the Shaw Bros. lot as an independent film. Just like *Fists of the White Lotus*, Lau Kar-leung was the choreographer, and was more than likely the film's director. Stephen Teo attributes this film to Lau Kar-leung: "*Shaolin and Wu Tang/ Shaolin yu Wu Dang* (1983) is a neglected work credited to Lau Kar-fai (Lau's adopted brother), but really directed by Lau himself under the pseudonym of 'Kung Fu Leong.'"[41] Teo notes the similarities to Lau's other films like *Dirty Ho*, and feels that it should be discussed as a Lau film. In *Shaolin and Wu Tang*, Gordon Liu's character once again has to train at the Shaolin temple in order to take revenge, and it does sometimes feel like a quasi-sequel to *The 36th Chamber of Shaolin*. This film was the inspiration for the RZA in the creation and name of the rap group the Wu Tang Clan.[42] Almost all of the English dubbed samples of kung fu movies from their debut album *Enter the Wu Tang (36 Chambers)* were taken from *Shaolin and Wu Tang*, and the "36 Chambers" part of the album's title was an homage to *The 36th Chamber of Shaolin*. I have discussed elsewhere how the grindhouse distribution of kung fu films in the United States had an influence on hip-hop as it was emerging in New York City in the 1970s and 1980s.[43] Many fans of the Wu Tang Clan probably heard the sampled dialogue from *Shaolin and Wu Tang* on the album first, before seeing the film itself. In the West, Gordon Liu and Lau Kar-leung's films were distributed with more sensational titles that played up the violence, so *The 36th Chamber of Shaolin* was titled *The Master Killer*.[44] Because of this, Gordon Liu became known in the West as the Master Killer, interchangeable with his name. Even the RZA and Quentin Tarantino refer to him as the Master Killer. His star image in the West is as the fighting monk from Shaolin, "The Master Killer."

Gordon Liu and Lau Kar-leung continued to make films together at Shaw Bros. until 1985 when the studio decided to shut down film production to concentrate on making TV programs for Run Run Shaw's television studio TVB.[45] One of the reasons that Shaw decided to shut down film production was that they were facing stiff competition from Golden Harvest and Cinema City, and these studios were now making modern films about contemporary life in Hong Kong that local audiences wanted to see.[46] The Shaw Bros. dream world of ancient China was now out of fashion. Gordon Liu told Bey Logan: "We had been making movies at Shaw Brothers for so long, we thought we would always be doing it!" Liu goes on to tell Logan that at that time, the film actors didn't work on TV, so they were only in a few kung fu shows.[47] Later on, Gordon Liu did become a star at TVB, as the station began to hire a lot of its old contract players from Shaw's to work on its television programs. Lau Kar-leung directed a modern police movie *Tiger on the Beat* (1988) for Cinema City, and Gordon had a supporting role as a villain. Both Gordon and Lau Kar-leung worked on modern police and gangster movies in the 1980s, but they did not have the same recognition as during kung fu's heyday. Shaw Bros. had begun to make films again in 1988, on a much smaller scale, and as a collaboration with TVB. They formed Cosmopolitan Films with TVB in 1988, and made films like the comedy *Justice, My Foot!* (1992), starring TVB star Stephen Chow and directed by TVB director Johnnie To. These films were much closer to TVB television shows than the old cinemascope Shaw Bros. films, often using familiar television stars and technicians from TVB. It is out of this new televisual way of filmmaking of Shaw Bros. that Lau Kar-leung made another Shaw film as a director in 2003, *Drunken Monkey* (2003), his first for the studio since 1985. Gordon Liu has a co-starring role as a policeman and kung fu hero, and he has an old school duel with Lau Kar-leung himself in the film. Because Shaw Bros. had focused on television for so long, the film has the look of a TV show. Despite the televisual look of the film, the choreography was still impressive, and utilized Gordon Liu performing Hung Gar as a hero once more.

It was around this same time that Gordon Liu's stardom would receive its biggest boost by being cast by Quentin Tarantino to play two different characters in both volumes of *Kill Bill*. In *Kill Bill: Volume 1*, Tarantino cast Gordon as Johnny Mo, the leader of the Crazy 88 Gang, who all wear outfits and masks like Bruce Lee wore as Kato in *The Green Hornet* (1966-1967). For *Kill Bill: Volume 2*, Tarantino cast Gordon Liu as Bai Mei, for his tribute to Shaw Bros. and *Fists of the White Lotus*. Tarantino told *Kung Fu Magazine* that he went to the Shaw Bros. studio, and wanted to film there, but found it too small for his purposes. He specifically mentions Gordon Liu climbing the stairs to get to the temple to fight Bai Mei as the scene he wanted to shoot at Shaw's. He also said he wanted Lo Lieh to play Bai Mei initially: "In fact, I was hoping to get Lo to play Bai Mei . . ., but he was sick at the time and then of course I was saddened that he passed away."[48] Tarantino said in an interview on the extras of *Kill Bill: Volume 2* that he then considered playing Bai Mei himself, but decided to cast Gordon Liu, because he considered it good career and cinematic symmetry that Gordon fought the character, and was now playing the role himself. Tarantino also had an immense admiration for Gordon Liu as a kung fu star, and knew he could pull off the role much better than he could. Both *Kill Bill* volumes were commercial hits, and were received well by critics. As Bai Mei, Gordon Liu teaches Uma Thurman's character at the temple at the top of the stairs the five point palm exploding heart technique, Tarantino's tribute to Gordon Liu, Lau Kar-leung, and the history of Hong Kong martial arts cinema, and Thurman uses this to kill Bill at the end of the film. These two films elevated Gordon Liu's international stardom once again, reminding viewers of the enduring power of Liu's image as the quintessential Shaolin hero and one of the greatest representatives of orthodox kung fu.

Notes

1   Richard Dyer, *Heavenly Bodies: Film Stars and Society* (London: Routledge, [1986] 2004).

2   Ibid., 2.

3   Ibid., 3.

4   Richard Dyer, *Stars* (London: BFI, [1979] 1998).

5 Geoffrey O'Brien, "Made in Hong Kong: The Films of Shaw Brothers Studio," Artforum (September 2004): 250–5. See also Sek Kei, "Shaw Movie Town's 'China Dream' and 'Hong Kong Sentiments,'" in *The Shaw Screen: A Preliminary Study*, ed. Wong Ain-ling (Hong Kong: Hong Kong Film Archive, 2003), 37–47.

6 Cheuk-to Li (ed.), *A Tribute to Action Choreographers: 30th Hong Kong International Film Festival Programme* (Hong Kong: Hong Kong International Film Festival Society, 2006), 183.

7 Shing-hon Lau (ed.), *A Study of the Hong Kong Martial Arts Film: The 4th Hong Kong International Film Festival* (Hong Kong: The Urban Council, 1980), 177.

8 Li, *A Tribute to Action Choreographers*, 183.

9 Bey Logan, *Hong Kong Action Cinema* (New York: Overlook Press, 1996), 49.

10 Dyer, *Stars*, 97–8.

11 Dyer, *Heavenly Bodies*, 10.

12 All direct quotes from Gordon Liu in this chapter are from the extras on this DVD release.

13 Lau Yam, "About Chu Yu-chai," in *Mastering Virtue: The Cinematic Legend of a Martial Artist*, eds. Po Fung and Lau Yam (Hong Kong: Hong Kong Film Archive), 113.

14 Hing Chao, "Lau Kar Leung's Hung Kuen Cinema: A Martial Arts Perspective," in *Lingnan Hung Kuen: Kung Fu in Cinema and Community*, ed. Hing Chao (Hong Kong: City University of Hong Kong Press, 2018), 35–6.

15 Roger Garcia, "The Autarkic World of Liu Chia-Liang," in *A Study of the Hong Kong Martial Arts Film*, 121.

16 Lau Kar-leung, "Interview with Lau Kar Leung: We Always Had Kung Fu," in *A Tribute to Action Choreographers*, 60.

17 Kar L. Lau, "Oral History Interview: Lau Kar-leung," *VHS* (1997).

18 "Interview with Lau Kar Leung," 61.

19 Po Yin Chung, "The Industrial Evolution of a Fraternal Enterprise," in *The Shaw Screen*, 7. See also David Bordwell, *Planet Hong Kong: Popular Cinema and the Art of Entertainment* (Cambridge, MA: Harvard University Press, 2000), 63.

20 Chung, "The Industrial Evolution of a Fraternal Enterprise," 7–8.

21 Eric Pellerin, "Bruce Lee as Director and the Star as Author," *Global Media and China* 4, no. 3 (2019): 339–47.

22 Olivier Assayas and Charles Tesson, "Interview with Lau Kar-Leung: The Last Shaolin," Cahiers du Cinema 362–3 (1984), http://www.stickgrappler.net/2013/07/interview-with-lau-kar-leung-last.html (accessed September 23, 2023).

23 Bordwell, *Planet Hong Kong*, 251.

24 Dyer, *Stars*, 129.

25 Chun Fai Lam, *Tid Sin Kuen: Iron Wire Fist* (Hong Kong: Lam Chun Fai Hung Kuen Academy Ltd., 2017), 49.

26 Chao, "Lau Kar Leung's Hung Kuen Cinema," 79.

27 Lam, *Tid Sin Kuen*, 49.

28 "Interview with Lau Kar Leung," 61.

29 David Chow and Richard Spangler, *Kung Fu: History, Philosophy, and Technique* (Orange, CA: Action Pursuit Group, 1977), 61.

30 Stephanie Chung, "The Industrial Evolution of a Fraternal Enterprise," in *The Shaw Screen: A Preliminary Study*, ed. Wong Ain-Ling (Hong Kong: Hong Kong Film Archive, 2003), 10.

31 Ibid.

32 Li, *A Tribute to Action Choreographers*, 24.

33 Garcia, "The Autarkic World of Liu Chia-Liang," 124.

34 Tony Rayns, "Resilience: The Cinema of Liu Jialiang," in *A Study of the Hong Kong Cinema in the Seventies: The 8th Hong Kong International Film Festival*, ed. Cheuk-to Li (Hong Kong: The Urban Council, 1984), 52.

35 Dyer, *Heavenly Bodies*, 5.

36 Logan, *Hong Kong Action Cinema*, 52.

37 Winnie Fu (ed.), *The Making of Martial Arts Films: As Told by Filmmakers and Stars* (Hong Kong: Provisional Urban Council, 1999), 75.

38 Garcia, "The Autarkic World of Liu Chia-Liang," 129.

39 Li (ed.), *A Study of the Hong Kong Cinema in the Seventies*, 156.

40 Stephen Teo, *Hong Kong Cinema: The Extra Dimensions* (London: BFI, 1997), 106.

41 Ibid., 107.

42 The RZA and Chris Norris, *The Wu Tang Manual* (New York: Riverhead Freestyle/The Penguin Group, 2005), 63.

43 Eric Pellerin, "Kung Fu Fandom: B-Boys and the Grindhouse Distribution of Kung Fu Films," in *The Oxford Handbook of Hip Hop Dance Studies*, eds. Mary Fogarty and Imani Kai Johnson (Oxford: Oxford University Press), 97–115.

44 Logan, *Hong Kong Action Cinema*, 50.

45 Chung, "The Industrial Evolution of a Fraternal Enterprise," 14.

46 Bordwell, *Planet Hong Kong*, 70–1.

47 Logan, *Hong Kong Action Cinema*, 54.

48 Quentin Tarantino and Craig D. Reid, "Kill Bill," *Kung Fu Magazine* (2003), https://www.kungfumagazine.com/index.php?p=article&article=482 (accessed September 23, 2023).

Chapter 6

Sammo Hung: The Kung Fu Comic's Sublime Body

Luke White

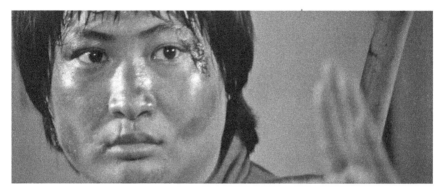

Figure 15 Sammo Hung as the "Fat Dragon." *Enter the Fat Dragon* directed by Sammo Hung. © Fung Ming Motion Picture Co. 1978. All rights reserved.

With his first credit in 1961, the Hong Kong Movie Database (as of 2022) lists Sammo Hung Kam-bo[1] as an actor in a staggering 192 films, as director of thirty-three, producer of forty-seven, and martial arts or action director of seventy-seven. Not only prolific and varied in his output, he has also been hugely influential, contributing to changes in choreographic, performance, and directorial style throughout a period that spans the rise and global proliferation of Hong Kong's martial arts cinema—Stephen Teo has called him "a kung fu man for all seasons."[2] Faced with this bewildering variety, my aim here will be first to offer a brief overview of Hung's significance, and then focus in on one aspect of his career. Within the context of this book, it is Hung's star persona, developed in roles in the kung fu comedy genre of the late 1970s, that is most significant. In understanding this, the central fact to consider is Hung's unusual appearance (Figure 15). Rather than a youthfully athletic, built body such as that of Bruce Lee or Jackie Chan, what made Hung an iconic figure was the seeming contrast between his rotund frame and his prodigious speed, agility, flexibility, and strength. After reviewing Hung's career, then, I will be analyzing the meanings of this unusual star body. This focus will allow us to further understand the threads through which Sammo has tied together his image not only as performer but also as choreographer and director.

The Body of Work: Sammo's Genre-hopping Corpus

Hung was born in 1952 and schooled from the age of nine in Beijing opera performance at Yu Jim-yuen's China Drama Academy. There, he was the "big brother" of a group of children who would also become martial arts legends, including Jackie Chan, Yuen Biao, Yuen Wah, and Corey Yuen.[3] Performers from the school's troupe would be loaned to movie studios for bit-part and stunt roles, and it was during this period that he received his earliest film credits. Hung's involvement grew rapidly and by the age of fourteen, he was assisting Han Yingjie on the choreography for King Hu's *Come Drink With Me* (1966), one of the films that launched the Shaw Brothers studio's "new action era" and gave impetus to the new genre of *wuxia* films that amplified the graphic violence of previous swordplays and paved the way for the kung fu film. Leaving the China Drama Academy at sixteen, he took up minor roles, performing and directing stunts and increasingly choreographing action for Shaw Brothers. He found work for several younger ex-students of the China Drama Academy— including Jackie Chan—giving them a leg up into the industry.[4] Hung became a favorite collaborator on Hu's movies. We see him, for example, in the famous forest fight of *A Touch of Zen* (1971). He was also the choreographer for Hu's *The Fate of Lee Khan* (1973) and *The Valiant Ones* (1975), where he also plays the principal villain.

Hung was also in on the ground floor when the new studio Golden Harvest was formed in 1970, taking on the job of house choreographer for their early action films and working with such stars as James Tien, Carter Wong, and Angela Mao. Where he appears in these, it tends to be as a "bad guy," his size making him a formidable opponent who foregrounds the skill and pluck of a smaller hero or heroine. However, Hung soon also took significant supporting roles—notably in *Hapkido* (1972). In the match at the very start of *Enter the Dragon* (1973), Hung played Bruce Lee's burly opponent, his no-nonsense approach to the physicality of combat (as well as his bulk and acrobatic skill) helping Lee set out a manifesto of his film-fighting philosophy: with both kickboxing and groundwork, it has as much in common with today's "MMA" as classic "kung fu."

For Golden Harvest, Hung also put together the slapstick action scenes for the Hui Brothers comedies. These included a brilliantly inventive fight in a restaurant kitchen in *Private Eyes* (1976) in which Michael Hui and an opponent go toe-to-toe using pans, woks, a swordfish, shark jaws, and even a string of sausages wielded in imitation of Bruce Lee's nunchaku. These hugely popular movies launched the dominance of humor over action at the Hong Kong box office throughout most of the 1970s. The significance of Hung's involvement in them should not be underestimated in accounting for the development of the hybridized kung fu comedy genre. This combined aspects of the Hui Brothers comic formula with acrobatic and martial performance styles derived from opera.[5] Although it remained largely a heroic film with prominent comic elements added, Hung's directorial debut *Iron-Fisted Monk* (1977) anticipated many elements of the comic action formula that Yuen Woo-ping and Jackie Chan would cement with the success the following year of *Snake in the Eagle's Shadow* and *Drunken Master*. In it, Hung's highly acrobatic action already draws more on the tumbling of opera than the performance of southern martial arts styles that had dominated the preceding years of kung fu's drive to display "traditional" kung fu. These acrobatics were interleaved with slapstick clowning and low, bodily humor. As well as his directorial debut, *Iron-Fisted Monk* was the first film in which Hung was the leading protagonist, and it marks the beginning of his establishment of a star persona.

In the coming years, Hung was a defining figure in the kung fu comedy, both in front of and behind the camera. *Magnificent Butcher* (1979), for example, built on the success of *Drunken Master* to cast him as a pupil of Wong Fei-hung, the character that Jackie Chan had played in that film. Helmed by the same director, it provided something close to an official sequel. In his directorial work, including *Dirty Tiger, Crazy Frog* (1978), *Knockabout* (1979), *Odd Couple* (1979), and *The Victim* (1980), Hung developed a comic world of dog-eat-dog competition, borrowed from the modern-day Hui Brothers comedies but now transposed back into a southern-Chinese rural past located somewhere toward the end of the nineteenth and the start of the twentieth centuries. The cynicism with which Hung's characters seek to get one over on each other has been noted by critics and read as reflecting the economic reality of laissez-faire capitalism in 1970s Hong Kong.[6] Within this fictional universe, Hung developed for himself a comic persona in equal part hapless everyman and cunning trickster.

Hung's action style in this period built on insights gained working with King Hu, who had been instrumental in making the camera itself as mobile as the performers, bringing it into the action rather than presenting combat as an event on a stage. Though also influenced by the long takes and clarity of Lau Kar-leung, Hung offered a cinematic fluidity where the dramatic movement or cutting of the camera added significantly to the visual impact and excitement of a scene. He also experimented with undercranking (filming at lower frame rates to create the effect of speeding up action) and "power powder" (where a small amount of talc is placed on clothing to be sent out in a cloud when impact occurs). These both added to the sense of frenetic violence, and Hung's choreography came to be known not only for its speed, intricacy, and precision but also for its viscerality: while other choreographers "faked" contact between performers, Hung insisted on contact, and on presenting it to the camera, often in slow motion.[7] Indeed, the intensity of their depictions of violence marks out Hung's comedies from Jackie Chan's. While Chan often sought to make movement dance-like,[8] Hung's films revel in physical damage, and this may well be part of his "cult" appeal. We see this with his two wing chun films, *Warriors Two* (1977) and *Prodigal Son* (1981), which are both fan favorites and hover at the boundary of comedy and brutality.[9] Where Chan increasingly made chases, acrobatics, and the creative use of everyday objects and environments central to his comedy style—allowing the crossover to a broader market—Hung remained closer to his kung fu roots. If they share a concern with the dexterous use of props, for Hung this took the form of dazzling work with an array of weapons.

The 1980s saw Hung teaming up with former opera-school classmates Jackie Chan and Yuen Biao, who collectively became known in Hong Kong as the Three Dragons. Their collaboration started with *Project A* (1983) and also included *Wheels on Meals* (1984) and *Dragons Forever* (1988). All three were involved in the highly popular Lucky Stars series, which was kicked off by *Winners and Sinners* (1983), directed by Hung. Alongside the martial arts of the Three Dragons, it included an ensemble cast of Hong Kong's most iconic comedians of the era. In this period, Hung also mixed kung fu comedy with the supernatural in *Encounters of the Spooky Kind* (1980) and *The Dead and the Deadly* (1982). As a producer, he initiated the craze for "hopping corpse" (*geongsi*) comedies with *Mr. Vampire* (1985).

When kung fu comedy's popularity waned, Hung nonetheless remained an important contributor to the martial arts genres that appeared in its wake. Hung's Vietnam War film *Eastern Condors* (1987) combined martial arts with gunplay and roused controversy about its levels of violence.[10] As a producer, he pioneered the "girls with guns" phenomenon with *Yes, Madam!* (1985), which gave Michelle Yeoh and Cynthia Rothrock their breakout action roles. When the trend turned toward wire-fu swordplays in the 1990s, Hung directed one of its finest examples, *Moon Warriors* (1992), and he provided the choreography for Wong Kar-wai's martial art-house classic, *Ashes of Time* (1994). Along with Yuen Woo-ping, he action directed *Kung Fu Hustle* (2004), and went on to choreograph the globally popular *Ip Man* (2008) and *Ip Man II* (2010). He returned to both directing and starring in 2016 with *The Bodyguard*.

Hung also contributed to the globalization of Hong Kong–style action with the TV series *Martial Law* (1998–2000), an action-comedy police drama which pioneered using Hong Kong stunt teams to provide fights for an American production. Evidencing the extent of his international appeal, with *Martial Law* Hung became the first East Asian to headline a US TV show.

The Work of the Body: Contextualizing Sammo's Performances

What emerges from thus reviewing Hung's oeuvre—aside from its multifaceted nature—are two key aspects of his star persona. First, there is the centrality of the comedy genre in forming it: this was key in Hung's rise to fame; it dominates his output in the era of his greatest prominence, and in it, the meanings of his star persona were established. The second aspect, however, seems to introduce a paradox. Though we might expect a comic performer to be involved with more "light-hearted" slapstick (and this is certainly a core element of Hung's performance skill), he is also known for the intense brutality and corporeal "realism" of his combat scenes. I have argued elsewhere that these two aspects are not in fact as opposed to each other as we may expect.[11] Here, I will analyze the ways this seeming contradiction takes form in Hung's star body.

However, as noted in this chapter's introduction, making sense of Hung's body as a "star text" must start with the apparent contradiction between his bulk and his athletic ability. This is all the more striking in the context of 1970s martial arts stardom. Hong Kong's star system in the 1950s and 1960s had been strongly oriented around female performers, even to the extent that they would take on male roles.[12] This changed in 1965, with the announcement by Shaw Brothers of a "new action era." This, it promised, would bring a new, gritty, and "realistic" action, in which life and death is decided, rejecting the mildness and "theatricality" of combat in prior films.[13] This was largely incited by Chang Cheh, a critic and scriptwriter who the Shaw executive took on as an advisor. Chang proposed that an ethos of *yanggang* (staunch masculinity) was necessary for Hong Kong to compete with the American and Japanese action films popular in Shaw's East and Southeast Asian market, which revolved around rugged male leads.[14] Chang developed and promoted a new stable of "manly" stars, placing them in prominent action roles. This entailed a change in the idea of the male martial arts hero as it had been imagined in films such as the popular Wong Fei-hung series of the previous two decades. Wong, played by Kwan Tak-hing, a man with a face that looked like he had been born old, embodied martial virtue as a mature Confucian patriarch. In contrast, Shaw's new stars—Jimmy Wang Yu, Lo Lieh, and Yueh Hua, for example—were young and glamorous, fashioned in the image of American popular culture. They reflected a broader cultural concern with youth and Westernization that was also seen in the phenomenon of the "youth film" of the 1960s and reflected Hong Kong's shift to an increasingly younger demographic.[15]

When Chang started to direct swordplays, his favorite star was Wang Yu, an ex-champion swimmer whose Olympian torso was often on display for the camera. With *The Chinese Boxer* (1970), Wang became the first star of the new genre of kung fu and the blueprint for its subsequent male heroes. In many ways, it is in comparison and contrast to Wang's image that Bruce Lee defined his own, out-muscling Wang with his built body and showing it off even more than his predecessor. Wang, Lee, and whole a generation of performers were marketed as idols and ideals for emulation: young, handsome, heroic, muscular, and physically capable, not to mention urbane, modern, and fashionable.

The focus on their *yanggang* bodies offers a way to understand the "realism" Shaw claimed for their films. With their intense stylization and melodrama, this clearly wasn't defined in terms of a naturalist aesthetic. Rather, grounded in the viscerality of combat, the on-display muscles of the genre's stars provided the terrain for an intensely sensory engagement with the cinematic spectacle of the body. It is in the materiality of the stars' and audiences' bodies that we might seek a form of realism—one encompassing the different registers of "authenticity" in performance that Leon Hunt has observed were central in kung fu cinema's reception.[16] The paradox here is that the star's body is at once a matter of intense *materiality* but also *ideal*. Kwai-Cheung Lo has thus discussed Hong Kong cinema's muscular bodies as having passed from physical presence into the "sublime."[17] This tension between the material and ideal is constitutive of the typical kung fu star's body, and this is something I will return to in my analysis of Hung.

The development of new images of the ideal, muscular, manly body also had resonance with longer histories of the Chinese martial arts. As the Qing dynasty collapsed at the end of the nineteenth century, reforming intellectuals described it as the "sick man of East Asia," a phrase that conflated masculinity, the individual body, and the health of the body politic. As Andrew Morris has detailed, one response to this was the development of China's physical culture, first importing Western exercises and then increasingly looking to its own martial traditions as a means of strengthening the bodies of its citizens and their fighting spirit, aiming to reinvigorate the nation as an industrial, political, and military force.[18] This concern with stamping order on the individual body (and hence on society) through physical culture's corporeal ideals was shared across the globe, and was pursued at special length by totalitarian states, both communist and fascist.

Male bodies were the particular battleground for such debates, with national transformation imagined in terms of masculine virility, reversing feminizing orientalist stereotypes. The appeal of the new masculinities of the martial arts stars of the late 1960s and early 1970s, an era in which militant ideas of decolonization and ethnic empowerment were sweeping the globe, was this sense of offering "positive" ideas of Chinese masculinity. Repeated anti-Japanese and anti-Western plots cemented these nationalist significations of the ideal, muscular, masculine kung fu body. But out of this comes a second contradiction: just as it hovered between the ideal and the material, the kung fu star body was a product simultaneously of Western consumerism (in its very production through the machinery of movie marketing, and its reliance on the aspirational imagery of advertising) and an anti-Western, nationalist message. Furthermore, it was both an image of modernist discipline and postmodern hedonism.

Sammo's Kung Fu Carnival

A number of critics have noted, however, that the kung fu comedy marked a movement away from nationalist concerns.[19] Identity in Hong Kong was increasingly negotiated in terms of the local rather than the national. The heady and turbulent 1960s were becoming a memory, and politics increasingly "disappeared" from public life in favor of a consumerism opened up by Hong Kong's growing economic success.[20] For many, the comedy marks a retreat from kung fu cinema's militant ethos, expressing instead the capitalist values increasingly dominant in Hong Kong.[21]

Rather than the ideal bodies of the start of the decade, the kung fu comedy offered the spectacle of a body much closer to the "grotesque realism" that Mikhail Bakhtin discussed as typical of medieval European carnival.[22] Like the carnival, kung fu comedies are filled with images of corporeal excess, and their humor revolves around "low" bodily functions: eating, shitting, puking, and farting. Rather than emerging from the perfected body of the virile male kung fu star, martial skill is connected to all kinds of aberrant bodies. The old, the ugly, the drunk or mad, cripples, women—and, yes, the fat—can all fight with fantastical ability. As martial and acrobatic performance itself was amplified to a breathtaking degree, the body involved seemed to belong less to aspirations toward the ideal than to a carnival logic of the excessive, marvelous, bizarre, or even freakish, evoking the fairground sideshow.[23]

But carnival is not without problems as a concept. It was overused to the extent that it became something of a theoretical cliché. Claims for carnival's "subversive" power need balancing by an awareness of the ways it functioned as much to reinforce as to undermine the social order it mocked.[24] Furthermore, there are problems in transposing an analysis based in the specifics of European culture to Hong Kong. However, as Hunt has noted, the match between carnival and kung fu comedy is too strong to ignore, and anthropologists have suggested that its grotesque mode, with roots in the ancient world, is observable as a broader pan-cultural phenomenon.[25] Certainly, a similar ribald humor is a significant element of the Chinese opera tradition in which Hung, along with many of those responsible for the kung fu comedy genre, was trained.[26] Furthermore, Bakhtin's account, written in Stalin's Soviet Union, was implicitly about modern-day power and its discontents, and some of the most compelling accounts of modern-day carnival have been in the context of colonial histories.[27]

The notion of carnival, then, may still be of use in thinking about Sammo's comic body. In carnival, the world of scarcity and oppression was temporarily overturned for a day of feasting and freedom, in which the hierarchies of the social order were upturned and everything elevated was brought down to earth for mockery. Kung fu comedy cinema offered something very similar for its working-class audiences. Rather than a hierarchical ontology of things in their proper, fixed places, on which authoritarian power rests, carnival celebrated becoming and transformation, the passage between bodies and orders as they exceeded their limits, asserting a wild dynamism inherent to the principle of life that resists all attempts to stamp form upon it.[28] Taking up this grotesque mode, the kung fu comedy similarly reversed the trend for the ideal, beautiful, ordered bodies of kung fu stardom, invested as these had been on the one hand in the modernist call to discipline and to reason's mastery of the physical, which had recently waned in ideological pull, and on the other in the ongoing reliance of consumerism on ideal images.

Enter the Fat Dragon

Sammo's rotund body is a prime example of this non-ideal carnival aesthetic of the kung fu comedy. It is telling that his breakthrough from supporting or antagonistic roles to that of protagonist only occurs within this new framework. Other stars of the genre also depart from the ideals of the previous moment: Jackie Chan, though athletic and muscular, does not have a typically handsome face: his nickname at opera school—redolent of carnival imagery—was "Big Nose."[29]

Hung's large frame implies the same prodigious appetites we meet in Rabelais's character Gargantua, whom Bakhtin places at the center of his analysis of carnival. Indeed, the carnivalesque nature of Hung's body as an on-screen image is made clear in many scenes. At the start of *Enter the Fat Dragon*, we are introduced to the character he plays, Ah Lung, a martial arts fanatic and obsessive Bruce Lee fan, feeding the pigs on his family farm. As Stallybrass and White argue, the pig, with its similarities to human flesh, is the archetypal carnival animal, straddling categories of cultural classification in ways that unsettle the hierarchies of the chain of being.[30] The cinematography lingers on the resemblances between the bodies of Ah Lung and his animals, and Hung plunges through their mass, crawling across their backs as the distinction between keeper and herd dissolves. Underlining the point, a humorously abrupt cut takes us from Ah Lung complaining about the excessive appetites of the creatures he is feeding to a shot in which he himself is pigging out on a plate of food. It is perhaps to alleviate the expense of his appetite that his father suggests he travel into the city of Hong Kong to help his uncle running a restaurant, and the action of the film—a "fish out of water" comedy in which the naïve bumpkin is faced with the world of the modern city—is initiated. The equation between Hung's body and that of the pig returns later in the film—and in fact persists across Hung's oeuvre. In *Warriors Two*, his character, "Porky," sells pork dumplings. In *Magnificent Butcher*, we are introduced to his character, Butcher Wing, wheeling a cart of pig carcasses to his stall, and then engaging in a dispute over them. In a later scene, he mistakes his teacher's direction for preparing marinaded pig trotters as instruction on an esoteric kung fu technique to make his own arms and hands invulnerable to injury.

A second scene involving pigs in *Enter the Fat Dragon*, however, clarifies the basic joke around which the film—and Hung's star persona—is posited. Having arrived in Hong Kong, Ah Lung comes across a stall selling sunglasses in a street market. He tries on several pairs, looking across at a poster of Bruce Lee, hoping to emulate the star's look in his iconic Persol Ratti shades (Figure 16). He gestures across the market and asks the stallholder: "Do I look more like him?" The camera follows the gaze of the slightly confused stallholder toward a cartoon image of a pig in glasses, also on display on the same wall. Slightly unsure of why Ah Lung would want to resemble this, he offers his cautious assent.

The stallholder's confusion sums up the comic premise of the film, which revolves around Sammo's/Ah Lung's mimicry of Bruce Lee in a series of fight scenes, replaying the ideal kung fu body of the star in carnival mode. Ah Lung's very name emphasizes this link. Lung translates as "dragon" and Lee's Cantonese stage name was, of course, Siu-Lung, "Little Dragon."[31] The "Ah," a modifier

Figure 16 Ah Lung (Sammo Hung) tries on a pair of sunglasses in hopes of looking like Bruce Lee. *Enter the Fat Dragon* directed by Sammo Hung. © Fung Ming Motion Picture Co. 1978.

indicating familiarity in address, already punctures the grand image of the dragon with its associations of royalty and the sublimely elemental. The comedy emerges from the collision of Bruce Lee's abilities, which seem in his films a manifestation of his perfect physique,[32] and Hung's overweight body. If Lee's body is sublime, then Sammo performs the short, carnival step from there to the ridiculous.

Hung's identification with Lee is also not confined to this film, and reiterated reference to Lee's prior "star text" became central to Hung's construction of his own. His Bruce Lee impersonations are repeated, for example, in *Millionaire's Express* (1986) and *Skinny Tiger and Fatty Dragon* (1990). He was brought in to choreograph the new action filmed to complete the 1978 release of Lee's unfinished *Game of Death*. Hung, furthermore, repeatedly came back to the depiction of the martial art Lee had studied, wing chun, not only in *Prodigal Son* and *Warriors Two*, but also through his choreography of Wilson Yip's biopics of Lee's teacher, Ip Man. Hung revisited the role of Lee's martial ancestor Wong Wah-bo, which he had played in *Prodigal Son*, in the television series *Wing Chun* (2006) and played Ip's teacher Chan Wah-shan in *The Legend Is Born: Ip Man* (2010). In these representations, the connection between Hung's and Lee's texts passes beyond the original comic gag and is played out across a range of genres or dramatic modes, as well as a range of professional roles, a fact I will return to later.

In thinking about *Enter the Fat Dragon*, however, a first task might be to understand further the nature of the humor. The laughter elicited may seem at first to follow the pattern described by Henri Bergson as the fundament of comedy: something high, ideal, or abstract—the work of the spirit—is brought down to earth by contact with the materiality of human existence. As Bergson expounds:

> When we see only gracefulness and suppleness in the living body, it is because we disregard in it the elements of weight, of resistance, and, in a word, of matter; we forget its materiality and think only of its vitality, a vitality which we regard as derived from the very principle of intellectual and moral life. Let us suppose, however, that our attention is drawn to this material side of the body; that, so far from sharing the lightness and subtlety of the principle with which it is animated, the body is no more than a heavy and cumbersome vesture, a kind of irksome ballast which holds down to earth a soul eager to rise aloft.[33]

This, indeed, echoes the satirical function of carnival's assault on the high through low humor. We see this mechanism staged in *Enter the Fat Dragon*'s sunglasses scene. In it, Lung clearly has "a soul eager to rise aloft"—dragon-like—but the "irksome ballast" of his heavy frame keeps him anchored close to earth, more pig than dragon. In the shape of the pratfall, this bathos is, indeed, a repeated device.

Early on, for example, Ah Lung fantasizes about being Bruce Lee while being rowed to Hong Kong. Imagining himself stamping on an opponent to finish him off as Lee does in *Enter the Dragon*, his face quivering with grand emotion, Lung is rudely awakened by the realization that he has put his foot through the bottom of the boat. With the boat sinking, Lung has to swim ashore and arrives in the city bedraggled and pathetic. Similarly, the "intellectual and moral" aspirations that Lung draws from his idol, in the form of his dreams of chivalric heroism, often backfire. When he puts down his food delivery to aid a woman by pursuing the purse-snatchers who have robbed her, he returns to find he has been robbed, too.

Of course, it is not precisely Bruce Lee himself who is the target of this comic deprecation. As his extended concern with Lee's image attests, Hung's performances are works of devotion, artefacts of a self-image constructed through his own fandom. This becomes clear within *Enter the Fat Dragon* in a scene where Lung gets work as an extra on a "Bruceploitation" film. Lung is contemptuous of the arrogant Bruce Lee lookalike who takes the lead role, Tseng Siu-lung (played by Tony Leung Siu-hung, brother of the real-life Lee "clone" Bruce Leung). The two come to fisticuffs, each performing their own impersonation of Lee's style (Figure 17). Lung, of course, is victorious, and the fight itself is, of course, a joke on the Hong Kong industry's continued exploitation of the dead star's image (as is the whole film). Beyond this, however, the scene seems to pose questions about the "truth" of Bruce Lee. It is not exactly Lee's sublime image itself which is mocked (though its peculiar replication across opponents is certainly a source of fun), but rather Tseng's belief that he can embody this. We could certainly read this in a Bergsonian manner as the "ballast" of Tseng's body failing at the transcendent task of assuming Lee's suppleness and grace. However, Hung's comedy seems more on the side of materiality than this would suggest. At stake in the opposition between the two opponents is the

Figure 17 Dragon vs Dragon: Ah Lung squares up to Tseng Siu-lung (Tony Leung Siu-hung) for a battle of the Bruce Lee clones. *Enter the Fat Dragon* directed by Sammo Hung. © Fung Ming Motion Picture Co. 1978. All rights reserved.

distinction between the image and substance of Lee: Tseng has the looks and movie dazzle of the kung fu star; however, it is the "fat dragon" who has the actual skill. The contest thus revolves around the question of "authenticity." If Lee's early death posed the question of whether he was "real" and the task of separating movie effects from fighting ability, Hung offers us a particular answer, separating out Lee's cinematic image and ideal body from the raw physicality of fisticuffs. Hung's "real" Lee is to be discovered in a corporeality that his own body has in seeming excess. Rather than being lodged in the ideal, martial power emerges from the same material body from which grotesque humor emerges. This reverses the "spiritualism" of Bergson: vitality—the grace, suppleness, and power of the martial artist—emerges not from the soul but from something rather like the carnival body.

This materialism, and the concern through it with "authenticity," draw together the comic and non-comic dimensions of Hung's oeuvre both in front of and behind the camera. His concern with brutal impact and the pratfall alike elevates the materiality of the performing body. Hung's large frame turns out to be an apt vehicle for expressing this, as it is all the more subject to gravity and momentum and serves to give an intense sense of the power that his weight can generate in flying kicks and grounded punches alike.

This concern with the materiality of combat also helps understand the role his emulation of Bruce Lee plays within his work as performer and choreographer. Corporeality becomes a mode in which to replay Lee's rejection of both graceful, operatic movement and "form" in martial arts in favor of street-fighting pragmatism. This is translated into Hung's concern with high impact choreography, and with what Wayne Wong has theorized through the notion of *shizhan* (combativeness), which he opposes to *zhenshi* (authenticity).[34] The latter term refers to the "authenticity" of tradition, which had been important in the Shaolin films of Chang Cheh and Lau Kar-leung. In contrast, *shizhan*, which Wong understands as drawing aesthetically from the works of Lee, names a concern with the pragmatics of violence, characterized in choreography by speed (*kuai*), brutality (*hen*), and precision (*zhun*). Wong's example of this is Donnie Yen's performance in the Ip Man films, the first two of which were choreographed by Hung. This *shizhan* aesthetic is more broadly found in Hung's oeuvre, a product of Hung's translation of Lee's street pragmatism into an action style revolving around corporeal materiality. Wong argues that the Ip Man films, bringing together wing chun traditions and philosophies with Lee's combative action aesthetic, unite *zhenshi* and *shizhan*. This is a longer concern across Hung's career, which synthesizes the operatic acrobatics in which he was trained, his interest in southern Chinese fighting styles, and Lee's sensibility for "combative" pragmatism, translated into the spectacle of bodily impact.

This embrace of materiality is also found in the nature of the laughter Hung's comedic work evokes. Here, rather than only a passage from lofty aspirations down into the mire of the body, which Bergson suggests is at the root of laughter, Hung takes us in the other direction too, and this seems quite in line with carnival's celebration of the corporeal. More central than his pratfalls or the slapstick punishment of the fool is the sense of wonder where Hung's "heavy and cumbersome vesture" rises to offer us the "gracefulness and suppleness of the living body." When Hung performs in the style and image of Bruce Lee, it is not to fail in the attempt or to affect clumsiness but to conjure the marvelous from his seemingly disjunctive flesh. One scene in *Enter the Fat Dragon* echoes the scenario from *Way of the Dragon* in which its hero Tang Lung confronts a group of foreigners who are causing trouble in a restaurant and laugh at Chinese kung fu. Like Tang Lung, Ah Lung takes the foreigners out onto the street to confront them, and Hung/Lung performs the same (already comedic) operatic kung fu dance that Lee performs, at the end beckoning his opponent forward. Every Bruce Lee fan knows what to expect next—the lightning-quick kick "dragon seeks path," which stuns his opponent. Puncturing this expectation in a moment of bathos, Sammo's Ah Lung stamps on his adversary's foot instead—but then, before we've quite done a mental double-take, executes the spectacular spinning kick with which Lee then finishes off his opponent, "dragon whips its tail," and does so with grace, speed, and power. The stamp becomes a moment of invention within a witty play on Lee's prior performance.

Hung, then, offers us something very different from the prior stardom of figures such as Bruce Lee. As a comic, Hung doesn't offer us a new ideal, but his performances work with and against the images he parodies and pastiches, taking them through the detour of the materiality of his body. As with carnival, there may be moments in this where the ideal is undermined, but it is also reiterated in Hung's very re-enactment of it. Like the women warriors discussed by Kwai-Cheung Lo, Hung—not exactly sick but the "fat man of East Asia," perhaps—re-performs an ideal masculinity from a position seemingly excluded from it, dramatizing not perfection but the struggle to attain it or valorize oneself in its terms.[35] Such struggle is dramatically and psychologically compelling, and in Lo's Lacanian terms, it might be seen as sustaining the "sublime" ideal not by attempting to fill its place but marking the impossibility of doing so by incongruously presenting himself in its stead.[36] Nonetheless, Hung's image also detaches kung fu's grace and power from normative bodies, highlights their artificiality, and situates them as objects for active play and meaning-making.

Postscript: Ghosts of the Fat Dragon

There are two prominent places where Hung's comic body finds its echo in recent cinema. The most literal is *Enter the Fat Dragon* (2020). In this, Donnie Yen wears a "fat suit" to simulate Hung's proportions, though the plot seems to have little to do with Hung's 1978 film of the same name besides the premise of a chubby protagonist with a Bruce Lee obsession and a loose connection to the tropes of *Way of the Dragon*. The other echo is in *Kung Fu Panda* (2008), which although it makes no direct reference to Hung nonetheless replays the basic joke of a rotund martial arts hero. Underlining the link, Hung's *The Bodyguard* (2016) has a villain say of his character in this, "Boss, he's like a kung fu panda!"

In both cases, changes in cinematic technology change the nature of the laughter. The materiality of Hung's performances was inherent to the conditions of production of 1970s Hong Kong action. This was rooted in the physical labor of stunt workers such as Hung, which substituted for the high-tech spectacle Hollywood was increasingly offering in this period.[37] The machismo of this competitive milieu also provides a condition of the violence of Hung's films—and, perhaps, the less-than-admirable aspects of sexism and homophobia that dog his directorial output. The broader context for these problematic aspects of Hung's output, of course, is the wider anxiety about Chinese or Asian masculinity discussed above, and the desire to strengthen, purify, and reassert this in the face of feminization and inferiorization that had been so central to the Hong Kong martial arts cinema in the previous decades.[38]

By contrast to the sheer physicality of the work of these stuntmen, however, both Yen's Fat Dragon and Disney's Kung Fu Panda are effects of the digital immateriality of CGI. *Kung Fu Panda*, with its reverent resurrection of tropes from kung fu comedy, certainly seems to replay the carnival fun of Hung's body, and retains a contrast between the light, airborne movement of the Furious Five and the emphatically weighty Po, whose Bergsonian body repeatedly falls, bounces, and wobbles, remaining subject to the laws of gravity and momentum in a way no other character in the film is. This, in fact, turns out to be the secret of his ultimate victory over the film's villain, and at a stretch we might even read the film as celebrating Po's carnival materiality as the source of his strength. However, there is no physicality here: as an audience, we also register any grace emerging from Po's soft body as an artefact of the multimillion-dollar technological infrastructure of Dreamworks' CGI machine. From one (slightly unkind) perspective, the banality of the film's "you can be anything you want" message itself is one that denies that materiality of life for a world and a self supposedly as fungible as the pixel.

In *Enter the Fat Dragon*, the padding and facial prosthetics that allow Yen to become overweight policeman Fallon Zhu are also complimented by computer graphics (especially in its climactic battle atop the Japan Radio Tower), making the film at points hardly less an animation than *Kung Fu Panda*. Yen, of course, moves with none of the cumbersomeness of a heavier physique, and wires accentuate his release from gravity. The marvel is once again that of the power of cinematic technology to transform bodies. Po and Zhu alike exemplify our condition of weightless being amid the digital flows of transnational culture and capital. Sammo Hung's sublime carnival physicality nonetheless haunts their image, calling us back to earth.

Notes

1 In early credits, Hung's nickname was more commonly rendered Samo, but after market research for *Martial Law* this was changed to Sammo to aid pronunciation for American audiences. It also renders more accurately the Cantonese name of the cartoon urchin, Sam Mo (Three Hairs), from which this was derived.

2 Stephen Teo, *Chinese Martial Arts Cinema: The Wuxia Tradition* (Edinburgh: Edinburgh University Press, 2009), 156.

3 Jackie Chan, *I Am Jackie Chan: My Life in Action* (London: Pan Books, 1999), 21–127.

4 Ibid., 117, 157–62.

5 Luke White, *Legacies of the Drunken Master: Politics of the Body in Hong Kong Kung Fu Comedy Films* (Honolulu: University of Hawai'i Press, 2020), 33–8.

6 Ting-ching Chan, "The 'Knockabout' Comic Kung-fu Films of Samo Hung," in *A Study of the Hong Kong Martial Arts Film*, ed. Shing-hon Lau (Hong Kong: Urban Council, 1980), 149.

7 Leon Hunt, *Kung Fu Cult Masters: From Bruce Lee to Crouching Tiger* (London: Wallflower, 2003), 40.

8 Aaron D. Anderson, "Asian Martial Arts Cinema, Dance, and the Cultural Languages of Gender," in *Chinese Connections: Critical Perspectives on Film, Identity and Diaspora*, eds. Tan See-Kam, Peter X. Feng, and Gina Marchetti (Philadelphia: Temple University Press, 2009), 192.

9 See Teo, *Chinese Martial Arts Cinema*, 156. See also Lam Chiu-wing, "Sammo Hung, the One and Only," in *Golden Harvest: Leading Change in Changing Times*, eds. Po Fung and Lau Yam (Hong Kong: Hong Kong Film Archive), 66.

10 Bey Logan, *Hong Kong Action Cinema* (London: Titan, 1995), 96.

11 White, *Legacies of the Drunken Master*, 82–105.

12 Leung Wing-Fai, "Multi-Media Stardom, Performance and Theme Songs in Hong Kong Cinema," *Canadian Journal of Film Studies* 20, no. 1 (2011), 44.

13 Peter Gravestock, "The Real and the Fantastic in the Wuxia Pian," *Metro Magazine* 148 (2006): 106–11.

14 Man-Fung Yip, *Martial Arts Cinema and Hong Kong Modernity: Aesthetics, Representation, Circulation* (Hong Kong: Hong Kong University Press, 2017), 88–92.

15 Poshek Fu, "The 1960s: Modernity, Youth Culture, and Hong Kong Cantonese Cinema," in *The Cinema of Hong Kong: History, Arts, Identity*, eds. Poshek Fu and David Desser (Cambridge: Cambridge University Press, 2000), 71–89.

16 Hunt, *Kung Fu Cult Masters*, 21–47.

17 Kwai-Cheung Lo, "Muscles and Subjectivity: A Short History of the Masculine Body in Hong Kong Popular Culture," *Camera Obscura* 13, no. 3 (1996), 106–207.

18 Andrew D. Morris, *Marrow of the Nation: A History of Sport and Physical Culture in Republican China* (Berkeley: University of California Press, 2004).

19 See Chan, "The 'Knockabout' Comic Kung-fu Films of Samo Hung," 149, and Hunt, *Kung Fu Cult Masters*, 102.

20 Ackbar Abbas, *Hong Kong: Culture and the Politics of Disappearance* (Minneapolis: University of Minnesota Press, 1997), 5.

21 See Chan, "The 'Knockabout' Comic Kung-fu Films of Samo Hung," 149, and Hunt, *Kung Fu Cult Masters*, 102.

22 Mikhail Bakhtin, *Rabelais and His World* (Bloomington: Indiana University Press, [1965] 1984).

23 White, *Legacies of the Drunken Master*, 38–41.

24 Peter Stallybrass and Allon White, *The Politics and Poetics of Transgression* (London: Methuen, 1986), 13–14.

25 Hunt, *Kung Fu Cult Masters*, 111.

26 Ashley Thorpe, *The Role of the Chou ("Clown") in Traditional Chinese Drama: Comedy, Criticism and Cosmology on the Chinese Stage* (Lewiston: Edwin Mellen Press, 2007).

27 Robert Stam, *Subversive Pleasures: Bakhtin, Cultural Criticism, and Film* (Baltimore: Johns Hopkins University Press, 1989), 123.

28 Bakhtin, *Rabelais and His World*, 32.

29 Suzi Feay, "Jackie Chan: An Unlikely Hero," *Independent* (November 25, 2005), https://www.independent.co.uk/news/people/profiles/jackie-chan-an-unlikely-hero-516884.html (accessed September 23, 2023).

30 Stallybrass and White, *The Politics and Poetics of Transgression*, 49–59.

31 The play on Lee's name is complicated by the fact that Hung's stage name as a child performer was Yuen Lung, so there is an element of self-referentiality here, too.

32 Lau Tai-muk, "Conflict and Desire: Dialogues between the Hong Kong Martial Arts Genre and Social Issues in the Past 40 Years," in *The Making of Martial Arts Films: As Told by Filmmakers and Stars* (Hong Kong: Hong Kong Film Archive), 32.

33 Henri Bergson, "Laughter," in *Comedy*, ed. Wylie Sypher (Baltimore: Johns Hopkins University Press, 1991), 90.

34 Wayne Wong, "Synthesizing *Zhenshi* (Authenticity) and *Shizan* (Combativity): Reinventing Chinese Kung Fu in Donnie Yen's Ip Man Series (2008–2015)," *Martial Arts Studies* 3 (2017): 72–89.

35 Kwai-Cheung Lo, *Excess and Masculinity in Asian Cultural Productions* (Albany: SUNY Press, 2010).

36 Lo, "Muscles and Subjectivity."

37 See Hunt, *Kung Fu Cult Masters*, 102. See also Lauren Steimer, *Experts in Action: Transnational Hong Kong-Style Stunt Work and Performance* (Durham, NC: Duke University Press, 2021).

38 Female characters in Hung's films—for example, in *Iron-Fisted Monk* or *Magnificent Butcher*—are often sexually assaulted by the films' villains to provide a reason for the hero's revenge, with the act presented as cinematic spectacle for a male gaze. *Encounter of the Spooky Kind* ends with its hero, played by Hung, beating his unfaithful wife brutally and mercilessly. In an article otherwise setting out to celebrate Hung's achievements, Lam Chiu-wing notes that although sexist representation is endemic in the industry, "the disdain for women in Sammo's film has to be the worst in all of Hong Kong productions" (Lam, "Sammo Hung, the One and Only," 68). For homophobia in Hung's work, see, for example, his combat with a team of transvestite assassins in *Twinkle, Twinkle, Lucky Stars* (1985). The effeminate Leung Yee-tai (played by Lam Ching-ying) in *Prodigal Son* might be Hung's most positive depiction of a queer character, but even here stereotypes predominate and form the occasion for numerous homophobic gags. That Hung's films harbor so much sexism and homophobia might well mark a limit to the extent that their carnivalization reverses and pluralizes the nationalist narratives of those films or the (ultimately patriarchal) hierarchies and fixed ontologies that their idealizations of the male body supported.

Chapter 7

Jackie Chan: A Stunting Star's Industrial Legacy

Lauren Steimer

Figure 18 Jackie Chan hanging out in Hollywood. *Rush Hour* directed by Brett Ratner. © New Line Cinema 1998. All rights reserved.

Introduction

A specter is haunting Hollywood. The image of Jackie Chan looms large for many of Hollywood's most prolific contemporary stunt coordinators. However,

Chan was not met with such a reverent reception when he first arrived on American sets to star in *Battle Creek Brawl* (1980). Hollywood was certainly not prepared for an action star known not only for doing his own stunts but also for choreographing all of the action. As Sylvia L. Martin has explained, the American film industry has a much more stratified relationship to on set labor than Hong Kong productions.[1] Chan experienced this rigidity through his interactions with stunt coordinators, stunt performers, and the directors of his early Hollywood-made films. Hollywood stars, for all their bluster and bravado, do not do their own stunts, and they certainly do not control action choreography or cinematographic choices during action scenes. Structurally, the Hollywood industry cannot easily accommodate stunting stars due to insurance constraints tied to funding for features and television. Chris Holmlund reminds us that "as one of the biggest global action stars, Chan's identity and appeal are complex. In many ways, his case is special."[2] As a result, there was and remains no Hollywood equivalent to Jackie Chan. While star theory points to the unique character or discursive formations that define individual stars, the star's identity and reception are also defined by the divisions of labor and regulatory structures underpinning the transnational media industries in which they work. This chapter brings industrial concerns to bear on the fighting star's image.

Jackie Chan has possibly received the most English-language scholarly attention of any Hong Kong star. Nevertheless, no author has addressed Chan's reception in Hollywood stunt communities from the 1980s to the present. Chan's authoritative control over action choreography and camera work was at odds with the division of media labor instilled in American stunt teams of the early 1980s. His style of martial arts choreography, fluid movement, wide framing, and requests to shoot multiple takes for fight scenes stood in stark contrast to American stunt craft traditions of the time, which emphasized brevity, simplicity, and the safety of the star. As a result, stunt performers who specialized in Asian martial arts traditions were marginalized in Hollywood stunt communities and often worked on low-budget or straight-to-video productions during this period. While these stuntmen had greater control of action choreography, that was because the films that they worked on had lower financial stakes.

After *The Matrix* (1999), Hollywood stunt work shifted toward including Asian martial arts spectacles in higher budget features. This transition allowed stuntmen to act as "action designers" or "fight coordinators." As these roles become increasingly formalized in Hollywood productions, more action designers pay homage to Chan through their fight choreography. First, this chapter addresses Chan's shifting reception in the Hollywood stunt industry via analyses of his working conditions during *Battle Creek Brawl*. Next, this piece considers Chan's culture of influence over action designers working in Hollywood, such as stuntman Jonathan "Jojo" Eusebio, via an analysis of the action design in Eusebio's film *Birds of Prey* (2020). Finally, the chapter concludes by examining

Chan's more considerable legacy within Hollywood action design history and among high-profile members of Hollywood stunt communities of practice.

Jackie Chan's early schooling from the age of seven in Peking Opera (*Jingju* 京劇) under a ten-year contract at the China Drama Academy (中國戲劇學校) in Hong Kong was a precondition to his work as an action film star due to the rigorous training Chan endured. Additionally, the stiff competition in the opera circuit caused Chan to look elsewhere for more gainful forms of employment.[3] The young Chan practiced martial arts, weapon work, acrobatics, and stretching daily to improve his flexibility, stamina, and core strength, all of which are necessary for successful performance in the opera. As recounted by Chan and other members of the "Seven Little Fortunes," students were beaten individually and collectively for any individual student's failure to perform to perfection during training.[4] Flexibility, stamina, and resilience to pain proved to be as valuable to Chan in his early movie career pursuits as his martial arts training. When Chan left the academy in the early 1970s, he sought work as a stuntman in Hong Kong productions. He could do so because of the network he built while at the China Drama Academy. The slightly older Sammo Hung had left the school first and was already working as a stuntman in the Hong Kong film industry. He helped his "little brother" find work as a stuntman on *wuxia* and *gongfu* films, both of which were popular in the early 1970s. The Shaw Brothers' tendency toward both genres and their constantly churning Fordist production system provided ample opportunity for Chan's professional development as a stuntman.

In the time Chan spent training as an opera performer in the 1960s, Hollywood's stunt community evolved beyond their disorganized training, evaluation, and certification systems into a much more regimented schema. While Hollywood stunt performers seemed to have perfected techniques for on-screen punching, falling, and horsemanship, they lacked a central governing organization to regulate certification and job placement. Working stunt performers were commonly members of the Screen Actors Guild (SAG), which had covered stunt workers since the union's formation in 1933. Even at its most conscientious, the union has historically struggled to meet the needs of stunt workers. The Stuntmen's Association of Motion Pictures (SAMP) was formed in 1961 to fill the breach left by a union that, by its definition, catered to actors. Unlike SAG, SAMP promoted the careers and concerns of stunt workers, stunt coordinators, and second unit directors. In the 1960s and early 1970s, the Screen Actors Guild often referred productions looking for stunt performers or coordinators directly to SAMP. The Stuntmen's Association of Motion Pictures was a fraternal organization designed to systematize the employment and expectations for stunt performers in Hollywood. Membership in SAMP was invite-only.

Invitations to join were at the behest of current members. Their network operated like a closed circuit, eliminating opportunities for talented outsiders. Much like the Hong Kong stunt industry in the 1960s, the Hollywood stunt industry was a nepotistically curated collection of primarily male professionals.

While the Hong Kong stunt industry employed a few women in the 1970s, most found work because of their connections to working stuntmen they knew from their Peking Opera academies. In Hong Kong and Hollywood, those already employed as stunt performers were the arbiters of talent or skill. There was and remains no formal test or documented list of qualifications to become a stuntman in either Hong Kong or Hollywood. These evaluation processes are in distinct contrast to the systems employed in the United Kingdom, the Republic of Ireland, and Australia, all of which require specific training and employ universal testing requirements for all applicants. At its inception, the Stuntmen's Association of Motion Pictures was an all-white and all-male organization. The group's unofficial regulation of the Hollywood stunt industry in the 1960s and 1970s effectively blocked many women and racial minorities from gainful employment as stunt workers. These groups formed their own professional stunt organizations in 1967, but continued to struggle for legitimacy and regular employment in the industry. The Stuntmen's Association also limited training access to those already linked to SAMP. Stunt workers outside SAMP trained within their own organizations, such as the Black Stuntmen's Association and the Stuntwomen's Association of Moving Pictures. Unlike SAMP, both organizations lacked proper training facilities. The members with the most experience on set would train new members to ensure performance quality, safety, and consistency.

Hollywood's Stuntmen's Association of Motion Pictures and Hong Kong's stunt community histories share the push toward professionalization and nepotistic and discriminatory selection processes in the 1960s and 1970s. However, they diverge on matters of training and on-screen performance. The cause for this break is less a cultural distinction, such as that between European styles of fighting and Asian forms of martial arts, and more an effect of different studio valuation systems, union regulations, and entertainment industry insurance mandates. Most theatrically released Hollywood films from the 1960s through the 1980s are likelier to feature European boxing styles than wushu or taekwondo. Still, the form of combat alone did not codify stunt performance techniques, camera placement, editing, and movement in the mise-en-scene. The primary schism between Hollywood and Hong Kong action design in the 1960s through the 1980s is the degree to which Hollywood ensconced the star from harm and offered up the stunt worker's body in return.

A Short Chronology of Hong Kong Action Design

The fortitude and complexity of Hong Kong's cinematic martial arts action design history is not a topic easily condensed and categorized into discrete eras of production. That being said, in an effort to distinguish this long history from the relatively recent evolution of martial arts action design in Hollywood, it is possible to break down Hong Kong cinematic action design into at least four distinct but related periods of development: the pre-classical period in Shanghai, the classical period in Cantonese and Mandarin cinema (1949–82), the post-classical period of advances in wirework and effects design (1983–2001), and the post-Handover period of mainland-ification (2002–present) in which many productions are shot and funded in mainland China with Hong Kong actors and action coordinators, and mainland stunt teams. I will discuss the first three periods in detail, as the fourth is of less import to this chapter's argument. These categories do not speak directly to genre or subgenre production, nor do they necessarily correspond to the rise of particular Hong Kong stars. Each of these moments is defined according to key developments and on set standards in action design labor and production.

The pre-classical period of martial arts action design aligns well with the production of martial arts serials by Shanghai-based studios in the 1920s and 1930s, what Zhang Zhen refers to as the "pre-consciousness" of Hong Kong action cinema.[5] During this period, productions required martial arts practitioners to work on set as trainers for the stars and also as background action. The stars commonly lacked formal long-term training in martial arts and had to be instructed in weapon work and fight scenes. While wirework was used in this era, the style and craftwork are quite rudimentary compared to modern harnesses, rig work, and character movement. Harnesses were similar to those used for stage productions and performers could only be moved up, down, screen left, or screen right. The harnesses lacked multiple pick points required for complex choreography. The actors lacked extensive training for complex maneuvers. Additionally, the rigging team used simple pulley designs and the line pullers only had to jump down off ladders and hold the actors aloft.

The classical period of Hong Kong cinematic action design begins in 1949 with the release of the first in a long series of Wong Fei-hung films starring Kwan Tak-hing. While there are certainly Cantonese martial arts films from the late 1930s, considering the ban on filmmaking during the Japanese occupation of Hong Kong (1941–5), the martial arts films made in the SAR prior to the occupation are few in number compared to those made during the postwar production boom.[6] The Wong Fei-hung series, introduced in *The Story of Wong Fei-hung: Part I* in 1949 (Wu Pang), utilized techniques that were common to Cantonese action design during the prewar period, including extensive training for lead actors in martial arts action and the presence of a coordinator, or "Dragon-Tiger Master," who would work with the lead actors to arrange the fight scenes and to perfect movement. This film had five credited martial arts consultants, including members of prominent martial arts schools and Peking Opera academies such as Yuen Wing-kwai and Wu Pang-hing. Some of the

Cantonese kung fu film production units worked in tandem with local martial arts academies to perfect the action on-screen so as to make it regionally accurate and marketable to Cantonese-speaking audiences.

While scholars often speak of a new era of Hong Kong *wuxia* filmmaking in the 1960s, the action design of that period inherits from old techniques common to Shanghai-produced martial arts serials of the 1920s and 1930s and the production structures of Cantonese kung fu films of the 1950s. By the rise of the major Mandarin studios in the 1960s, the organizational structure of Hong Kong action design had already been cemented. Martial arts coordinators, today referred to as "Action Directors," have become required elements for major studio productions. They were not the equivalent of stunt coordinators in the US production context. Martial arts coordinators or consultants experience much more respect from the director and crew. Martial arts coordinators were not necessarily in charge of the entire stunt team or of elements of action design outside of fight work and wirework, but to the extent that stunts intersected fight design. The Mandarin *wuxia* films relied heavily on wirework in the 1960s. Though the art form had not evolved much, the stunt workers who were hired to perform in wires were often Peking Opera-trained performers, who could move in a much more dexterous fashion than the action actors of the 1930s. As the Mandarin studios offered steady work, certain martial arts coordinators honed their craft in this era and became more hotly desired for the effects that they could produce. The formulaic nature of the studio system codified the workplace standards for action design on set.

The largest break between Hong Kong cinematic action design traditions and those of the classical era begins in 1983 with the production and release of Tsui Hark's *Zu Warriors from Magic Mountain*. This film ushered in the post-classical era with Fung Hak-on's new wire rig design that allowed for movement in all directions. It provided greater freedom of movement for actors and stunt performers. Harness design also evolved in relation to these new possibilities. These elements did not arise in a cultural vacuum as Hong Kong media workers exchanged ideas, techniques, and tools with other transnational production teams. This is a common practice in stunt industries worldwide. Action coordinators borrow, steal, and adapt techniques from other units. In this instance, Fung's team stole and perfected a technique that they had observed in Hollywood's *Superman* (1978). The actors and stunt team from *Zu Warriors from Magic Mountain* moved across the screen aided by divergent movement rigs and amplified by the film's visual design work. These two elements, dynamic wirework movement and industry-leading visual effects, became central elements of post-classical era Hong Kong cinematic action design.[7]

The temporal divisions between these three eras are loose and permeable. The project of creating such a timeline is doomed to, at the very least, minor failures because cinematic technique, organization structures, and work habits do not evolve along a tidy timeline. Media production rarely bends to clean periodization because histories of transnational exchange and work cultures are messy habits. As Sylvia J. Martin explains, Hong Kong film production cultures are defined by their flexibility.[8]

The Classical Era of Hollywood Action Design

From the 1910s through the early 1950s, Hollywood action design slowly accumulated a series of standard techniques. In the years between the silent movie serials and the dawn of sound, many performers transitioned from work in the circus, rodeo, air show, or Wild West Show circuit to sporadic employment as stunt doubles or as non-descript stunt performers.[9] Over time, the most consistently employed stunt workers developed a system to avoid injury to both actors and the stunt team. These performers passed down this knowledge to their children and extended families. This clan network structure was likely inherited from the performance cultures of live entertainment that both predate and inform Hollywood action, such as the circus and the rodeo.[10] This education framework is expected in craft traditions. Techniques are passed down through generations, and family members generally work in the same line of work. The practices of this early period began to formalize in the 1950s and became more codified as SAMP took control of the industry. The classical era of Hollywood action design begins during this period.

The increase in B-pictures and television Westerns during the 1950s and 1960s and the creation of the Stuntmen's Associate of Motion Pictures in 1961 systematized action production based on three principles: brevity, simplicity, and the safety of the star. Stunt performers trained in delivering and receiving a punch. They employed two techniques still used to this day: stacking and selling. Stacking, also called "focus stacking," uses blocking and focal length to compress the space between fighters to fabricate contact visually. Selling is performatively responding to an actual or perceived hit. These methods protect actors and stunt workers and make the action seem dynamic to audiences. There is enough distance between actors and stunt performers to complete a full arm swing. The stunt worker turns their head away from the punch and allows the head to swing briefly back toward the impact, to create the impression of recoil from the fabricated impact. This system permits multiple short takes of the same simple action and reaction. Cinematographers can expeditiously acquire the coverage they need; ideally, no one is harmed during the shoot.

These techniques infiltrated the Hong Kong stunt community via Robert Wise's blockbuster 1966 Hollywood film *The Sand Pebbles*. While the film was shot in Hong Kong, many local stuntmen found work on the production. On this shoot, a teenage Jackie Chan learned the Hollywood style of on-screen combat. Chan describes the process as follows: "The American stuntmen had to teach the Hong Kong stuntmen how to react properly to movie punches, and how to throw the punches. We learned how to do our reactions and our action from the American stuntmen.[11] *The Sand Pebbles* shoot was a formative experience for many Hong Kong stuntmen. According to Chan, before the arrival of that production in Hong Kong, stuntmen used traditional strikes and blocks from their martial arts training in the Peking Opera. He admits that his style shifted after the film and that he "really learned my action, my punch, a lot of my punches in the movies, I really learned from American stuntmen."[12] This shift in Hong Kong action design added shorter edits between shots and direct engagement with the camera. Before this moment, many Hong Kong productions filmed action in long or medium long shots. There was a frontality to the performance, as though the action was taking place on an opera stage. His introduction to the American system of action design encouraged Chan (and many others) to explore the three-dimensionality of the screen image by combining long shots and long takes of martial arts combat with dynamic, quick cuts between punches thrown and received. The search for the origin of any particular action design style leads the scholar on a circuitous path. Questions of cultural appropriation become conceptually convoluted by the process of exchange fostered through transnational stunt networks. Nevertheless, though American focus stacking and selling techniques changed action design in Hong Kong, this cultural appropriation did not produce adverse financial effects for Hollywood. The reverse cannot be said for Hollywood's shift toward Hong Kong-style action in the last two decades, as the Hong Kong box office has been flooded with big-budget top-earning US action imports, edging out local competition.

Classical period Hollywood action design was able to protect the star and manufacture the perception that the star hit hard enough to knock a man off-kilter and sometimes off his feet in one blow. The masculine heroes of Hollywood cinema do not retreat and are not objects of ridicule. Mark Gallagher has argued that "US action films conventionally highlight the normative qualities of their male heroes—such as whiteness, heterosexuality, and physical dominance. In addition, such films consistently avoid locating their protagonists as targets of comedy or in other feminizing situations."[13] Gallagher's point, which he links to the narrative structure of US action films, is equally applicable to the fight scenes. Action design and narrative trajectory are mutually reinforcing determinants of characterization. The heroes of the classical period of Hollywood action design hit hard and hit first.[14] In fact, the stunt workers in these films exaggeratedly perform impact and injury to reinforce the physical dominance of the star. As Gallagher attests, the characters Jackie Chan plays in his Hollywood films are likelier to be walloped, avoid being hit, or run away.[15] Chan may have been trained in the fundamentals of the classical Hollywood style of action design, but he could never fully conform to the masculine image of a Hollywood action star. Chan's star image is informed not simply by the characters he embodies but by how they fight.

The Opposite of a Hollywood Action Star

Liam Neeson, for instance, is not an action star, but they can use a small shot and make him become an action star. There's actor action star and there's action star. It's different. Now, Liam Neeson is an actor action star. First, he can act and his action is easy. There's easy action and difficult action. . . My kind of action is the difficult action. But the audience doesn't know that. They just want to see good or bad, that's all![16]

The global cinematic success of Bruce Lee, while cut short, would have implications for Chan's career in Hong Kong in the early to mid-1970s and his early work in Hollywood. Jackie Chan was among the many Hong Kong stars marketed as Bruce Lee's successor. Many scholars, critics, and Chan have commented on this era of his career as disastrous. In interviews, Chan is eternally deferential to Lee's star image as a severe and hard-hitting martial artist. Chan positions himself, by comparison, as a comedian. Golden Harvest's contract with Chan in the mid-1970s mimicked the structure of Bruce Lee's contract with the studio. Once Chan transitioned successfully to kung fu comedy, he could recast his star persona as distinct. However, contractually speaking, Chan never entirely stepped out of Bruce Lee's shadow. Like Lee, Chan had control over choreography regardless of who was paid to direct his films. This system worked for Lee in Hong Kong because action/fight coordinators were respected figures on set. Directors worked with or even catered to the whims of the fight coordinator. Generally, Hollywood did not have fight coordinators on theatrically released productions in the 1970s and 1980s. Directors often trusted a second unit director and stunt coordinator to plan the fight and the shots. A Hollywood stunt coordinator did not choreograph an elaborate fight scene. Most hits were planned in a shot-reaction shot format in medium close-up. Wider shots of short duration could be used to demonstrate a giant brawl or used for establishing shots. The distinctions between the Hollywood and Hong Kong division of action labor on set ensured that *Battle Creek Brawl* would feature fight scenes that satisfied neither Hong Kong nor Hollywood audiences.

The division of active labor on set and the styles of action design in *Battle Creek Brawl* are distinct from the working conditions and action design common to Chan's Hong Kong films in that Hollywood stars have minimal input into the action design process, and fight scenes are choreographed to be shot quickly, to avoid injury. The production culture of *Battle Creek Brawl* was somewhat like Chan's later work, and the fight scenes, while slow and poorly choreographed, are vaguely similar to Chan's Hong Kong fight work. Director Robert Clouse had worked with Bruce Lee on *Enter the Dragon* (1973) and was familiar with Golden Harvest's satellite production model, with the star in control of action choreography. Though Clouse and Chan fought over some of the action scenes, Chan had more input into the design of the fight scenes in this film than he did for either *Cannonball Run* (1981) or *The Protector* (1985).

Battle Creek Brawl was shot in Texas and the American Southwest and featured some prominent martial artists, including Gene LeBell and Pat E. Johnson. However, most of the men that Chan engaged with during the fight scenes were Hollywood stuntmen. Their reactions are poorly timed to Chan's hits. It is not that these stunt performers were untrained. Stuntman Loren Janes, one of the founders of the Stuntmen's Associate of Motion Pictures, had taught a teenage Chan the American action design system on the set of *The Sand Pebbles.* Now Chan was acting as his supervisor even though Chan had no standing in the Hollywood stunt community.

Chan's Hong Kong fight scenes showcase his flexibility, stamina, and core strength. To do so requires much longer takes than the American standard for fight scenes. The other stunt workers on the production included long-standing SAMP members like Diamond Farnsworth, Tom Morga, and George Fisher. All of them were trained according to the Hollywood system and would have been caught off guard at the learning curve required to produce Chan's long take, multi-fight beat sequences. A fight beat is a choreographed point of contact, intentional miss, or near-miss. Classical period Hollywood action design is often just a single beat or three beats at most. The American stuntmen Chan worked with on *Battle Creek Brawl* would have found these scenes, such as the first fight scene in the alley behind the Kwan family's restaurant, unnecessarily complex and taxing. The fight sequence begins with three shots and two simple fight beats:

- Shot 1: Chan's Jerry Kwan lands a comedic tomato to the face of the man in the blue suit (one fight beat).
- Shot 2: Jerry's father scolds him.
- Shot 3: The same stuntman pratfalls over a bag of food (one fight beat)

This series of beats follows standard classical period Hollywood action design techniques. The beats are not complex and can be easily performed and memorized. The most complicated element thus far is that the fight is staged in depth instead of one-on-one. This means the stuntmen in the background must continue acting while the beats are hit in the foreground. At this point, the fight scene transitions to something similar to Chan's Hong Kong fight work.

- Shot 3 (cont.): Jerry is grabbed from behind by the stuntman in the tan suit (one fight beat).
- Shot 3 (cont.): The man in the tan suit punches Jerry in the face, and Chan sells the hit by spinning away from the direction of the punch (one fight beat).
- Shot 3 (cont.): The stuntman in the black suit slaps Jerry, and Chan jumps back slightly (one fight beat).
- Shot 3 (cont.): Jerry and the man in the black suit wrestle. Jerry kicks the man in tan and pushes the man in black to the wall (one fight beat).
- Shot 3 (cont.): The man in the blue suit charges and punches at Jerry, and Chan ducks (one fight beat).
- Shot 3 (cont.): The man in the blue suit hits Jerry with his left arm extended, and Chan sells the hit (one fight beat).
- Shot 3 (cont.): Jerry pushes the man in the blue suit (one fight beat).

This single shot features eight fight beats. All are delivered more slowly than is typical in Chan's Hong Kong films, and all involve traditional moves used in classical period Hollywood action design. No punches or extended arms to the face make contact, and all stuntmen and Chan propel themselves through the space to sell hits. This is a complex fight for a Hollywood film from this period because of the high fight beat count, but it does not showcase Chinese martial arts, and the delivery is slow. The scene progresses to quicker shots with low fight beat counts in which Chan delivers a comedic performance, and the stuntmen move little in comparison. The scene would have challenged the stuntmen because of the high beat count and the fact that they had to work with the film's star during the scene. The function of stunt performers in Hollywood is to keep the stars safe. This scene, while far from Chan's most dynamic in his long career, asks much from the American stunt team: allow the star to choreograph the action; execute long strings of fight beats in a long take in a wide shot; protect the star at all costs. As Chan points out, there are "actor action stars" in Hollywood, and their work is comparatively "easy." The reason for this is that stars need to be protected from injury. If a star is injured, production shuts down, whereas if a stunt worker is injured, they bring in a replacement. The function of stunt workers in Hollywood is to make action scenes safe for cast and crew because, as experts, they use techniques perfected by their local industries.

The Post-classical Era of Hollywood Action Design: The Rise of the Fight Coordinator

If you look at movies, really, before *The Matrix*, they were barroom brawls, and quick punches, and, you know, *Rocky*—as kind of boxing fights. But there were really no mainstream big-budget Hollywood martial art films. They didn't exist yet.[17]

Following the global success of Bruce Lee in the 1970s, more Hollywood films featured some Asian martial arts techniques. However, the martial arts action film as a genre was generally considered a low-budget or direct-to-video market. Because these films had a lower profile in the industry, the production culture was less rigid. Martial artists found work as stuntmen on these films. Most stunt coordinators in the 1980s and early 1990s were not experts in Asian martial arts, and for this reason, they permitted martial arts-trained stuntmen and stuntwomen to choreograph the action on set. It was common for a fight to be choreographed by the stuntman, who would teach the star a small series of fight beats right before the camera began rolling. These scenes were hastily constructed, and martial arts-trained stunt performers were allotted more creative freedom because the coordinators did not consider these scenes serious stunt work. Before the 2000s, most martial arts fight design in Hollywood films was crafted ad hoc. The Screen Actors Guild, stunt organizations, and the Academy of Motion Picture Arts and Sciences did not recognize "fight coordinator" as a job. Stunt workers were not paid more for performing in this capacity. As stuntman, coordinator, and action auteur Chad Stahelski articulates, the industry changed after the success of *The Matrix*.

The production culture of *The Matrix* was for martial arts-trained Hollywood stunt workers. The fight coordinator for the film, Yuen Woo-ping, was a renowned Hong Kong action filmmaker from a prominent Peking Opera clan and was treated with reverence on set by the Wachowski sisters. Yuen choreographed and directed previsualizations or "previz" fight scenes, which were used as templates for camerawork, editing, movement, and mise-en-scene during the film's production process. Fight scenes were carefully plotted and rehearsed, first with the stunt team and later with the actors long before production. This system was standard in Hong Kong, where the terms "martial arts choreographer," "action choreographer," and "action director" are commonly used to describe the position Yuen held, each denoting a slightly higher status. The film's financial success caused Hollywood to value martial arts fight choreography more. Chad Stahelski, who worked as Keanu Reeves' stunt double on *The Matrix*, describes how in the Hollywood system, "fights in movies used to just be 'swing and punch and swing and punch' and you just move the camera around so much that you just hope something connects. (laughs) Martial arts has become such a mainstream thing now that you can't fake that kind of thing."[18] Hollywood refashioned Asian martial arts fights as necessary components of action design for big-budget films in various action-adjacent genres. This move, in turn, ushered in a new era of Hollywood action design in which the creative input of the "fight choreographer" was highly favored, and their work was recognized as a spectacular means to financial success and as well as award-worthy.

Though the production culture of *The Matrix* may have heralded the post-classical era of Hollywood action design, audiences soon tired of *wuxia*-styled wirework spectacles. In the two decades that followed, action design teams learned to balance wire effects with earthbound martial arts techniques. The rise in status of the fight coordinator and the need for preplanning in the form of previz videos of the fight scenes meant that coordinators like Jojo Eusebio had greater control over production. Eusebio describes cinematography and editing choices as part of the purview of the fight coordinator: "There is more to choreography and fights, stunt action, or action design than just doing the choreography. You've got to control how it's shot. You've got to control how it's edited. You've got to have [an] influence on those things."[19] The recognition of fight coordinators as a required and supervisory part of the Hollywood stunt team allowed martial arts experts like Eusebio to change how Hollywood action scenes were both shot and edited. With this newfound power, Eusebio organized his fight scenes around the same principles as Jackie Chan: fluid movement, wide framing, and playful use of objects from the mise-en-scene as weapons.

Eusebio's final group fight scene in the Booby Trap Fun House in *Birds of Prey* is reminiscent of Jackie Chan's Hong Kong action fight scenes. It is also more similar to Chan's Hong Kong action design aesthetics than any of Chan's fights from his early Hollywood films like *Battle Creek Brawl*. Eusebio wanted the actresses to be visible during the fight scene and choreographed the action during their five months of training for the fight scenes. The actresses trained daily, and Margot Robbie learned to roller skate for two scenes, including this fight scene. Eusebio wanted to avoid using stunt doubles because that choice would limit longer takes and wider shots with the actresses faces in view. Much like Chan, the actresses were visualized actively fighting on screen and limited trick shots. The most complex part of the fight takes place on a rotating carousel. The shots that precede this segment show dynamic movement in the form of jumps and flips off moving funhouse obstacles. Throughout this scene, the actresses are sometimes substituted with their stunt doubles for more sophisticated maneuvers. All the action in this scene before the carousel Many-Hits-Many group fight comprises short one to three-fight beat sequences and quick edits between shots. Once Robbie's Harley Quinn is outfitted in roller skates at the center of the carousel, the elaborate fight begins. The camera tracks right for a longer take while the carousel spins to the left as four adult actresses fend off the team of stuntmen with three to four fight beats each. The actresses use the large hands attached to the carousel to fling stuntmen from the spinning platform, an oversized mallet to hit them in the head and stomach, and arrows to stop any forward movement. This style of action design would be unthinkable in earlier eras of Hollywood stunt history. *Birds of Prey*'s director Cathy Yan explains that the longer shots and complex fight beat chains were designed to evoke Jackie Chan's Hong Kong work: "Jonathan Eusebio, who's our stunt coordinator, we really got along, and we talked a lot about Jackie Chan movies and how practical it was and how you weren't cutting really quickly. You're kind of staying on it and staying on the action."[20] The action design was an integral part of the film, and Yan envisioned the narrative, characterization, and fight scenes as fully integrated elements. Much like fight coordinators on most Hong Kong productions, Eusebio had input on the entire creative process for the fight scenes, not just the choreography.

The new era of Hollywood action grants fight coordinators more oversight into the creative process. However, the action design often betrays its Hollywood roots in that shot duration is, on average, much shorter, and stunt doubles cover more elaborate moves. The star still must be protected at all costs. Even so, the third era of Hollywood action design is increasingly and intentionally reminiscent of Chan's work in Hong Kong. One reason is that the most in-demand fight coordinators work for months with actors to prepare for fight scenes in stunt gyms designed for this purpose. These facilities are a relatively new phenomenon and are often run by esteemed stuntmen trained in martial arts whose careers flourished after *The Matrix*. These training gyms are ideal spaces to practice long fight beat chains while propelling upward by gymnastics spring floors and protected from falls by pads and boxes. Fights are no longer composed haphazardly for the camera. In this new era, Jackie Chan's Hong Kong fight aesthetics are held on high by Hollywood's top fight coordinators like Jeff Imada, James Young, Chad Stahelski, Davis Leitch, Andy Cheng, Philip J. Silvera, and Jojo Eusebio. Animated by more than admiration for Chan's craft, these fight design artists have pushed the US film and television industries toward wider shots, longer fight beat chains, and more elaborate movement. This new generation has transformed the American action landscape, and the result looks very similar to what you might expect from a Jackie Chan film from Hong Kong in the 1980s or 1990s.

Notes

1   Sylvia J. Martin, *Haunted: An Ethnography of the Hollywood and Hong Kong Media Industries* (New York: Oxford University Press, 2017), 97–114.

2 Chris Holmlund, "Celebrity, Ageing, and Jackie Chan: Middle-aged Asian in Transnational Action," *Celebrity Studies* 1, no. 3 (2010), 99.

3 Pui-Lun Chan, "Act Like Jackie Chan: The Cinematic Legacy of Jingju Training Schools in Hong Kong," *TDR: The Drama Review* 62, no. 2 (2018), 115.

4 Jackie Chan, *I am Jackie Chan: My Life in Action* (New York: Ballantine Books, 1998), 51–2.

5 Zhang Zhen, "Bodies in the Air: The Magic of Science and the Fate of the Early 'Martial Arts' Film in China," *PostScript* 20, nos. 2–3 (Winter-Spring 2001), 51–4.

6 David Desser, "The Kung Fu Craze: Hong Kong Cinema's First American Reception," in *The Cinema of Hong Kong: Cinema, Arts, Identity*, eds. Poshek Fu and David Desser (Cambridge: Cambridge University Press, 2000), 31–2.

7 Fung Hak-on, "The Bearable Lightness of Wire: A Milestone for the Wire," in *A Tribute to Action Choreographers: 30th Hong Kong International Film Festival Programme*, ed. Cheuk-to Li (Hong Kong: Hong Kong International Film Festival Society, 2006), 141.

8 Martin, *Haunted*, 111.

9 A stunt double stands in for a named character during dangerous performance segments. A non-descript stunt role, or "ND," often serves as background action or an unnamed antagonist.

10 Clan networks are common in stunt communities around the world. Often, members of the clans with the longest lineage in the field get the most work and retain a power over their local stunt communities.

11 Chan quoted in John R. Little and Curtis F. Wong (eds.), *Jackie Chan and the Superstars of Martial Arts: The Best of Inside Kung Fu* (New York: McGraw-Hill, 1998), 112.

12 Ibid.

13 Mark Gallagher, "Rumble in the USA: Jackie Chan in Translation," in *Film Stars: Hollywood and Beyond*, ed. Andy Willis (Manchester, UK: Manchester University Press, 2004), 123.

14 This tendency is celebrated by fans of these characters. For example, Star Wars originalists often proclaim "Han shot first" in reference to the edited version of *Star Wars: Episode IV: A New Hope* (1977), in which Han Solo now only fires when fired upon.

15 Gallagher, "Rumble in the USA," 116.

16 Jackie Chan quoted in Tara Karajica, "Jackie Chan on Why Hollywood Isn't Producing Good Martial Arts Films Anymore," *Indiewire* (April 28, 2015), https://www.indiewire.com/2015/04/jackie-chan-on-why-hollywood-isnt-producing-good-martial-arts-films-anymore-62584 (accessed September 23, 2023).

17 Chad Stahelski, "Interview with Cale Schultz," *87Eleven Action Design Podcast* (May 17, 2019).

18 That Shelf Staff, "Interview: Chad Stahelski & David Leitch," *That Shelf* (October 24, 2014), https://thatshelf.com/interview-chad-stahelski-david-leitch (accessed September 23, 2023).

19 Jojo Eusebio, "Interview with Cale Schultz," *87Eleven Action Design Podcast* (June 3, 2019).

20 Hoai-Train Bui, "How Jackie Chan and John Wick Inspired the Action Sequences in *Birds Of Prey*," *Slashfilm* (February 3, 2020), https://www.slashfilm.com/572053/birds-of-prey-fight-scenes-cathy-yan (accessed September 23, 2023).

Chapter 8

Michelle Yeoh: Combating Gender

Kyle Barrowman

Figure 19 Yim Wing Chun (Michelle Yeoh) invents a new martial art and a new model of womanhood. *Wing Chun* directed by Yuen Woo-ping. © Century Pacific 1994. All rights reserved.

Since the 2018 release of the surprise hit *Crazy Rich Asians*, continuing through the blockbuster success of the 2021 box-office record-breaking Marvel film *Shang-Chi and the Legend of the Ten Rings*, and culminating with the 2022 release of the even more surprising and even bigger popular and critical hit *Everything Everywhere All at Once*, it would be an understatement to say that Michelle Yeoh is experiencing a remarkable resurgence. Known for years the world over as—to borrow the description of her character by Awkwafina's character in *Shang-Chi*—"an awesome, magical kung fu goddess," and now known the world over as a Golden Globe- and Oscar-winning actress, Yeoh did the press rounds throughout the 2023 awards season, and she took the opportunity on multiple occasions to reflect on her forty-year journey through international stardom. In particular, she has found it amusing how often the people interviewing her make comments to the effect that their parents or grandparents are so excited that they are interviewing her.[1] The implication is that older or more "hardcore" fans of cinema, specifically of Hong Kong action cinema, will know Yeoh and her work well, whereas younger or more "casual" fans will have become acquainted with Yeoh for the first time only recently. Indeed, while there is plenty of intertextual amusement to be appreciated in Awkwafina's character's description of Yeoh's character in *Shang-Chi*, as well as in the multiversal depiction of Yeoh's character Evelyn Wang's alternate action star identity in *Everything Everywhere All at Once*, there is at the same time something frustrating about imagining fans who are witnessing Yeoh's tremendous success who are incapable of situating it as the culmination of four decades of work as an action icon. To this end, rather than focus on her recent popular and critical successes, in this chapter I will plot the coordinates of Yeoh's journey from an aspiring dancer to an international action heroine, focusing in particular on her formative years in Hong Kong cinema and on her fascinating work in the 1980s and 1990s.

Interestingly, though not all that surprisingly given their physical affinities, the biographies of numerous Hong Kong martial arts cinema stars include backgrounds in dance. Not only did the first major female action icon of the classic Shaw Brothers *wuxia* films, Cheng Pei-pei, have a background in dance, but even Bruce Lee was a Crown colony Cha-Cha champion in Hong Kong in his youth. In this respect, Yeoh's trajectory from dance to martial arts is not that anomalous. However, unlike many of her genre peers, Yeoh was no mere hobbyist, nor was dance merely one among many facets of a broader theatrical training; on the contrary, Yeoh began training ballet in Malaysia at the age of four, and she went to college at the Royal Academy of Dance in London where she was preparing for a career as a dancer. Unfortunately, a back injury nixed those plans, and she wound up on the beauty pageant circuit instead, winning Miss Malaysia in 1983. This new notoriety landed her a TV commercial opposite Jackie Chan, and he and Sammo Hung thought that she would be a great addition to their films. Soon enough, Yeoh would make her film debut in Hung's 1984 comedy *The Owl vs. Bumbo*. Initially cast as merely a pretty face, Yeoh's second appearance in one of Hung's films would be more physically demanding: in *Twinkle, Twinkle, Lucky Stars* (1985), Yeoh plays a judo instructor who humorously handles Richard Ng's character but who is unable to defeat the "big fellow" Hung.

In addition to the speed with which she learned Cantonese, which demonstrated her sincerity to those around her in wanting to pursue a career in the Hong Kong film industry, Yeoh's eagerness to take on more physically challenging, action-centric roles gave Hung an idea, which he pitched to Dickson

Poon, with whom he had founded the production company D&B Films. The idea was to have a sub-genre of female-led action vehicles. The brilliance of the idea was proven very quickly, as Yeoh, in her third film, starred alongside American martial arts champion Cynthia Rothrock (soon to become an action icon herself[2]) in the film *Yes, Madam!* (1985). This is the film that gave birth to the "girls with guns" cycle of Hong Kong action films. Historically speaking, *Yes, Madam!* is an important film not only for its female leads, but also for its modernization of martial arts action. Helping to bring Hong Kong action from out of the historical/mythological settings of such classic *wuxia* and kung fu films as *The One-Armed Swordsman* (1967), *A Touch of Zen* (1971), *Fist of Fury* (1972), and *The 36th Chamber of Shaolin* (1978), *Yes, Madam!* is one of several key films—along with Jackie Chan's *Police Story* (1985) and *Police Story 2* (1988) and John Woo's *A Better Tomorrow* (1986), *A Better Tomorrow II* (1987), and *The Killer* (1989)—that brought Hong Kong action cinema into the present day and into contemporary urban environments. In the context of Yeoh's career, however, *Yes, Madam!* is important for a different reason: it marked the first time, but importantly not the only time, that she appeared in a film in which her character is forced to tackle issues related to gender.

To be clear, my language here (preferring "in which her character is forced to tackle issues related to gender" to "in which Yeoh chose to tackle issues related to gender") is not accidental. Though there have been scholars who have argued for an "actor as auteur" perspective, on the basis of which we are encouraged to consider actors to be as crucial to the creative process as (if not more crucial than) writers, producers, or directors, I do not subscribe to this methodological perspective.[3] It is true that there are actors who go to great lengths to choose specific projects and to work with specific cast and crew in order to create/perpetuate a particular persona. Far from the days of the Hollywood studio system and the contract player who just did the projects that were assigned to them, innumerable actors have carefully sifted through material with the intention of shaping for themselves their own star texts. From Steve McQueen through Tom Cruise up to Millie Bobby Brown, there have been countless actors who have taken active roles (including even becoming producers and starting their own production companies) in shaping their careers, and some even act as true collaborators during the production process. I do not wish to dispute this; I merely wish to clarify that this is the exception rather than the rule, and that what it takes for an actor to ascend to the status of auteur is truly exceptional. In the case of Michelle Yeoh, she does not rise to the level of auteur. She did not produce her own films, nor did she ever write or direct her own films. In fact, it would take nearly two decades, until her 2002 film *The Touch*, for Yeoh to take on a bigger role and receive story and producer credits in addition to her acting.

Yet, having drawn this methodological/terminological line, even though I do not consider Yeoh an auteur, I do not consider here a mere actor, either. This is one of the many perplexities investigated by Stanley Cavell in *The World Viewed*, in which he takes the opportunity to explore the nature of *acting* (which is a definable practice) versus the nature of *stardom* (which is an indefinable phenomenon). Consider the following passage, the significance of which will reverberate through—indeed, which will anchor—this entire chapter:

> An exemplary screen performance is one in which, at a time, a star is born. After *The Maltese Falcon* we know [Humphrey Bogart as] a new star . . . His presence in [*The Maltese Falcon*] is who he is, not merely in the sense in which a photograph of an event is that event; but in the sense that if [this film] did not exist, Bogart would not exist, the name "Bogart" would not mean what it does . . . But it is complicated. A full development of all this would require us to place such facts as these: Humphrey Bogart was a man, and he appeared in movies both before and after the ones that created "Bogart." Some of them did not create a new star (say, the stable groom in *Dark Victory*) . . . but [still] are related to that [star] and may enter into our later experience [of his films]. And Humphrey Bogart was both an accomplished actor and a vivid subject for a camera. Some people are, just as some people are both good pitchers and good hitters; but there are so few that it is surprising that the word "actor" keeps on being used in place of the more beautiful and more accurate word "star"; the stars are only to gaze at, after the fact, and their actions divine our projects.[4]

In line with Cavell's thinking in this passage, *Yes, Madam!* is the film in which, quite literally, a star was born. But what is significant about Michelle Yeoh's star vehicles? In such films as *Yes, Madam!*, *Royal Warriors* (1986), *Magnificent Warriors* (1987), *Police Story 3: Supercop* (1992), *The Heroic Trio* (1993), *Tai Chi Master* (1993), *Wing Chun* (1994), and *The Stunt Woman* (1996)—which films I contend make up the first distinct *phase* or *stage* of her career—what are the salient aspects of performance, character, and theme that come together to make "Michelle Yeoh" mean what it does? Just as James Cagney's 1930s gangster films created a star persona that all of his subsequent films (whether crime films, melodramas, musicals, or comedies) would be related to and forced to contend with, and just as Clint Eastwood has spent the last half-century reworking/reflecting on the star persona created in his Western and cop action films in the 1960s and 1970s, the first decade of Michelle Yeoh's career resulted in the creation of a particular star text.[5] Every film that she made subsequent to *The Stunt Woman*, the film that marks the close of the first phase of her career inasmuch as it signals the possibility of her shifting from single young woman characters to older mother characters—that is, every film from *Tomorrow Never Dies* (1997) and *Crouching Tiger, Hidden Dragon* (2000), through *Memoirs of a Geisha* (2005) and *Crazy Rich Asians*, up to *Boss Level* (2021) and *Everything*

Everywhere All at Once—has reflected back on or extended the persona that initially emerged in her early Hong Kong work. The Cavellian question, then, is: *what does* "Michelle Yeoh" *mean*? How should we (and how should we not) understand the winding road of her career, and how do her major films relate to/comment on/elaborate on each other to where, together, they make legible a distinctive star text?

In this chapter, I will argue that the Michelle Yeoh star text can be interpreted with reference to a conception of *combating gender*. It is my contention that Yeoh's characters represent challenges to conventional notions of what a woman is/should be (what a woman should and should not look like, how a woman should and should not act, what roles women can and cannot take on, etc.) and that the frequency with which she played such characters in her films created a star persona that was so *femininely* powerful that she challenged the conventions of action cinema and effectively redefined the woman warrior archetype. And, if her performance in *Everything Everywhere All at Once* is any indication, she is as committed as ever to playing characters who redefine what women can do on the screen and, by extension, what women can aspire to be and do off the screen. This, then, is my understanding of the Michelle Yeoh star text, and it will be the task of this chapter to demonstrate its validity and value, which I will do with reference to the pioneering scholarly work of Andrew Britton on the pioneering female star Katharine Hepburn.

To my mind, Britton's analysis of the Hepburn star text is the gold standard in star studies, but my purpose in adducing his work in the present context is because the way that he approached Hepburn promises many equally fascinating insights if Yeoh is approached the same way, for both stars are famous for their iconoclastic feminism. Methodologically speaking, Britton admirably refused to reduce Hepburn to one character type or to force her career into one clear teleology. Contrariwise, Britton segmented Hepburn's career in order to better understand and appreciate the historical specificity of her work at distinct points in her career—he analyzed films in which a father-daughter dynamic is central, as in such films as *A Bill of Divorcement* (1932), *Sylvia Scarlett* (1935), and *The Philadelphia Story* (1940); in which a community of women forms and is foregrounded, as in such films as *Little Women* (1933), *Quality Street* (1937), and *Stage Door* (1937); in which Hepburn teams up with Spencer Tracy, as in such films as *Woman of the Year* (1942), *Adam's Rib* (1949), and *Pat and Mike* (1952); and in which she plays "old maids," as in such films as *The African Queen* (1951), *Summertime* (1955), and *The Rainmaker* (1956). Though he maintained that there is a discernible through line to Hepburn's career—his overarching argument is that "Katharine Hepburn is the only star of the classical cinema who embodies contradictions (about the nature and status of women) in a way that not only resists their satisfactory resolution in a stable, affirmable ideological coherence," but who also "continually threatens to produce an *oppositional* coherence which is registered by the films as a serious ideological threat" inasmuch as her presence "is always more radical than her films" given how she "forces her films to go in directions they cannot possibly follow, adopt strategies they cannot fully sustain, raise issues they cannot adequately resolve"[6]—he nevertheless insisted on focusing on each phase in its temporal and cultural specificity so as to avoid allowing the "shadow, more or less pronounced," of one phase to obscure the contours of another.[7]

This, in my estimation, is the best way to approach Michelle Yeoh's career. Following Britton's lead in his assertion that "each phase [of a star's career] can be regarded as a specific attempt to solve the problems produced by the ideological material organized in the persona,"[8] it is worth approaching Yeoh's early films as a distinct phase in her long career, specifically as the phase in which her ideologically radical presence destabilized traditional film narratives— as happens in *Yes, Madam!* and *Wing Chun*—while at the same stabilizing her image as the most radical woman warrior. As a first step toward unpacking all of this, it is worth spending a little time initially with Yeoh's first starring vehicle, *Yes, Madam!*. It is in this film that many of the most important threads in Yeoh's star text were weaved together for the first time. First, at the most general level, Yeoh's character is a strong and independent woman. This is not unique to Yeoh, but it establishes not merely the type of character she will most often play, but the type of woman she is most keen to portray. Second, and more specifically, her character is a woman in a position of power and who is in charge of many people, including many men, all of whom respect her intelligence and her abilities but some of whom find it difficult to relate to her as (what they think of as) a woman. Despite the radicality of the "girls with guns" cycle of Hong Kong actioners and the genuinely positive influence that *Yes, Madam!* (and its female knight errant precursors and its women warrior descendants) had on the action genre as a whole, Yeoh's (and Rothrock's) presence is nevertheless, like Hepburn's presence, more radical than the films in which she appears.

In the course of Yeoh's character Ng's investigation into who murdered her lover, she winds up partnered with Rothrock's character Carrie Morris; together, they follow the comedically inept tail of a group of criminals who have gotten tangled up with crime kingpin Tin Wai-Keung (James Tien), a triad boss who always manages to slip through the cracks of the justice system. The climactic showdown at Tin's house culminates in Ng and Morris taking out Tin's muscle, Dick (Dick Wei) and Mad Dog (Fat Chung), but unfortunately for our heroines, the microfilm that contained the evidence of Tin's guilt is destroyed, leaving them as police officers with no ground to arrest their quarry. Worse still, Tin alleges that Ng and Morris are trespassing and have been harassing him and attacked him in his home, which prompts the by-the-book police chief (Melvin Wong) to arrest Ng and Morris instead of Tin (Figure 20). As Ng and Morris, the two agents of justice, and Strepsil (John Sham) and Aspirin (Hoi Mang), the two small-time

Figure 20 Despite being officers of the law, Senior Inspectors Ng (Michelle Yeoh) and Morris (Cynthia Rothrock) learn the painful lesson that some men are above the law. *Yes, Madam!* directed by Corey Yuen. © D&B Films 1985. All rights reserved.

crooks who obtained the evidence of Tin's criminal activities, are being led out of Tin's house, Aspirin learns of the death of his and Strepsil's friend Panadol (Tsui Hark). In a fit of rage, he grabs a police officer's gun and, with Strepsil holding back the nearby officers to keep them from intervening, gets vigilante justice by shooting down Tin.

The interesting twist at the end of *Yes, Madam!* carries with it some unfortunate ideological implications. Despite both Ng's and Morris' excellent police credentials (both having trained at Scotland Yard, both working as top officers in their respective countries, and both solving the case and apprehending Tin by themselves with no police backup), they are unable to bring the criminal to justice. Indeed, they are not even able to secure vigilante justice. It is the criminals—the *male* criminals—who put an end to Tin, while the police officers—the *female* police officers—are arrested by the police chief—the *male* police chief—quite as if he is reprimanding the female officers for their "excessive" (re: masculine) zeal. Though *male* cops bending (if not breaking) the law in pursuit of justice (and/or revenge) is a standard component of action cinema—witness the likes of Jackie Chan (e.g., *Police Story* [1985]), Arnold Schwarzenegger (e.g., *Raw Deal* [1986]), Sylvester Stallone (e.g., *Cobra* [1986]), Steven Seagal (e.g., *Out for Justice* [1991]), Bruce Willis (e.g., *Die Hard* [1988]), and Donnie Yen (e.g., *Flash Point* [2007]) bucking the system and taking matters into their own hands, always violently and often extrajudicially—the *female* cops in *Yes, Madam!* are not allowed to bring the criminal to justice. The result is a film the end of which feels rushed, perfunctory, and downright silly—in Britton's words, this is a paradigmatic example of a film that is taken in a direction it cannot follow, that adopts strategies it cannot fully sustain, and in which the "emergency exit" of the *deus ex machina* vigilante shooting is impeded so much that the film all but unravels under the weight of its ideological contradictions.[9]

The pressure applied to action conventions by virtue of Yeoh's presence, however, would only increase. This is evidenced by a later film like *Wing Chun*, which is more successful than *Yes, Madam!* in its attempt to integrate the "feminine" and the "masculine" in Yeoh's character, but in which there are still deep tensions that director Yuen Woo-ping is unable to resolve.[10] *Wing Chun* also happens to be the film from Yeoh's early career that has received the most sustained scholarly attention, no doubt due to the profundity of its thematic interests, although, as I will argue, its true radicality has yet to be acknowledged or appreciated, nor has it been properly situated in the context of Yeoh's career.[11] In *Wing Chun*, Yeoh plays the title character Yim Wing Chun. Forced by a bandit into marriage at a young age, Wing Chun runs away from her marital obligations—much to the chagrin of her father—and learns martial arts from *sifu* Ng Mui (Cheng Pei-pei), who teaches her pupil not only how to defend herself but how to integrate the many aspects of her identity as a female fighter. At the point at which the film begins, Wing Chun is known as the fiercest fighter in her village, but only certain people know that she is a woman. Others, especially outsiders, see her decidedly not feminine clothing and her ostensibly masculine fighting prowess and assume that she is a man, while those who know that she is a woman resent her superior fighting prowess and find her abilities threatening to their manhood. When a young woman named Charmy (Catherine Yan Hung) arrives in the village with an older, sickly husband (who dies shortly after their arrival), she is set upon by local bandits who plan to kidnap her (and the second-in-command, Flying Monkey [Cui Ya-hui], intends to force her to marry him). Wing Chun intervenes and protects Charmy, and Wing Chun's aunt, Abacus Fong (Kingdom Yuen), invites Charmy to work for her as a waitress in her restaurant. The three women establish a routine, which is when a new arrival named Leung Pok-to (Donnie Yen) arrives in the village looking for a girl named Wing Chun. Apparently, he and Wing Chun knew each other when they were children, and he has spent the years since then looking for her with the intention of marrying her. As an outsider, he also assumes that Wing Chun is a man, mistaking the feminine Charmy for the Wing Chun he used to know.[12] It is only over time, as Pok-to and Wing Chun spend more time together defending Charmy from the bandits, and in particular from Flying Monkey's older brother and bandit leader, the devastating fighter Flying Chimpanzee (Norman Chu), that Pok-to realizes his mistake and reconnects with the Wing Chun he came in search of, while, for Wing Chun's part, all the time that she spends with Pok-to brings up inside of her feelings that she has not felt in a great many years, and it forces her to reconsider what she wants out of life, and indeed who she wants to be in life.

In the words of Sasha Vojković, the films of Yuen Woo-ping feature "some of the most extraordinary action women in the history of cinema, culminating with the legendary martial arts heroine Wing Chun" in the film of the same name, in which Woo-ping provides a "simplistic, yet incredibly empowering (albeit imaginary) solution to the (far from resolved) crisis of femininity."[13] To my mind, not only is there nothing simple about the solution proffered by Woo-ping in *Wing Chun*, but I would argue further that, to the extent that the "crisis of femininity" is not yet resolved, the conclusion of *Wing Chun* is also (*necessarily*) unresolved. Given Wing Chun's backstory, having been kidnapped and taken as the intended wife of a bandit whom she fled and which experience led her to learn martial arts to defend herself, the fact that she is in a position now to defend Charmy—that is, to protect Charmy from the same fate that befell her when she was a young girl—is a way for her to overcome her earlier trauma. By "repeating" the same scenario of a young girl being hounded by a vicious bandit who plans to force her into a marriage of which she wants no part, but this time being able to protect the young girl and prevent her from having to endure such subjugation, Wing Chun at the same time "rescues" *herself* and is able thereby to *reclaim her feminine identity*. Indeed, as Vojković rightly points out, Wing Chun "reclaims her subjectivity by inventing her own fighting method," namely, the martial art of Wing Chun, which is to say that she reclaims her subjectivity "by *fighting like a woman*."[14] Rather than fight the more powerful Flying Chimpanzee head-on, matching strength with strength, she uses subtler techniques to nullify and overcome his superior strength. (In a rather on-the-nose sequence, Flying Chimpanzee takes out a very large spear, the intimidating tool of his with which he plans to dominate Wing Chun, while, for her part, Wing Chun uses two small daggers, and as they fight in a confined space, Flying Chimpanzee's large spear is rendered impotent [Figure 19]. These associations/connotations go a long way toward explaining why Wing Chun is often thought of as a "feminine," or "soft," martial art, and indeed why its creation myth prominently features women warriors.[15]) On character terms, however, the moment that Wing Chun takes the advice of her *sifu* and creates her own style of fighting—and, by extension, her own way of existing in the world as both a woman and a warrior—is equally the moment that she integrates her identity and reembraces her womanhood. This, however, is only one side of the coin vis-à-vis the crisis of femininity. If Wing Chun has resolved to her own satisfaction her personal identity crisis, there remains the task of creating a space for herself—her *new* self—in patriarchal society.

In Vojković's account, Wing Chun's creation of a new martial art, and by extension of a new way of being a woman warrior, is a simple—and, allegedly, a *successful*—resolution to the crisis of femininity and thus to the film. No longer does Wing Chun have to deny herself (to) her childhood sweetheart; it is once she has embraced her true self and fought as a woman that she is not only able to vanquish the villain, but able finally to enter into a healthy relationship. Benjamin

Judkins reads the film similarly, though his account of Wing Chun's character arc (and its alleged resolution) is far more sophisticated in my estimation than Vojković's, not least because of his comprehensive knowledge of Wing Chun and Chinese martial history. Scholars in the West have historically latched on to (as Vojković does) the cross-dressing tendencies and trans potentialities of the Hong Kong woman warrior figure, often interpreting such characters as Butleresque "queer" characters who foreground the performative nature of gender.[16] Judkins, however, rejects this line of interpretation. Instead, with reference to the legendary figures of Hua Mulan and Qiu Jin, Judkins argues that such Westernized queer readings are "divorced from a solid understanding of Chinese martial culture" and its "close association with the quest for masculinity." As Judkins explains, "Mulan and Qiu Jin dressed as men not in an attempt to emulate Western modes of queer behavior, but to demonstrate their attainment of 'martial virtue' within the [martial arts] community." In short, even though it is theoretically en vogue to read things queerly, it is important to note that neither Mulan nor Qiu Jin were "rebelling against the gender hierarchies of society" as traditional feminist theorists or contemporary queer theorists would have it;[17] on the contrary, they were "attempting to change their place in the social structure while leaving its essential form [i.e., its gender politics, binaries, and hierarchies] intact."[18]

This is an important point for Judkins to register because it not only introduces greater historical and cultural accuracy into the conversation, but it also brings into clearer focus what he considers to be the even greater radicality of *Wing Chun*, on which he expounds in the following insightful passage:

> On the surface [*Wing Chun* may seem to be] a "get back in the kitchen" sort of a story . . . [but] it manages to achieve more real pathos than most Kung Fu films . . . Rather than acknowledging the primacy of [the] deeply flawed patriarchal system [from which Wing Chun fled as a young girl] she rejects it entirely. She is no longer willing to concede that martial virtue is a subspecies of masculinity . . . Rather than accepting a "conservative" set of values, Yim Wing Chun totally upends the carefully cultivated gender hierarchy. Once she has done that there is no longer any reason to continue dressing as a man or to reject her fiancé. Only by totally and violently challenging the constraints of society could Yim Wing Chun find a way to live a "normal life."[19]

Interestingly, this same gender dialectic is at work in the Hepburn star text. In her early career through the 1930s, Hepburn (in)famously experienced a series of box-office flops which led to her being labeled "box-office poison," ostensibly the death knell for her career. Taking her future into her own hands, Hepburn went back to the stage, developed a project for herself that she believed would "rehabilitate" her image in the eyes of the public, and returned to the silver screen with *The Philadelphia Story*, the film that did exactly what Hepburn wanted it to do—it set her up for another five decades of acting, during which time she won an additional three Oscars and became one of the biggest stars in the history of Hollywood, and it ultimately provided the urtext for her popular films in the 1940s and 1950s with Spencer Tracy. In *The Philadelphia Story* (and, subsequently, in *Woman of the Year*, *Adam's Rib*, and *Pat and Mike*), Hepburn's strong and independent female character must be "tamed" or "subdued" and "(re)educated" in what it means to be a woman, and the only person who can do this is a man. In *The Philadelphia Story*, it is Cary Grant's character who helps Hepburn's character become a "proper" woman capable of being a good wife. In such later films as *Woman of the Year*, *Adam's Rib*, and *Pat and Mike*, meanwhile, it is the characters played by Spencer Tracy who tame, or at least temper, Hepburn's dynamic female characters.

In *Woman of the Year*, Hepburn plays political columnist Tess Harding and Tracy plays sports reporter Sam Craig. Their romance plays out as an "opposites attract" story, but it is significant that Sam's character does not need to change anything about his personality or his job to make his and Tess's marriage work; on the contrary, it is Tess who is forced to realize that, for all of her education and culture, the "great woman" is not a woman at all, and if she hopes to be a good wife and to have a successful marriage, she must get (back) into the kitchen and (re)learn what that entails. The final set-piece of the film even literally places Hepburn in the kitchen, where she fails in screwball comedy fashion to do such simple tasks as make coffee and waffles. In an effort to avoid painting all of Hollywood history with the same brush (vis-à-vis charges of irredeemable sexism/misogyny), it warrants mentioning that *Woman of the Year* is an impressively and admirably progressive film as far as 1940s films go, particularly in the way that Sam rejects the "housewife"/"professional" binary that Tess has misguidedly internalized and explains to her that he does not want her to forsake her identity as Tess Harding in order to become Mrs. Sam Craig, but rather wants her to be both a great woman and a great wife, which means learning how to be Tess Harding-Craig. (This, in my estimation, is the crux of the crisis of femininity, and while ideologically we have yet to resolve the tensions that it generates, that *this* is the crisis experienced by Hepburn in *Woman of the Year* and by Yeoh in *Wing Chun* is central to the present argument.) Nevertheless, for as much as we can discriminate contextually, taking care to accurately interpret and conscientiously evaluate each individual film and its ideological content, there is something unmistakably conservative (if not oppressive) in the way that *Woman of the Year* resolves, and this inherent ideological conservatism vis-à-vis gender politics becomes even more problematic in a later film like *Pat and Mike*.[20]

One of the most popular films that Tracy and Hepburn made together, *Pat and Mike* is arguably the most radical of their films (and arguably of all of Hepburn's films) vis-à-vis gender, thus making it of particular relevance to the present consideration of Michelle Yeoh's radicality, inasmuch as I am keen to trace a historical line from Hepburn to Yeoh with regards to the power of the most radical female star texts to challenge gender politics in the cinema. In *Pat and Mike*, Hepburn plays superstar athlete Patricia "Pat" Pemberton and Tracy plays her manager Mike Conovan. At one point late in the film, Mike has the squeeze put on him by two crooks who want Pat to take a dive. Seeing that Mike is about to get beat up, Pat intervenes: an expert in self-defense in addition to golf and tennis, Pat easily dispatches the two thugs with a series of wrist locks, strikes, and chokes, much to Mike's embarrassment.[21] Compounding Mike's emasculation, when all parties are taken into police custody and forced to explain/reenact the encounter, Pat again demonstrates her martial skill, while Mike is forced to stand idly by and admit that he did (because he was capable of doing) nothing.[22] By the end of the film, feeling that he has lost his man card, Mike is given the opportunity—intentionally, by Pat—to play the role of knight in shining armor. Determined to ditch her overbearing fiancé Collier (William Ching), Pat spends much of the film avoiding him while falling in love with Mike. When Collier makes his last stand, rather than authoritatively telling him to leave and that their relationship is over, and rather than physically removing him despite her clearly displayed ability to do so, Pat conspicuously pretends to be a mere damsel in distress: she calls for her brave defender Mike, who bursts into the room to protect his lady from this usurper. (In a hilarious sequence of attempted gallantry, Mike has no idea what to do to Collier, so he tries to replicate the move that he saw Pat do earlier when she pulled the feet out from under one of his attackers. In essence, Mike's model of masculine fighting prowess, which model he tries—and fails—to emulate in the course of defending his lady's honor, *is his lady* Pat.) The clever bit in this sequence is the way that Pat is so conspicuously performing: she tells Mike (in a hushed, girlish voice) that Collier "frightened" her, which is why she called him, otherwise she would have had no idea what to do to protect herself. So over the top is her performance that Mike sees through it: he laughs and remarks, "I think you can take care of yourself," even admitting, "I bet you could lick me." But what solidifies their relationship, their *true* partnership beyond manager and athlete, is when Mike says to her, transcending the (non-) issue of who could lick whom, "I'll tell you one thing I *do* know: Together, we can lick 'em all," which is him accepting their differences (or, more accurately, accepting *her* differences from what he has always believed a woman is/should be) and thereby overcoming his feelings of inadequacy/insecurity.

Juxtaposing a Hepburn film like *Pat and Mike* to a Yeoh film like *Wing Chun* may appear to support a reading of the latter that is in line with Vojković's and Judkins' readings. However, while I find much in each of their readings insightful and persuasive, I think that both Vojković and Judkins fall into the trap of reading *Wing Chun* too optimistically. To be sure, aspects of character and plot between *Pat and Mike* and *Wing Chun* line up quite neatly—most notably, Pat's/Wing

Figure 21 Wing Chun (Michelle Yeoh), Pok-to (Donnie Yen), and the persistence of gender trouble. *Wing Chun* directed by Yuen Woo-ping. © Century Pacific 1994. All rights reserved.

Chun's physical superiority to Mike/Pok-to, which far from deterring Mike/Pok-to from pursuing Pat/Wing Chun is that which they find the most attractive and ultimately celebrate and even love about them—but these two films are not equivalent, and to interpret *Wing Chun* as if it resolved everything as neatly as *Pat and Mike* would be to miss the most radical aspects of each film. Significantly, neither Vojković nor Judkins addresses the moment at the end of *Wing Chun* when, having married Pok-to, Wing Chun prepares to ride off into the sunset with her new husband. Pok-to, on horseback, sees Wing Chun speaking to Charmy. They lock eyes, deeply in love and each eager to begin their new life together as husband and wife, and then all of a sudden Wing Chun leaps into the air and jumps onto her horse beside Pok-to. The crowd around them applauds the feat, but Pok-to leans over and whispers to Wing Chun, "Be more feminine." Despite being described by Vojković as "the one male person who is not threatened by Wing Chun's fighting skills,"[23] this final exchange between Pok-to and Wing Chun introduces a crack in the foundation of what both Vojković and Judkins see as a fully resolved narrative and character arc (Figure 21).

Counter to such overly optimistic readings of *Wing Chun*, I contend, first, that *Wing Chun* is a profoundly ambivalent film, and second, that *Everything Everywhere All at Once* effectively closes the gap that prevents *Wing Chun* from achieving its sought-after resolution by virtue of its multiverse plot which grants the male/husband and female/wife characters a plethora of identities all of which must be integrated in order for their marriage and their family to stay together. To the first point, consider that by the end of *Wing Chun*, at which point Wing Chun has successfully integrated the component parts of her identity as a woman and as a warrior, and at which point she has officially married her long-adoring and supportive suitor Pok-to, Woo-ping seems to have brought his film to the exact same point that George Cukor had brought *Pat and Mike* at the point of Pat's defense of Mike. It is to the latter film's credit that Pat's performance as the damsel in distress is so conspicuous inasmuch as it is Cukor critiquing through satire the playacting that is required of women to "fit" in patriarchal society; it is also to the film's credit that it not only sanctions but celebrates Mike's radical acceptance of Pat. However, it must still be acknowledged that, regardless of how empty the gesture, the woman was still required to make such a gesture, she was still required to prostrate herself *in some way* before the man and take up a patriarchally sanctioned, non-threatening position in the gender hierarchy. *Wing Chun* is distinguished by the fact that Yeoh's character makes no such gesture, and thus there is no resolution to be had. Unlike Hepburn's characters in such films as *Woman of the Year* and *Pat and Mike*, Yeoh's character Wing Chun does not prostrate herself before her man. Pok-to's knee-jerk reaction to Wing Chun's aerial display jumping on the horse is to admonish her and to insist that she be more feminine. This is exactly how Mike reacts to Pat after he witnesses her combative display. In *Pat and Mike*, Pat's response is to acquiesce, whereas in *Wing Chun*, Wing Chun does not acquiesce. Where does this leave her, the newlyweds, the film, the genre, and indeed the genders? Once this subtle crack in the stability of this ostensibly "progressive" relationship is introduced and the "resolution" radically undermined, the film immediately ends, offering no solution to the persistent "gender trouble" that, if this exchange between husband and wife is any indication, will persist beyond the end credits. *Wing Chun* in effect poses, without answering, the question: can this/any man accept this/any woman who is so committed to combating gender norms?[24]

This, then, is everything that feeds into Yeoh's performance in *Everything Everywhere All at Once*, a film which incorporates every element of her star text from every phase of her career and in which her character is forced to integrate into one identity the many faces not just of "Woman," inasmuch as she alternates between identities as a housewife, a businesswoman, a movie star, a lesbian, etc., but also of "Michelle Yeoh." Far from representing a case study in oppression and stifled emancipatory glory, however, which was Britton's ultimate verdict on the career of Katharine Hepburn, the career of Michelle Yeoh is distinguished by the admirable way that she has retained her fighting spirit in her roles from *Yes, Madam!* up to *Everything Everywhere All at Once*, and importantly without sacrificing or denouncing her feminine identity on the one hand or capitulating to patriarchal subjugation on the other. Whether her characters are punished for their transgressions, as they are in *Yes, Madam!* and *Heroic Trio 2: Executioners* (1993), or whether they persist through adversity in their quests for a more meaningful feminine existence, as they do in *Wing Chun* and *The Stunt Woman*, Michelle Yeoh is a monument to grace under pressure, maintaining one's dignity in the face of hardship, and having the courage of one's convictions.

Indeed, to the extent that, as I argued at the outset of this chapter, *Everything Everywhere All at Once* is the culmination of Yeoh's four decades of action stardom, it rather neatly combines every thread of Yeoh's star text, while at the same time, as I alluded to earlier, resolving the crises of both masculinity and femininity by virtue of its science fiction conceit. This was in large part intentional, for Daniel Kwan and Daniel Scheinert did not merely create her character to be an amalgam of her many characters from the different phases of her career; they even initially planned on naming the character "Michelle" to solidify the connection between character and star.[25] But it goes beyond the amusing intertextuality of seeing a fictional character's alter ego mirror the actor's real-life star image. In *Everything Everywhere All at Once*, Michelle Yeoh was afforded the opportunity to showcase everything that has made her the star that she is, everything that she is capable of as an actress and as an action hero, and everything that has informed her star text, all in one film. If the early phase of her career can be read as her playing characters at odds with their environments—characters suffering from identity crises who struggle to reconcile their identities as women and as warriors, who yearn for a different way of living and who hope to be able to create a different world in which to live—then *Everything Everywhere All at Once* affords her the opportunity to synthesize these currents. And, thanks to the multiverse plot element, this splintering of identity, this need to integrate the many aspects of her personhood that make her who she is, this persistent and persisting crisis of femininity in inhospitable patriarchal contexts, is literalized on the level of the plot such that Evelyn Wang the character's integration of all the Evelyn Wangs she has been and could be is equally Michelle Yeoh the star's integration of all the Michelle Yeohs she has been, could be, and in time might very well become.

In his poetic portrait of Greta Garbo, the early film theorist Béla Balázs discussed the way that Garbo's beauty was "a beauty of suffering; she suffers life and all the surrounding world," which is to say that her beauty was "in opposition to the world," it stood out as "a protest against this world" and thus as a clarion call for a better, more hospitable world.[26] Taking the baton from Garbo, Hepburn's star text was more active, she fought against the world in which she was expected to prostrate herself, but she could only fight so hard for so long. Michelle Yeoh represents the third stage in this evolution of female stardom. Her star text is literally that of a fighting star, of a woman eager to combat—and capable of combating—gender norms with respect to cinematic and cultural conventions. She has played single young women and romantic partners, old maids and housewives, warriors and mothers, and in so doing she has created a powerful and inspiring image of both stardom and of womanhood. All of which is to say that Michelle Yeoh always has been and always will be everything everywhere all at once, and her star shines as brightly over the history of Hong Kong martial arts cinema as it does over the future of international action filmmaking.

Notes

1   For instance, in Lucy Feldman's *TIME* write-up, Feldman not only recounts this experience of Yeoh's, she even corroborates it by admitting that her own mother tagged along with her on the interview so that she could meet Yeoh. See Lucy Feldman, "Michelle Yeoh: *TIME* 2022 Icon of the Year" (2022), https://time.com/icon-of-the-year-2022-michelle-yeoh (accessed September 23, 2023).

2   For information on Cynthia Rothrock's stardom and reception, see Meaghan Morris's chapter on her in this volume.

3   The pioneering work on actors as auteurs is Patrick McGilligan's study of James Cagney in his *Cagney: The Actor as Auteur* (New York: Da Capo Press, [1975] 1980), while, in the realm of martial arts cinema, Eric Pellerin has extended this line of thinking with respect to Bruce Lee in his "Bruce Lee as Director and the Star as Author," *Global Media and China* 4, no. 3 (2019): 339–47, https://journals.sagepub.com/doi/epdf/10.1177/2059436419873337 (accessed September 23, 2023). For my part, while I share Laurence F. Knapp's fascination with what he calls "starteurs," the stars who become filmmakers and who consciously work through aspects of their own star texts like Charlie Chaplin, Clint Eastwood, and Woody Allen, I do not extend this to the art of acting as if acting were itself a form of authorship. I do not think that it is. Cf. Knapp's *Directed by Clint Eastwood* (Jefferson, NC: McFarland, 1996) and my "Bruce Lee: Authorship, Ideology, and Film Studies," *Off-screen* 16, no. 6 (2012), https://offscreen.com/view/bruce_lee_authorship_part_1 (accessed September 23, 2023), and "A Plea for Intention: Stanley Cavell and Ordinary Aesthetic Philosophy," *Movie: A Journal of Film Criticism* 9 (2021), 75, n.6, https://warwick.ac.uk/fac/arts/scapvc/film/movie/movie_issue9_apleaforintention.pdf, (accessed September 23, 2023). See also Wayne Wong's chapter in this volume, in which he persuasively argues that Kwan Tak-hing qualifies as an auteur given his involvement in shaping his characterization of Wong Fei-hung.

4   Stanley Cavell, *The World Viewed: Reflections on the Ontology of Film* (Cambridge, MA: Harvard University Press, [1971] 1979), 28–9.

5   To clarify, I will oscillate throughout this chapter between such terms as star *texts*, *personas*, and *images*. Though different scholars in the past have latched on to different terms for different reasons, I mean to keep all these terms and ways of thinking about stars in play in an effort to signal the multifaceted nature of stardom as a phenomenon and stars as unique entities.

6   Andrew Britton, *Katharine Hepburn: Star as Feminist* (New York: Columbia University Press, [1984] 2003), 8.

7   Ibid., 213.

8   Ibid.

9   Ibid., 8.

10 Indeed, while pursuing this route would take me too far afield, it is helpful to conceptualize *Wing Chun* as, in line with Robin Wood's formulation, an "incoherent text" (Robin Wood, "The Incoherent Text: Narrative in the 70s," in *Hollywood from Vietnam to Reagan. . . and Beyond* [New York: Columbia University Press, {1986} 2003], 41–62): As I will argue in my reading of the film, *Wing Chun* is a film "in which the drive toward [ideological coherence] has been visibly defeated," and not due to a lack of either effort or intelligence, but rather, due to the "strains, tensions, and contradictions" that exist culturally and which feed into—and, in the case of incoherent texts, problematize to extreme degrees—all art (ibid., 42).

11 In addition to then-contemporary remarks made by Bey Logan on the one hand (see his *Hong Kong Action Cinema* [London: Titan Books, 1995]) and Tony Williams and Yingjin Zhang on the other (see their "Michelle Yeoh," *Encyclopedia of Chinese Film*, ed. Yingjin Zhang [London: Routledge, 1998], 382–3), investigations have been conducted more recently by Lisa Funnell (see her *Warrior Women: Gender, Race, and the Transnational Chinese Action Star* [Albany, NY: State University of New York Press, 2014]), Benjamin Judkins (see his "Yim Wing Chun and Gender: The Stories of Ip Man and Yuen Woo-ping in a Comparative Perspective," *Kung Fu Tea* [2021], https://chinesemartialstudies.com/2021/01/21/yim-Wing Chun-and-gender-the-stories-of-ip-man-and-yuen-woo-ping-in-a-comparative-perspective-2 [accessed September 23, 2023]), Luke White (see his *Legacies of the Drunken Master: Politics of the Body in Hong Kong Kung Fu Comedy Films* [Honolulu: University of Hawai'i Press, 2020]), and, most extensively, Sasha Vojković (see her *Yuen Woo-ping's Wing Chun* [Hong Kong: Hong Kong University Press, 2009]). My interest in *Wing Chun* was first ignited, however, by Luke White and Susan Pui San Lok's presentation "Through the Window: Wing Chun as Woman Warrior" at the 2015 Martial Arts Studies Conference held at Cardiff University.

12 Abacus even has Charmy wear the clothes that Wing Chun used to wear when she had Charmy's job in her aunt's restaurant, which is one of the reasons why Pok-to mistakes her for Wing Chun, but which also serves as one of the many ways that Woo-ping codes Charmy as the younger, feminine version of Wing Chun. Indeed, Woo-ping throughout the film positions the three women—Wing Chun, Abacus, and Charmy—as three different versions, or instantiations, of Woman. Wing Chun is the ferocious fighter who is strong and independent, but there is a sadness to her that stems from her renunciation of her femininity; Charmy is sweet and beautiful, but she lacks strength and has all of her life been dependent on men; and Abacus is smart and independently wealthy, but her calculating business savvy has altered men's perceptions of her as a vicious shrew whom they alternately fear and scorn. Wing Chun, in essence, is tasked with uniting these different "strands" together in one personality, while Woo-ping's inability to unite these strands within this character in a manner that satisfies the male characters speaks to our cultural—that is, to patriarchal society's—ideological inability to countenance such mongrel womanhood.

13 Vojković, *Yuen Woo-ping's Wing Chun*, 3.

14 Ibid., 16.

15 For more elaborate discussions of Wing Chun and Chinese martial history, see Benjamin Judkins' blog, *Kung Fu Tea*, and his and Jon Nielson's *The Creation of Wing Chun: A Social History of the Southern Chinese Martial Arts* (Albany, NY: State University of New York Press, 2015).

16 Though an exploration of the increasingly fertile and fascinating intersections of gender studies (including queer and trans studies) and Sinophone studies would take me too far afield, the following seems worth mentioning. First, for an indication of the importance of Butler to studies of the woman warrior archetype, see Vojković, *Yuen Woo-ping's Wing Chun*, 15–17, 112, 118, and Funnell, *Warrior Women*, 4–5, 168. Second, for an indication of Butler's importance in broader studies of gender vis-à-vis martial arts stars, see Kwai-Cheung Lo, *Excess and Masculinity in Asian Cultural Productions* (Albany: State University of New York Press, 2010), 108; Sabrina Qiong Yu, *Jet Li: Chinese Masculinity and Transnational Film Stardom* (Edinburgh: Edinburgh University Press, 2012), 80; and White, *Legacies of the Drunken Master*, 139. Third, for an indication of Butler's importance in even broader studies of gender vis-à-vis Sinophone media, see Siu Leung Li, *Cross-Dressing in Chinese Opera* (Hong Kong: Hong Kong University Press, 2003), 106–7, 180–1; Howard Chiang and Alvin K. Wong, "Introduction: Queer Sinophone Studies, Interdisciplinary Synergies," in *Keywords in Queer Sinophone Studies*, eds. Howard Chiang and Alvin K. Wong (London: Routledge, 2020), 3; and Song Hwee Lim, *Celluloid Comrades: Representations of Male Homosexuality in Contemporary Chinese Cinemas* (Honolulu: University of Hawai'i Press, 2006), 130. While some contemporary scholars have begun to try to think about gender beyond familiar Butlerian coordinates—most notable here is Howard Chiang's *Transtopia in the Sinophone Pacific* (New York: Columbia University Press, 2021)—the fact remains that Butler looms large over virtually all scholarly discussions of gender, for better or worse. For my part, I want to stress that to accurately assess a film like *Wing Chun* it is necessary, to borrow from Chiang, to challenge the "ahistorical universality commonly assumed in leading theorems of gender" in order to add "transcultural texture to the variability" of gendered experiences and, by extension, gendered representations. Cf. Chiang, *Transtopia in the Sinophone Pacific*, 14.

17 Indeed, as Siu Leung Li sagaciously points out, in the story of Mulan as it was told in Xu Wei's influential sixteenth-century play *Maid Mulan Joins the Army in Her Father's Stead*—which play Li avers "had a great influence on the representation of women in Chinese drama by later playwrights, both male and female" (Li, *Cross-Dressing in Chinese Opera*, 85)—"Mulan's crossing of gender lines is only provisional." There is, in Li's estimation, "an oppositional dynamic of containment and subversion at work" in this play, on the basis of which such "transgressive" actions as Mulan unbinding her feet in order to be an effective fighter never rise to the level of threatening the "Confucian gender system," for, as Li explains:

> "[The] foot-binding motif [in *Maid Mulan Joins the Army in Her Father's Stead*] is not found in the original 'Ballad of Mulan' which dates back many hundreds of years to a period when foot-binding was not yet prevalent. It is common knowledge today that the bound foot as a fetish signified the ultimate subjugation of women in late imperial China. Xu's insertion of the most oppressive patriarchal constraint on women is itself revealing enough . . . [for] Mulan, in order to put herself in the shoes of a man, has to undo (although only temporarily) the containment of the patriarchy epitomized in foot-binding. The undoing of the fetish unleashes the female from male control and renders her power that surpasses man's . . . Yet unbinding her feet causes her to worry about how she will get married when she returns from the battlefield with a pair of enlarged feet. Readers and spectators in the past would feel relieved when Mulan immediately tells of a magical soaking treatment that can re-shrink the feet to the size of the 'golden

lotus' . . . In this way, the unconscious feminine subversion is immediately contained by naturalized masculine values and this is further illustrated by the theme of chastity running through the whole play. Mulan gets her parent's consent to playact as her father's double only on the condition that she keeps her virginity — the most valuable price of women as commodities of exchange in the imperial past . . . The androgynous body is immediately kept in check by the non-deflowered female body within, and her subordination to [the patriarchy] is taken for granted" (Li, *Cross-Dressing in Chinese Opera*, 85–6).

It is my contention that a similar oppositional dynamic is discernible in *Wing Chun*, though Yeoh's role in the film absolutely threatens the conventional gender system and *this* is what marks her out as such a radical presence in a film that is not as bold in upending said system as its main character is.

18 Judkins, "Yim Wing Chun and Gender."

19 Ibid.

20 My insistence on analyzing media texts in their specificity, on a case-by-case basis and with respect to their temporal and cultural contexts, is an attempt to avoid the sort of reductive theorizing and inaccurate criticism that I critique and caution against in my "Contesting Feminism: Pedagogical Problems in Classical Hollywood Cinema, Feminist Theory, and Media Studies," *Feminist Media Studies* (2023), https://www.tandfonline.com/doi/full/10.1080/14680777.2023.2268305 (accessed February 2, 2024). On the subject of classical Hollywood romantic comedies, meanwhile, I discuss their gender politics in more detail in my "Reconsidering Remarriage: Stanley Cavell and the Vicissitudes of Genre," *New Review of Film and Television Studies* (2023), 21(4), https://www.tandfonline.com/doi/abs/10.1080/17400309.2023.2246350?journalCode=rfts20 (accessed September 23, 2023).

21 Though it is beyond the scope of the present chapter, it is worth mentioning that this fight scene from *Pat and Mike* is an important point on the timeline of martial arts action in the history of Hollywood cinema. For a broader analysis of representations of martial arts in classical Hollywood cinema, see my "Grappling with History: Martial Arts in Classical Hollywood Cinema," *Kung Fu Tea* (2015), https://chinesemartialstudies.com/2015/08/06/guest-post-grappling-with-history-martial-arts-in-classical-hollywood-cinema (accessed September 23, 2023).

22 Interestingly, after they leave the police station, when Pat is desperate to understand what she did to upset Mike, he laments the way that in building her up into a star athlete he inadvertently created a "Frankenstein monster," and he refers to her as "Mrs. Frankenstein" before explaining that he wants "a 'he' to be a *he* and a 'she' to be a *she*." This speaks quite clearly and directly to the mongrel womanhood that I mentioned earlier with respect to Wing Chun, as well as to the persistent difficulty in our societies through time — and, particularly, the difficulties of men — to reconcile such (assumed-to-be) mutually exclusive qualities as beauty/femininity and strength/masculinity in their apprehensions of/relationships with women. Indeed, this problem is universal, as evidenced by Daniel Aranha Pedersen's poignant Danish short film *Swollen* (2023), in which Lina (Mariana Awela) is a mixed martial artist whose passion for fighting alienates her boyfriend Mikkel (Thomas Dalmo Nommensen). Across time and across cultures, this problem has plagued and continues to plague people, and it will rear its head every time actions are prescribed according to — or proscribed on the basis of — gender.

23 Vojković, *Yuen Woo-ping's Wing Chun*, 29–30.

24 To add one more layer of ideological confusion, one could argue that the closest that *Wing Chun* comes to answering this question is by virtue of the end credits song which Woo-ping chose to play the film out. Once the end credits begin to roll, with no solution in sight to the gender trouble that ostensibly awaits the newlywed couple, the song that plays the film out consists of the following lyrics: "Who's the one you love? / Who's the one that hurt you? / Who's asking you to be in his arms? / Who cares about your dreams? / Who understands your plight? / Who touches your heart? / If a woman always waits for you till late at night / Not regretting her youth passing her by / She's devoted her life to you / A woman falls in love easily and is emotionally fragile / A woman never knows how low she can fall / For a woman, love is her soul / She could devote her life to someone she loves." On the one hand, if this song is meant to capture the journey of Wing Chun, it fails to do so, for she did not devote herself to Pok-to and then sacrifice her youth in order to wait for him. If anything, it was the other way around, with Pok-to devoting himself to Wing Chun and sacrificing his youth in his quest to reunite with her. (Wing Chun is also quite clearly not the image of a "fragile" woman however that term is defined.) Quite the contrary, Wing Chun willingly pursued the life of a warrior, and she even tells Pok-to plainly at one point in the film that she never regretted her decision to do so, even though she knew that in pursuing a warrior lifestyle she may well have foreclosed the possibility of ever being in a relationship. On the other hand, if this song is meant to lay out the future marital bliss that awaits the newlywed couple on the other side of the end credits, their final exchange would seem to undercut this, for it is not clear that Wing Chun can—or wants to—"devote her life" to Pok-to, at least not if such "devotion" entails giving up the warrior component of her identity. Here, again, is that oppositional dynamic of containment and subversion alluded to by Li vis-à-vis Mulan, with the connection between Woo-ping's film and Xu Wei's play even more pronounced inasmuch as the gender containment is enacted on the level of song: In *Maid Mulan Joins the Army in Her Father's Stead*, Mulan maintains her femininity by promising to return not only to her conventional gender role, but also to return having kept her virginity, singing before leaving, "Be at ease, mother / I'll return to you a virgin daughter," and then singing upon her return home, "Returning to you the same non flower-bearing bud." Cf. Li, *Cross-Dressing in Chinese Opera*, 86.

25 Yeoh vetoed this idea because, while she obviously wanted to connect to the character as an actress—and while countless actors have done this by playing characters whose first name is the same as theirs, from Jackie Chan often playing characters named Jackie to Jack Nicholson often playing characters named Jack—she also wanted viewers (that is, everyone who is *not* Michelle Yeoh) to be able to connect with the character; as Yeoh herself put it: "This story is not about me . . . [it] is about many people—mothers, aunties, women out there who walk by you in the supermarket unnoticed. They never have a voice. They're never the superheroes" (see Nicholson, "The Year of Michelle Yeoh"). Ironically, one could argue that, in this way, the story actually *is* about Michelle Yeoh, who has not always had a voice and not always been acknowledged/appreciated for being the superhero—and superstar—that she has always been.

26 Béla Balázs, *Theory of the Film: Character and Growth of a New Art* (London: Dennis Dobson, [1948] 1952), 286–7.

Chapter 9

Cynthia Rothrock: Fame, Style, and the Video Star

Meaghan Morris

Figure 22 Cynthia Rothrock in her fighting stance. *Lady Dragon* directed by David Worth. © Rapi Films/Cinematic Collection 1992. All rights reserved.

Never a particularly talented actress, Rothrock has some skill as a screenfighter but wasted her potential in low-budget, no-brain productions like the appalling *Triple Cross* (1993) or *Guardian Angel* (1994).

DAVID WEST[1]

Honor and Glory [1992] and *Undefeatable* [1993] made money because Cynthia Rothrock was so famous all around the world at that time. She's the only American girl who can fight! So, the people like her.

GODFREY HO CHI-KEUNG[2]

The long and varied career of the American martial arts champion and actress Cynthia Rothrock presents a complex case for a discussion of film stardom and reception. First, her fame has fluctuated over time with spiraling audience uptakes of technological change. In a 2014 interview, she remarked that popularity comes and goes in both movies and styles of martial arts: "They are really popular and then they aren't at all, so it goes in cycles."[3] She spoke from experience. Fifty-seven years old at the time, she already had three phases of stardom behind her: live performance and competition in the early 1980s, Hong Kong cinema from 1985 to 1990, and US-based direct to video (DTV) action in the 1990s. Then came the "quiet period of time from 2004-2010ish that seemed to hit a lot of the action icons of the 90's video market."[4] Between 2004 and 2012, Rothrock made just one new film, Pau Martínez's *Bala Perdida (Lost Bullet*, 2007). Returning to the screen with supporting roles in *Santa's Summer House* (2012), *Badass Showdown* (2013), and *White Tiger* (released in 2017), she went on to make minor appearances in two or three low-budget films a year before the COVID-19 pandemic closed production early in 2020. However, during this phase of low-key film activity she broadened her fan base through, on the one hand, the martial arts "event" industry with its lavish awards ceremonies and Halls of Fame inductions,[5] and, on the other hand, through exuberant participation in social media platforms and online sites.[6]

These activities have now generated a cyber-based phase of stardom. As Rothrock herself points out, platforms such as YouTube and the growth of streaming services have created new audiences for her Hong Kong classics, while boutique distribution companies such as Eureka Entertainment (UK), 88 Films (UK), and Vinegar Syndrome (USA) are remastering some of her films for high-quality Blu-ray editions.[7] This latest popularity upswing brought Rothrock's film profile full circle in my part of the world when the booking options for her "First Australian Tour" in February 2023 included, along with photo ops, a private dinner, and a martial arts seminar, a rare theatrical screening of her first Hong Kong film, *Yes, Madam!* (1985). Preceded by a "Kungfu Retrospective Live Q&A" with Rothrock on stage, this film festival-style experience was framed by the Art Deco picture palaces of the Hayden Orpheum Theater (built 1935) and the Astor

Theater (1936), heritage-listed havens of cinephilia in Sydney and Melbourne, respectively.[8] A clear case of the corporate production of stardom,[9] Rothrock's Sydney itinerary also exemplified the power of her star image to articulate socially disparate fan communities. On the other side of the city from the affluent, Anglo-dominant, "North Shore" harbor setting of the Orpheum in Cremorne, her seminar was hosted by Zeus Martial Arts Academy in Marrickville, a densely multi-ethnic urban center with an immigrant working-class base and a hipster overlay in Sydney's inner west.

A second layer of complexity arises with an effort to set boundaries to Hong Kong martial arts cinema itself. On the production side, the transnational flows of capital and creativity that engage much film scholarship now[10] were foundational for cinema in colonial Hong Kong conditions. Nourished in the 1920s by "a variety of American influences"[11] that linked Hong Kong to Shanghai,[12] this cinema was formed by "an *interflow* of people and resources"[13] that shaped from the 1930s an export-oriented industry serving diverse overseas Chinese audiences[14] and engaging with film production in Taiwan, Japan, Korea, and the Philippines.[15] While novel, the casting for "international flavor"[16] that brought Rothrock and other foreign fighters to Hong Kong in the 1980s built on long-standing practices of multilateral exchange and appropriation that led some in the 1990s to work on films elsewhere because they were seen as Hong Kong stars.[17] Rothrock's signature film *Lady Dragon* (1992), a revenger riff on the Hong Kong kung fu pedagogy template, was co-directed by David Worth (*Kickboxer*, 1989) and Ackyl Anwari for Rapi Films in Indonesia.[18] Yet, in the slippage from production to consumption contexts that marks video circulation, *Lady Dragon* now appears in a list of top five *American* DTV action films of the 1990s.[19]

The aesthetic as well as industrial knock-off culture that drives the martial arts genre is thus significant in terms of reception, because among the fans who relish reviving classic scenarios and stars are new generations of film and martial arts practitioners.[20] The reinvention of *Yes, Madam!* as a theatrical experience for Rothrock's 2023 Australian tour highlights how the consumption-driven aspect of stardom[21] feeds new industrial initiatives; the event creator, Dan Delts, recalls that this aspect of his business began with a "light bulb" moment when a friend wished that his son could watch on the big screen "all those movies that we grew up watching on VHS."[22] Certainly, *Yes, Madam!* was projected on celluloid in Hong Kong's cavernous popular cinemas in 1985, not sourced from a Blu-ray transfer for a niche cultural event.[23] The reinvention technologically enabled by the latter, however, is primarily social as fans gather with strangers in public space to share a big screen communal experience.

In this chapter, I explore what was distinctive about Rothrock's stardom in the Hong Kong-based phase of her film career, why she thrived there as she did, and how her creative response to changing reception conditions has transcended the ups and downs of a cyclical popularity. In part because of her adventurous approach to taking her martial arts practice into new media contexts, those conditions over the years have included doubt from some critics that she was really a film star at all.

Cynthia Rothrock vs. Cindy Law Fu Lok: Dissociative Stories of Fame

Cynthia Rothrock's Hong Kong career had rare features.[24] If Western critics tend to exaggerate the freedom that women enjoyed to play action leads in Hong Kong after the late 1960s "masculinization" of its martial arts cinema,[25] we may also under-estimate the force of racial exclusiveness in that cinema's social imaginaries.[26] Most *gweilos* ("white ghosts") are recognized only collectively for playing disposable heavies, arrogant opponents, shady business dealers, and the British cops or American agents who anchor Hong Kong action in a world of foreign threat.[27] African-American men played similar roles to whites: Jim Kelly's casting as a hero with Bruce Lee in *Enter the Dragon* (1973) was a sign of global marketing, as was Kareem Abdul-Jabbar's role as Mantis in Lee's unfinished *The Game of Death* (1972). Far more typical of the period is the role of the kickboxing champion Peter "Sugarfoot" Cunningham as the unnamed "Black Assassin" who slaughters a family in Corey Yuen Kwai's *Righting Wrongs* (a.k.a. *Above the Law*, 1986). However, this film included highly visible roles for two white women: Rothrock as "Cindy Si Yai-li," a tough cop, and Karen Sheperd as "Karen," an assassin. Both women were recently retired karate champions, but Rothrock's character had a personality, a Chinese name, a speaking role (dubbed, of course), significant screen time, and second billing after the star, Yuen Biao.

As Leon Hunt points out, Rothrock was "the only white martial artist to make the transition from heavy . . . to leading roles."[28] As "Law Fu Lok," she was the first white woman to co-star in a Hong Kong feature (*Yes, Madam!* with Michelle Yeoh) and the first white person to headline a Hong Kong film, *The Blonde Fury* (a.k.a. *Lady Reporter*, 1989). She also enjoyed relative longevity as a pan-Asian film personality. While Karen Sheperd made two Hong Kong films, Rothrock made fourteen for Hong Kong entrepreneurs between 1985 and 2000 as well as her four Hong Kong-influenced films in Indonesia.[29] At the same time, Rothrock shares three characteristics with average "*gweilos* in Hong Kong cinema." First, it is still difficult to find out much that is detailed about the full range of her Asian work from scholarly English sources; typically, critics have noted that Hong Kong gave her much better scope to perform but then discuss in more detail the films that she made in America.[30] Second, Rothrock did not come to Hong Kong from Hollywood. Like most of the heavies, she fell into film in the mid-1980s because of her participation in an American martial arts culture that was deeply influenced by Bruce Lee but had its own inclusive ethos that shaped the *possibility* of Lee's career.[31] Third, unlike Jean-Claude Van Damme and Chuck Norris, who also began their film careers in Hong Kong, Rothrock has not played even a minor role in Hollywood; the closest she came was *Irresistible Force*, a TV pilot film co-starring Stacy Keach and directed by Kevin Hooks for CBS Entertainment.[32] However, in addition to her eighteen Asian films she has appeared in forty-odd low-budget/DTV films produced mostly by North American independents.

All this adds up, one would think, to an exceptional achievement. However, reading about Cynthia Rothrock can leave you wondering whether she has a twin sister, a double life, or a dissociated personality. One Cynthia Rothrock, called "Cindy" by her favorite director, Corey Yuen Kwai, and in several of her films,[33] is a martial arts legend of the 1980s who became a huge international film star by the early 1990s, "so famous all around the world at that time" according to Godfrey Ho Chi-keung. The subject of media articles worldwide,[34] she was the first woman to rate cover stories in *Black Belt* and *Inside Kung Fu* magazines and became the object of adoring fan websites in the 1990s, featuring today in YouTube galleries of her best fight scenes.[35] In contrast, the other Cynthia Rothrock is famous for *not* being famous. Found primarily in academic studies and upscale journalism rather than the fan and martial arts sites in which the success story thrives, the second Rothrock is "the biggest star you never heard of,"[36] as the *New York Times* perhaps too memorably put it. This Rothrock merely "began" her acting career in Hong Kong (a phase quickly glossed over), and then "wasted her potential in low-budget, no-brain productions," as David West put it in the first epigraph, ending up in "the ghetto of exploitation."[37] Even Rikke Schubart, a sympathetic feminist critic, framed her study with this question: "Failed Female Hero? 'Queen of Martial Arts' Cynthia Rothrock."[38]

Within the terms of the Rothrock "failure story," the two personalities connect as successive phases in a star biography: Rothrock returned to the USA in 1990 to make two *China O'Brien* films directed for Golden Harvest by Robert Clouse of *Enter the Dragon* fame, and it was all downhill from there. While the overlap in her activities at this time was more complex than this, there is no doubt that as a powerful female fighter Rothrock faced casting and other obstacles in the USA that restricted and therefore *changed* what she could do on-screen. On her own account, her agent's overtures would meet such responses as "Can she be the hero's girlfriend?"[39] and "women in the lead roles of action films wouldn't sell."[40] Schubart lists also the "unlucky timing" of her return when Hollywood was bursting with new action stars and digital modes of creating action; her lack of "classical Hollywood beauty" or training as an actress; her age; her refusal at this time to undress for erotic spectacle; and a stocky body trained, unlike those of Linda Hamilton and Sigourney Weaver, "for fight and not for show."[41]

This story rests on several dubious assumptions: that martial arts film is a low genre unknown to the readers of the New York Times ("the biggest star you never heard of"); that Hong Kong films are always better than low-budget American films; and that any Hollywood fame is "bigger" than an Asia-based reputation, regardless of the scale and reach of the latter. I have argued elsewhere that US martial arts films are often best understood as melodramas of working-class gender and ethnicity, not as failed Hong Kong wu da pian,[42] and in my view some of Rothrock's films are among the best of their kind: Fight to Win (1987), Tiger Claws (1991), Rage and Honor (1992), and Outside the Law (2001). My interest here, however, is in the pressure that drives the "failure" version of the Rothrock star biography to produce a rivalrous mode of comparison between Hong Kong and American action cinemas that tugs our attention toward a critique of the United States. Naoki Sakai (1997: 15–16) calls this West-privileging mode of comparison "co-figuration," and in the context of Rothrock criticism it underlies the account that goes from Hong Kong cinema in the 1980s (pretty good but not much to say) to American low-budget in the 1990s (pretty bad and much more to say), creating the dissociative relation between her two star personae.[43]

The Rothrock success story does not recognize failure: fan-based and "pan-Asian" in a sense that includes sensibilities in the West,[44] it has no need for a Hong Kong-Hollywood binary, asking rather whether any movie from anywhere is any good. An outcome of this fan culture in recent years has been the Internet-driven "discovery" of Rothrock's Hong Kong films by lovers of 1990s US-made DTV that enabled a Blu-ray release of Yes, Madam! in 2023. In contrast with West's equal opportunity contempt for Richard W. Munchkin's US Rothrock video, Guardian Angel (1994), and an "appalling" Indonesian film, Ackyl Anwari's Triple Cross (a.k.a. Angel of Fury, 1990), the online critical encyclopedia of genre film, Bleeding Skull, declares: "Rothrock's immense filmography has been criminally overlooked for decades. The time for her universal conquest is now. And the unhinged Indonesian battle-epic known as Angel of Fury is the best place to start."[45]

In full agreement, I follow the Rothrock success story because fan-oriented discourses are often more exacting at the level of detail and more measured in their judgment of specific films than academic accounts seeking to apply general principles of representation critique. From this, it follows that I do not have to ask, with Schubart, "Why, then, is Cynthia Rothrock not a movie star?"[46] My premise is rather that she was a movie star for a significant Asian phase of her martial arts career and remains a global video star to this day.

A Career in Showing Fight

Cynthia Rothrock had "achieved celebrity" status in the US martial arts world before she came to Hong Kong.[47] Born in 1957 in Wilmington, Delaware, she grew up in Scranton, Pennsylvania, where at the age of thirteen she hesitantly took up karate in a health club belonging to the parents of a friend.[48] Progressing rapidly once she decided to practice, she began competing professionally from 1981 and retired in 1985 as a five-time undefeated World Karate Champion in Forms and Weapons competition, open then to men as well as women. Famously, in 1983, Rothrock was spotted on the cover of a karate magazine by a talent coordinator for a Kentucky Fried Chicken commercial, and the fun of making this ad along with watching Jackie Chan movies with her instructor Shum Leung put films in the back of her mind as a someday aspiration.[49]

In 1983, however, Rothrock was focused on training to keep her undefeated status while performing as a member of Ernie Reyes Sr.'s West Coast Demonstration Team. Reyes had a successful business in mixed martial arts including Eskrima, wushu, and kickboxing seminars from Benny Urquidez. Their

Although she's best-known for forms and weapons, Cynthia Rothrock was a sparring champion in her early days.

Figure 23 Cynthia Rothrock in her competition days. © Cynthia Rothrock. All rights reserved.

brand was promoted by the "Demo Team," a touring troupe making innovative use of pop music to enhance martial arts display. The story of the early days of the Team has them piling into a 1977 yellow Dodge van to tour California on weekends, cramming six to eight people in a hotel room like any hopeful American rock or pop band of the period. A nice anecdote has Rothrock screaming as a burglar stole a boom box with the Team's precious demo tape of the Bee Gees' "Staying Alive": "What would the West Coast Demo Team do without generations of music?"[50] This high-performance life blending athletic and aesthetic currents of 1980s American pop culture suited and honed Rothrock's talents. Undoubtedly, she is a formidable martial artist, having gained seven black belts in distinct disciplines (tang soo do, taekwondo, eagle claw, wushu, northern Shaolin, ng ying kung fu, and pai lum white dragon kung fu). However, the Forms and Weapons competitions in which she excelled are non-combat, choreographed practices involving a stylized exhibition of the *singular* martial body's capacities. So, while it is true that Rothrock's body is trained "for fight and not for show," it is more precise to say that Rothrock was trained to "*show fight*"—that is, to demonstrate what a fighting woman's body could do, and her most unusual attainment as a woman was her skill with weapons. This background, along with the contacts she made through Ernie Reyes Sr., put her in an ideal position to drift into the new martial arts cinema evolving at the time between California and Hong Kong.

On the Hong Kong side, led by Golden Harvest, producers longing to break into the American market were cruising for talent around the US martial arts scene.[51] In a much-repeated story, Rothrock recalls that Reyes received a call from Paul Maslak, then editing *Inside King Fu* magazine, to say that producers from Ng See Yuen's Seasonal Film Corporation were auditioning to find the next Bruce Lee. It was agreed that Reyes could bring women along as well, although this "next Bruce Lee" was supposed to be a Caucasian man.[52] On Rothrock's account, after doing form, weapons, self-defense, and fighting, the director Yuen Kwai insisted on choosing her.[53] However, instead of being whisked over to instant stardom in the kung fu capital of the world, Rothrock heard nothing from Hong Kong for the next eighteen months.[54] While Ng See Yuen is famous for taking risks with unknown actors, notably the young Jackie Chan, Bey Logan notes that, "as ever, N.G had recognized [Rothrock's] talent without ever really knowing what to do with it."[55] It seems likely that Maslak, who would later direct Rothrock himself in *Sword of Justice* (1996), continued Seasonal's quest for a Caucasian male star. As the casting director for Ng See Yuen's production of *No Retreat, No Surrender* in 1986, Maslak discovered Kurt McKinney and Jean-Claude Van Damme.[56]

Rothrock's break finally came when the ABC network news anchor, Peter Jennings, saw a newspaper story about her effort to maintain her undefeated championship status and invited her onto his show. Sammo Hung then called to ask "'Who is this girl that has a Hong Kong contract?' because technically they were going to forget about me."[57] In July 1985, Hung flew Rothrock to Hong Kong to make *Yes, Madam!* for D&B Films, a new company owned by the retail magnate, Dickson Poon.[58] Instead of seeking another Bruce Lee, D&B planned to combine Rothrock with another newcomer, Michelle Yeoh, to launch into the market with a "battling babes" variation on the buddy cop film then becoming the rage in Hollywood after *48 Hours* (1982) and *Beverly Hills Cop* (1984).[59] *Yes, Madam!* also took inspiration from the locally popular *Charlie's Angels* TV show (1976–81) and the contemporary action comedy of Eric Tsang's *Aces Go Places* (1982) and Sammo Hung's *Wheels on Meals* (1984).[60] This development came as a surprise to Rothrock who expected to be wearing braids and silken sleeves in a period kung fu movie.[61]

Yes, Madam! kicked off a trend for "girls with guns" movies that lasted several years.[62] For her part, Rothrock was flying back and forth during production to compete for her fifth successive title in the USA. Her account of this gives insight into the labor involved in Hong Kong cinema's transnational traffic in "people and resources":[63]

> That was tough because I'd get in from Hong Kong, compete the next day and then fly back to Hong Kong for work on the following day! I didn't know then what I was going to do with films. I thought it was going to be a one-time thing. I did this movie, it was an experience in my life, and thought I would go back to teaching martial arts in the schools I had. The movie was a big hit, it broke box-office records, so I got another offer to do one more right after that. So, I stayed and completed two movies. I thought, I like this and maybe it's going to be my career for the time being.[64]

This casual reminiscence also highlights how the experience of making a film "one-time" inflected Rothrock's thinking toward cinema as one activity placed "for the time being" on an open-ended spectrum of martial arts-based activities, rather than breaking dramatically with her former life in the mode of a film star "discovery" myth.

With her fifth title secured, Rothrock settled into the Hong Kong action film world, where she performed with some of the city's leading or emerging talents: Yuen Biao, Kenny Bee, Sammo Hung, Sibelle Hu, Tsui Hark, Andy Lau, Michiko Nishiwaki, Sandra Ng, Yukari Oshima, Lydia Shum, Eric Tsang, Yuen Wah, and Michelle Yeoh. She also worked for directors who now enjoy international recognition: Yuen Kwai (*Yes, Madam!*; *Righting Wrongs*; *No Retreat, No Surrender 2: Raging Thunder*, 1988; *The Blonde Fury*, co-directed with Mang Hoi); Sammo Hung (*Millionaire's Express*, a.k.a. *Shanghai Express*, 1986); and Wong Jing (*Magic Crystal* a.k.a. *Jade Crystal*, 1986). Embedded in the action film community rather than flying in briefly as an imported star, Rothrock was also cast in films by deeply local industry figures. She made *The Inspector Wears Skirts* (1988) for Wellson Chin with Jackie Chan as producer, and *City Cops* (1989) for Lau Kar-wing, younger brother of the director Lau Kar-leung, and adopted brother of the actor Lau Kar-fai (Gordon Liu). The action director for her last film made in the city of Hong Kong, Chin's *Prince of the Sun* (1990), was Yuen Tak, one of Yu Jim Yuen's Seven Little Fortunes troupe with Jackie Chan, Corey Yuen, Yuen Biao, Yuen Wah, and Sammo Hung.

This was a boom period for Hong Kong film exports[65] and most of these films were widely seen, with Rothrock's fights earning great esteem. For Chinese styles specialist Blake Matthews, *Yes, Madam!* and *Righting Wrongs* are among "the greatest action films of all time,"[66] while Logan lists Rothrock twice in the "Ten Best Hong Kong Comedy Fights" for *Magic Crystal* with Richard Norton and *The Inspector Wears Skirts* with Jeff Falcon.[67] In her second film, *Millionaire's Express*, she had the honor of a solo comic fight with Sammo Hung, who said that "Cynthia made a tremendous impact . . . It wasn't just that she was a Western woman doing martial arts, but that she was performing Chinese kung fu so well!"[68]

Mobile workers have variable ways of deciding at different times what counts as home base in their lives. Rothrock moved back to Los Angeles in 1988 and Raymond Chow's decision to send her to Utah in 1990 to make two *China O'Brien* films was a pivotal moment with the fad for foreign fighters fading in Hong Kong. However, the industrial base of an actor is not the same thing as personal location and *China O'Brien* was not Rothrock's first Hong Kong film made with an American cast and an American style of simplified fight choreography.[69] That was the film she finally made for Ng See Yuen, *No Retreat, No Surrender 2*. A follow-up to Seasonal's first "Caucasian Bruce Lee" film, this film was set in Thailand, featured another new white male (Loren Avedon), and gave Rothrock a comic role as a cranky helicopter pilot. Nor did her Hong Kong career end neatly with *China O'Brien*, a modest but, on video, enduring success in which she played the sweet, avenging daughter of a murdered small-town sheriff. From 1991 to 1993, she made films for diverse companies across locations in Canada and Australia as well as Indonesia, and two of these, *Honor and Glory* (1992) and *Undefeatable* (1993), were made in the US by the notorious Hong Kong "ninja" director, Godfrey Ho Chi-keung.[70]

The director of some sixty B-movies, Ho (a.k.a. "Hall") was infamous for generating dozens more Z-grade movies by splicing together re-used B-movie footage while adding new scenes and lunatic touches of kitsch (roller-skating ninjas, for example). This cut-and-paste technique allowed him to fabricate four or five films for the price of one. Following in the tracks of Golden Harvest and Seasonal a decade earlier, but by-passing both theatrical release and the Hong Kong market in favor of an American DTV release, Ho contacted Rothrock because she was "bankable" as "the only American girl who can fight!" She made a limited appearance in *Honor and Glory*, a film she describes as "horrible,"[71] then in *Undefeatable* she played the central role of a street-fighter whose sister is murdered by a demented martial artist. Ho duly created for the Asian market a variant of *Undefeatable* called *Bloody Mary Killer* with added footage of Yukari Oshima, a sub-plot featuring Robin Shou as the son of a fugitive from Hong Kong ICAC, and a different mood as emphasis shifts to "little" characters linking the Shou and Rothrock stories.[72]

A third film by Ho, *Manhattan Chase* (2000), cast Rothrock in a minor role in her last Hong Kong film as a cop in a kidnap-caper starring Loren Avedon. It failed; peaking in the 1993–4 season,[73] but faced with a wave of new technologies, the DTV industry was hit by the Asian financial crisis of 1997–8 and the entire US video market was struggling by the end of the decade.[74] Ironically, Rothrock's Hong Kong profile undermined her at this point. Reflecting on the ultimately fatal cost of his dependence on the US video market, Ho claimed that *Manhattan Chase* could not work in Hong Kong without a famous *American* actor: "B grade American movies cannot be released in Hong Kong, because there are no names like Tom Cruise."[75]

Styles of Stardom

What was it to "star" in the Hong Kong martial arts cinema of the 1980s? To be *seen* as a star in this context of production and reception was not necessarily to play dramatic lead roles or to achieve the lofty status of a singular "heavenly body,"[76] although Hong Kong cinema in general has fabricated those with some

Figure 24 Cynthia Rothrock showcasing her fighting ferocity. *Righting Wrongs* directed by Corey Yuen. © Golden Harvest 1986. All rights reserved.

success (Jackie Chan, Chow Yun-fat, Andy Lau, Tony Leung Chiu-wai, and now Michelle Yeoh, for example). In Rothrock's film heyday, however, to "star" was first and foremost to perform complex fights and risky stunts collaboratively with a long-suffering professionalism. The spotlit fighting star was created by a crew that enabled and perfected his or her performance. As Leon Hunt points out, kung fu comedy at this time was based in the collective experience and "relentlessly cruel training" of former Opera performers turned stuntmen.[77] Ann Hui's *Ah Kam* (*The Stunt Woman*, 1996) portrayed the brutally patriarchal familialism of film production at this time (while ironically exposing its star, Michelle Yeoh, to serious injury[78]).

Knowing nothing about how films anywhere were made, Rothrock took the brutality for granted.[79] No doubt her toughness and talent as a competitive fighter as well as her "Demo Team" background and her trouper's lack of "*gweilo* character*" (egotism) helped her adapt to the insular, guild-like culture of the Hong Kong filmmaking world.[80] Retelling her own stories of bruising mishaps,[81] she stresses that she fitted in because of her willingness to work through pain: "I tried hard, I did everything they said, I got hurt, I didn't cry . . . I wasn't what they thought, like 'Ooh, I broke a nail' . . . I gave a hundred and ten per cent in the fights."[82] Her frequent co-star Richard Norton, an Australian martial artist active in Hong Kong from 1985 to 1997, similarly ascribes his success there to an uncomplaining compliance with whatever the stunt crews required.[83]

A related aspect of Hong Kong martial arts stardom in this era was the joy as well as the pain of being the focus of choreographic perfectionism for protracted periods of *time*. A rich online archive of dialogue between martial artists cooped up in pandemic lockdown in 2020 now complements the studies we have of the differences between classic Hong Kong and Hollywood "action technologies"[84] and their regimes of expert practice.[85] Rothrock, Norton, and the younger Scott Adkins concur that the literally painstaking process of perfecting a single fight that evolved over many days and even weeks, instead of spending most production time on the drama as they did in the US, created incomparable action spectacles in the days before CGI.[86] Among those scenes were Rothrock's heavily anthologized "one against many" fights, such as her pole-fighting display in *Yes, Madam!* (a thirty-day shoot) and the exquisite brawl on rope scaffolding in *The Blonde Fury*. The defining unit of stardom was the fight scene itself, not character priority in the fictional set-up, and the formal perfection of Rothrock's scenes allowed them to slide effortlessly into the halls of fame on YouTube a quarter of a century later.

Nevertheless, if her abilities and a pitch-in disposition helped Rothrock assimilate quickly, the narrative situations in which her skills were mobilized were shaped by a need to explain the characters that she did play on-screen. Easy to typecast in the law enforcement roles normalized for *gweilos* in British colonial times, she played a cop in six of her eight city-based productions (exceptions being the Bandit in *Millionaire's Express* and a Buddhist monk in *Prince of the Sun*), and in four of her six off-shore films. More justification was needed, however, not because she was a woman fighting men (routine in Hong Kong cinema) but because she was a white woman playing a *good* cop who fought bad *Chinese* men. In *Yes, Madam!*, *Righting Wrongs*, and *City Cops*, this racialized awkwardness is comically defused for the audience when local men make crude remarks about the ugly body, rough skin, or "third class nightclub" looks of the *gwei por* (sub-titled as "white bitch" or "foreign chick"), only to discover that, thanks to the magic of post-sync sound, she speaks Cantonese.

Typecasting served Rothrock well, although she herself has expressed yearnings for "costumes" (as in *Prince of the Sun*) and to play "anything that isn't me!" David Bordwell argues that in popular cinema "genres demand character types, so stars must to some degree match fixed roles,"[87] and even in the US, Rothrock's fictional repertoire was mostly limited to fighter variations. This "true to life" proximity between screen roles and a star also holds for Richard Norton: typecast as a heavy in films, he made his living as a bodyguard to global music stars for many years.[88] However, the flat and prosaic acting style that Rothrock brought to dramatic scenes allowed her to perform very effectively the blunt, bossy, Anglo-American "typicality" enjoyed by local audiences. Stereotypes are always powerful producers of bonding through social recognition, in affirmative as well as discriminatory ways, and Hong Kong popular culture prizes typicality in everyday as well as on-screen life. Its vernacular cinema long retained in its poetics that "overstatement of character" that Harold Meyerson traces from early Hollywood to the 1930s, contrasting the "readability" of character actors to the "opacity" of classic stars like Greta Garbo, Gary Cooper, or Marlene Dietrich.[89] Some Hong Kong dramatic stars such as Leslie Cheung and Anita Mui have shared the latter's "blank" power to attract emotional projection from fans. However, like the Chinese opera traditions from which it drew,[90] martial arts cinema in the 1970s and 1980s was all about readability, riotously offering audiences a recognition carnival of the "simple inner essences" infusing social and ethnic stereotypes.[91]

At the same time, both Rothrock and Norton had signature moves of the kind that Meyerson calls a character "refrain."[92] Like Norton's trademark question "Painful?" sadistically delivered after a nasty blow, Rothrock's scorpion kick personally typified *her* rather than any particular role.[93] For Richard Dyer, the Western film star's individuality is unstably shaped by the socially typical in a "lurching from one formulation of what being human is to another."[94] In a different cultural context, typical Hong Kong martial arts stars may lurch toward complicating moments of individuation. Rothrock's cops had different qualities and ways of relating to the local community as well as to their partners. As a fighting star, she was always cast as a good cop in the sense of siding with the law, but she did not always play a nice person. Hunt notes that Rothrock "is often an abrasive presence in her Hong Kong films"[95] and this is especially true of *Yes, Madam!* where, as Carrie Morris, she embodies colonial arrogance in her dyad with Michelle Yeoh's diplomatic Inspector Ng. Morris is violent, unsubtle, and hostile to Chinese until Ng's courage and the vulnerable silliness of three rogues called Panadol (Tsui Hark), Aspirin (Mang Hoi), and Strepsil (John Shum) lead her to care about their fates. Cindy Morgan in *The Magic Crystal* is a simple essence of "good guy," protecting a small boy and a cute alien rock from Richard Norton's fiendish Russian, Karov, but Cindy Si in *Righting Wrongs* is a seriously flawed character, brutal and obtuse with a self-righteous myopia about corruption in Hong Kong that brings tragedy in three of the film's four endings.[96] In later films, for a local audience now familiar with "Cindy," Rothrock's cops are emotionally involved in local Chinese life. Madam Law in *The Inspector Wears Skirts* and Cindy in *The Blonde Fury* are tough professionals who fly in and out of the city but remain embedded in enduring female friendships. The job-focused Cindy of *City Cops* even crosses a sensitive social boundary to have an implied affair with her male partner, Kau Tai (Shing Fui-on).

To the extent that these films do individualize Rothrock, her odd partnerships allow her to act as a foil for pungent comment on Hong Kong society. Kwai-Cheung Lo points out that her characters have affinity with the life-ways of bumbling "little men" in contrast with new rich yuppies of the 1980s, whether the latter be heroes or villains.[97] When the *gwei por* sides with the little men against an ineffective or corrupt local authority, the films can both revel in and laugh at a demotic sexism, racism, and homophobia while also slinging off at the greed and hypocrisy of the Hong Kong status quo. In *The Inspector Wears Skirts*, male senior cops sneer at an Arab dignitary's sexism before forming a women's commando group to guard his wife so they can profit from his wealth. More conventionally, Cindy in *City Cops* saves her mission from a clueless boss by threatening to reveal his peccadilloes and his corruption, while her foreignness enables a stream of satirical quips as locals patronize her ignorance. Kau teaches her: "Hong Kong's not like the States. Information is not free, you've got to pay for it here."

As well as drawing on the Hollywood buddy-cop and girl-group "angels" formats, Rothrock's films more significantly work in the *pak-dong* (partner) comedy tradition initiated in the 1970s by the Hui brothers.[98] The influence of such comedies as *The Private Eyes* (1976) and *Security Unlimited* (1981) on the martial arts cinema was profound, not least on the sublime kung fu slapstick associated with Jackie Chan[99] as well as the *mo lei tau* ("silly talk") unleashed by Stephen Chow, and this influence highlights a difficulty that many Western critics have with Rothrock's and other Hong Kong martial arts films of this period. The problem is not simply that they mix action with comedy and drama with slapstick and farce, although this is the familiar lament of action fans whose sense of aesthetic propriety no longer tolerates the melodramatic and vaudevillian traditions of Western popular theater. A bigger obstacle is that the comedy in these films is often untranslatably verbal, with inventive Cantonese jokes constituting "the local audience as a privileged hermeneutic community."[100] When an online review stub in English describes *City Cops* as "14 bearable minutes, the other 70 or so totally uninteresting," it identifies the ratio of action scenes to Cantonese language performance.[101]

In another mark of the Hui brothers' influence on Rothrock's films, Cindy's warmest interactions are often with her girlfriends, families, people on the street, and minor characters such as the inept cop "Bad Egg" (Yuen Kwai) and his frustrated father Uncle Tsai (Wu Ma) in *Righting Wrongs*. The fictional worlds she inhabits are crowded with the "little" comic figures often read by outsiders as gratuitous and grating as they take up screen time, but who offer delicious moments of social recognition to a Hong Kong-literate audience: for example, the rigid policing of trivial offences by a vicious parking officer while the rule of law in the city collapses (*Righting Wrongs*); the lazy reporters faking stories and the nurse callously stealing a patient's food (*The Blonde Fury*); and the incompetent, bullying school teacher who works only for gambling money (*Prince of the Sun*).

A cultural transfer enabling Rothrock to star in this kind of comedy without much Cantonese was her willingness to fool around with old school American screwball comedy.[102] Untrained in delivering dialogue until after her return to the USA, she had a talent for mimetic "silent" performance; she plays comic scenes as well as her fights with the gusto that she calls "a hundred and ten per cent."[103] This did not serve her well in her 1990s US films, where she relied too often on facial muscles to signify shifts in mood. In Hong Kong comedies, however, she "fits in" even when her role is not that of a comic lead: she thrives in Wong Jing's "bacchanalian" pop inventiveness in *Magic Crystal*,[104] and in *Prince of the Sun* she plays a stylish monk who guards the Buddha reincarnated as an annoying little boy hiding out from the minions of evil in a gambling addict's apartment, haunted by cranky ghosts. A culturally pitch-perfect translation of Michael Ritchie's film with Eddie Murphy, *The Golden Child* (1986), *Prince of the Sun* rivals *City Cops* as Rothrock's Hong Kong film least appreciated by her Western fans.[105] However, with Conan Lee playing a good-hearted illegal immigrant from mainland China, and with Eddie Murphy's manic energy spread across all the minor characters while Rothrock as the "odd" savior stays cool, it does a brilliant job of screwballing the frenetic mood and financial panic racking Hong Kong as 1997 approached.

Rothrock's characters are often *goofy* and, perhaps more than any other performance feature, her comic gusto distinguishes Rothrock's stardom from the work of other *gweilo* martial artists working in Hong Kong cinema at this time, with the exception of Richard Norton who also visibly enjoys playing the fool; their partnership works beautifully because neither tries to dominate or preserve their dignity on-screen. Other Western performers may cite Jackie Chan as a primary influence, but most are more impressed by Chan's stunts and risk-taking realism[106] than by his uptake of the slapstick tradition of Western silent and early sound cinema.[107] Preoccupied with burdens of empire rather than the plight of little people, Hollywood action at this time was light years away from the legacies of Charlie Chaplin and Buster Keaton; when Rothrock was making *Millionaire's Express* and *Magic Crystal*, Tom Cruise was making *Top Gun* (1986), Chuck Norris was a patriot in *Invasion U.S.A.* (1985), and Jean-Claude Van Damme was preparing Newt Arnold's exciting, camp, and utterly humorless *Bloodsport* (1988). Rothrock's gender and Norton's nationality set them off-center for that Hollywood action imaginary,[108] but in their Hong Kong films they occupy an "outsider-inside" position that relays a foreign gaze while opening up for wider audiences the comically warm, parochial worlds that their characters inhabit.

Along with her fighting skills, the performance traits that made Cynthia Rothrock a Hong Kong martial arts film star were her toughness, her love of challenges, her readiness to have a go at anything, her team spirit, and an infectious comic verve. These carried over to some extent in her US work, although after *China O'Brien* her DTV films had a darker, more monochrome tenor and a tendency at first to make her the sidekick of some male "newbie with a fraction of her screen presence."[109] As always, she tried hard, didn't cry, and with *Undefeatable*, *Guardian Angel*, and *Sword of Justice*, she achieved lead roles in three of the great B-action classics of the decade. Today, her ability to combine the category of "champion martial artist" with that of comedian or "goof" has allowed her to become a cross-media star with her YouTube channel offering extreme sports as well as training videos, and "behind the scenes" shorts with stories from her Hong Kong years; she is a fine interviewer, featuring Samuel Kwok, Vincent Lyn, and Scott Adkins in her "Rothrock and Roll" pandemic tapes, and giving her goofiness free rein with hilarious bloopers that are not about injuries but silly mistakes in online conversation. In 2023, the scale of her cyber-fanbase allowed her to crowd-fund her own film, *Black Creek*, through Kickstarter and Indiegogo; a "martial arts Western" with a cast of US martial arts film superstars (including Billy Blanks, Richard Norton, Don "The Dragon" Wilson, and Benny "The Jet" Urquidez), this project broke new ground with an incentives scheme for backers that allowed fans to participate in the production.[110] Meanwhile, her classic Hong Kong martial arts stardom has been revived not only by Blu-ray companies but by a generation of Internet-based film critics for such sites as *Comeuppance Reviews*, *Direct to Video Connoisseur*, *Girls with Guns*, *It's a Beautiful Film Worth Fighting For*, *Screen Anarchy*, and *Vern's Reviews on the Films of Cinema*. As a Rothrock fan of thirty years standing myself, I concur with one of these sites, *Bleeding Skull*: "The world could use seven-hundred more Cynthia Rothrocks. Since that's not possible, it's our duty to canonize everything about the one that we do have."[111]

Notes

1   David West, *Chasing Dragons: An Introduction to the Martial Arts Film* (London: I. B. Tauris, 2006), 214–15.

2   Arnaud Lanuque, "Interview with Ninja director Godfrey Ho," *Hong Kong Cinemagic* (2007), http://www.hkcinemagic.com/en/page.asp?aid=230&page=0 (accessed September 23, 2023).

3   Raj Khedun, "Interview with Cynthia Rothrock, part 2," *Kung-Fu Kingdom* (January 25, 2014), https://kungfukingdom.com/interview-with-cynthia-rothrock-part-2 (accessed September 23, 2023).

4   Tom Jolliffe, "Cynthia Rothrock: The First Lady of International Action," *Flickering Myth* (August 2, 2021), https://www.flickeringmyth.com/2021/08/cynthia-rothrock-the-first-lady-of-international-action (accessed September 23, 2023).

5   Recent examples are: the Munich Hall of Honours 2022 "Celebrity of the Year" award, https://www.youtube.com/watch?v=jPcH5qhJE-s&ab_channel—anfredHaempel; the Italian "Martial Hero Award," 2018–21, https://martialheroaward.com/master/gm-cynthia-rothrock/; and the USA "2022 Century Martial Arts Lifetime Achievement Award," https://www.youtube.com/watch?v=HnDF4johFr8&t=55s&ab_channel=CynthiaRothrock (all accessed September 23, 2023). She was also the invited special guest at the 2023 "Who's Who in the Martial Arts Hall of Honors Legacy Weekend" Awards presentation in Las Vegas, https://www.whoswhointhemartialarts.com (accessed August 9, 2023).

6   At my time of writing she is on Facebook at https://www.facebook.com/CYNTHIAROTHROCK, with an older page at https://www.facebook.com/cyndi.rothrock; Instagram, @officialcynthiarothrock and @cynthiarothrockladydragon; Twitter, https://twitter.com/cynroth; and YouTube, https://www.youtube.com/@CynthiaRothrockChannel. Her official website is http://www.cynthiarothrock.com.

7   Cynthia Rothrock, "Cynthia Rothrock Interview: Martial Arts Goals," *Art of One Dojo* (June 21, 2022), https://www.youtube.com/watch?v=9EFAWJ89ldo&ab_channel=ArtofOneDojo (accessed September 23, 2023).

8   See "Dan Delts Fan Experiences," https://dandelts.com.au/dan_delts (accessed September 23, 2023). Dan Delts does up-market events creation for sports and action stars as well as corporate celebrities, acting as "personal appearance managers" in Australia for Steven Seagal, Michael Jai White, Daniel Bernhardt, and Bolo Yeung as well as Cynthia Rothrock.

9   Richard Dyer, *Stars* (London: BFI, [1979] 1998), 10–12.

10 See Esther C.M. Yau (ed.), *At Full Speed: Hong Kong Cinema in a Borderless World* (Minneapolis: University of Minnesota Press, 2001); Meaghan Morris, Siu Leung Li, and Stephen Chan Ching-kiu (eds.), *Hong Kong Connections: Transnational Imagination in Action Cinema* (Hong Kong: Hong Kong University Press, 2005); and Leon Hunt and Leung Wing-Fai (eds.), *East Asian Cinemas: Exploring Transnational Connections on Film* (London: I. B. Tauris, 2008).

11 Law Kar and Frank Bren, *Hong Kong Cinema: A Cross-Cultural View* (Lanham, MD: The Scarecrow Press, 2004), 87.

12 Stephen Teo, *Hong Kong Cinema: The Extra Dimensions* (London: BFI, 1997), 3–28.

13 Law Kar, "The American Connection in Early Hong Kong Cinema," in *The Cinema of Hong Kong: History, Arts, Identity*, eds. Poshek Fu and David Desser (Cambridge: Cambridge University Press, 2000), 59.

14 See Stephen Teo, "Local and Global Identity: Whither Hong Kong Cinema?" *Senses of Cinema* 7 (2000), https://www.sensesofcinema.com/2000/asian-cinema/ hongkong (accessed September 23, 2023), and Poshek Fu (ed.), *China Forever: The Shaw Brothers and Diasporic Cinema* (Urbana and Chicago: University of Illinois Press, 2008).

15 See Law Kar (ed.), *Border Crossings in Hong Kong Cinema*: *The 24th Hong Kong International Film Festival* (Hong Kong: Leisure and Cultural Services Department, 2000).

16 Kwai-Cheung Lo, *Excess and Masculinity in Asian Cultural Productions* (Albany: State University of New York Press, 2010), 130–1.

17 Thomas Barker, "Exploiting Indonesia: From *Primitives* to *Outraged Fugitives*," *Plaridel* 11, no. 2 (2014), 16.

18 Ekky Imanjaya, *The Cultural Traffic of Classic Indonesian Exploitation Cinema*, PhD diss. (University of East Anglia, 2016), 121.

19 Emilie Black, "Best 90s Direct-to-Video Action Movies," *JoBlo* (September 18, 2022), https://www.joblo.com/best-90s-direct-to-video-action-movies (accessed September 23, 2023).

20 See David Desser, "The Martial Arts Film in the 1990s," in *Film Genre 2000: New Critical Essays*, ed. Wheeler Winston Dixon (Albany: State University of New York Press, 2000), 77–110.

21 Dyer, *Stars*, 17–18.

22 "I met Van Damme in Hong Kong then this happened! Interview with Dan Delts (part 1)," *Viking Samurai* (December 6, 2022), https://www.youtube.com/ watch?v=4aSfG5Po6UM (accessed September 23, 2023).

23 Dan Delts, personal correspondence, December 30, 2022. *Yes Madam!* was released on Blu-ray by Eureka Entertainment on December 12, 2022.

24 In this and the following section, I draw on my earlier "What can a *gwei por* do? Cynthia Rothrock's Hong Kong Career," *Inter-Asia Cultural Studies* 13, no. 4 (2012), 1–17.

25 Man-Fung Yip, *Martial Arts Cinema and Hong Kong Modernity* (Hong Kong: Hong Kong University Press, 2017), 85.

26 On the earlier period of female-dominated swordplay films, see Tony Williams, "Hong Kong Martial Arts Women," *Asian Cinema* 17, no. 1 (2006): 155–65; Lo, *Excess and Masculinity in Asian Cultural Productions*, 107–40; Lisa Funnell, *Warrior Women: Gender, Race, and the Transnational Chinese Action Star* (Albany: State University of New York Press, 2014); and Yip, *Martial Arts Cinema and Hong Kong Modernity*. On the casting of Western foreigners, Funnell notes "the racial assumption that martial arts is a Chinese and/or Asian-based form of combat" (Funnell, *Warrior Women*, 38–9).

27 In Cantonese, the term *gweilo* ("white ghost") applies strictly to Caucasian men. In Hong Kong English its referential range is more flexible, often subsuming the more insulting term for a white woman, *gwei por*. African-American men are "*hak gwei*" ("black ghost"). Unlike *gweilo*, these terms do not pass into everyday Hong Kong

English. For interviews with foreigners who played structural roles in the film industry, see "Gweilos, Foreigners in HK Cinema," *Hong Kong Cinemagic*, http://www.hkcinemagic.com/en/cat.asp?catid=23&did=88 (accessed September 23, 2023).

28 Leon Hunt, *Kung Fu Cult Masters: From Bruce Lee to Crouching Tiger* (London: Wallflower Press, 2003), 123.

29 See Sheperd's archived website, https://web.archive.org/web/20150310114308/http://karensheperd.com/karate-divaland/history. The most reliable version of Rothrock's filmography is http://www.imdb.com/name/nm0001686 (both accessed September 23, 2023).

30 See Yvonne Tasker, *Spectacular Bodies: Gender, Genre, and the Action Cinema* (London: Routledge, 1993), 24–6; Andy Willis, "Cynthia Rothrock: From the Ghetto of Exploitation," in *Film Stars: Hollywood and Beyond*, ed. Andy Willis (Manchester: Manchester University Press, 2004), 174–88; and Rikke Schubart, *Super Bitches and Action Babes: The Female Hero in Popular Cinema*, *1970–2006* (Jefferson, NC: McFarland, 2007), 144–65.

31 See my "Learning from Bruce Lee: Pedagogy and Political Correctness in Martial Arts Cinema," in *Keyframes: Popular Film and Cultural Studies*, eds. Matthew Tinckcom and Amy Villarejo (London: Routledge, 2001), 171–86. See also Paul Bowman, *Theorizing Bruce Lee: Film-Fantasy-Fighting-Philosophy* (Amsterdam: Rodopi, 2010), 37–42.

32 According to Rothrock, the proposed TV series was canned by CBS because of anxiety about screen violence in the USA at the time. See "Cynthia Rothrock: Irresistible Force," Cynthia Rothrock YouTube Channel (July 18, 2020), https://www.youtube.com/watch?v=QKdYlKrRlvo&t=515s&ab_channel=CynthiaRothrock (accessed September 23, 2023).

33 For Rothrock's assessment of her Hong Kong directors and co-stars, see her interview "Action Overload: An Interview with Cynthia Rothrock," on the Dragon Dynasty DVD release of *Above the Law* (2007), http://www.youtube.com/watch?v=YqjeGodF6jo (accessed December 16, 2022). See also *Profiles*. Her character was called "Cindy" in *The Magic Crystal*, *Righting Wrongs, The Blonde Fury*, and *City Cops.*

34 Al Cirboni, "Cynthia Rothrock," *Martial Arts* (August 29, 2021), http://j2n-ma.blogspot.com/2012/08/cynthia-rothrock.html (accessed September 23, 2023).

35 The best of the classic fan websites, "The Cynthia Rothrock World Order," closed by mid-2011. At my time of writing, Rothrock's official website and Fan Club with a portal to her Martial Arts Association is at https://www.cynthiarothrockofficial.com and the best compilation overview of her work and life, with connections to interviews and podcasts, is Rothrock's YouTube channel: https://www.youtube.com/@CynthiaRothrockChannel.

36 Andy Meisler, "The Biggest Star You Never Heard Of," *The New York Times* (July 3, 1994), https://www.nytimes.com/1994/07/03/movies/television-the-biggest-star-you-never-heard-of.html (accessed September 23, 2023).

37 Willis, "Cynthia Rothrock."

38 Schubart, *Super Bitches and Action Babes*, 144–65.

39 Meisler, "The Biggest Star You Never Heard Of."

40 Joe Yanick, "An Oral History of PM Entertainment, a Low-Budget High-Octane American Dream," *Hopes&Fears* (January 7, 2016), http://www.hopesandfears.com/hopes/culture/film/217129-an-oral-history-of-pm-entertainment (accessed December 19, 2022).

41 Schubart, *Super Bitches and Action Babes*, 162–4.

42 See my "Transnational Imagination in Action Cinema: Hong Kong and the Making of a Global Popular Culture," *Inter-Asia Cultural Studies* 5, no. 2 (2004): 181–99.

43 Naoki Sakai, *Translation and Subjectivity: On "Japan" and Cultural Nationalism* (Minneapolis: University of Minnesota Press, 1997), 15–16.

44 David Desser, "Hong Kong Film and the New Cinephilia," in *Hong Kong Connections*, 205–21.

45 Joseph A. Ziemba, "*Angel of Fury* (1992)," *Bleeding Skull: Exploring Otherworldly Cinema Since 2004* (July 2, 2015), http://bleedingskull.com/angel-of-fury-1992 (accessed September 23, 2023). It is also worth noting that there is a title confusion in Rothrock's oeuvre. As Matthew Poirier points out, the 1990 *Angel of Fury* is a recut and redubbed version of the Indonesian *Triple Cross*. The later film known as *Lady Dragon 2* (1993) in the US is titled *Angel of Fury* (1993) in the UK. See Poirier's "*Angel of Fury* aka *Triple Cross*," *Direct to Video Connoisseur* (March 5, 2022), http://dtvconnoisseur.blogspot.com/2022/03/angel-of-fury-aka-triple-cross-1990.html (accessed September 23, 2023).

46 Schubart, *Super Bitches and Action Babes*, 192.

47 Chris Rojek, *Celebrity* (London: Reaktion Books, 2001), 18.

48 Scott Adkins, "The Art of Action 12: Cynthia Rothrock," *Scott Adkins YouTube Channel* (September 20, 2020), https://www.youtube.com/watch?v=DsMFdrOQTsY&t=1213s&ab_channel=ScottAdkins (accessed September 23, 2023).

49 See "Cynthia Rothrock Kentucky Fried Chicken Ad (1983)," https://www.youtube.com/watch?v=TkGYrkzkueo&t=31s&ab_channel=bmuz (accessed September 23, 2023). On idolizing Jackie Chan, see "Cynthia Rothrock and Richard Norton Q&A," *Black Belt* (May 7, 2020), https://www.youtube.com/watch?v=7NdJUswqU78&ab_channel=CynthiaRothrock.

50 See "Ernie Reyes," *Ernie Reyes' West Coast World Martial Arts Association*, https://erniereyes.com/about-us/ernie-reyes (accessed September 23, 2023).

51 Michael Curtin, *Playing to the World's Biggest Audience: The Globalization of Chinese Film and TV* (Berkeley and Los Angeles; University of California Press, 2007), 54.

52 See *Profiles: Featuring Cynthia Rothrock* (2007), DVD, USA: Quest Media Entertainment.

53 Adkins, "The Art of Action 12: Cynthia Rothrock."

54 *Profiles*.

55 Bey Logan, *Hong Kong Action Cinema* (London: Titan, 1995), 157.

56 See my "Learning from Bruce Lee."

57 *Profiles*.

58 On the flexible relations between Hong Kong independent production companies orchestrated by the "gatekeeping" of Raymond Chow at Golden Harvest, see Curtin, *Playing to the World's Biggest Audience*, 47–67.

59 See Jeffrey A. Brown, "Bullets, Baddies and Bad Guys: The 'Action Cop' Genre," *Journal of Popular Film and Television* 21, no. 2 (1993): 79–87, and Neal King, *Heroes in Hard Times: Cop Action Movies in the U.S.* (Philadelphia: Temple University, 1999).

60 On the long-running exchange between Hong Kong cinema and generations of *Charlie's Angels* production, see Sherrie A. Inness, *Tough Girls: Women Warriors and Wonder Women in Popular Culture* (Philadelphia: University of Pennsylvania Press, 1999); Marc O'Day, "Beauty in Motion: Gender, spectacle and action babe cinema," in *Action and Adventure Cinema*, ed. Yvonne Tasker (London: Routledge, 2004), 201–18; and Lisa Funnell, "Assimilating Hong Kong Style for the Hollywood Action Woman," *Quarterly Review of Film and Video* 28, no. 1 (2010): 66–79.

61 Adkins, "The Art of Action 12: Cynthia Rothrock."

62 See Lisa Funnell, "Fighting for a Hong Kong/Chinese Female Identity: Michelle Yeoh, Body Performance, and Globalized Action Cinema," in *Asian Popular Culture in Transition*, eds. L. Fitzsimmons and J. Lent (London: Routledge, 2012), 172–3, and Thomas Podvin and David Vivier, "Interview with HK Film Historian Law Kar," *Hong Kong Cinemagic* (December 1, 2005), http://www.hkcinemagic.com/en/page.asp?aid=309&page=3 (accessed September 23, 2023).

63 Kar, "The American Connection in Early Hong Kong Cinema," 59.

64 David Pearce, "A Foot in Your Face: Cynthia Rothrock," *Fatal Visions* 14 (1993), 24.

65 Grace Leung and Joseph Chan, "The Hong Kong Cinema and its Overseas Market: A Historical Review, 1950–1995," in *Fifty Years of Electric Shadows*, ed. Law Kar (Hong Kong: Urban Council, 1997), 146.

66 Blake Matthews, *It's All About the Style: A Survey of Martial Arts Styles Depicted in Chinese Cinema* (USA: CreateSpace Independent Publishing Platform, 2013), 25.

67 Logan, *Hong Kong Action Cinema*, 142.

68 Sammo Hung quoted in ibid., 157.

69 See Darren Murray, "Hong Kong Goes West—When Hong Kong Film Makers Attempt to Break the Western Market—Part 2," *Screen Anarchy* (February 24, 2017), https://screenanarchy.com/2017/02/hong-kong-goes-west---when-hong-kong-film-makers-attempt-to-break-the-western-market---part-2-contrib.html (accessed September 23, 2023), and Craig D. Reid, "Fighting without Fighting: Film Action Fight Choreography," *Film Quarterly* 47, no. 2 (1994): 30–5.

70 For more details on the forty-odd ninja films attributed to Ho, see http://en.wikipedia.org/wiki/Godfrey_Ho.

71 Adkins, "The Art of Action 12: Cynthia Rothrock."

72 Two other "Rothrock" films were generated in this way. Ho's *Angel the Kickboxer* (1993) includes footage from *Honor and Glory*, and Phillip Ko Fei's *Set Me Free* (2001) uses Ho's *Manhattan Chase* (2000). See *Hong Kong Movie Database*, https://hkmdb.com/db/people/view.mhtml?id=6283&display_set=eng.

73 Frederick Wasser, *Veni, Vidi, Video: The Hollywood Empire and the VCR* (Austin: University of Texas Press, 2001), 185.

74 M. Ray Lott, *The American Martial Arts Film* (Jefferson, NC: McFarland, 2004), 199, 205–9.

75 Lanuque, "Interview with Ninja director Godfrey Ho."

76 Richard Dyer, *Heavenly Bodies: Film Stars and Society* (London: Routledge, [1986] 2004).

77 Hunt, *Kung Fu Cult Masters*, 102.

78 Jim McLennan, "*The Stunt Woman (Ah Kam)*," *Girls with Guns* (December 7, 2013), https://girlswithguns.org/stunt-woman-ah-kam (accessed September 23, 2023).

79 Adkins, "The Art of Action 12: Cynthia Rothrock."

80 Lisa Odham Stokes and Michael Hoover, *City on Fire: Hong Kong Cinema* (London: Verso, 1999), 26–7.

81 "Cynthia Rothrock: On-Set Injuries," *Cynthia Rothrock YouTube Channel* (December 19, 2020), https://www.youtube.com/watch?v=dHwhUp0WEiY&ab_channel=CynthiaRothrock (accessed September 23, 2023).

82 Rothrock, "Action Overload."

83 See Scott Adkins, "The Art of Action 11: Richard Norton," *Scott Adkins YouTube Channel* (August 28, 2020), https://www.youtube.com/watch?v=fODw921IOHc&ab_channel=ScottAdkins (accessed September 23, 2023). Co-starring with Rothrock in *The Magic Crystal* (1986), two *China O'Brien* films (1990–1) and two *Rage and Honor* films (1992–3), Norton worked with Sammo Hung on *Twinkle, Twinkle, Lucky Stars* (1985) and *Millionaire's Express* (1986), and with Jackie Chan in *City Hunter* (1993) and *Mr. Nice Guy* (1997).

84 See Leon Hunt, "The Hong Kong/Hollywood Connection: Stardom and Spectacle in Transnational Action Cinema," in *Action and Adventure Cinema*, 269–83, and Reid, "Fighting without Fighting."

85 Lauren Steimer, *Experts in Action: Transnational Hong Kong-Style Stunt Work and Performance* (Durham, NC: Duke University Press, 2021).

86 See Adkins, "The Art of Action 11" and "The Art of Action 12"; Cynthia Rothrock, "Rothrock & Roll with the Punches: Cynthia Rothrock & Scott Adkins," *Cynthia Rothrock YouTube Channel* (October 4, 2020), https://www.youtube.com/watch?v—rt47Td7Lqk&ab_channel=CynthiaRothrock (accessed September 23, 2023).

87 David Bordwell, *Planet Hong Kong: Popular Cinema and the Art of Entertainment* (Cambridge, MA: Harvard University Press, 2000), 157.

88 Adkins, "The Art of Action 11."

89 Harold Meyerson, "The Character Actor: His Rise and Pratfall," *Film Comment* (November-December 1977), 7.

90 Sai-shing Yung, "Moving Body: The Interactions between Chinese Opera and Action Cinema," in *Hong Kong Connections*, 21–34.

91 Meyerson, "The Character Actor," 8.

92 Ibid.

93 First used by Norton in *Twinkle, Twinkle, Lucky Stars*, "Painful?" is referenced by Scott Adkins in *Accident Man* (2018). See Adkins, "The Art of Action 11: Richard Norton." Rothrock first used the scorpion kick in *Yes, Madam!* (1985). See Rothrock, "Cynthia Rothrock Interview: Martial Arts Goals."

94 Dyer, *Heavenly Bodies*, 16.

95 Hunt, *Kung Fu Cult Masters*, 123.

96 In the original Hong Kong ending, Cindy dies and so does Yuen Biao's vigilante hero, Jason Chan. Consistent with the film's pessimistic vision of Hong Kong's corrupt public institutions, this ending was booed by Taiwan audiences who wanted the characters to live. Rothrock was recalled to shoot an alternative ending in which she survives and Jason is jailed for his murders. There are also two endings in which one lives and the other dies. See https://www.movie-censorship.com/report.php?ID=698057 (accessed September 23, 2023).

97 Lo, *Excess and Masculinity in Asian Cultural Productions*, 129–30.

98 See Law Kar, "Michael Hui: A Decade of Sword Grinding," in *A Study of the Hong Kong Cinema in the Seventies*, ed. Cheuk-to Li (Hong Kong: Hong Kong International Film Festival, 1984), 65–8; Greg Dancer, "Film Style and Performance: Comedy and Kung Fu from Hong Kong," *Asian Cinema* 10, no. 1 (1998): 42–50; Jenny Kwok Wah Lau, "Besides Fists and Blood: Michael Hui and Cantonese Comedy," in *The Cinema of Hong Kong*, 158–75; and Luke White, *Legacies of the Drunken Master: Politics of the Body in Hong Kong Kung Fu Comedy Films* (Honolulu: University of Hawai'i Press, 2020), 35. For a film directly inspired by the *Charlie's Angels* model, without the Hui Brothers inflections that I see as significant in Rothrock's films, see Teresa Woo's *Angel* (a.k.a. *Iron Angels*, 1987), starring Moon Lee and Yukari Oshima.

99 See the wonderful kitchen brawl from *The Private Eyes* with nunchaku sausage strings, a swordfish, and a set of "jaws": https://www.youtube.com/watch?v=Zsn9XnfNz2s&ab_channel=LilyHuang (accessed September 23, 2023).

100 Linda Chiu-han Lai, "Film and Enigmatization: Nostalgia, Nonsense, and Remembering," in *At Full Speed*, 232.

101 http://www.sogoodreviews.com/reviews/c8.htm#citycops (accessed September 23, 2023).

102 Laleen Jayamanne, *Toward Cinema and Its Double: Cross-Cultural Mimesis* (Bloomington: Indiana University Press, 2001), 200–1.

103 Rothrock, "Action Overload."

104 Bordwell, *Planet Hong Kong*, 175.

105 See Andrew Skeates, "*Prince of the Sun*," *Far East Films* (May 15, 2015), https://www.fareastfilms.com/?review_post_type=prince-of-the-sun (accessed September 23, 2023), and Blake Matthews, "*Prince of the Sun* (1990)," *It's a Beautiful Film Worth Fighting For* (March 10, 2022), https://abeautifulfilm.blogspot.com/2022/03/prince-of-sun-1990.html (accessed September 23, 2023).

106 Herb Borkland, "Cynthia Rothrock—Honor & Cuteness," *Fightingarts.com* (n.d.), http://www.fightingarts.com/reading/article.php?id=596 (accessed September 23, 2023).

107 Kyle Barrowman, "Origins of the Action Film: Types, Tropes, and Techniques in Early Film History," in *A Companion to the Action Film*, ed. James Kendrick (Hoboken, NJ: Wiley-Blackwell, 2019), 11–34.

108 Morris, "Transnational Imagination in Action Cinema."

109 Vern, "*Tiger Claws*," *Vern's Reviews on the Films of Cinema* (April 21, 2022), https://outlawvern.com/2022/04/21/tiger-claws (accessed September 23, 2023).

110 See Cynthia Rothrock, "Cynthia Rothrock's *Black Creek*: A Martial Arts Western," *Art of One Dojo* (March 3, 2023), https://www.youtube.com/watch?v=siFwBGZrYAI&ab_channel=ArtofOneDojo (accessed September 23, 2023).

111 Ziemba, "*Angel of Fury* (1992)."

Chapter 10

Jet Li: A Career in Three Acts

Andy Willis

Figure 25 Jet Li prepares for battle. *Fist of Legend* directed by Gordon Chan.
© Golden Harvest 1994. All rights reserved.

Introduction

A film star's image and persona are not fixed in aspic. This means that those who are able to sustain a career as a star across a number of decades often have certain phases that reflect their popularity, their geographical transitions, and, as that career progresses, their aging. Given the significant changes that have affected the Hong Kong film industry over the past four decades, any stars, such as the subject of this chapter Jet Li, who emerged during the 1990s have had to negotiate those shifts if they wanted to maintain a star profile. Given this, as Gary Bettinson argues, "one adjective is recurrently invoked to characterize Hong Kong stars: flexibility."[1] This echoes the sentiment put forward by Tony Williams, when he notes that such a description seems particularly appropriate to describe the stardom of Jet Li. Comparing him to other stars, he states that Li is notably a "flexible and adaptable actor whose persona crosses more cultural and geographic boundaries," and one who is "more adaptable to changing historical and industrial circumstances."[2] Sabrina Yu makes a similar point when she argues that "Li is one of the most flexible and adaptable Chinese stars because his career has crossed numerous cultural and geographical boundaries, from mainland China to Hong Kong, from East to West and from Hollywood to Europe."[3]

In this chapter, I intend to explore three major phases in the career of Jet Li: his initial rise to stardom in the Hong Kong industry of the 1990s, his transition to international productions in the USA and France in the late 1990s and early 2000s, and finally his return to East Asia and the emerging blockbusters of the mainland China film industry in the twenty-first century. While none of these phases is fixed—Li made films in Hong Kong as he was working more internationally in the early twentieth century, for example—they do offer a prism through which one can consider Li's stardom alongside, or as part of, the major changes experienced by the Hong Kong film industry in this period. In her study of Li, Yu argues that the transitional aspects of the performer's persona are present from the beginning. He is a mainland Chinese actor who built his career in Hong Kong where he would be considered a star but also an outsider, who then moved to international productions where the range of roles were limited, before moving on to mainland Chinese blockbusters where he could be celebrated as a Chinese star. In each of these phases, I will consider how these contexts, as well as audiences' reactions to them, impacted upon the potential meaning of Jet Li, martial arts film star.

The Emergence of Jet Li: Hong Kong Cinema in the 1990s

Jet Li first found martial arts success as a national wushu champion in mainland China during the 1970s. He had begun training at the age of eight and started to represent his country at eleven. Such was his success that he was selected to perform his skills in front of the American President Richard Nixon at the White House in 1974.[4] Li's first appearances in feature films were a trio that centered on the martial arts of the Shaolin Temple and were shot on location in mainland China at the Henan temple.[5] These were *Shaolin Temple* (1982), *Kids from*

Shaolin (1984), and *Martial Arts of Shaolin* (1986). It is his appearance in these films with their lengthy training, practice, and display sequences that established Li as a performer who was also a skilled martial artist in his own right. Moving more clearly into the Hong Kong industry following these appearances Li worked with the production company Sil-Metropole, directing himself in the Second World War-set *Born to Defend* (1986). The relative disappointment of this film at the Hong Kong box-office saw Li make a smaller action oriented film next. *Dragon Fight* (1989) saw the emerging performer acting alongside another future Hong Kong superstar, Stephen Chow. While again showcasing his performance skills, this film again failed to fully connect with Hong Kong audiences. There is some suggestion that this lack of connection between Li and filmgoers in Hong Kong was due to his perceived status as a mainland performer and therefore an outsider, something Sabrina Yu suggests was enhanced by his inability to speak Cantonese and the need to dub his performances into that language. Yu also suggests that these combined at this time to question his status as a bona fide Hong Kong star.[6] Whatever the complexities of being a mainland performer in Hong Kong during the decade leading up to the handover of 1997, Jet Li would become a major star by playing a well-known character from local cinema history in a film series that would be a major success at the box-office.

It was Jet Li's next role following *Dragon Fight* that would establish him as a major figure within the Hong Kong film industry of the 1990s. As a number of those who have written about Li have noted, his rise to Hong Kong film stardom has been closely linked with his playing a number of already well-established, almost mythical characters within Hong Kong cinema. The first of these was the legendary martial arts figure Wong Fei-hung. A real-life character who was known as a Chinese patriot, he had been portrayed in a series of films in the 1950s, 1960s, and 1970s by Kwan Tak-hing before Li was cast in the role for director Tsui Hark's *Once Upon a Time in China* (1991).[7] This film and its two immediate sequels, *Once Upon a Time in China II* (1992) and *Once Upon a Time in China III* (1993), played a significant part in the revival of the *wuxia* film during this period, reimagining the genre for the decade leading up to Hong Kong's handover from the colonial rule of Great Britain to the People's Republic of China. David Bordwell has noted that Tsui Hark's champions have described him as a "key innovator and modernizer"[8] of the era and notes that Stephen Teo has called the films' engagement with Chinese history "nationalism on speed."[9] Linking the film's production to the emerging anxiety regarding the future of Hong Kong after the handover, Tony Williams has argued that casting Li ensured that the film "raised questions of continuity and change."[10] It was in this initial period of Li's stardom that his persona intersected with the wider social and political apprehensions of the moment.

Given these weighty concerns, Jet Li's initial emergence into Hong Kong cinema stardom was a subtle one. *Once Upon a Time in China* opens with shots of a traditional Lion Dance upon the deck of a ship that is one of many in the harbor. There is a cut to a camera tracking along the deck, which stops to frame Jet Li sitting watching the spectacle, his cream-colored costume standing out from the reds of the gathered soldiers and the dark blue of his companion. The camera returns to the dance before cutting back to Li and moving slightly to ensure he is center of the frame, clearly the main focus. Following a return to the celebrations on deck, a group of French soldiers on a nearby ship mistake the firecrackers being used as part of the festivity on the ship as shots being fired, and open fire themselves, hitting the head of the Lion and killing the martial artist within. Responding to this, Li's Wong Fei-hung jumps to save the head and then joins in the dance revealing his excellent, almost otherworldly martial arts skills. The emergence of the star, complete with numerous shots that frame him from a low angle suggesting his importance, in the opening of this film clearly links Li's evolving persona to the idea of tradition, here in the form of the character of Wong Fei-hung and the fact that he saves the dance through his excellent martial arts skills. Made at the beginning of the pivotal decade of the 1990s, the film has a clear nationalistic agenda, which will become attached to a number of roles Li plays as the 1990s progress. As Williams notes:

> The *Once upon a Time in China* series represents one of the major achievements of 1990s Hong Kong cinema. Focusing on the character of legendary martial artist Huang Fei-hong, the series differs from its predecessors by dealing with issues central to contemporary Hong Kong as it reached the end of one historical epoch and moved toward another. In 1997, Hong Kong lost its status as a British crown colony and became reunified with mainland China.[11]

The credit sequence of *Once Upon a Time in China*, which shows Li's Wong Fei-hung training the black flag army on a beach in order for them be ready to protect the nation from foreigners and their unequal treaties. This sequence is repeated, although arguably with subtly different meaning, across the films of the series maintaining the link between nationalist sympathies, martial arts skills, character, and star persona. As his career progresses, the link between martial arts skills and star persona becomes a definitive characteristic of the film star "Jet Li," and one that will not be broken whatever the context within which the actor is working.

In *Once Upon a Time in China II*, following a pre-credit sequence establishing the White Lotus sect and their belief in magic's ability to protect them from pain and gunfire as well as their naïve nationalistic excesses, Wong Fei-hung is once again shown training the black flag army on a beach. In this iteration, the shots of training are intercut with ones showing Wong traveling on a steam train. The sequence opens with a shot from a low angle of Li's Wong sitting thoughtfully before turning to the training and then offering another shot, moving closer, of Wong on the train. The sequence then continues to cut between the two spaces, ensuring that here in the second film of the series audiences are now presented with a much clearer sense that Li is the star and hero of the film. His character, in contrast to the violence and blind destruction of the White Lotus, is protective of the nation (the black army flags wielded on the beach read: "Protect your family and country") but not backward looking, something shown in this sequence by his embracing of technology such as the steam train on which he travels. Therefore, at a time of anxiety regarding Hong Kong's reunification with China, the role of Wong connects Jet Li with a paternalistic version of Chinese nationalism, one that is reassuring and ultimately not the threat that some at the time feared.

By becoming so associated with a character such as Wong Fei-hung, Li places his stardom in a lineage of Hong Kong martial arts characters and film performers. As the 1990s progressed, Li would take on the roles of other established figures that would assist in this in the public imagination. Following his role as Wong, Li would take on the role of another legendary figure, Fong Sai-yuk, in two films: *Fong Sai-Yuk* (1993) and *Fong Sai-Yuk 2* (1993). Fong had been a character in a variety of Hong Kong films including *The Adventures of Fong Sai Yuk* (1950) and a number of Shaw Brothers productions that highlighted Shaolin style martial arts such as *Heroes Two* (1974) and *Shaolin Temple* (1976). By accepting the role of Fong, Li further develops his stardom as something that is part of a longer lineage of martial arts film stardom. If his playing Fong evokes local stars such as Alexander Fu Sheng, who often played the role at Shaw Brothers, his role as Chen Zhen in *Fist of Legend* (1994) invited comparison with one of martial arts cinema's greatest stars, Bruce Lee. Lee had played the character of Chen Zhen in *Fist of Fury* (1972), a film that carried strong Chinese nationalist tendencies in its portrayal of the character's struggle against racism. Given this, *Fist of Legend* seems once again to link the star to Chineseness as the reunification of China and Hong Kong loomed on the horizon. In taking this series of roles, Li's star image can be seen to assume an added layer, that of a protector of Hong Kong cinema's legacy. This is something that particularly suited his wider persona which, unlike Jackie Chan's, tended toward the serious and straight-faced. For Jet Li, it seemed being part of a lineage of martial arts cinema was significant.

The Hong Kong release of *Fist of Legend* was supported by a poster that simply showed Jet Li standing alone, emphasizing his heroic role in the film. It also confirmed his bankability at the local box-office. After a series of films that saw Li play contemporary and historical leads, including a return to Wong Fei-hung in *Once Upon a Time in China and America* (1997), the star would seek to make a name for himself in America, initially taking a supporting role as the villain Wah Sing Ku in *Lethal Weapon 4* (1998).

International Appeal and the Idea of "Authenticity"

The lead-up to the handover of Hong Kong to China in 1997 saw a number of Hong Kong film practitioners relocate to the US and try their hand within American cinema. This can be attributed to an anxiety among the film community, reflecting that present in the wider population, regarding the political future of Hong Kong following the handover as well as fears over the potential impact that political shift may have on levels of production. By the late 1990s, American cinema was open to the inclusion of Hong Kong practitioners as the influence of their filmmaking was becoming apparent. Leon Hunt, writing in 2004, has argued that "Hollywood has assimilated three kinds of 'Hong Kong action': the high-octane gunplay of John Woo, the stunt-filled action-comedy of Jackie Chan and Sammo Hung, and the 'wire fu' of historical martial arts films like *Once Upon a Time in China*."[12] While these aspects are certainly identifiable within American films generally in terms of style, they do not fully explain the more difficult transfer of Hong Kong film stars and their personas into the US.

The firmament of Hollywood film stars seems to have only a limited number of spaces for international actors to take-up. This is particularly the case when these performers are not cast to, or chose not to, "pass" as American. In these cases, stars are closely identified with traits that Hollywood seems to consider as essentially representative of their national or regional identity. Across American film history, examples of stars whose persona has complemented this casting/ performance trend have included: David Niven's creation of the essential Englishman; Yves Montand's 1960s creations of a Hollywood take on the gallic lover; Omar Sharif's generic North African or Arab; and Antonio Banderas's more contemporary version of the Latin lover. While none of these performers managed to break out of such essentialist roles as they were cast in by Hollywood, many, notably Montand and Banderas's, have explored much more diverse parts in their non-Hollywood films. The limited casting of these stars stands against the multiple roles taken by an actor like Anthony Quinn who throughout his career portrayed a gallery of nationalities and identities (Greek, Spanish, Arab, and Native American, for example) in Hollywood films.

Given the US box-office success of *Lethal Weapon 4*, the turn of the twenty-first century offered Jet Li the opportunity to be cast in a number of Western films. Given the restrictions on the roles offered to international performers, he entered a period of his career where he would play a number of broadly speaking "Chinese" characters, many of which were defined unsurprisingly by their martial arts skills. Li entered the international market at a similar time as another key Hong Kong martial arts star, Jackie Chan. Given that there was a limited number of "foreign" roles on offer in Hollywood, Li's persona had to offer something slightly different to Chan's. While the pair appeared in American films in the same year, the latter was to bring his long-standing comedic skills and persona to *Rush Hour* (1998) and *Rush Hour 2* (2001), while Li would remain rather stone-faced and serious in roles such *Romeo Must Die* (2000) and *Cradle 2 the Grave* (2003).

Leon Hunt discusses the ways in which martial arts film fans, faced with these films, saw Li as losing his authenticity during this period. In this formula, Li's star status and persona was representative of Hong Kong cinema's martial arts heritage, and his international film appearances were actually potentially destroying that legacy. However, for international audiences for action films, those less well versed in the style and history of Hong Kong films, Jet Li's presence was still a signifier of "authenticity," something for them still drawn from his history in Hong Kong films. Many of these more general fans of action films were not the same hardcore fans of Hong Kong films who had questioned Li's embracing of technology to create cinematic spectacle. These were rather those who celebrated such cinematic spectacle and saw Li's star presence as an essential component of it. For them, Li was a signifier of "real" martial arts skills, particularly when compared to the likes of Hollywood actors such as Keanu Reeves in the Matrix films. It was the embracing of Li by such international action movie audiences, as opposed to martial arts film fans, that allowed him to have a more robust international period than most other Hong Kong émigrés apart from perhaps Jackie Chan.

The question of authenticity in regard to Jet Li is something that seems to circulate in a number of almost contradictory ways. This suggests that Li's star persona functions slightly differently in various contexts, meaning that any understanding of it must be based on placing the star into the contexts within which that persona operates. For example, while Li may signify authenticity for more general film audiences, Hunt argues convincingly that one can begin to separate the idea of Jet Li and authenticity in the context of Hong Kong cinema. Discussing Li and the celebrated fight between his character Wong Fei-hung and Donnie Yen's Iron Robe Yim that takes place amid bamboo scaffolding and alleyways in *Once Upon a Time in China II*, he states that "kung fu stardom is no longer the centre of 'authenticity.'"[13] In his argument, Hunt echoes Ackbar Abbas in suggesting that cinematic technique had supplanted the performance skills of the star, citing Yuen Woo-ping's wirework, Tsui Hark's editing, camera speed, and framing.[14] Hunt puts forward the notion that in the era when Li became a major star it is the performer's filmic "presence" rather than their actual martial arts skills that actually differentiates the star from the proficient martial arts performer. In this regard, Li's films contain a number of instances where, in fighting mode, the star is framed in a shot where the camera moves toward him, thus helping to create a sense of presence through cinematic technique as Hunt argues, rather than using the fixed shot designed to observe and capture performance skills associated with martial arts cinema in earlier eras of Hong Kong film production. A good example of this can be found a number of times within the extended fight sequence in *Once Upon a Time in China II* mentioned above. In Hunt's argument, Li represents a contemporary, post-new wave martial arts star. His presence embraces new technologies in a manner that is the antithesis of the old school "primitive" cinematic style of martial arts fight cinematography so adored by many fans of the genre.[15] It was this notion of "presence," and the changing meaning of Jet Li as a martial arts star, that allowed him to transfer into another arena successfully: the international action film.

Jet Li and "Hip-hop Kung Fu"

The early twenty-first century saw the production of a number of mid-budget action films in Hollywood that drew on martial arts and gave prominent roles to performers drawn from the field of black music, such as singer Aaliyah and rapper DMX. This cycle of films, which include the Jet Li vehicle *Romeo Must Die* and the Steven Seagal vehicle *Exit Wounds* (2001), was labeled by co-producer of the aforementioned films Dan Cracchiolo as "hip hop kung fu."[16] A number of these works became successful at the box-office, with Li's follow up to *Romeo Must Die*, the 2003 film *Cradle 2 the Grave*, making US$17.1 million over its opening weekend and landing at the top of the box-office charts before, according to boxofficemojo.com, making just under US$35 million at the US box-office. The only previous sustained US box-office success for films that involved martial arts and had lead Chinese actors had occurred in the early 1970s during the "kung fu craze" spearheaded by Bruce Lee. The impact of this is highlighted by David Desser, who argues that the popularity of Hong Kong kung fu films in America hit an all-time high in 1973 when, "on May 16, 1973, *Fists of Fury*, *Deep Thrust: The Hand of Death*, and *Five Fingers of Death* were ranked 1, 2, and 3, respectively, on *Variety's* list of the week's top box-office draws."[17]

Significantly, after making his first appearance in a Hollywood film as the villain in *Lethal Weapon 4*, Li co-starred in two of the most successful of these "hip hop kung fu" films, *Romeo Must Die* and *Cradle 2 the Grave*. As an already established East Asian star, Li's presence gave these films the potential for international success as well as appealing to the US fans of martial arts cinema. One other significant thing had happened at this time that heightened the potential of these films to move closer to the mainstream: the release and success of *The Matrix* in 1999. For general action film audiences martial arts were now a central component of the pleasures on offer. Li offered a clear version of this that as explored earlier signified authenticity.

Romeo Must Die was the first major hit of the cycle. Marketed, in the frenzy of a post-*Matrix* cashing-in period, as "from the producer of *The Matrix*," Joel Silver, it was also the first lead role in a US film for Li. In the context of a US production such as *Romeo Must Die*, Li's star persona promised "real" martial arts action for a general audience. The fact that the producers were aware of various potential audiences' demands for authenticity is reflected in their employment of Li's long-time collaborator and fight designer Corey Yuen as fight choreographer for the film. Indeed, co-producer Silver admits that he had first become aware of Li as a star from his appearances in the *Once Upon a Time in China* series.[18] Silver had already used Hong Kong kung fu legend Yuen Woo-ping as the fight choreographer on *The Matrix* and so was aware of what technicians from the Hong Kong tradition of martial arts cinema may bring to his projects in terms of both production values and audiences' desire for "authenticity" when it came to martial arts-based fight sequences. With this in mind, Silver and director Andrzej Bartkowiak were able to combine more traditional American action film elements such as shoot-outs and car chases with Hong Kong cinema martial arts fighting content. Together, they developed what Hunt has termed "MTV-style Hong Kong action,"[19] a style that was continued in the second film of this cycle to star Li, *Cradle 2 the Grave*.

One of the more striking things about Jet Li's move into international productions is the fact that he made many more of them over a sustained period of time than comparable stars who emerged from Hong Kong cinema such as Chow Yun-fat whose career, as discussed below, did not progress as much in Hollywood where he made merely three features in the late 1990s. In addition to the "hip hop kung fu" cycle, Li also starred in American productions such as *The One* (2001) and *War* (2007) as well as European films that were seeking an international market. Most notably in the latter were the Luc Besson-produced French films *Kiss of the Dragon* (2001) and *Unleashed* (2005). Working through the EuropaCorp company, Besson had become a major figure in a new kind of French action cinema that was shot in English and designed to appeal to international audiences. According to Isabelle Vanderschelden, "EuropaCorp is the French film production group created in 2000 by director Luc Besson and Pierre-Ange Le Pogam, a former producer of Gaumontmajor."[20] The aim of the company was to break away from what could be considered insular French production traditions. As Vanderschelden notes regarding their work and approach:

> Some are co-productions, such as *Le Baiser mortel du dragon/The Kiss of the Dragon*, *Danny the Dog* or *The Transporter*. They have substantial budgets and are shot in English. These films favour mainstream generic conventions and appropriate trendy Hollywood (and Hong Kong) formulae, rather than exploring the aesthetic issues traditionally associated with French cinema. Hence, they have often received criticism for their lack of substance as purely commercial ventures.[21]

Lisa Purse sees EuropaCorp as an organization that "adopts a model similar to that of a Hollywood studio (endeavoring to control both production and distribution), and has a track record of offerings that combine an international cast and hybrid, if formulaic, mainstream genres and forms."[22] *Kiss of the Dragon* was one of their earliest attempts to create an international product that utilized an international cast and was aimed at a youthful global market, and the fact that Jet Li was an essential part of the film's "package" reflects how the star had now become a more global action film commodity. It is therefore important to acknowledge this when discussing Jet Li's third act—his return to China. Now, as a major film star, he brought with him a more complex persona, one that potentially made meaning in slightly different ways depending on the contexts in which it was being utilized and which of his films audiences had consumed.

A Return to Chinese Cinema

As well as occurring in the shadow of the handover, Jet Li's work outside the Hong Kong film industry had coincided with a notable decline in local film production in Hong Kong and the emergence, and then domination, of co-productions with the industry of the Chinese mainland. This phenomenon was driven by the rapidly expanding theatrical market in mainland China which proved financially attractive to Hong Kong practitioners who looked to design products that could exploit it. This was further facilitated in 2004 with the introduction of the Closer Economic Partnership Arrangement (CEPA), which made co-productions with Hong Kong and their access to the China market easier.

The mainstream China market of the early twenty-first century also proved to be one where film stars still held sway in terms of appeal to audiences and box-office returns. A good example of how this might impact the career of a Hong Kong star is the case of Chow Yun-fat. As already noted, Chow was a major star across East Asia since the mid-1980s, and like Li had left for Hollywood at the time of the handover. After a number of under-performing mid-budget American action films such as *The Replacement Killers* (1998) and *The Corruptor* (1999), Chow played the King in *Anna and the King* (1999) alongside Jodie Foster. According to boxofficemojo.com, this film also proved to be something of a disappointment at the box-office, making just under US$114 million worldwide against a budget of US$92 million. Following these, Chow was offered the lead in director Ang Lee's homage to the *wuxia* film, *Crouching Tiger, Hidden Dragon* (2000). Gathering together a cast of stars that also included Cheng Pei-pei, Michelle Yeoh, and Zhang Ziyi, the film proved to be a major international box-office success, making US$213.5 million worldwide.

One of the producers of *Crouching Tiger, Hidden Dragon*, was Hong Kong-based Bill Kong of Edko films. Kong was also one of the producers of another multi-star film *Hero* (2002). Another international success ($177. 3 million), in this case the star roster included Jet Li, alongside Tony Leung Chiu-wai, Maggie Cheung, Zhang Ziyi, and Donnie Yen. By including such stars, the film is carefully designed to bring together a number of high-profile performers whose appeal it can be argued intersect with a variety of potential audiences for the film outside China where they were all recognizable and well-established. Leung and Cheung had strong East Asian appeal, but were also known in international arthouse circles due to their collaborations with director Wong Kar-wai. Zhang had established herself with mainland and international arthouse audiences working firstly on Zhang Yimou's *The Road Home* (1999) before having an international breakout with *Crouching Tiger, Hidden Dragon* and *Rush Hour 2*. Yen had by this time forged a career made-up of supporting roles and lower-budget action films, and had also tried his hand in Hollywood appearing in small roles and assisting with fight choreography in *Highlander: Endgame* (2000) and *Blade II* (2002). Among action fans Yen was still known for his fight with Jet Li in *Once Upon a Time in China II*, so a new collaboration had appeal. Given that there was clearly a lot of star power on the film, *Hero* was marketed in America as if it was solely a vehicle for Li, reflecting his marketability in that territory.

The decision to focus on Li is certainly reflected in the manner in which Miramax constructed a trailer for *Hero*'s release in the USA. While Leung, Cheung, Zhang, and Yen were all significant box-office attractions in East Asia with significant roles in the film, Miramax chose to focus on Li for their US trailer. For example, the trailer opens with a moment with Cheung and Leung sitting watching Li display his sword skills. The first clear shot of the actor's head and shoulders is that of Li as he faces toward the camera. He is then shown alone facing a barrage of arrows drawing his sword. The rest of the trailer contains a number of moments from across the film that center on Li with inter-titles stating: "Jet Li . . . His strength . . . will defy an empire . . . and his courage . . . will unite a nation."

This focus on Li as the main star of *Hero* is also reflected in the UK poster for the film's release in 2004. Here Li's head and shoulders in a side profile dominate the frame. These elements support the idea that in the West, Jet Li was a known star with a set of clear connotations, even if his box-office bankability was in mid-budget action films and large-scale foreign imports, centered on the perceived authenticity of his martial arts skills. While Li's martial arts skills are still central to *Hero*, the film's perceived nationalist politics, which is articulated rather bluntly by Jia-xuan Zhang,[23] hark back to the films that established Li's stardom, particularly the *Once Upon a Time in China* series. This aspect of Li's persona, someone not of Hong Kong but of China, which had initially made him an outsider to some in Hong Kong, now enabled the actor to re-establish himself as a major star of twenty-first-century cinema emerging from China. In addition, the success of *Hero* in mainland China proved the continued importance of film stars in that territory, and confirmed Jet Li as one of the most significant and as a major box-office attraction within that market. Li would now make a number of martial arts driven epics targeted primarily at the China market, such as *The Warlords* (2007) in which he starred alongside Andy Lau and Takeshi Kaneshiro, which created a sense that he was now something of an elder statesman of Chinese cinema. Since making *The Warlords*, Li's film choices have seen the actor move easily between the different production contexts that reflect the three phases of his career that I have outlined above. In doing so, he has successfully worked across international film industries in a manner that makes him one of the few truly global stars not to emerge from the Hollywood film industry. Reflecting this, he finally co-starred with another global star, Jackie Chan, in *The Forbidden Kingdom* (2008) and returned to playing Hollywood villains in *The Mummy: Tomb of the Dragon Emperor* (2008), a role that harked back to his international breakout in *Lethal Weapon 4*.

The ease with which Li is able to now navigate international film production suggests that perhaps the actor has entered a new phase of his career, one that more than anything reveals how his star persona, conceivably more than any other film star who emerged from the Hong Kong industry, has been able to become flexible enough to work in two very different star-heavy films: the Chinese propaganda epic *The Founding of a Republic* (2009) and the celebration of old school Hollywood action movies *The Expendables* (2010). While the latter confirmed that Li is one of the few Hong Kong or Chinese film stars of international renown, perhaps nothing proves this as much as the fact that when Disney was looking for a star with the gravitas and appeal to play the Emperor of China in their live action *Mulan* (2020), a film they hoped to intersect a number of markets, they selected Jet Li. The continued success of Li as a film star is therefore due to his ability to mean a variety of things at different moments, to remain flexible, and to allow filmmakers to draw on these various elements as they see fit.

Notes

1   Gary Bettinson, "Commentary: Hong Kong Stars and Stardom," in *A Companion to Hong Kong Cinema*, eds. eds. Esther M.K. Cheung, Gina Marchetti, and Esther C.M. Yau (Hoboken, NJ: John Wiley & Sons, 2015), 379.

2   Tony Williams, "Under 'Western Eyes': The Personal Odyssey of Huang Fei-Hong in *Once Upon a Time in China*," *Cinema Journal* 40, no. 1 (2000), 8.

3   Sabrina Qiong Yu, *Jet Li: Chinese Masculinity and Transnational Film Stardom* (Edinburgh: Edinburgh University Press, 2012), 5.

4   Ibid., 7.

5 Leon Hunt, *Kung Fu Cult Masters: From Bruce Lee to Crouching Tiger* (London: Wallflower, 2003), 73.

6 Yu, *Jet Li*, 7.

7 Stephen Teo, *Hong Kong Cinema: The Extra Dimensions* (London: BFI, 1997), 170.

8 David Bordwell, *Planet Hong Kong: Popular Cinema and the Art of Entertainment* (Cambridge, MA: Harvard University Press, 2000), 135.

9 Ibid., 139.

10 Williams, "Under 'Western Eyes,'" 4.

11 Ibid.

12 Leon Hunt, "The Hong Kong/Hollywood Connection: Stardom and Spectacle in Transnational Action Cinema," in *The Action and Adventure Cinema*, ed. Yvonne Tasker (London: Routledge, 2004), 269.

13 Hunt, *Kung Fu Cult Masters*, 42.

14 Ibid.

15 Ibid., 46.

16 See Cracchiolo's interview on the special feature "The Making of *Exit Wounds*" on the DVD.

17 David Desser, "The Kung Fu Craze: Hong Kong Cinema's First American Reception," in *The Cinema of Hong Kong: History, Arts, Identity*, eds. Poshek Fu and David Desser (Cambridge: Cambridge University Press, 2002), 20.

18 See Silver's interview on the special feature "The Making of *Exit Wounds*" on the DVD.

19 Hunt, *Kung Fu Cult Masters*, 23.

20 Isabelle Vanderschelden, "Luc Besson's Ambition: EuropaCorp as a European Major for the 21st Century," *Studies in European Cinema* 5, no. 2 (2009), 91.

21 Ibid., 94.

22 Lisa Purse, *Contemporary Action Cinema* (Edinburgh: Edinburgh University Press, 2011), 173.

23 Jia-xuan Zhang, "*Hero*," *Film Quarterly* 58, no. 4 (2005): 47–52.

Chapter 11

Zhang Ziyi: An Alternative Female Action Stardom and The Logic of Indeterminacy

Dorothy Wai Sim Lau

Figure 26 Zhang Ziyi avenging her father. *The Grandmaster* directed by Wong Kar-wai. © Annapurna Pictures 2013. All rights reserved.

Introduction

Zhang Ziyi, a Chinese A-lister who has a martial arts background but whose screen roles span a wide array of genres including romance and melodrama, distinctively impresses the world audience with her fighting heroine characters and spectacular dynamism. After her debut appearance in Zhang Yimou's *The Road Home* (1999), the actress rose to stardom in Ang Lee's Hollywood-produced martial arts hit, *Crouching Tiger, Hidden Dragon* (2000). Co-starring with prominent action stars Chow Yun-fat and Michelle Yeoh, Zhang vividly played a wild, self-centered, and headstrong swordswoman named Jen who is able to display spectacular kineticism and an energetic physique, electrifying the audience with her personality. The phenomenal success of the film won Zhang her first role in Hollywood the next year, as a henchwoman of an underworld boss in *Rush Hour 2* (2001), a star vehicle featuring Jackie Chan. After championing a promising start to her acting career, Zhang was cast in a roster of Chinese or pan-Asian co-productions including *Zu Warriors* (2001), *Musa* (2001), *Hero* (2002), *House of Flying Daggers* (2004), *The Banquet* (2006), and *Forever Enthralled* (2008). All these titles were period blockbusters that required the actress's acrobatic skill and corporeal agility to various degrees. Zhang's non-action features—such as *2046* (2004), *Memoirs of a Geisha* (2005), and *Sophie's Revenge* (2009)—capitalized on her association with the martial arts genre.[1] In 2013, Zhang's compelling yet contentious martial arts persona was overtly reinvigorated in Wong Kar-wai's *The Grandmaster* (2013), a cinematic realization of the auteur's vision of the grandmaster Ip Man. The film centrally features a female martial artist named Gong Er (played by Zhang Ziyi) to retell the story of the wing chun master. As an utterly fictional character, absent in other Ip Man movies, Gong Er is an imperative character in both diegetic and extradiegetic terms, propelling the plot and cementing Zhang's status as a martial arts performer. In view of such a prolific profile in action cinema, however, Zhang can hardly be categorized and appraised under the rubrics of martial arts stardom in any conventional sense. While Zhang establishes a charismatic action appeal on-screen, the appeal is perplexed by affectivity and a transcendental sensibility, the qualities that are more emotional and spiritual than corporeal, shaping an elusive and equivocal image. Her star phenomenon illuminates parameters other than body-focused choreography and the physical prowess of representing and interpreting the female fighter identity. This chapter, hence, serves as an exploratory effort of Zhang's alternative martial arts stardom and its representational politics against the backdrop of transnational blockbuster filmmaking and technological intervention.

One premise of this chapter is that the traditional paradigm of approaching and appraising female martial arts personae which emphasizes dexterity, precision, and clarity seems insufficient in an era marked by multiply coded and hypermediated bodies on-screen. Scholars have examined the expansion of the popular action image from local or regional markets to the transnational connections in recent decades. Since the 1970s, Hong Kong martial arts films and stars have been a widely circulated cultural export, and one which heralded aspirations in the West. Chinese icons such as Bruce Lee, Jackie Chan, Jet Li, Donnie Yen, and Chow Yun-fat are successful border-crossers to Hollywood, perpetuating their hyper-mobility, martial artistry, and chivalric image, the salient aspects of their established personae. The 1990s witnessed the rise of the global entertainment economy and technological innovations, which reconstructed action personae, making them more presentable to a worldwide audience. The martial arts icons, all of whom hew closer to the prototype of Hollywood's action heroes, reveal little of the culturally indigenous orientation of martial arts in Chinese-language cinema and appeal more to "global" motifs and morals.[2] The prevalent use of CGI in blockbuster filmmaking, furthermore, expands the reach of the cinematic kung fu and martial arts personalities, allowing those talents who do not know martial arts to play kung fu masters. This advance signaled the emergence of a new visual vocabulary that provided novelty to martial arts aficionados while questioning the authentic kinetic bodies.

While martial arts film is a predominantly male-oriented space, Zhang Ziyi's crossover precedents—such as Michelle Yeoh and Cheng Pei-pei—are acclaimed for their hard-fighting image and knight-errantry, highlighting their capacity to compete with their male counterparts. Gunplay, kung fu, and martial arts are established as masculine genres composed of male-focused narratives. A female cycle of the genres emerged in the 1970s (King Hu's *xia nu* swordplay films) and 1980s (Hong Kong's gunplay), which opened up a new horizon for the construction and reception of martial arts identities. Arguing in the context of refocusing female stars in the action genre, Lisa Funnell postulates that transnational action films portray flexible subjects, who are able to represent and appropriate multiple, fluid, and contradictory identities. Funnell attempts to deconstruct the East-West binarism that has troubled many discussions of the Western imagination of China, rejecting reductive readings that merely critique the reification of the Other in the Western popular discourse. She, nonetheless, ponders how the global appeal of Chinese action stars has widely shaped and perplexed the production of gendered and racialized identities in Hollywood.[3] Following Funnell's postulation, this chapter posits indeterminacy as a modality for reimagining female fighting personae on-screen and negotiating the worth of the kinetic performance. Focusing on Zhang Ziyi as an example, this chapter employs *Crouching Tiger, Hidden Dragon* as a point of departure, navigates through *Hero*, and then scrutinizes *The Grandmaster*. I argue that Zhang's martial arts presence is romanticized and virtualized; this presence is shaped by the authorial intent of Wong Kar-wai, resulting in an indeterminate subjectivity. By so doing, the analysis sheds light on alternative approaches from the action- or body-oriented and violence-driven approaches that are sustained in the patriarchal structure of inquiring about martial arts personae.

Scholarship reveals that studies of Zhang Ziyi are largely situated in the transnational context of Chinese filmmaking and stardom through the lenses of new femininity,[4] linguistic flair,[5] and scandal.[6] Only scant critical attention is devoted to her martial arts persona. To fill the gap, this chapter examines how Zhang Ziyi's martial arts image evolves in conjunction with affective motivations, transcendental sensibilities, and virtualized aesthetics on screen as well as how the logic of indeterminacy provides emergent tropes to the rhetorics of female crossover stardom. Hence, this account serves as an addition to the current literature of Zhang Ziyi's starscape and female fighting stardom in the cultural and technological junctures more broadly.

The Logic of Indeterminacy and Zhang Ziyi's Martial Arts Being

This chapter intervenes in the explorations of female star identities by probing Zhang's martial arts-based starscape through the conceptual lens of indeterminacy. While the conception of determinacy has attained overwhelming influence in Western philosophical inquiry, recent scholarship indicates an increasing recognition of the significance of indeterminacy.[7] In Greek, the determinate signifies "limit" and the indeterminate "negation," or "unlimited."[8] In his discussion of the Transcendental Ideal, Immanuel Kant formulates the principle of determination underpinned on the modularity of determinability: "every concept, in regard to what is not contained in it, is indeterminate [*unbestimmt*], and stands under the principle of determinability: that of every two contradictorily opposed predicates only one can apply to it, which rests on the principle of contradiction."[9]

Following Kant's logical thread, every concept can be made determinate by applying only one side of the pair of oppositions to the concept. It is implied that if both predicates were applied to the same concept, indeterminacy arises. The Greek philosopher Parmenides, in an elaborate note, illuminates the thought of being. He argues that the multiplicity of existing things and their mutant forms and motions are but an appearance of a single eternal reality ("Being"), thus giving rise to the Parmenidean principle that "all is one." For Parmenides, the determinate is *one*: it is just Being, and it does not exceed its own limit.[10] The indeterminacy of Non-being is *dissolution into many*: it is and it is not.

Taking cues from Kant and Parmenides, I hypothesize Zhang Ziyi as an indeterminate subject on which seemingly contradictory attributes can predicate. I posit two sets of attributes including: first, corporeality and spirituality; and second, reality and virtuality. Both sets of contrasting attributes are enveloped and mobilized by Wong Kar-wai as an auteur when they pivoted on the discourse generated by *The Grandmaster*. I delineate how Zhang's fighting persona puts at the forefront a set of ethereal motivations and shapes a sublime performance, as well as how it is mediated by the use of cinematographic spectacle and CGI. I contend that Zhang's screen embodiment mediates varied and divergent star subjectivities and values in the Hong Kong-Chinese nexus, portending a new martial arts Being which destabilizes the reality of determinacy comprising clarity, adroitness, and kineticism in a crossover frontier. Whereas literature has asserted that indeterminacy is the negation of *determinatus*, which signifies "limit,"[11] I reject such a convenient claim. Instead, I argue for not a negation but a negotiation, which denotes a process, or a becoming operating as a condition of an infinite quantity of epistemological orientations and interpretations. The indeterminacy reverberates the very idea of cinema functioning as a public sphere, with the term "public" implying "a discursive matrix or process through which social experience is articulated, interpreted, negotiated and contested in an intersubjective, potentially collective and oppositional form."[12] Movie stars are one of the vehicles in such a process. As Richard Dyer posits, movie stars represent shared cultural values and attitudes as well as promote a certain ideology.[13] By virtue of being experienced and individuated (embodying a general social norm in a unique image), stars serve to defuse the political meanings that form the inevitable yet potentially explosive or offensive point of departure of all media messages. By identifying stars' cinematic presence as a site for interrogating conflicting social values, this chapter wrestles with the limit of indeterminacy in the context of film stardom, exploring to what extent fighting heroines in pan-Chinese co-productions represent action performances and scrutinizing body politics in new light. To its critical end, this chapter charts novel contours of the production and reception of Chinese female martial arts stardom.

From *Crouching Tiger* to *Hero*: Zhang Ziyi's Early *Xia Nu* Appeal

Zhang Ziyi's image in *Crouching Tiger, Hidden Dragon* can be regarded as a twenty-first-century extension of the 1960s and 1970s "woman warrior" image, unfolding feminist themes and suggesting neoliberalist impulses. As a renewed "crossover" form of new-style *wuxia pian*, *Crouching Tiger* proves that the imaginary space generated by martial arts films can be adapted for a transnational audience with or without a background knowledge of Chinese history, through a conscious translation of the local into the global in the production process.[14] Co-starring with Michelle Yeoh and Cheng Pei-pei, notable action actresses from two different generations, Zhang Ziyi plays a heroine who is "active, mobile, physically strong,"[15] embodying the spirits of chivalry and righteousness. Copious studies have offered a feminist reading of Jen, Zhang's character, who is dedicated to the pursuit of freedom with her attempts to break free from social constraints in the patriarchal *jianghu* world, even at the expense of her aristocratic privileges. Her youthful spirit is established in contrast to another mature heroine in the film, Michelle Yeoh's Yu Shu Lien, who dedicated herself to a lifelong pursuit of honor and justice, without discovering the consequences of unfulfilled love until her final days. Chinese audiences generally consider the female consciousness and the notion of individualism as "part of the West's cultural fabric," becoming tools to attract Western audiences.[16] Jen's westernized, hybrid imaginary is, moreover, mimicked and reproduced in other media like celebrity endorsements. Consider the popular Visa card commercial which features Zhang as a diner in a Chinese restaurant who complains that "the soup is too salty,"[17] followed by a high-caliber fight that erupts between the Asian heroine and the white knives- and choppers-wielding chefs. The advertisement presents Zhang as a powerful choreographed agent, capitalizing on her established screen appeal as a martial arts film star in the service of the Visa brand. This, too, hints at the mounting significance of Chinese stars in global commercial and cultural markets.

Zhang Ziyi's multivalent embodiment continues in the martial arts epic *Hero* (2002), which stresses emotionality more than physicality. With an impressive cast of bankable Chinese stars including Tony Leung Chiu-wai, Maggie Cheung, Jet Li, and Donnie Yen, *Hero* is the first movie from mainland China to become a global sensation, securing its historical status in the Chinese-language cinema.[18] The ensemble film presents a *Rashomon*-like story unraveled in an array of flashbacks, suggesting the instability of meaning and the indeterminacy of such ideas as truth, righteousness, and peace in the discursive frame of politics and power.[19] Set in ancient China, the plot depicts the Emperor Qin who becomes the target of three assassins, Long Sky (Donnie Yen), Broken Sword (Tony Leung Chiu-wai), and Flying Snow (Maggie Cheung), until a warrior named Nameless (Jet Li) paradoxically emerges to defend him. Zhang Ziyi, who was in her second role both in a Zhang Yimou movie and in the martial arts genre, plays one of the two key female characters called Moon, a faithful student of Broken Sword. In the film, Zhang only has fifteen minutes of screen time.[20] Yet her exceptionally brief appearance gives gravity in specific terms of augmenting the potential of *xia nu*'s emotional appeal. The immediate function of Zhang's role pertains to the ambiguous relationship that her character Moon develops with Broken Sword, which relationship sunders the alliance between Broken Sword and Flying Snow. Moving beyond the diegesis, Moon exhibits the function of magnifying affectivity, as she is able to appeal to audience identification. This occurs in the final flashback scene, in which Flying Snow engages Broken Sword in a duel. Flying Snow kills Broken Sword and then ends her life with the same sword as Moon manages to arrive, seeing the two lovers lie fallen together. The function of Moon in this scene is to witness and to mourn.[21] As the camera captures, Moon's cries are silenced, muffled, and intensified in a gradual manner. Her emotional appeal permits the viewers to engage in this romanticized yet tragic moment through the eyes of Moon. This engagement is later extended to the narrative of *tian xia*, the film's pivotal theme.[22]

The female fighter image of both Flying Snow and Moon is tied to romantic imaginary and emotional undercurrents. As Louise Edwards notes, the heroine model in *Hero* extends the twentieth-century typology of a "romancing" woman warrior.[23] The right to love and the importance of romantic love to individual happiness was a crucial motif in twentieth-century storytelling.[24] Moreover, the narrative of *Hero* seems to present the two heroines in a way that they fight in unstable emotional states, unlike their male counterparts.[25] Two instances include Moon in her confrontation with Flying Snow in avenging the death of Sword as well as Flying Snow in her fight with Nameless facing circles of the Qin troops.

These sequences indicate their inability to tread beyond the technical virtuosity to achieve a broader spiritual horizon demanded by superb warriors. The heroines' emotional precariousness is expressed through the highly lyrical visuals, Zhang Yimou's famous signature. One may observe that the spectacular fight between the two rival heroines exemplifies the director's "color narrative" (colors as the key narrative elements)[26] and smooth camera movement. Iconography including fallen leaves and flowy clothes romanticizes the scene, making the female body a vehicle of ephemerality more than gravity. In an abstract and emotional threshold, the female fighters are rigorously engaged in each other. As Robert Ebert asserts, *Hero*, with sporadic insertions of brutality, displays "how the martial arts genre transcends action and violence and moves into poetry, ballet and philosophy."[27]

The Grandmaster: An Ip Man-themed Auteurist Epic that Configures a Female Fighter

A rich flow of emotions in the construction of a female fighting persona infuses *The Grandmaster*, an epic that reconfigures the tale of Ip Man in Wong Kar-wai's own tropes. As Wong expresses, Ip Man is a figure who often seems mysterious to Wong Kar-wai even after several movies that have been made about the wing chun master.[28] He came to the project primarily because of his curiosity about the iconic Bruce Lee, who is famously the kung fu disciple of Ip Man. The production of Wong's epic coincided with the trend of producing Ip Man-themed movies in the late 2000s and 2010s in Hong Kong cinema. Other installments of the Ip Man cycle mostly cast martial artists to play the titular role, markedly in two Donnie Yen vehicles, *Ip Man* (2008) and *Ip Man 2* (2010), followed by the prequel *The Legend Is Born: Ip Man* (2010), featuring Denise To (Hong Kong martial artist-actor), and the spin-off *Master Z: Ip Man Legacy* (2018), starring Max Zhang (Chinese actor-wushu athlete).[29] Taking a different tack, Wong cast his favorite actor, Tony Leung Chiu-wai, even though he does not know kung fu. Considering his stature and the high-profile nature of the project, Leung's harsh martial arts training in preparation for the role, as well as his philosophical approach to playing the character, became popular topics in entertainment news.[30] Leung's Ip Man persona appears gentle and erudite rather than physically driven, matching his status as a profound and spirited actor. Wong's conscious casting of Leung is premised on the auteur's reading of Ip Man: a martial artist more like an aristocrat who likely engages in combat more as an artist than as a fighter,[31] echoing Gary Bettison's remark that Wong "both roughens the Ip Man legend and assimilates it to his authorial program."[32] Reprising the Ip Man brand, *The Grandmaster* was released in different cuts in different places—including Hong Kong, mainland China, Europe, and the United States—to cater to sundry commercial and festival markets.[33] The film's worldwide gross is approximately USD63 million, becoming Wong's most commercially successful theatrical release by far.[34]

Wong made *The Grandmaster* as a dialogue with the wushu tradition chiefly by projecting a vision of *jianghu*, a ubiquitous imaginary in the martial arts genre.[35] Literally meaning "rivers and lakes," and, by extension, "all corners of the world," *jianghu* is an imagined space populated with martial arts heroes (*xia ke*) or heroines (*xia nu*) bound together by a code of honor (*xia*).[36] Habitually translated as "the martial arts world," the *jianghu* connotes the image of a wandering life, "beyond the reach of the government [which] has for a long time been recognized as a key to understanding the Chinese popular imagination."[37] Wong Kar-wai is renowned for his long-time connection with *jianghu*. As scholarly works and biographical accounts tell, he grew up immersed in the culture propagated by martial arts films and novels and his own universe is richly coded by the forms borrowed from or inspired by the notion of *jianghu*.[38] In the auteur's oeuvre, titles like *Ashes of Time* (1994) use the world of *jianghu* to tell a *wuxia* tale with novel insight. Based on a four-volume saga by martial arts novelist Louis Cha, who modernized the long-standing genre in the 1950s, *Ashes of Time* recalibrates the genre by exploring the subjectivity of time, the impossibility of returning to the past, and difficulties in relationships through profound dialogues and visual aesthetics instead of combat choreography.[39]

The Grandmaster proves Wong's renewed passion in *jianghu*, reinventing representational politics so that women can take center stage. Part of the film's storytelling and the construction of the Ip Man persona are driven by the hero's interaction with Gong Er. Gong Er is a fictional character, a strong-willed and independent martial arts expert who strives to defy the limits of society.[40] Wong's choice to introduce a "fake" figure in the "real" story of a wing chun master intriguingly underscores questions pertaining to the mythic origins of this martial art itself. According to Benjamin Judkins and Jon Nielson (2015), wing chun, similar to many southern Chinese arts, is a key example of how martial arts bear a "creation myth" that conveys inhabitants' lived experience and are usually considered as a kind of social construction, which guides the performance of the art and the actions of the community.[41] The traditional wing chun creation myth centrally revolves around a female fighter named Yim Wing Chun. As the only disciple of Ng Mui, a Buddhist nun with ties to the Shaolin Temple,[42] Yim purportedly built on her master's teachings and developed for herself the martial art style now known as wing chun. Furthermore, the persona of Yim bears certain features of the heroines cited in the legends of Fujianese White Crane and Chuka Shaolin—for example, Fang Qi Niang and Leow Fah Shih Koo[43]—indicating the possible proximity, in both mythological and stylistic terms, between different martial arts in southern China.

Wong's invention of Gong Er continues the imaginary of female fighters and is inspired by female martial artists in the Republic era, as well as polished and competent "Renaissance women" including the renowned Soong sisters.[44] As Ip Man's rival-comrade, the heroine challenges Ip Man to regain her family's honor while being emotionally attached to him.[45] The reality of the emotional relationship and the forbidden romance leads to some profound dialogues about the meaning of life, intensifying the existentialist temper of the narrative.[46] In addition to the romantic entanglement, Gong Er's martial bagua expertise diversifies the martial arts representations of Ip Man movies. Whereas wing chun is a relatively rigid system with moves that are "plain and nondescript,"[47] in Wong's words, Gong Er's action involves more "dramatic moves and turns,"[48] which are performed by Zhang with rhythm and flexibility.

Beauty, Romanticism, Spirituality

The Grandmaster's female embodiment of jianghu pivots on Wong Kar-wai's evocation of nostalgia as a state of emotion, which constitutes the auteur's Romantic methodology.[49] According to Margaret Hillenbrand, the nostalgia of Wong's films is linked to "states of love, or, more precisely, lovesickness."[50] Wong's nostalgic ethos is manifested in the film's nonlinear supply of affect that cuts across the representational planes of romanticism and beauty. Critics are inclined to describe Wong's oeuvre as "beautiful and intimate,"[51] although the auteur has denied a conscious intention to create beautiful shots or films.[52] In The Grandmaster, Wong concentrates on the beauty of the past and the historicity of kung fu, unveiling the interlacing of yearning with choreography. Wong romanticizes the past, celebrating clichéd Confucian virtues of honor, loyalty, and filial responsibility while juxtaposing them to modern times.[53] Cinematographically, Wong uses slow motion and close-ups to strengthen the atmospheric tension in combat scenes. Fluid and elusive, Gong Er's adroit moves become a visual tool to guide the audience between the past and the present, alongside Leung-as-Ip's soulful voiceover which offers insights into the art of wing chun.

The presence of *The Grandmaster*'s heroine vacillates between realms of spirituality and corporeality, premised on but not limited to the ostensibly antithetical positions of the two attributes. Philosophical traditions in the West have seen a long-standing distinction between the body and the soul, contending that the body is dismembered and separated from the spiritual.[54] Recent decades have witnessed an emergence of a diversity of views that unfolds a tendency of fusing body and spirit. Philosophers such as John Dewey and Martin Heidegger strive to collapse the distance between body, mind, and world by diffusing the barrier of the subject/object duality.[55] The discourse of martial arts being, incarnated by Zhang Ziyi in *The Grandmaster*, corroborates the bodily stamina and fighting dexterity of Gong Er but it does not suggest that the corporeal and the spiritual are determinately contesting modalities. Rather, it is inclined to an open-ended, flexible, and erratic appeal, which underscores the potential significance of spirituality in reconfiguring the female fighter persona.

Spirituality informs the mode of poetics of *The Grandmaster*, shaping the sublime being of Gong Er and enabling spectators' emotional access to the heroine. Gong Er's sublime being reaches its apotheosis in the film's ending, which features the bed-ridden heroine and her recollections of childhood. The flashback shows the young Gong observing her father practicing the "sixty-four hands" technique in the snow. The scene segues into the adult Gong duplicating the kung fu moves under the bright sunshine, indicating how she grew up in the shadow of the patriarch and painfully endeavored to perfect his techniques. Captured in a montage of close-ups, bird's-eye-view shots, and wide shots in slow motion, the heroine's kinetic presence is intercut with extreme close-ups of snowflakes, branches, and plum blossoms, suggesting that kung fu harmonizes with nature.[56] The montage is paired with another strand of her memory featuring an indoor scene of Gong Baoshan instructing his young daughter with some bagua moves. Zhang-as-Gong's voiceover emerges and guides the audience to revisit her past. The self-narration ends with the line (spoken in a calm yet melancholic tone): "From my father, I discern not *zhao* (tactic) but *yi* (righteousness). Those were my happiest days." (在我爹身上，我看到的不是招，而是義，那是我最開心的日子) This implies that Gong Er's perception of martial arts transcends materiality to reach metaphysicality, revealing a kind of contentment that is irretrievable.

Competent yet vulnerable, Gong Er displays an immaterialized presence, which is coded by fatalism. According to Sandy Lo, the beauty of the heroine does not refer to the beauty of chivalry, as many other martial arts narratives unfold, but is the beauty shaped by her inability to free herself from the potential constraints of fate.[57] If *Crouching Tiger* portrays Zhang-as-Jen as able to free herself eventually, *The Grandmaster* seems to suggest the opposite. In many scenes of *The Grandmaster*, the heroine shows her ruminative resolution to continue her father's legacy, but the resolution is thwarted by her subsequent predicament. The final flashback reveals Zhang-as-Gong as absorbed and trapped by her memory, shaping a fighting persona along the axes of pain and suffering, and making it appear more tragic than naïve. In this scene, the camera rests on a medium close-up of the heroine, wearing a gratified smile and tearful eyes, looking at someone out of the frame. Zhang's performance denotes a sense that she is freeze-framed in her own time and unfolds a sense of immortality or a "superhuman agency,"[58] in Stephen Teo's terms, resonating with a recurring thesis of Wong's oeuvre, "Romanticism is eternal."[59]

Virtualizing the Heroine's Presence

The Gong Er persona is romanticized and de-essentialized by technologized spectacle, buttressing the fluid, amorphous potentials of the female fighter image in martial arts cinema. Since the 2000s, blockbuster martial arts or kung fu productions—such as *House of Flying Daggers* (2004) and *Kung Fu Hustle* (2004)—have developed a common language, which is promoted by digital technologies and constitutes a new "cinema body,"[60] the ultimate spectacle of our cinematic experience of martial arts films. The phenomenon also leads to debates such as how technology enhances or hinders the conventional mode of martial arts screen representations. In *The Grandmaster*, certain scenes display CG-mediated visuals, which virtualize the narrative space and displace martial arts identities.[61] Consider the frequently quoted train terminal scene, the climactic confrontation between Gong Er and Ma San (Max Zhang), reportedly one of three key fight scenes in the film for Wong during production.[62] Set in 1940, the scene portrays Gong Er seeking vengeance from Ma San, Gong Baoshan's renegade disciple who killed the old master and usurped the daughter's place in the household (this plot point contributes to the heroine's fatalistic character arc). The heroine appears as a femme-fatale-like fighter, described by New-York-based film journalist Anne-Katrin Titze as "a martial arts Anna Karenina with fur cuffs."[63] As the combat ends, Gong Er defeats Ma and takes back the Gong school, but she is severely injured in the process.

Martial authenticity is shown in the scene. In the duel, Gong Er deploys the graceful but deadly bagua, which is derived from the established martial arts system.[64] bagua involves many adept turns and hand positions, allowing the combatant to use different angles of defense and attack.[65] Ma uses the crushing-fist technique of xingyiquan (shape and intent fist), a style bearing a military root and employing full-body coordination to instigate bursts of power that can turn the fighter into a human weapon.[66] The styles used by Gong Er and Ma San encapsulate the two sides of old Gong's legacy, for each of them inherits a strand of their school's skill. Ma was able to merge the two styles, which is what many practitioners have endeavored to do, because the styles complement each other well.[67]

The martial arts bodies of Gong Er and Ma San are, at times, troubled by the overt technological mediation in cinematic and digital terms. According to Wong Kar-wai, the essence of the moves is captured by precise cinematography.[68] This strategy seems reminiscent of certain preceding auteurs, such as King Hu who is well-known for his use of camera work, which augments the dynamism and fluidity of Cheng Pei-pei's movements in *Come Drink with Me* (1966).[69] Rather than emphasizing the number of moves that appear unbroken and are completed within a single take, as Leon Hunt's cinematic authenticity suggests, the fight at the train station requires editing to present the moves of Zhang Ziyi, focusing on not how real but how poetic they look.[70] As Bill Desowitz points out, Wong Kar-wai orchestrates the fights as "silent ballets," characterized by the presence of smoke and snow that highlights "an element of poetry."[71] Likewise, Steven Boone extrapolates that the movie's combat sequences in general are tremendously poetic, like "majestic dances" and "philosophical conversations."[72] Such a mix of martial and dance components is stipulated by Zhang's slim and flexible body-build, mirroring her status as a youth dance champion.[73]

The virtual spectacle apparently erases codes of martial authenticity, making it less culturally oriented and more globally pleasing. In his analysis of the cultural politics of kung fu, Siu-leung Li remarks upon the "disappearance of kung fu,"[74] describing the emergence of a more universal action choreography that disseminates transnationally, best typified by Hollywood's famous sci-fi extravaganza, *The Matrix* (1999). It facilitates the transition from the focus on the heroic body (representation of "real" kung fu) to the special effects (so-called "wire fu").[75] Li contends that the new kung fu aesthetic illustrates a "dilemma of representation," originating from the tensions between "the tradition and the modern, the mimetic and the non-mimetic modes of discourses [that] are coexistent and co-extensive in the filmic imaginary."[76] This dilemma gives rise to the "incoherence, contradictions and instabilities of its meanings in circulation."[77] The tensions involved here point to reflections about the reality of indeterminacy which do not designate any form of the idealized virtual body. As Zhang Ziyi is not a martial artist, her kinetic body has not been a locus to authenticate kung fu. Nor does her body delineate a realm to make kung fu stabilized in its representation when CGI is applied to it.

This forms an interesting contrast to the fighting persona of Michelle Yeoh in the Hollywood sensation, *Everything Everywhere All at Once* (2022), co-directed by Daniel Kwan and Daniel Scheinert. In this action-packed sci-fi hit, Yeoh plays an aging Chinese-American immigrant named Evelyn who runs a laundromat with her husband and begins an adventure in multiverse realities in which she possesses the ability to fight. Obviously, the casting of Yeoh capitalizes on the actress's established image as a transnational Asian icon who can fight and perform stunts by herself. However, most of the action in this movie is digitally generated, and the technologized spectacle marginalizes and trivializes Yeoh's kinetic persona. Moreover, the narrative does not provide a space for (authentic) kung fu to appear, which problematizes if it does not negate the character's agency as a (trained, cultivated) fighter. Ironically, Yeoh-as-Evelyn did appear as an action movie celebrity, but it only exists as fantasy in one of the alternative universes to which the heroine's mind is led. If Zhang's character in *The Grandmaster* serves to facilitate an interrogation of presence and absence, appearance and disappearance, which results in a character whose very existence is indeterminate, then Yeoh's persona in *Everything Everywhere All at Once* effectively signals the disappearance of martial agency, of the training and cultivation required to be(come) a martial artist, which invites further explorations of how cinematic martial arts can/should be understood and how action stars can be (re)configured on-screen. In an era when CGI is virtually ubiquitous in action films, the kinetic mimicry is eclipsed by the conscious aestheticization and staging of digital spectacles, while female embodiment epitomizes its potential to transcend models of representation in cultural, generic, and gendered terms. As Vivian Lee expounds: "to say the spectacle is the hero is not to reiterate the predominance of homogenizing technology over human action or agency; rather, it implies an ongoing inquiry into the dynamics between technology, cultural production, and the lived and imagined realities of contemporary society."[78]

Conclusion

Zhang Ziyi's diversely coded, culturally ambivalent fighting persona demonstrates the global currency of martial arts identities and distinguishes her from other female fighting stars. By trading in absence and uncertainty, Zhang appears as an indeterminate subject in martial arts cinema with an image that reveals apparently contradictory attributes: corporeality and spirituality as well as reality and virtuality. As exemplified in her early appearances in *Crouching Tiger, Hidden Dragon* and *Hero*, Zhang has engineered an appeal that showcases other dimensions than the physical vigor and hyper-kinetic movements of martial arts films. Emphasis is often put on emotional undercurrents and the lyrical visuals in combat scenes. The agile yet vulnerable persona continues in *The Grandmaster* and is largely driven by the authorial intent of Wong Kar-wai. As an epic vindicating the auteur's treatment of Ip Man and his execution of romantic authorship, the film reinvents the *jianghu* imaginary in which women can position themselves at center stage. Eminently romanticized, Zhang's *xia nu*-style personification of Gong Er is marked by ethereal consciousness, diversifying the female fighter image. Her persona exhibits a mutating stardom with an absence of determinacy, portending a new representational order for the genre of martial arts cinema in the digital mediascape.

Notes

1   Leung Wing-Fai, "Zhang Ziyi: The New Face of Chinese Femininity," in *East Asian Film Stars*, eds. Leung Wing-Fai and Andy Willis (Basingstoke: Palgrave Macmillan, 2014), 65.

2   Vivian Lee, "Virtual Bodies, Flying Objects: The Digital Imaginary in Contemporary Martial Arts Films," *Journal of Chinese Cinemas* 1, no. 1 (2006): 11.

3   Lisa Funnell, *Warrior Women: Gender, Race, and the Transnational Chinese Action Star* (Albany: State University of New York Press, 2014), 15–17.

4   Leung, "Zhang Ziyi."

5   Dorothy Wai Sim Lau, "On (Not) Speaking English: The 'Phonic' Personae of Transnational Chinese Stars in the Global Visual Network," *Journal of Chinese Cinemas* 12, no. 1 (2018): 20–40.

6   Dorothy Wai Sim Lau, "Asian Celebrity Capital in Digital Media Networks: Scandal, Body Politics and Nationalism," in *Media in Asia: Global, Digital, Gendered and Mobile*, ed. Youna Kim (London and New York: Routledge, 2022), 139–51.

7   Gregory S. Moss, "The Emergent Philosophical Recognition of the Significance of Indeterminacy," in *The Significance of Indeterminacy: Perspectives from Asian and Continental Philosophy*, ed. Robert H. Scott and Gregory S. Moss (New York: Routledge, 2018), 1–47.

8   Ibid., 1.

9   Immanuel Kant, *Critique of Pure Reason*, ed. and trans. Paul Guyer and Allen W. Wood (Cambridge: Cambridge University Press, [1781/1787] 1998), 553.

10   Moss, "The Emergent Philosophical Recognition of the Significance of Indeterminacy," 2.

11   Ibid., 5.

12   Miriam Hansen, "Early Cinema, Late Cinema: Permutations of the Public Sphere," *Screen* 43, no. 3 (1993), 201.

13   Richard Dyer, *Stars* (London: British Film Institute, 1979).

14   Jinhua Dai, "Order/Anti-Order: Representation of Identity in Hong Kong Action Movies," in *Hong Kong Connections: Transnational Imagination in Action Cinema*, eds. Meaghan Morris, Siu Leung Li, and Stephen Ching-Kiu Chan (Hong Kong: University of Hong Kong Press, 2005), 93.

15   Rong Cai, "Gender Imaginations in *Crouching Tiger, Hidden Dragon* and the *Wuxia* World," *Positions: East Asia Cultures Critique* 13, no. 2 (2005), 448.

16   Huaiting Wu and Joseph Man Chan, "Globalizing Chinese Martial Arts Cinema: The Global-Local Alliance and the Production of *Crouching Tiger, Hidden Dragon*," *Media, Culture & Society* 29, no. 2 (2007), 209.

17   AusTVemporium, "Zhang Ziyi 'Salty Soup' Visa Commercial" (2008).

18   Haizhou Wang and Ming-Yeh T. Rawnsley, "*Hero*: Rewriting the Chinese Martial Arts Film Genre," in *Global Chinese Cinema: The Culture and Politics of* Hero, eds. Gary D. Rawnsley and Ming-Yeh T. Rawnsley (New York: Routledge, 2010), 92.

19   Lee, "Virtual Bodies, Flying Objects," 18.

20   Olivia Khoo, "Fifteen Minutes of Fame: Transient/Transnational Female Stardom in *Hero*," in *Global Chinese Cinema: The Culture and Politics of* Hero, eds. Gary D. Rawnsley and Ming-Yeh T. Rawnsley (New York: Routledge, 2010), 121–32.

21 Ibid., 124.

22 Ibid.

23 Louise Edwards, "Twenty-First Century Women Warriors: Variations on the Traditional Theme," in *Global Chinese Cinema*, 71.

24 Chang-Tai Hung, "Female Symbols of Resistance in Chinese Wartime Spoken Drama," *Modern China* 15, no. 2 (1989): 151–6.

25 Edwards, "Twenty-First Century Women Warriors," 72.

26 Xioyi Fu, "A Look at the Color Narrative in 'Hero,'" *Newhouse Insider* (November 13, 2017), https://newhouseinsider.syr.edu/2017/11/a-look-at-the-color-narrative-in-hero (accessed September 23, 2023).

27 Roger Ebert, "Astonishing 'Hero' Transcends the Martial Arts Genre," *RogerEbert. com* (August 26, 2004), https://www.rogerebert.com/reviews/hero-2004 (accessed September 23, 2023).

28 Kar Wai Wong and John Powers, *WKW: The Cinema of Wong Kar Wai* (New York: Rizzoli, 2016), 262.

29 Another Ip Man movie that stars a non-martial artist as the title role is *Ip Man: The Final Fight* (2013). This Herman Yau-directed epic casts veteran actor Anthony Wong Chau-san, who does not practice kung fu, as the aged wing chun master.

30 Laura Hertzfeld, "'The Grandmaster': Ziyi Zhang on Her Intense Kung Fu Training Schedule," *Entertainment Weekly* (August 21, 2013), https://ew.com/article/2013/08/21/the-grandmaster-ziyi-zhang (accessed September 23, 2023).

31 Wong and Powers, *WKW: The Cinema of Wong Kar Wai*, 265.

32 Gary Bettinson, *The Sensuous Cinema of Wong Kar-wai: Film Poetics and the Aesthetic of Disturbance* (Hong Kong: Hong Kong University Press, 2015), 128.

33 David Bordwell, "THE GRANDMASTER: Moving Forward, Turning Back," *Observations on Film Art* (March 25, 2018), http://www.davidbordwell.net/blog/2013/09/23/the-grandmaster-moving-forward-turning-back (accessed September 23, 2023).

34 Ibid.

35 Bérénice Reynaud, "Wong Kar-wai and His *Jianghu*," in *A Companion to Wong Kar-wai*, ed. Martha P. Nochimson (Sussex: Wiley-Blackwell, 2015), 82.

36 Ibid., 80.

37 Stephen Ching-Kiu Chan, "Figures of Hope and the Filmic Imagery of Jianghu in Contemporary Hong Kong Cinema," in *Between Home and World: A Reader in Hong Kong Cinema*, eds. Esther Cheung and Yiu-wai Chu (Hong Kong: Oxford University Press, 2004), 301.

38 Reynaud, "Wong Kar-wai and His *Jianghu*," 80–1.

39 Richard James Havis, "Hong Kong Martial Arts Cinema: How *Ashes of Time*, Star-Studded Wong Kar-wai Film, Gained Classic Status," *South China Morning Post* (April 16, 2020), https://www.scmp.com/lifestyle/entertainment/article/3079994/hong-kong-martial-arts-cinema-how-ashes-time-star-studded (accessed September 23, 2023).

40 Wong and Powers, *WKW: The Cinema of Wong Kar Wai*, 263. "Gong Er" literally means "Mister Two." It is a convention to call successful women Mister. See Reynaud, "Wong Kar-wai and His Jianghu," 107.

41 Benjamin Judkins and Jon Nielson, *The Creation of Wing Chun: A Social History of the Southern Chinese Martial Arts* (Albany, NY: State University of New York Press, 2015), 27–9.

42 "Ng Mui—The Nun Who Invented the Martial Arts Wing Chun," *Our Ancient History* (February 14, 2020), https://www.phdeed.com/articles/ng-mui-nun-who-invented-martial-arts-wing-chun (accessed September 23, 2023).

43 NICO, "Fang Qi Niang and the White Crane style of Yong Chun," *Kung Fu Coffee Break* (December 30, 2021), https://martialartscultureandhistory.com/en/fang-qi-niang-and-the-white-crane-style-of-yong-chun (accessed September 23, 2023), and Benjamin Judkins, "Wing Chun and the Hakka Arts: Is There a Connection?," *Kung Fu Tea* (September 28, 2012), https://chinesemartialstudies.com/2012/09/28/wing-chun-and-the-hakka-arts-is-there-a-connection (accessed September 23, 2023).

44 Reynaud, "Wong Kar-wai and His *Jianghu*," 93. As the daughters of banker and Methodist minister Charlie Soong, Ai-ling Soong, Chingling Soong, and Mei-ling Soong received their education at Wesleyan College in the United States when the Republican era began. The three women respectively married Hsiang-hsi Kung (China's finance minister in the Kuomintang [KMT] government), Sun Yat-sen (the first president of the Republic of China), and Chiang Kai-shek (the leader of the Kuomintang), shaping their distinctly vital roles in both China and Taiwan. See Reynaud, "Wong Kar-wai and His *Jianghu*," 107.

45 Hertzfeld, "'The Grandmaster.'"

46 Peter Glagowski, "World of Wong Kar-wai: *The Grandmaster*," *Flixist* (December 19, 2020), https://www.flixist.com/the-grandmaster-world-of-wong-kar-wai (accessed September 23, 2023).

47 Wong and Powers, *WKW: The Cinema of Wong Kar Wai*, 265.

48 Ibid.

49 Stephen Teo, "Wong Kar-wai's Genre Practice and Romantic Authorship: The Cases of *Ashes of Time Redux* and *The Grandmaster*," in *A Companion to Wong Kar-wai*, 522–39.

50 Margaret Hillenbrand, "Nostalgia, Place, and Making Peace with Modernity in East Asia," *Postcolonial Studies* 13, no. 4 (2010): 394.

51 David Poland, "*The Grandmaster*, Director Wong Kar Wai," in *Wong Kar-Wai: Interviews*, eds. Silver Wai-ming Lee and Micky Lee (Jackson: University Press of Mississippi, 2017), 157.

52 Jake Mulligan, "Interview: Wong Kar-wai," in *Wong Kar-Wai: Interviews*, 162–3. Wong Kar-wai's original response reads, "I never want to make beautiful pictures. I just want to make sure it's right"; "No . . . No. I'm not going to frame a beautiful shot [for the sake of beauty]."

53 Debadrita Sur, "Exploring Art and Action through Wong Kar-wai Film 'The Grandmaster'," *Far Out Magazine* (July 24, 2021), https://faroutmagazine.co.uk/wong-kar-wai-film-the-grandmaster (accessed September 23, 2023).

54 Pauline Phemister, "Corporeal Substances and the 'Discourse on Metaphysics,'" *Studia Leibnitiana* 33, no. 1 (2001): 68.

55 "Corporeality and Spirituality in the Avant Garde," *The Amoeba Weeps* (n.d.), https://www.huckhodge.com/corporeality-and-spirituality-in-th (accessed September 23, 2023).

56 Teo, "Wong Kar-Wai's Genre Practice and Romantic Authorship," 538.

57 Sandy Hsiu-chih Lo, "Light and Shadow of *Jianghu*: Peering into the Contemporary Political Mythology in *Crouching Tiger, Hidden Dragon*, *Hero* and *The Grandmaster*," in *The Politics of Memory in Sinophone Cinemas and Image Culture: Altering Archives*, eds. Hsiao-yen Peng and Ella Raidel (London and New York: Routledge, 2018), 176.

58 Teo, "Wong Kar-Wai's Genre Practice and Romantic Authorship," 538.

59 Ibid., 527.

60 Lee, "Virtual Bodies, Flying Objects," 13.

61 Poland, "*The Grandmaster*, Director Wong Kar Wai."

62 Bilge Ebiri, "Director Wong Kar-Wai Explains Three Key Scenes from *The Grandmaster*," *Vulture* (August 23, 2013), https://www.vulture.com/2013/08/wong-kar-wai-explains-three-scenes-from-the-grandmaster.html (accessed September 23, 2023). The other two key scenes refer to the opening scene of Ip Man fighting in the rain and the flashback of Gong Er's childhood.

63 Anne-Katrin Titze, "The Precision of a Master: Wong Kar Wai on Making *The Grandmaster*," *Eye For Film* (August 18, 2013), https://www.eyeforfilm.co.uk/feature/2013-08-18-wong-kar-wai-in-conversation-about-the-grandmaster-feature-story-by-anne-katrin-titze (accessed September 23, 2023).

64 Bordwell, "THE GRANDMASTER."

65 starspawn, "Comment on Annapurna Pictures, 'THE GRANDMASTER Train Fight,'" 2020.

66 Ibid.

67 Bordwell, "THE GRANDMASTER." .

68 Titze, "The Precision of a Master: Wong Kar Wai on Making the Grandmaster."

69 Funnell, *Warrior Women*, 59.

70 Leon Hunt, *Kung Fu Cult Masters: From Bruce Lee to Crouching Tiger* (London: Wallflower Press, 2003).

71 Bill Desowitz, "Cinematographer Le Sourd Talks Anatomy of 'The Grandmaster' Train Fight," *IndieWire* (January 14, 2014), https://www.indiewire.com/2014/01/cinematographer-le-sourd-talks-anatomy-of-the-grandmaster-train-fight-194173 (accessed September 23, 2023).

72 Steven Boone, "*The Grandmaster*," *RogerEbert.com* (August 23, 2013), https://www.rogerebert.com/reviews/the-grandmaster-2013 (accessed September 23, 2023).

73 "Zhang Ziyi," *People* 62, no. 10 (June 9, 2004).

74 Siu Leung Li, "Kung Fu: Negotiating Nationalism and Modernity," *Cultural Studies* 15, no. 3–4 (2001), 537.

75 Ackbar Abbas, *Hong Kong: Culture and the Politics of Disappearance* (Hong Kong: Hong Kong University Press, 1997), 31–2.

76 Li, "Kung Fu," 522.

77 Ibid.

78 Lee, "Virtual Bodies, Flying Objects," 25.

Chapter 12

Donnie Yen: Authenticity, Nationalism, and the Bruce Lee Legacy

Leon Hunt

Figure 27 Ip Man (Donnie Yen) defends the tradition of Chinese martial arts from Gunnery Sergeant Barton Geddes (Scott Adkins). *Ip Man 4: The Finale* directed by Wilson Yip. © Mandarin Motion Pictures 2019. All rights reserved.

Introduction

At the end of *Kung Fu Jungle* a.k.a. *Kung Fu Killer* (2014), just before the end credits, there follows a lengthy dedication to a parade of stars, stunt performers, directors, fight choreographers, and other filmmakers, including the film's star Donnie Yen, "for upholding the fine tradition of Hong Kong action cinema." Most of these people have made cameos in the film, including former Golden Harvest boss Raymond Chow, Shaw Brothers star David Chiang (now John Chiang), directors Kirk Wong and Andrew Lau, producer Ng See-yuen, and fight choreographers Yuen Bun and Tung Wai. Others—some of whom are no longer with us—appear on film posters or in action on TV screens, for example, Jackie Chan and celebrated Shaw Brothers director/fight choreographer Lau Kar-leung. Inevitably, given Donnie Yen's well-known admiration for him, one of these absent friends is Bruce Lee, delivering a flying kick in the original Hong Kong film poster for *The Big Boss* (1971).

This is a rousing, crowd-pleasing end to the film, and probably also a heartfelt one. Few in what is left of the Hong Kong film industry have done more to keep alive that "tradition" than Donnie Yen, a tradition that he himself is very much a part of, whether taking on Jet Li's Wong Fei-hung in *Once Upon a Time in China II* (1991), playing the venerable Wong's father in *Iron Monkey* (1993), or playing Ip Man in the popular four-part film series. But while Donnie Yen is the last major Chinese martial arts star, he also represents a separation between "Hong Kong action cinema" as a known global brand of cinema and Hong Kong as "Special Administrative Region." In two earlier essays,[1] I characterized Donnie Yen's stardom as "belated"; he had largely been a supporting player during Hong Kong cinema's last "golden age" of the early 1990s and was not enough of a brand name to be part of the Hollywood exodus of the late 1990s (although he has appeared in a number of Hollywood films, usually in secondary roles). His period of major stardom has coincided with a period during which Hong Kong's post-handover status has moved from "constrained autonomy" to "assimilationist direct rule,"[2] and Yen is a controversial figure in Hong Kong. While the boycott of *Mulan* (2020) went beyond Yen alone to the political statements made by its female lead Liu Yifei and filming taking place in Xinjiang amidst human rights abuses of the Uyghur people, *Ip Man 4: The Finale* (2020) drew ire for statements made by producer Raymond Wong, co-star Danny Chan (ironically playing Bruce Lee, whose "Be water" motto had been adopted by the Occupy movement), but above all for Yen sharing the stage with Xi Jinping at the Gala celebrating the anniversary of the handover in 2017.[3] In addition, Yen had posted footage of himself with Xi alongside a celebratory message about Hong Kong's return to the "Motherland." The #boycottIpMan4 campaign posted spoilers on social media, casting the film as "epitomizing the China-leaning nature of Hong Kong-Chinese collaborations that cater to the Chinese audiences' tastes at the expense of the Hong Kong audience."[4] Thus, on the one hand, he stands as the last star of his kind, possessing both the physical skills and star presence to embody *wuxia* and kung fu stardom, while, on the other, he manifests the "soft" power of kung fu being allied to the "hard" colonizing power of global China.

Whether Yen's political stance arises out of genuine conviction or pragmatism, there are equal dangers in whitewashing it—as Western celebrations of his films sometimes do—and reading the films too readily as straightforward manifestations of pro-Beijing propaganda. In any case, they need to be situated within the longer narrative of Yen's career. In his analysis of Jackie Chan's move from local to global stardom, Steve Fore characterizes it as a process of "disembedding," drawing on Anthony Giddens' notion of "the 'lifting out' of social relations from local contexts of interaction and their restructuring across indefinite spans of time-space."[5] While Chan's earlier films located his persona in a set of meanings and values specific to Hong Kong, his persona became "progressively more diffuse and less emphatically tied to a specific cultural space,"[6] leading ultimately to him finally becoming a Hollywood star. Yen's trajectory is almost the reverse of this, a case of *re-embedding.* He renounced his American citizenship in 2009 and while he continues to work in Hollywood, recently making a strong impression in *John Wick: Chapter 4* (2023) alongside Keanu Reeves, he presents himself in interviews as in no great need of American cinema, dismissing his role in the *Star Wars* film *Rogue One: A Star Wars Story* (2016) as an Orientalist cliché.[7] "I am fighting for the Chinese people," he insists in interviews,[8] but this is far from a unified embedding, split between an idea of "Hong Kong action cinema" and a nationalism that Ho-Fung Hung characterizes as "a mystical Han-centric Chinese community bounded by racial blood ties," one that has increasingly moved away from the handover promise of "one country, two systems" to a "one country" ideology that seeks to de-emphasize or even erase a distinct Hong Kong identity.[9]

Yen was born in Guangdong but, like Bruce Lee before him, grew up in the United States. His mother Mark Bow-sim was a renowned martial artist who ran the Chinese wushu Research Institute in Boston. He later joined the Beijing wushu team in which Jet Li had become a national champion. He was scouted by Yuen Woo-ping during a visit to Hong Kong and was seen as a potential rival to Jackie Chan. In fact, Yen's film debut, *Drunken Tai Chi* (1984), is a kung fu comedy that proceeds along similar lines as those for which Chan had become famous, most notably the Woo-ping-directed and Chan-starring kung fu comedy *Drunken Master* (1978). Woo-ping used Yen not only as a performer but also as a fight choreographer, and Yen would often choreograph his own fight scenes. Yen's most typical films from this period belong to the hybrid of comedy, action, and martial arts in which Chan, Sammo Hung, and others specialized. *Tiger Cage* (1988), *In the Line of Duty 4* (1989), and *Tiger Cage 2* (1990) register less as individual films than episodes in a cyclical "cinema of attractions"—watching Yen's fight scenes in those three films out of context, one could be forgiven for thinking that they all come from the same film (he even has the same opponent in all three, Michael Woods, a student of Yen's mother). Yen's character "Crazy Dragon" endures a series of comic indignities in *Tiger Cage 2*, handcuffed to Rosamund Kwan in the early half of the film, at one point urinating down his own leg while trying to relieve himself while still attached to her, before turning into a martial arts master for the climactic fights with Woods and others. Woo-ping has remained an important collaborator in Yen's career, up to and including the later Ip Man films, and they have done some of their best work together.

Like Jet Li, Yen fell into the orbit of producer-director Tsui Hark during the 1990s revival of kung fu and *wuxia* films. But unlike Li, and for whatever reason, Yen did not seem to be regarded as a leading man, except on television, where in 1995 he starred in a remake of Bruce Lee's *Fist of Fury* (1972), the first time his admiration for the late star manifested explicitly on-screen. Yen's most memorable film role during this period is the Qing commander who comes into conflict with

Wong Fei-hung in *Once Upon a Time in China II.* Not only are the duels with Jet Li at the peak of Hong Kong fight choreography—fighting with poles and a deadly length of wet cloth—but Yen brought subtle complexity to his villainous role. *Iron Monkey* remains a fan favorite, with a more central role for Yen as Wong Kei-ying, father of the more celebrated hero Wong Fei-hung, but the frantic undercranking of the camera perhaps sells short the genuine speed and precision that Yen possesses. There was a notable gulf between the appreciation of Yen in Western fan cults surrounding Hong Kong action cinema and his secondary status in the local film industry. Bey Logan singles him out in his *Hong Kong Action Cinema* as the standout talent among the "new dragons,"[10] and he is a prominent figure in Lisa Odham Stokes and Michael Hoover's book *City on Fire*.[11] In 1990, the fanzine *Eastern Heroes* brought him to the UK for the "Dragon Discovered" tour, including an appearance at London's cult repertory cinema the Scala.[12] But when the "Hong Kong exodus" took place in the late 1990s, Yen was not enough of a brand name for Hollywood to see him as the equal of Li, Chan, Chow Yun-fat, or Michelle Yeoh. Toward the end of the decade, he set up his own production company, Bullet Films, to direct and star in two films, *Legend of the Wolf* (1997) and *Ballistic Kiss* (1998), but neither were commercial successes.

Three key films set a new direction for Donnie Yen's career. In *Hero* (2002), he was once again Jet Li's opponent in what was a cameo role, but one with the added prestige of the new arthouse *wuxia* films. *SPL: Sha Po Lang* (2005) was a crime drama along similar lines to the successful *Infernal Affairs* trilogy (2002–3) but incorporated martial arts scenes in a "back-to-the-basics" style that played to his strengths.[13] For the first time, Yen added grappling techniques from mixed martial arts (MMA), including joint locks and chokeholds, into his fight scenes, something that has remained a component in his modern-day action films. In doing so, he revived a tradition of "authenticity"[14] that had been less prominent in 1990s kung fu and *wuxia* films (despite the participation of Jet Li and others). Yen embodied the "aura of the kung fu body"[15] in which a "cultural imaginary" of empowering martial arts skill is manifested in a performer who to some extent represents the promise of the real.[16] Bruce Lee had first embodied this ideal— both a "real" martial artist with no need of cinematic trickery and a Chinese hero fighting for his people as in *Fist of Fury* and *The Way of the Dragon* (1972). "I'm a big fan of Bruce Lee, more than anybody out there," Yen had once said in an interview. "If I don't play Bruce Lee, who is going to play Bruce Lee in Hong Kong? Who's going to portray these solid martial arts abilities with the same kind of stature? Nobody else."[17] Finally, there was *Ip Man* (2008), in which Yen would find his defining role as the Wing Chun Grandmaster most famous for being Bruce Lee's teacher, much as Li had with Wong Fei-hung. It is little wonder that these are the most written-about of Yen's films,[18] bringing together the new nationalism of post-handover Hong Kong-China cinema, the preoccupation with Bruce Lee, and a return to the authentic that allowed Yen to both play and *be* a true kung fu hero.

Leaving aside his work in Hollywood, Yen's output over the last twenty years has largely fallen into three categories. He has been prolific in a cycle of *wuxia* films, including an English-language sequel to Ang Lee's sensational *wuxia* film *Crouching Tiger, Hidden Dragon* (2000) entitled *Crouching Tiger, Hidden Dragon: Sword of Destiny* (2016), in which Michelle Yeoh reprised her role from the original film and which was directed by Yuen Woo-ping. He has continued to make modern-day action films that incorporate martial arts fight scenes. And finally, there is the revival of the classic kung fu film in the Ip Man series. I want to focus here particularly on the latter two categories for two reasons. Firstly, these are films that have traditionally relied rather more on the "authentic" martial arts performance skills of their lead actors, whereas the more fantastical feats of the *wuxia pian* feature special effects more consistently and prominently. Secondly, these are generic traditions that can be said to "belong" more properly to Hong Kong cinema, whereas the *wuxia pian* has been pan-Chinese in its development, originating in Shanghai, travelling to Hong Kong and Taiwan before becoming fully transnational in the new millennium. The kung fu film, admittedly a retrospective category when mapping its longer tradition, is usually seen to have begun with the showcasing of authentic Southern styles in the Cantonese Wong Fei-hung series that began in 1949. The hybrid action film, on the other hand, is part of the legacy of the cosmopolitan Hong Kong cinema that emerged in the 1980s. These are both endangered traditions—how will the Hong Kong crime film adapt to the National Security Law and its interpretation of "subversion," and what will become of the kung fu film when there is no one like Yen to headline it? These are the traditions that Yen, for now, is committed to keeping alive.

Managing Bruce Lee: Ip Man and Other Stories

Where Jackie Chan constructed his star persona in opposition to Bruce Lee, and Jet Li also cut a very different figure even when remaking *Fist of Fury* as *Fist of Legend* (1994), Yen's admiration for Bruce Lee has been visible both in the roles he has played (Chen Zhen, Ip Man) and in continuing the legacy of physical authenticity that in many ways runs counter to dominant fashions in contemporary martial arts cinema. Sometimes this has taken the form of virtual impersonation, as when playing Chen Zhen in the *Fist of Fury* TV series and *Legend of the Fist: The Return of Chen Zhen* (2010). The latter dresses Yen in signature Bruce Lee outfits (the white suit from *Fist of Fury*, Kato's mask and outfit from *The Green Hornet*), equips him with his iconic weapon (the nunchaku), while Yen throws in some of Lee's battle cries but also performs his own signature moves such as his mid-air double and triple kicks. More recently, he donned a fat suit in a remake of *Enter the Fat Dragon* (2020), originally a film starring and directed by Sammo Hung in 1978 that parodied the "Bruceploitation" industry of performers such as Bruce Li/Ho Chung-tao and Dragon Lee. Yen's use of MMA techniques in his fight choreography, arguably his most distinctive contribution to Hong Kong action, can also be seen as a link to Bruce Lee, whose hybridized jeet kune do is often claimed as a forerunner of MMA. Lee's fight with Kareem Abdul-Jabbar in *The Game of Death* (1972) now plays like an MMA-style battle: less graceful than most of Lee's action scenes, it is an ugly scrap that ends with Lee choking his opponent to death. Some of Yen's films are "haunted by Bruce Lee . . . *structured* by Bruce Lee . . . *induced* by Bruce Lee,"[19] but this coalesces most strikingly in the Ip Man series.

Yen has a fellow Bruce Lee star-fan in Stephen Chow Sing-chi, the comic star who is also a credible action performer in films such as *Kung Fu Hustle* (2004), in which he wears Lee's white shirt and black trousers from *Enter the Dragon* (1973) for the climactic action scenes. Chow's channeling of Lee can be seen as the desire to "reincarnate into one's favourite screen personas" in a "nostalgic style,"[20] and this is sometimes true of Yen, particularly when playing Chen Zhen. In *Legend of the Fist*, "Bruce Lee" is, at various points, a narrative reference point, a signature outfit or weapon, and, at one point, outright impersonation: Yen performs Lee's war cries solely in the dojo fight that restages the one from *Fist of Fury.* In the final fight with the Japanese master, after getting the worst of the initial round, Yen's Chen Zhen triumphs with moves that owe little to Lee. He performs different iterations of "Lee" in the course of the film, like the guises that his character adopts in his anti-Japanese resistance, but also sometimes operates without them. The difference between Chow and Yen with regard to Lee is that while Chow can more than carry an action scene, as in Yuen Woo-ping's choreography for *Kung Fu Hustle*, his reputation does not rest on them; Chow's invocations of Lee are an affectionate homage. Yen, on the other hand, seeks to continue the legacy by also establishing his own place within it as the "natural" successor to Lee.

A further connection between Lee and Yen is a tradition within the Hong Kong kung fu film (more so than in the *wuxia pian*) of nationalism, anti-colonialism, and anti-foreign sentiment. On the face of it, the anti-colonialism of the Ip Man films might not seem that different from that of the classic kung fu films of the 1970s, including Lee's. As the films travel internationally, there might even be some positives in seeing colonial Britain (as in some recent Indian films) presented as cartoon villain, condescending and corrupt. Lee is often positioned, ambiguously or contradictorily, in relation to nationalism, while at the same time representing an international outlook, both Chinese and Chinese-American. The question of Lee's belonging has been the subject of considerable debate and disagreement. Lau Tai-muk interprets his muscular presence as "a substitute for the strong but 'vanishing' motherland,"[21] while Ackbar Abbas interprets Lee's nationalism as trading on "*memories* of slights and insults suffered in the past . . . as if there were no idea who the 'enemy' really was."[22] In Yen's Ip Man films, the picture might be partial—the original colonizer is the villain, while the new one is implicitly cast as liberator in its absence—but they are very explicit about who the enemy is.

A consistent formula in the Ip Man series is that there are two conflicts to resolve—a local one involving a rival *sifu* and a more serious one with a foreign aggressor. A deleted scene reveals that originally these two conflicts would unite in the first *Ip Man* (2008), the defeated northern fighter who challenges Ip in the early scenes becoming an informer for the Japanese, who shoot him when he is no longer useful. Instead, he returns as a reformed character in *Ip Man 2* (2010), with one deaf ear from his earlier encounter with Master Ip. This will become the pattern for the series. In *Ip Man 2*, Sammo Hung's rival Hung Gar teacher Master Hung is not only hostile but working as a "go-between for the foreigners," the corrupt and racist British. But not only are their differences resolved, but Ip Man will avenge Hung's fatal match with the arrogant boxer Twister (Darren Shahlavi). Cheung Tin Chi in *Ip Man 3* is motivated by both ambition and his own poverty (he is a rickshaw puller and single father) to challenge Ip Man for the title of Wing Chun Grandmaster. Once again, this leads him to work for the villains and foreigners, but Cheung is ultimately a sympathetic, if flawed, character. Unusually, their match forms the climax of the film, with the foreign threat settled earlier for reasons I shall come back to. In *Ip Man 4: The Finale* (2019), Ip must resolve a conflict with Master Wan (Yue Wu), both a Wing Chun Grandmaster and head of the Chinese Benevolent Association in San Francisco's Chinatown, from whom Ip needs a letter of recommendation for his son to study in an American school. Wan is disapproving of Bruce Lee teaching kung fu to foreigners, including *Chinese Gungfu: The Philosophical Art of Self Defense* (1963), his cheaply produced instruction book that has been reprinted for many Lee fans over the years. Master Wan tells Ip the story of Dong Guo, who saved a wolf from hunters only to be eaten by it in place of the expected gratitude. And in some ways, the film seems to agree with the story's message—the US marines in the film have appropriated Japanese karate to the extent that it is presented as being "American." The film's main villain, a racist gunnery sergeant played by the martial arts star Scott Adkins, is hostile to Chinese kung fu as a "foreign" martial art being taught to the marines, but he combines karate with rhetoric about (implicitly white) American supremacy. The question of interacting with foreigners is left unresolved in the film—even Bruce's excitable African-American student works conflictedly with the immigration department harassing the Chinese. The spread of kung fu via Bruce Lee's rise to stardom and its adoption by the military is presented as a desirable form of soft power at the same time that Ip Man decides that he prefers his son to remain in Hong Kong for his education, having witnessed the endemic racism in America.

Yen has characterized his Ip Man as "essentially a nerd who fights well,"[23] and he lost weight to reduce his muscular frame to play the role. But Yen's Ip—in contrast with the romantic and melancholy version played by Tony Leung in Wong Kar-wai's *The Grandmaster* (2013)—might more accurately be seen as a combination of Wong Fei-hung, the Confucian man of virtue, and Bruce Lee's Chen Zhen, facing up to those who see China and the Chinese as the "Sick Man of Asia." The second half of the first *Ip Man* restages *Fist of Fury*, particularly in the dojo fight as Ip defeats and injures numerous karatekas. As Paul Bowman observes, the film elides the real reason for Ip's departure from Fo Shan to Hong Kong— Chinese communists, rather than Japanese invaders.[24] Episodes 2 to 4 will be set wholly (2 and 3) or partly (4) in the Hong Kong of 1950, 1959, and 1964 respectively, although the final film will jump forward to 1972 in its final scene as Bruce Lee arrives at his *sifu*'s funeral. "You know the foreign devils run Hong Kong," complains Kent Cheng's police officer in *Ip Man 3*, an explicit anti-colonial stance that also informs one of Yen's non-martial arts films, *Chasing the Dragon* (2017), a biopic of the Hong Kong gangster Ng Sik-ho (known as "Crippled Ho"). But while the Crown Colony can now be presented—indeed, *has to be presented*—as a corrupt empire imprisoning and exploiting Hong Kong Chinese, these films are also nostalgic for that period. *Chasing the Dragon* features the Kowloon walled city and shares with *Ip Man 4* paradigmatic shots of CGI planes flying low over Kowloon.

Siu Leung Li discerns in certain kung fu films "an underlying self-dismantling operation that denies its own effectiveness in modern life."[25] For Ip Man or Chen Zhen to convincingly oppose the Japanese occupation of Fo Shan or Shanghai, rules of engagement within a defined space must stipulate that guns be kept out of the conflict. But another question haunts the kung fu imaginary in addition to its threatened obsolescence—how effective is Chinese kung fu and the Chinese kung fu body against foreign (particularly Western) fighters and their martial arts? In the case of Bruce Lee, his white opponents prove relatively straightforward, too locked into their rigid karate forms to be able to handle his martial ingenuity—only Kareem Abdul-Jabbar proves a more formidable opponent over whom Lee barely triumphs. And while Abdul-Jabbar's ethnicity (and considerable height) sets him apart from the likes of Chuck Norris and Bob Wall, he also embodies a more abstract problem for Lee by not belonging to any recognizable style of fighting. There is a long tradition of bringing Western martial artists, sometimes from competitive backgrounds, into Hong Kong martial arts films—Yen's duels with Michael Woods in his early films, for example. The Japanese General in *Ip Man* is shown to be no match for Master Ip, but Darren Shahlavi's Twister in *Ip Man 2* and Scott Adkins' Barton Geddes in *Ip Man 4* initially look too strong for wing chun to counter effectively. How can a close-range fighting style handle their reach and power? In addition, we have already seen them destroy Master Hung (in Part 2) and Master Wan (in Part 4), both of whom have fought stalemate duels with Ip Man. What these films seem to reiterate is that most Chinese fighters and most Chinese kung fu will stand no chance against these powerful *gweilos*—only Ip Man can find a way of breaking them down and only after taking considerable punishment himself. But most telling of all is his duel with the character played by Mike Tyson in *Ip Man 3*, an iconic face-off that might put us in mind of Lee's Colosseum fight with Chuck Norris in *Way of the Dragon.* However, it might also remind us that Bruce Lee was preoccupied with an even more celebrated boxer, Muhammad Ali. The official Bruce Lee website sells T-shirts that mock up a bout between "The Dragon" and "The Greatest," and there are anecdotes about Lee claiming that he intended to fight Ali one day, but others of him conceding that Ali would probably have killed him with one punch. This is also bound up with the question of Lee's status as a "real" fighter, something that is less of an issue for Yen—"We are not martial arts fighters who want to make films," he says in an interview included with the Blu-ray of *Flash Point*, "we are filmmakers who are very good at martial arts." Quentin Tarantino's *Once Upon a Time . . . in Hollywood* (2019) imagines a fight on the set of *The Green Hornet* between Lee (arrogant, boastful) and the stuntman played by Brad Pitt, a confrontation prompted in part by Lee claiming that he would "cripple" Muhammad Ali in a fight. Pitt's character, a former marine and trained killer, dismisses kung fu fighters as "dancers." The fight is inconclusive after one round won by each, but it isn't looking good for Bruce—Pitt seems to have the measure of him, and Tarantino seems to be reasserting the superiority of American army-trained combat over fancy foreign fighting and film stars who mistake their on-screen invincibility for the real thing.

Having identified Ip Man as the best Chinese martial artist, Tyson lays down the challenge—"Let's see whose fists are fastest, yours or mine," a line of dialogue used to promote the film in the trailer. But Master Ip is not actually required to defeat him—the challenge is to last three minutes with him, which he does. It is easy to imagine the off-screen reasons for this resolution—Tyson is no Chuck Norris, willing to be the punchbag for a kung fu star, while Yen must preserve the invincibility of the titular hero. Thus, the scene used to promote the film is not its climax, appearing instead some two-thirds of the way through, giving us time to forget that there is someone who the invincible kung fu master cannot beat. Tyson's character is an ambiguous one, ostensibly the real villain of the film (with the support of the British) in wanting to buy up a school for its real estate value (the arrival of American capital) and willing to use intimidation and violence. But he also knows some Cantonese and seems to have a Chinese wife and daughter, who he immediately goes to after his duel with Ip, their standoff sufficient for him to back off. If Ip "wins," it is not by triumphing in combat but through the importance of family that the films also assert—his wife is at this point dying of cancer.

Bruce Lee, as we have seen already, weaves in and out of this series as a reference point, but he is also a growing narrative presence. Bowman calls him an "absent presence" in the first film, confined to being channeled in the dojo scene and acknowledged as Ip's most famous pupil in on-screen text at the end of the film.[26] By *Ip Man 4*, I would suggest that he can be seen as a kind of "present absence." Lee makes his first appearance as a child, already making his cocky nose-thumbing gesture, at the end of *Ip Man 2*; he tries again to persuade Master Ip to teach him at the start of *Ip Man 3* before teaching him cha-cha toward the end of the film so that he can dance with his dying wife. But *Ip Man 4* begins with Lee at the Long Beach Tournament—the first historically verifiable event in the series since the Marco Polo Bridge incident in *Ip Man*—but immediately fictionalizes it by having his *sifu* visit to see him spar and demonstrate his famous one-inch punch. Ip Man has two problem "sons" in the film, both known in different ways to have perpetuated his legacy—his soon-to-be-famous pupil and his actual son, Ip Ching, now a difficult teenager who he plans to send abroad (a plot point that blurs Lee and the younger Ip). There is a scene familiar from every Bruce Lee biopic where he is challenged and already has all his movie mannerisms in place. Then there is the matter of his book *Chinese Gungfu*, which Ip is presented with by two different people—Lee's African-American student who arrives in Hong Kong to invite him to San Francisco, and a disapproving Master Wan. The objection of older émigré Chinese to Lee teaching foreigners is a familiar strand in the Lee biography and various Lee biopics, but the matter of teaching foreigners is displaced onto the Chinese-American marine Staff Sergeant who wants to teach kung fu to marines and meets a different kind of resistance. Lee then disappears from the main body of the film, reappearing only to provide refuge to Chinese being harassed by immigration officers. In a telling moment, the refugees complain about the lack of recognition for the Chinese contribution to America and lack of equality, then one of them pauses and apologizes to Bruce for going too far. The implication is that, despite the film's insistence that "All Chinese are One Big Family," Bruce isn't quite the same as the rest of them, and the impression is reinforced by his lack of participation in the fight back. It is Ip Man who will defeat Geddes and assert that Chinese must stand up for themselves. Lee becomes absent again until paying his respects to his deceased master in the final scene. This seemingly marks an important point in Yen's negotiation of his relationship with Lee through various iterations of nationalism and authenticity. The resulting effect is of a separation between Ip Man and Bruce Lee in a series of films that largely put their faith in a "father" generation, whereas a Hong Kong that is still "young" is vulnerable to both foreigners and its own unruliness.

Surviving the Kung Fu Jungle: Yen's Modern-day Action Films

Read in this way, the Ip Man films along with *Chasing the Dragon* seem to align most evidently with a pro-Beijing stance, at least to a degree. But that is not the whole story of Yen's more recent output. Even more than the classic kung fu film, which largely takes place in Qing-era or early Republican China, the modern-day action film that mixes kung fu, gunplay, and often comedy is a distinct Hong Kong tradition, and also one that plays to all of Yen's strengths, whereas he is forced to play against his natural charisma (and his full range of martial arts ability) as Ip Man. He had shone in the Yuen Woo-ping directed action films of the 1980s, even if they were inevitably overshadowed by the films of Jackie Chan and others. *SPL* gave Yen a new lease of life as an action star, its narrative modelled on *Infernal Affairs* and displaying an unusual care with script construction and focusing on flawed police heroes—this is a subgenre with an uncertain future under Hong Kong's new anti-subversion laws. But it was also a vehicle for Yen's physical talents, shown to the full in two standout fight sequences—an alleyway confrontation with the assassin played by Wu Jing and a climactic face-off with Sammo Hung's gang boss. This type of action had not been seen in Hong Kong cinema for a while. In *Flash Point* (2007), *Special I.D.* (2013), and *Raging Fire* (2021), he plays a cop who is in some way in conflict with his superiors, sometimes a "rogue cop" with a short fuse. In *Raging Fire*, Yen's Cheung Sung-bong is after a group of former cops jailed for having killed a suspect during interrogation who now carry out a series of brutal robberies. But he is also in conflict with police top brass and business elites who oversee a culture of clientelism. As in *SPL*, where his character regrets a violent incident in his past, Yen plays a straight-edged cop in contrast with more corruptible colleagues. In all of these films, his MMA-inspired fight techniques are incorporated into the hand-to-hand action scenes.

The most interesting of Yen's recent modern-day films, *Kung Fu Jungle*, seeks to bridge the gap (not necessarily wide to begin with) between the classic kung fu film and the modern-day action film. It is again a crime film, but this time Yen is not playing a cop. Hahou Mo is a fight instructor to the police who is jailed for

Yin on the inside and yang on the outside.

Figure 28 Former martial arts champion Hahou Mo (Donnie Yen) outlines his fighting philosophy. *Kung Fu Jungle* directed by Teddy Chan. © Emperor Motion Pictures 2014.

killing his opponent in a challenge match. This time we are not in the world of compromised police officers or organized crime, but rather a serial killer narrative—in the words of the film's alternative English title, a kung fu killer. The killer Fung Yu-sau (Wang Baoqiang), born with a disability (an atrophied leg) that he has turned into a strength, is killing a series of martial arts masters in an ordered sequence that Hahou Mo immediately recognizes—specialists in fist, leg, grappling, weapons, and internal energy. This places Yen's character in a position not dissimilar to a Hannibal Lecter-type figure (he is allowed a briefly sinister smile), albeit a more benign version, the imprisoned killer who alone understands the mind of an active killer. By playing out the challenge between rival masters as a serial killer narrative, *Kung Fu Jungle* in its own way returns to the question of kung fu's place in the modern world. Fung Yu-sau is driven by the belief that "Martial arts is meant to kill"—what else is it for otherwise? He listens to the opera "Conquer the Five Battles" on a tape recorder and writes the names of his targets in Chinese calligraphy—his pathology manifests as a denial of modernity. Both "killers" are connected in different ways to mainland China and both are border-crossers in the course of the film. Fung came to Hong Kong from Hebei at the age of sixteen and speaks Mandarin. He has crossed the border over a period of twenty years, but while we are told that his main base is on the mainland, he is tracked to his grandmother's house in Tai O on Lantau island where his wife's ashes are waiting. Thus, in clan family terms, he is connected to Hong Kong, specifically a dark and archaic Hong Kong that must be eliminated from the modern Special Administrative Region.[27] Hahou Mo, on the other hand, is from Ip Man's old territory, Fo Shan, where he ran a kung fu school, the Six Mergence Sect. When he returns to Fo Shan, it is given an idyllic glow by the cinematography, a rural retreat from the high-rise modernity of Hong Kong. But he is no Ip Man—at least not yet—and begs forgiveness from his deceased master for his challenges to other sects. He wears a cord on his wrist, like Bruce Lee's medallion in *The Big Boss*, to remind him not to fight. Returned to prison at the end of the film, where he reinvents himself as a *sifu* dispensing health advice, he says in voiceover, "The thought of being number one never occurred to me again." But before that, he must inevitably fight Fung, who has worked his way through all the other great exponents of their respective styles (including a Hong Kong action star). They fight with fists and feet and then huge bamboo poles spilled from a lorry in the middle of a busy freeway, heavy vehicles speeding past and at one point over them. But it is ultimately a bullet that settles things—Charlie Yeung's police inspector shoots Fung while Hahou Mo is unconscious, which both allows him to adhere to his commitment to not kill and confirms once again the anachronistic presence of kung fu in the technological modern world.

This admittedly preposterous narrative allows for not only the maximum number of fight scenes and kung fu styles but also a reconnecting of the kung fu film to its Southern origins; Fo Shan is a relatively uncontroversial mainland location, albeit deployed in the service of a pro-China subtext. And then, of course, there is the film's end-credit tribute to this tradition of filmmaking, which gives the film an elegiac flavor.

"The Fine Tradition of Hong Kong Action Cinema"

Bruce Lee was not the first Chinese martial arts star, but he was the first of his kind, the first to manifest the "aura of the kung fu body." This is a very specific tradition that Yen has sought to keep alive alongside his commitment to the Hong Kong action cinema tradition more broadly, while at the same time negotiating the legacy of Lee in relation to his own bid for the kung fu star pantheon. The role of Ip Man and the incorporation of MMA would be central to that negotiation, both providing ways of invoking Lee without merely impersonating or paying homage to him. But he also belongs to a different moment in the history of Hong Kong and Hong Kong cinema to that of Lee—his nationalism registers differently, and while Lee's Westernized outlook complicated his Hong Kong belonging, Yen's pro-China stance inevitably compromises his status as savior of the Hong Kong action tradition. Much the same is true of Jackie Chan for similar reasons, although the peak of his stardom coincided with a less turbulent era. Now sixty at the time of writing, Donnie Yen remains productive and a formidable performer on-screen. But another specter hovers over some of his recent films—in the death of Ip Man (from cancer) at the end of Part 4, in the tribute to the late director Benny Chan at the end of his final film, *Raging Fire*, in the dedication to a "fine tradition" at the end of *Kung Fu Jungle*. As Hong Kong cinema's final kung fu star, some of the controversies surrounding Yen might make his legacy difficult to assess. There is no doubting his continuing dedication to "the fine tradition of Hong Kong action cinema," however long it might have left, but he is also complicit in the growing divide between that tradition and Hong Kong itself.[28]

Notes

1   Leon Hunt, "Too Late the Hero? The Bittersweet Stardom of Donnie Yen," in *East Asian Film Stars*, eds. Leung Wing-Fai and Andy Willis (Edinburgh: Edinburgh University Press, 2014), 143–55, and "Dragons Forever," in *The Chinese Cinema Book*, eds. Song Hwee Lim and Julian Ward (London: BFI/Palgrave Macmillan, 2018), 189–99.

2   Ho-fung Hung, *City on the Edge: Hong Kong Under Chinese Rules* (Cambridge: Cambridge University Press, 2022), 117.

3   Karen Chu, "Hong Kong Protestors Boycott 'Ip Man 4' for Donnie Yen and Producers' Pro-Beijing Stance," *The Hollywood Reporter* (December 23, 2019), https://www.hollywoodreporter.com/news/politics-news/hong-kong-protesters-boycott-ip-man-4-1264759 (accessed September 23, 2023).

4   Ibid.

5   Anthony Giddens quoted in Steve Fore, "Life Imitates Entertainment: Home and Dislocation in the Films of Jackie Chan," *At Full Speed: Hong Kong Cinema in a Borderless World*, ed. Esther C.M. Yau (Minneapolis: University of Minnesota Press, 2022), 117.

6   Ibid.

7   Zaneta Cheng, "Donnie Yen," *Prestige Hong Kong* (January 2018), https://www.zanetacheng.com/donnie-yen-cover-story-prestige-hong-kong-jan-18 (accessed September 23, 2023).

8   Rebecca Davis, "Donnie Yen Lauds Hong Kong's Return to China as He Starts New Films, 'Sleeping Dogs,' 'Golden Empire,'" *Variety* (July 7, 2020), https://variety.com/2020/film/asia/donnie-yen-mulan-sleeping-dogs-hong-kong-national-security-law-1234699338 (accessed September 23, 2023).

9   Hung, *City on the Edge*, 131.

10   Bey Logan, *Hong Kong Action Cinema* (London: Titan, 1995), 173.

11   Lisa Odham Stokes and Michael Hoover, *City on Fire: Hong Kong Cinema* (London: Verso, 1999).

12   Rick Baker, "Donnie Yen—A Dragon Discovered," in *The Essential Guide to Eastern Heroes*, ed. Lisa Tilston (London: Eastern Heroes Publications, 1995), 28–30.

13   Lisa Funnell, "Hong Kong's It/*Ip Man*: The Chinese Contexts of Donnie Yen's Transnational Stardom," in *Transnational Stardom: International Celebrity in Film and Popular Culture*, eds. Russell Meeuf and Raphael Raphael (New York: Palgrave Macmillan, 2013), 125.

14   See my *Kung Fu Cult Masters: From Bruce Lee to Crouching Tiger* (London: Wallflower Press, 2003).

15   Siu Leung Li, "The Myth Continues: Cinematic Kung Fu in Modernity," in *Hong Kong Connections: Transnational Imagination in Action Cinema*, eds. Meaghan Morris, Siu Leung Li, and Stephen Chan Ching-kiu (Hong Kong: Hong Kong University Press, 2005), 60.

16   Siu Leung Li, "Kung Fu: Negotiating Nationalism and Modernity," *Cultural Studies* 15, nos. 3–4 (2001), 516.

17   Donnie Yen quoted in Lisa Odham Stokes and Michael Hoover, "An Interview with Donnie Yen," *Asian Cult Cinema* 29 (2000), 55–6.

18   See Wenhu Hong, "Myth of Hegemonic Masculinity: A Study of Donnie Yen's Movie Images," *Comparative Literature: East and West* 16, no. 1 (2012): 83–92, and Stevey Richards, "The Patriotic Narrative of Donnie Yen: How Martial Arts Stars Reconcile Chinese Tradition and Modernity," *Celebrity Studies* 10 no. 2 (2019): 276–84.

19   Paul Bowman, *Beyond Bruce Lee: Chasing the Dragon through Film, Philosophy, and Popular Culture* (London: Wallflower Press, 2013), 167.

20   Vivian P.Y. Lee, *Hong Kong Cinema since 1997: The Post-Nostalgic Imagination* (New York: Palgrave Macmillan, 2009), 118.

21 Lau Tai-muk, "Conflict and Desire—Dialogues between the Hong Kong Martial Arts Genre and Social Issues in the Past 40 Years," in *The Making of Martial Arts Films—As Told by Filmmakers and Stars*, ed. W. Fu (Hong Kong: Provisional Urban Council, 1999), 33.

22 Ackbar Abbas, *Hong Kong: Culture and the Politics of Disappearance* (Minneapolis: University of Minnesota Press, 1997), 30.

23 Kit Yan Seto, "Fighting Fit," *The Star* (April 23, 2010).

24 Bowman, *Beyond Bruce Lee*, 169.

25 Li, "Kung Fu," 516.

26 Bowman, *Beyond Bruce Lee*, 167.

27 I am indebted to Meaghan Morris here for her observations on Fung's family background.

28 Many thanks to Meaghan Morris, Kyle Barrowman, and the two anonymous readers for comments and suggestions on this chapter.

Index

The letter *f* following an entry indicates a page with a figure.

Abdul-Jabbar, Kareem 166, 226
"About Chu Yu-chai" (Lau Yam) 96
Aces Go Places (Tsang, Eric) 171
acting/actors
    actor action stars 135, 137
    actor as auteur 145
    Cavell, Stanley 146
    character 175
    method 82
    national traits 192
    performance 82–6
    skills 26–7
    typicality 175
action design 128, 130–5, 136–7, 139,
    140
action directors 132 *see also* fight
    coordinators
Action Figures (Gallagher, Mark) 6–7
action films 6, 82
action stars 135
actor action stars 135, 137
Adam's Rib (Cukor, George) 147, 153
Adventures of Fong Sai Yuk, The (Hung
    Chung-Ho) 191
African Queen, The (Huston, John) 147
Ah Kam (*The Stunt Woman*) (Hui, Ann)
    174
Ali, Muhammad 227
Anderson, Aaron 15
Angry River, The (*Gui nu chuan*) (Huang
    Feng) 63
Anna and the King (Tennant, Andy) 196
anti-colonialism 224–5, 226
Ashes of Time (Wong Kar-wai) 112, 208
At the End of Daybreak (Ho Yuhang) 78,
    87, 88*f*
attire 31–3

authenticity 82–4, 86, 102, 112, 114,
    120, 193, 195, 211, 212, 222, 223

Badass Showdown (DeCoteau, David)
    164
Bagua 209, 211
Bakhtin, Mikhail 115–16
Bala Perdida (*Lost Bullet*) (Martinez, Pau)
    164
Balázs, Béla 2–3, 157
Ballistic Kiss (Yen, Donnie) 222
Banderas, Antonio 192
Bandhauer, Andrea and Royer, Michelle
    Stars in World Cinema 5
Banquet, The (Feng Xiaogana) 202
Bartkowiak, Andrzej 195
    Cradle 2 the Grave 192, 194, 195
    Exit Wounds 194
    Romeo Must Die 192, 194, 195
Batman television series 45–6
Battle Creek Brawl (Clouse, Robert) 128,
    135–7, 139
Bazin, André 3–4
being 204
Bergson, Henri 118, 119, 120
Besson, Luc 195
Better Tomorrow, A (Woo, John) 145
Better Tomorrow II, A (Woo, John) 145
Beverly Hills Cop (Brest, Martin) 171
Big Boss, The (Lo Wei) 44, 63, 64, 219,
    230 see also *Fists of Fury*
Bill of Divorcement, A (Cukor, George)
    147
Birds of Prey (Yan, Cathy) 128, 139–40
Black Creek (Lanier, Shannon C.) 178
Black Stuntmen's Association 130
    Highlander: Endgame 197

Blade II (del Toro, Guillermo) 197
blaxploitation films 70
Blonde Fury, The (Mang Hio) 166, 174,
176, 177
Bloodsport (Arnold, Newt) 178
Bloody Mary Killer (Ho Chi-keung,
Godfrey) 173
bodies 114–15, 118
aberrant 115–18
Bergson, Henri 118, 119, 120
Hung, Sammo 116–18, 120, 121–3
Kung Fu Panda 122–3
Lee, Bruce 117–18, 120, 121
materiality 114, 118, 120, 121, 122
and soul 210
technology 212
Bodyguard, The (Hung, Sammo) 112,
122
Bogart, Humphrey 2, 146
Bold, the Corrupt, and the Beautiful, The
(Yang Ya-che) 78, 90
Bordwell, David 15
Born to Defend (Li, Jet) 189
Boss Level (Carnahan, Joe) 146
Bowman, Paul 7, 226, 227
Brave Archer, The (Chang Cheh) 81
Britton, Andrew 147–8, 149
Broken Oath (*Po jie*) (Jeong Chang-hwa)
62, 72
*Bruce Lee's Fighting Method: Self-
Defense Techniques* (Lee, Bruce)
53–4

Cagney, James 146
Cange (*Song of Sadness*) (Chiu Shu-San)
29
Cannonball Run (Needham, Hal) 136
carnival 115–20, 122
Cavell, Stanley 1–2
World Viewed, The 1–2, 146
celebrities. *See* stardom
CEPA (Closer Economic Partnership
Agreement) 86, 196
Cha, Louis 208
Challenge of the Masters (Lau Kar-leung)
98–100
Chan, Jackie 35, 68, 112, 127f–40,
220–1
appearance 116
authenticity 82–3
Battle Creek Brawl 128, 135–7, 139

Cannonball Run 136
choreography 128, 135
disembedding 220–1
Drunken Master 35, 98, 111, 221
fighting skills 136
Forbidden Kingdom 198
Hung, Sammo 129
influence of 177–8
Lee, Bruce 135
opera 81, 95, 129
Police Story 145, 149
Police Story 2 145
Project A 112
Protector, The 136
Rush Hour 127f, 192
Rush Hour 2, 192
Sand Pebbles, The 134, 136
Snake in the Eagle's Shadow 98,
111
stunts 128, 129
Three Dragons, the 112
training 129, 134–5, 136
in United States 128, 192–3
Western films 192–3
Chang Cheh 81, 98, 113, 114
Brave Archer, The 81
One-Armed Swordsman, The 145
Shaolin Martial Arts 97
yanggang 81, 113
Chao, Hing 99
Chaplin, Charlie 3
Charlie's Angels television show 171
Chasing the Dragon (Wong Jing) 226,
228
Cheung, Maggie 197
China 72, 79, 196, 198, 203, 206
foreign threats 226–7
Hong Kong and 220, 221
human rights 220
Ip Man films 228
jianghu 208
martial arts history 114
masculinity 114–15
nationalism 221
China Doll trope 66
China O'Brien films (Clouse, Robert) 167,
172, 178
Chinese Boxer, The (Wang Yu, Jimmy)
114
Chinese Film Stars (Farquhar, Mary and
Zhang, Yingjin) 5

Chinese Gungfu: The Philosophical Art of Self Defense (Lee, Bruce) 225, 228
choreography 83, 97, 102, 138–9, 212
   Dirty Ho 103
   fights 128
   time 174
Chow, Stephen 224
   Kung Fu Hustle 112, 211, 224
Chow Yun-fat 80, 195, 196
   Anna and the King 196
   Corruptor, The 196
   Crouching Tiger, Hidden Dragon 196
   Replacement Killers, The 196
Chung, Stephanie 100
cinema. *See* film
cinematography 212
City Cops (Lau Kar-wing) 172, 175, 176, 177
City on Fire (Stokes, Lisa Odham and Hoover, Michael) 222
Cleopatra Jones (Starrett, Jack) 70
Cleopatra Jones and the Casino of Gold (Bail, Charles) 70
Closer Economic Partnership Agreement (CEPA) 86, 196
Clouse, Robert 136
   Battle Creek Brawl 128, 135–7, 139
   China O'Brien films 167, 172, 178
   Enter the Dragon 15, 41*f*, 44, 48*f*, 52, 53, 62, 63, 66, 69, 70, 110, 166, 224
Cobra (Cosmatos, George P.)149
Coffy (Hill, Jack) 70
colonialism 224–5, 226
Come Drink With Me (Hu, King) 110, 212
Companion to Hong Kong Cinema, A (Cheung, Esther M.K., Marchetti, Gina and Yau, Esther C.M.) 6
Confucianism 30, 31, 32, 33
Confucius
   Liji (The Book of Rites) 33
   Spring and Autumn Annals, The (*Chunqiu*) 31
Corruptor, The (Foley, James) 196
Cradle 2 the Grave (Bartkowiak, Andrzej) 192, 194, 195
Crazy Rich Asians (Chu, Jon M.) 143, 146
Crazy Shaolin Disciples (Yau Ka Hung) 103

creation myths 209
Crouching Tiger, Hidden Dragon (Lee, Ang) 146, 196–7, 201–2, 205–7, 210, 213, 223
Crouching Tiger, Hidden Dragon: Sword of Destiny (Yuen Woo-ping) 223
cultural nationalism 30–1, 34–5, 36
Cunningham, Peter "Sugarfoot" 166

dance 78, 83, 144
Dark Victory (Goulding, Edmund) 2, 146
Daxia Gan Fengchi (*The Knight*) (Tsong Lam) 22, 35
Dead and the Deadly, The (Wu Ma) 112
Deep Throat (Damiano, Gerard) 65
Deep Thrust: The Hand of Death (Huang Feng) 194
Delts, Dan 165, 179 n. 8
determinacy 204–5
Die Hard (McTiernan, John) 149
Dirty Ho (Lau Kar-leung) 85, 99, 102–3, 104
Dirty Tiger, Crazy Frog (Hung, Sammo) 111
Dobson, Tamara 70
"Dragon Discovered" tour (*Eastern Heroes*) 222
Dragon Fight (Tang, Billy) 189
Dragon/Wuxia (Chan, Peter) 89*f*
Dragons Forever (Hung, Sammo and Yuen, Corey) 112
Driskell, Jonathan
   Film Stardom in Southeast Asia 5
Drunken Master (Yuen Woo-Ping) 35, 98, 111, 221
Drunken Monkey (Lau Kar-leung) 105
Drunken Tai Chi (Yuen Woo-ping) 221
duels 49
Dyer, Richard 79, 99, 101
   Heavenly Bodies 2, 94
   Stars 2, 94

East Asian Film Stars (Leung Wing-Fai, and Willis, Andy) 5
Eastern Condors (Hung, Sammo) 112
Eastern Heroes
   "Dragon Discovered" tour 222
Eastwood, Clint 146
Eight Diagram Pole Fighter, The (Lau Kar-leung) 78, 85
"Encoding/Decoding" (Hall, Stuart) 50

Encounters of the Spooky Kind (Hung, Sammo) 112
Enter the Dragon (Clouse, Robert) 15, 41*f*, 44, 48*f*, 52, 53, 62, 63, 66, 69, 70, 110, 166, 224
Enter the Fat Dragon (Hung, Sammo) 109*f*, 116–20, 121, 223
Enter the Fat Dragon (Tanigaki, Kenji and Chang, Aman) 121–3, 223
Enter the Wu Tang (36 Chambers) (Wu Tang Chan) 104
EuropaCorp 195–6
Eusebio, Jonathan "Jojo" 128, 139, 140
    Birds of Prey 128
Everything Everywhere All at Once (Kwan, Daniel and Scheinert, Daniel) 143, 144, 146–7, 155, 156, 157, 212–13
Executioners from Shaolin (Lau Kar-leung) 100, 103
Exit Wounds (Bartkowiak, Andrzej) 194
Expendables, The (Stallone, Sylvester) 198

Fairbanks, Douglas 29
Farquhar, Mary and Zhang, Yingjin
    Chinese Film Stars 5
Fate of Lee Khan, The (Hu, King) 110
fiction 47
fight coordinators 128, 135, 138, 139, 140, 195 *see also* action directors
Fight to Win (Fong, Leo) 168
fighting skills 26, 28
film 2 *see also* kung fu comedy
    action 6, 82
    affective power 51–2, 55
    blaxploitation 70
    buddy cop 171
    budgets 70–1
    choreography 83
    cinematography 212
    cut-and-paste technique 172
    exchange and appropriation 165
    export 165, 172, 202
    French 195–6
    global/regional production 71–2
    hip hop kung fu 194
    Hong Kong cinema 6, 165, 168
    Hong Kong martial arts cinema 5–7, 15–16
    James Bond influence 68, 69, 70

kung fu cinema 5–7, 15–16, 35, 36 n. 1
    language 177
    martial arts 6
    MTV-style Hong Kong action 195
    popularity 194
    real kung fu 22–3
    reality and 46–7, 50–1, 54, 55–6
    reception 165
    special effects 212
    technique 193–4
    technology 83. 203, 211, 212–13, 223
    violence in 42, 112
    wuxia 22, 26, 64, 110, 132, 189, 223
Film Stardom in Southeast Asia (Driskell, Jonathan) 5
film studies 50
    snobbery 6
film theory 15
"First Australian Tour" (Rothrock, Cynthia) 164–5
Fiske, John 82
Fist of Fury (*Jing wu men*) (Lo Wei) 26, 34, 35, 36, 64, 145, 191, 222, 223, 224, 226
Fist of Fury television series 221, 223
Fist of Legend (Chan, Gordon) 27, 35, 187*f*, 191, 223
Fists of Fury (Lo Wei) 194 see also *Big Boss, The*
Fists of the White Lotus (Lo Lieh) 103
Five Fingers of Death (Chung Chang-Wha) 194
Flash Point (Yip, Wilson) 149, 227, 229
Fong, Mona 98
Fong Sai-yuk 191
Fong Sai-Yuk (Yuen, Corey) 191
Fong Sai-Yuk 2 (Yuen, Corey) 191
Forbidden Kingdom (Minkoff, Rob) 198
Fore, Steve 220
Forever Enthralled (Chen Kaige) 202
48 Hours (Hill, Walter) 171
Founding of a Republic, The (Huang Jianxin and Han Sanping) 198
Foxy Brown (Hill, Jack) 70
Fung Hak-on 132
Funnell, Lisa 203

Gabin, Jean 3–4
Gallagher, Mark 135
    Action Figures 6–7

Game of Death (Lee, Bruce) 52, 118, 166, 224

Garbo, Greta 3, 157

Garcia, Roger 101, 102

Gelü Qingchao (*Romance of the Songsters*) (Sunn, Joseph) 28–9

gender 65–7, 145, 161 n. 22

   combatting 147, 148–9, 150–7

Geraghty, Christine 79

Golden Child, The (Ritchie, Michael) 177

Golden Harvest film studio 63, 67–8, 70–1, 72, 110

Grandmaster, The (Wong Kar-wai) 201*f*, 202, 204, 207–12, 213, 226

Green Hornet, The television show 43, 44, 45–6, 105, 223, 227

Grier, Pam 70

Guan Yu 22, 31

Guangong Yuexia Shi Diaochan (*General Kwan Seduced by Diaochan Under Moonlight*) (Chiu Shu-Sun and Kwan Man-Ching) 22

Guardian Angel (Munchkin, Richard W.) 164, 168, 178

Hall, Stuart

   "Encoding/Decoding" 50

Hapkido (*Heqi dao*) (Huang Feng) 61*f*, 62, 63, 64, 65, 66*f*, 71, 110

Happiness (Lo, Andy) 78, 88

Heavenly Bodies (Dyers, Richard) 2, 94

Hepburn, Katharine 67, 147–8, 152–3, 157

   Adam's Rib 147, 153

   African Queen, The 147

   Bill of Divorcement, A 147

   Little Women 147

   Pat and Mike 147, 153–5, 156

   Philadelphia Story, The 147, 153

   Quality Street 147

   Rainmaker, The 147

   Stage Door 147

   Summertime 147

   Sylvia Scarlett 147

   Woman of the Year 147, 153, 156

Hero (Zhang Yimou) 197, 202, 206–7, 213, 222

Heroes Two (Chang Cheh) 191

Heroic Trio, The (To, Johnnie) 146

Heroic Trio 2: Executioners (To, Johnnie and Ching Siu-tung) 156

Highlander: Endgame (Aarniokoski, Doug) 197

Himalayan, The (*Mizong sheng shou*) (Huang Feng) 62, 72

hip-hop 104

hip hop kung fu 194

Ho Chi-keung, Godfrey 172–3

   Bloody Mary Killer 173

   Honor and Glory 164, 172, 173

   Manhattan Chase 173

   Undefeatable 164, 172, 173, 178

Hollywood 4, 5, 97, 167–8, 178 *see also* United States

   action design 133–5, 136–7

   actors' national traits 192

   inclusion of Hong Kong film practitioners 192

   labor relations 128

   normative male heroes 134

   stunt industry 127–8, 129–30, 133–40

homophobia 122

Hong Kong 80, 86, 90, 115, 189

   action design 130–4

   China and 220, 221

   cinema 6, 165, 168

   corruption 226

   film practitioners relocating to United States 192

   handover 189, 192, 220

   Once Upon a Time in China 190

   Once Upon a Time in China II 191

   social mobility 80, 86, 90

   society 176

   stardom 78, 79–81, 90

   stunt industry 130–4, 174

Hong Kong Action Cinema (Logan, Bey) 222

Hong Kong martial arts cinema 5–7, 15–16

Honor and Glory (Ho Chi-keung, Godfrey) 164, 172, 173

House of Flying Daggers (Zhang Yimou) 202, 211

How Wong Fei-hung Defeated the Tiger on the Opera Stage (Wu Pang) 21

Hu, King 111, 212

   Come Drink With Me 110, 212

   Fate of Lee Khan, The 110

   Touch of Zen, A 110, 145

   Valiant Ones, The 110

Huang Feng
    Angry River, The (*Gui nu chuan*) 63
    Hapkido (*Heqi dao*) 61*f*, 62, 63, 64,
       65, 66*f*, 71, 110
    Himalayan, The (*Mizong sheng shou*)
       62, 72
    Lady Whirlwind (*Tie zhang xuanfeng
       tui*) 62, 63, 64, 65 see also *Deep
       Thrust: The Hand of Death*
    Opium Trail, The (*Hei lu*) 63, 64, 66
    Shrine of Ultimate Bliss, The (*Tie
       jingang da po Ziyang guan*) 62,
       68*f*–9, 70–1, 72
    Tournament, The (*Zhong tai quantan
       sheng si zhan*) 62, 71–2
    When Taekwondo Strikes (*Taiquan
       zhen jiuzhou*) 62, 64, 71
Hui, Kara 77*f*–91, 88*f*
    acting skills 78, 87–9
    aging 87–90
    At the End of Daybreak 78, 87, 88*f*
    authenticity 83–4
    awards 78, 84, 87, 88, 89
    biography 81
    *Bold, the Corrupt, and the Beautiful,
       The* 78, 90
    Brave Archer, The 81
    dance skills 78, 83, 85
    Dirty Ho 85
    Dragon/Wuxia 89*f*
    Eight Diagram Pole Fighter, The 78,
       85
    family 81
    fighting skills 78, 83, 84, 85, 89
    Happiness 78, 88
    health 86
    Inspector Wears Skirts, The 85–6
    as *jincao yanyuan* 87
    Lady is the Boss, The (*zhangmen ren*)
       84–5
    later career 87–90
    Legendary Weapons of China
       85–6
    Martial Club (*Wuguang*) 85
    My Young Auntie (*zhangbei*) 77*f*, 78,
       79, 84
    personification 86
    Rigor Mortis 78, 87–8
    social mobility 90–1
    Tracey 78, 88
    training 78, 83

Hui, Michael
    Private Eyes 111, 176
    Security Unlimited 176
Hui Brothers 111, 176, 177
Hung, Sammo 109*f*–23, 117*f* 119*f*
    appearance 109*f*–10, 113, 116–18,
       120, 121, 122
    authenticity 82
    body 116–18, 120, 121–3
    body of work 110–13
    Bodyguard, The 112, 122
    carnival 116–21
    Chan, Jackie 129
    as choreographer 110–11, 112, 118,
       120
    Come Drink With Me 110
    comedy 111–12, 113, 116–19,
       120–2, 176–8
    Dead and the Deadly, The 112
    as director 111–12
    Dirty Tiger, Crazy Frog 111
    Dragons Forever 112
    Eastern Condors 112
    Encounters of the Spooky Kind 112
    Enter the Fat Dragon (1978) 109*f*,
       116–20, 121, 223
    Enter the Fat Dragon (2020) 121–3
    Fate of Lee Khan, The 110
    female characters 124 n. 38
    Game of Death 118
    Hapkido 110
    homophobia 122
    Ip Man 112, 118, 120
    Ip Man 2 112, 118, 120
    Iron-Fisted Monk 111
    Knockabout 111
    Kung Fu Hustle 112
    Lee, Bruce 117–18, 119–21
    Legend is Born: Ip Man, The 118,
       120
    Magnificent Butcher, The 111, 117
    Martial Law television series 112–13
    materiality 114, 118, 120, 121, 122
    Millionaires Express 27, 118, 172,
       175, 177
    Moon Warriors 112
    Mr. Vampire 112
    Odd Couple 111
    *Once Upon a Time in China and
       America* 191
    opera 81, 110

Owl vs. Bumbo, The 144
Private Eyes 111
problematic aspects 122, 124 n. 38
Prodigal Son 112, 118
Rothrock, Cynthia 170–1, 172
sexism 122
shizhan 120
Skinny Tiger and Fatty Dragon 118
Three Dragons, the 112
Touch of Zen, A 110
training 64, 110
Twinkle, Twinkle, Lucky Stars 144
Valiant Ones, The 110
Victim, The 111
violence 112, 113, 120, 122
Warriors Two 112, 117, 118
Wheels on Meals 112, 171
Winners and Sinners 112
Yeoh, Michelle 144–5
Hung Gar kung fu 93–4, 96–7, 98, 99
Hunt, Leon 22, 114, 166, 174, 192,
        193–4, 212
    Kung Fu Cult Masters 6

impersonation 27
In the Line of Duty 4 (Yuen Woo-ping) 221
indeterminacy 203–5, 206, 212, 213
Infernal Affairs trilogy (Lau, Andrew and
        Mak, Alan) 222, 229
injury 137, 174
Inosanto, Dan 52
Inspector Wears Skirts, The (Chin,
        Wellson) 85–6, 172, 176
Invasion U.S.A. (Zito, Joseph) 178
Invincible Eight, The (*Tian long ba jiang*)
        (Lo Wei) 63
Ip Man (Yip, Wilson) 33, 34, 36, 112, 118,
        120, 207, 222, 224–6, 228
Ip Man 2 (Yip, Wilson) 112, 118, 120,
        207, 224–6, 228
Ip Man 3 224–5 (Yip, Wilson) 224–6, 227,
        228
Ip Man 4: The Finale (Yip, Wilson) 219*f*,
        220, 224–6, 227–8, 231
Iron-Fisted Monk (Hung, Sammo) 111
Iron Monkey (Yuen Woo-ping) 220, 222
Irresistible Force (Hooks, Kevin) 167

Jade Bow, The (Chang Hsin-Yen and Fu
        Qi) 97
James Bond influence 68, 69, 70

Janes, Loren 136
Japan 1
Jeong Chang-hwa
        Broken Oath (*Po jie*) 62, 72
        King Boxer (*Tianxia diyi quan*) 63
jianghu (the martial arts world) 208, 209
jincao yanyuan (gold leaf actors) 87
John Wick: Chapter 4 (Stahelski, Chad)
        221
Judkins, Benjamin 151–2, 154–5
Justice My Foot! (To, Johnnie) 104

Kant, Immanuel 204
Kelly, Jim 166
Kids from Shaolin (Chang Hsin Yen)
        188–9
Kill Bill film series (Tarantino, Quentin) 62,
        95, 103
Kill Bill: Volume 1 (Tarantino, Quentin)
        103, 105
Kill Bill: Volume 2 (Tarantino, Quentin)
        103, 105
Killer, The (Woo, John) 145
King Boxer (*Tianxia diyi quan*) (Jeong
        Chang-hwa) 63
Kiss of the Dragon (Nahon, Chris) 195,
        196
KMT (Kuomintang) party 34
Knockabout (Hung, Sammo) 111
Kong, Bill 197
Kracauer, Siegfried 4
kung fu, disappearance of 212–13
Kung Fu Cult Masters (Hunt, Leon) 6
kung fu cinema 5–7, 15–16, 35, 36 n. 1
kung fu comedy 98, 111–12, 115–116,
        122, 176–7
        Hung, Sammo 111–12, 113, 116–19,
        120–2, 176–8
kung fu craze
        South Korea 71
        United States 63, 70
Kung Fu Hustle (Chow, Stephen) 112,
        211, 224
Kung Fu Jungle (Chan, Teddy) 219–20,
        229*f*–31
kung fu master, the 30
Kung Fu Panda (Stevenson, John and
        Osborne, Mark) 122–3
kung fu stars 19
"Kungfu Retrospective Live Q&A"
        (Rothrock, Cynthia) 164–5

Kuomintang (KMT) party 34
Kwan Tak-hing 19*f*–36, 25*f*, 32*f*
   acting skills 27–30, 35
   apothecary business 33–4
   authenticity 82
   calligraphy 33–4
   as choreographer 24
   Confucianism 30, 31, 32, 33, 113
   cultural nationalism 30–1, 34–5, 36
   family and upbringing 28
   fighting skills 20, 21–6, 28, 29–30, 35
   fund-raising activities 34–5
   KMT party 34
   literary image 31, 33
   martial training 31, 96–7
   opera 20, 22, 23, 28–9, 31, 82
   United States tour 28–30
   whips 29–30
   Wong Fei-hung films 20–2, 23, 24, 27,
     30–6, 95–6, 101–2, 113, 131

Lady Dragon (Worth, David and Anwari,
   Ackyl) 163*f*, 165
Lady is the Boss, The (*zhangmen ren*)
   (Lau Kar-leung) 84–5
Lady Whirlwind (*Tie zhang xuanfeng tui*)
   (Huang Feng) 62, 63, 64, 65 see
   also *Deep Thrust: The Hand of
   Death*
Lam Sai-Wing 24, 96
language 177
Lau, Dorothy Wai Sim 7
Lau Cham 24, 93–4, 95, 96
Lau family 25, 95
Lau Gar Ban 100
Lau Kar-leung 23, 81, 85, 96, 97
   Challenge of the Masters 98–100
   as choreographer 96, 97, 99, 102,
     103
   as demanding director 102
   Dirty Ho 85, 99, 102–3, 104
   Drunken Monkey 105
   Eight Diagram Pole Fighter, The 78, 85
   Executioners from Shaolin 100, 103
   Fists of the White Lotus 103
   Hung Gar kung fu 98, 99
   Jade Bow, The 97
   Lady is the Boss, The (*zhangmen ren*)
     84–5
   Lau Gar Ban 100
   Legendary Weapons of China 85

Liu, Gordon 97–9, 100, 102
Martial Arts of Shaolin 189
Martial Club (*Wuguang*) 85
My Young Auntie (*zhangbei*) (Lau
   Kar-leung) 77*f*, 78, 79, 84
pedagogy 100
Shaolin and Wu Tang 103–4
Shaw Brothers film studio 98, 99, 100
Skinny Tiger and Fatty Dragon 118
Spiritual Boxer, The 98, 99
36th Chamber of Shaolin, The 93*f*–4,
   99, 100–1, 104, 145
Tiger on the Beat 104
Lau Yam
   "About Chu Yu-chai" 96
Lazenby, George 68*f*–9, 75 n. 23
Lee, Bruce 26, 35, 41*f*–56, 45*f*, 135, 226
   Abdul-Jabbar, Kareem 226
   affective power 51–2, 56
   Ali, Muhammad 227
   authenticity 82
   Big Boss, The 44, 63, 219, 230
   body 117–18, 120, 121
   *Bruce Lee's Fighting Method:
     Self-Defense Techniques* 53–4
   *Chinese Gungfu: The Philosophical Art
     of Self Defense* 225, 228
   choreography 135
   Chow, Stephen 224
   contract decisions 97
   death 42, 68, 69
   depiction in *Once Upon a Time . . . in
     Hollywood* 42–5*f*, 46, 52
   effective techniques 52, 56
   Enter the Dragon 15, 41*f*, 44, 48*f*, 52,
     53, 62, 69, 224
   exploitation 119
   fighting skills 41–2, 46–9, 50, 51–4,
     55, 56, 64
   fighting style 95, 120
   Fist of Fury 26, 34, 35, 191, 222,
     224
   Game of Death 52, 118, 166, 224
   Green Hornet, The television show 43,
     44, 45–6, 105, 227
   Hollywood Walk of Fame star 1*f*
   Hung, Sammo 117–18, 119–21
   Ip Man films 227–8
   lessons of 52
   "Liberate Yourself from Classical
     Karate" 52

Longstreet television show 44, 52, 53
nationalism 224–5
physicality 114
real fighting 49–50, 52, 64
shizhan 120
sidekicks 46–9, 50, 51–4, 56
studies 50
Ting Pei 69
training 53, 54–5, 68
Way of the Dragon, The (*Meng long guo jiang*) 44, 52, 64, 121, 222, 227
Yen, Donnie 219, 221, 222, 223, 224, 231
Legend is Born: Ip Man, The (Yau, Herman) 118, 120, 207
Legend of the Fist: The Return of Chen Zhen (Lau, Andrew) 223, 224
Legend of the Wolf (Yen, Donnie) 222
Legendary Weapons of China (Lau Kar-leung) 85
Lethal Weapon 4 (Donner, Richard) 191, 192, 194, 198
Leung Chiu-wai, Tony 197, 208
Leung Wing-Fai and Willis, Andy *East Asian Film Stars* 5
Leung Wing-heng 24
Li, Jet 27, 33, 35, 187f–98
    authenticity 82, 83, 192
    Born to Defend 189
    Chinese market 197–8
    Cradle 2 the Grave 192, 194, 195
    Dragon Fight 189
    fighting skills 190, 197
    Fist of Legend 27, 35, 187f, 191, 223
    flexibility 188
    Fong Sai-Yuk 191
    Fong Sai-yuk 191
    Fong Sai-Yuk 2 191
    Forbidden Kingdom 198
    Founding of a Republic, The 198
    Hero 197–8
    hip hop kung fun 194
    international success188, 193, 194, 195–8
    Kids from Shaolin 188–9
    Kiss of the Dragon 195, 196
    language 189
    Lethal Weapon 4 191, 192, 194, 198
    as martial arts competitor 188
    Martial Arts of Shaolin 189

Mummy: Tomb of the Dragon Emperor, The 198
Once Upon a Time in China 27, 33, 35, 189–90, 197
Once Upon a Time in China II 189, 190–1, 193, 194, 197
Once Upon a Time in China III 189, 197
Once Upon a Time in China and America 191
One, The 195
Romeo Must Die 192, 194, 195
Shaolin Temple 27, 83, 188–9
technology, use of 83
Unleashed 195
War 195
Warlords, The 198
Western films 192–3
Wong Fei-hung 189–91
Li, Siu Leung 160 n. 17, 212
"Liberate Yourself from Classical Karate" (Lee, Bruce) 52
Liji (The Book of Rites) (Confucius) 33
Little Women (Cukor, George) 147
Liu, Gordon 93f–105
    biography 95
    Challenge of the Masters 98–100
    Crazy Shaolin Disciples 103
    Dirty Ho 102–3
    Drunken Monkey 105
    Executioners from Shaolin 100, 103
    Fists of the White Lotus 103
    Hung Gar kung fu 93–4, 96–7, 98, 99
    Kill Bill film series 95, 103, 105
    Kill Bill: Volume 1 103, 105
    Kill Bill: Volume 2 103, 105
    Kwan Tak-hing 95–6
    Lau family 95
    Lau Gar Ban 100
    Lau Kar-leung 97–9, 100, 102
    as the Master Killer 104
    Shaolin and Wu Tang 103–4
    Shaolin Martial Arts 97
    skill 99, 101
    television 104
    36th Chamber of Shaolin, The 93f–4, 99, 100–1
    Tiger on the Beat 104
    training 96–7, 101
    Young Vagabond 103
Lo Lieh 105
    Fists of the White Lotus 103

Lo Wei
   *Big Boss, The (Tangshan
      daxiong)/Fists of Fury* 44, 63, 64,
      194, 219, 230
   Fist of Fury (Jing wu men) 26, 34, 35,
      36, 64, 145, 191, 222, 223, 224,
      226
   *Invincible Eight, The (Tian long ba
      jiang)* 63
Logan, Bey
   Hong Kong Action Cinema 222
Longstreet television show 44, 52, 53

McDonald, Paul 79
Magic Crystal (Wong Jing) 172, 176, 177,
   178
Magnificent Butcher, The (Yuen Woo-
   ping) 24, 33, 111, 117\
Magnificent Warriors (Chung, David) 146
*Maid Mulan Joins the Army in Her
   Father's Stead* (Xu Wei) 160 n, 17,
   162 n. 24
Maltese Falcon, The (Huston, John) 2,
   146
Manhattan Chase (Ho Chi-keung,
   Godfrey) 173
Mao Ying, Angela 61f, 62–73, 66f, 68f
   Angry River, The (Gui nu chuan) 63
   Broken Oath (Po jie) 62, 72
   China Doll trope 66
   Enter the Dragon 66
   fighting skills 64–5, 72
   gender politics 65–7
   Golden Harvest film studio 63
   Hapkido (Heqi dao) 61f, 62, 63, 64,
      65, 66f, 71
   Himalayan, The (Mizong sheng shou)
      72
   *Invincible Eight, The (Tian long ba
      jiang)* 63
   kicks 65, 72
   *Lady Whirlwind (Tie zhang xuanfeng
      tui)* 62, 63, 64, 65
   opera 63
   Opium Trail, The (Hei lu) 63, 64, 66
   pigtail knockers 65, 66f
   power, lack of 67
   as Queen of Kung Fu 73
   *Queen's Ransom, A (E tan qun ying
      hui)* 75 n. 23
   as sexual object 65–6, 70

   *Shrine of Ultimate Bliss, The (Tie
      jingang da po Ziyang guan)* 62,
      68f–9, 70, 72
   training 64
   *When Taekwondo Strikes (Taiquan
      zhen jiuzhou)* 62, 64, 71
   market expansion 71
martial arts 21
   history 114
martial arts films 6
   real kung fu 22–3
Martial Arts of Shaolin (Lau Kar-leung)
   189
Martial Club (Wuguang) (Lau Kar-leung)
   85
Martial Law television series 112–13
masculinity 81, 113, 114–15, 122, 134,
   152, 203
Maslak, Paul 170
   Sword of Justice 170, 178
Massumi, Brian
   Parables for the Virtual 56
Master Z: Ip Man Legacy (Yuen Woo-
   ping) 207
*Mastering Virtue: The Cinematic Legend
   of a Martial Artist* (Po Fung and Lau
   Yam) 96
materiality 114, 118, 120, 121, 122
Matrix, The (Wachowskis, the) 128, 138,
   139, 193, 194, 195, 212
media platforms 164
Memoirs of a Geisha (Marshall, Rob) 146,
   202
Mencius (Mencius) 33
Meyerson, Harold 175
Millionaires Express (Hung, Sammo) 27,
   118, 172, 175, 177
minority groups 130 *see also* women
mizong 72
MMA 224
Montand, Yves 192
Moon Warriors (Hung, Sammo) 112
Morgan, Andre 67
Mr. Vampire (Lau, Ricky) 112
muay thai 71–2
Mulan 152, 162 n. 24
Mulan (Caro, Niki) 194, 220
*Mummy: Tomb of the Dragon Emperor,
   The* (Cohen, Rob) 198
Münsterberg, Hugo 15
Musa (Kim Sung-su) 202

My Young Auntie (*zhangbei*) (Lau
    Kar-leung) 77f, 78, 79, 84

nationalism 30–1, 34–5, 36, 114–15,
    190–1, 221, 224
Neeson, Liam 135
Nepal 72
Ng See Yuen 170
Niven, David 192
No Retreat, No Surrender (Yuen, Corey) 170
No Retreat, No Surrender 2 (Yuen, Corey)
    172
Norton, Richard 174, 175, 177, 178
nostalgia 209, 224, 226

Odd Couple (Hung, Sammo) 111
Once Upon a Time in China (Tsui Hark)
    27, 33, 35, 189–90, 192, 197
Once Upon a Time in China II (Tsui Hark)
    189, 190–1, 193, 194, 197, 220,
    221
Once Upon a Time in China III (Tsui Hark)
    189, 197
Once Upon a Time in China and America
    (Hung, Sammo) 191
Once Upon a Time . . . in Hollywood
    (Tarantino, Quentin) 42–5f, 47, 52,
    54, 227
    reality 50
    as sidekick movie 45–6
One, The (Wong, James) 195
One-Armed Swordsman, The (Chang
    Cheh)145
opera 28, 63, 81, 82
    comedy 115–16
    martial arts in 23
Opium Trail, The (*Hei lu*) (Huang Feng) 63,
    66
Out for Justice (Flynn, John) 149
Outside the Law (Montesi, Jorge) 168
Owl vs. Bumbo, The (Hung, Sammo) 144

Parables for the Virtual (Massumi, Brian)
    56
Parmenides 204
Pat and Mike (Cukor, George) 147,
    153–5, 156
performance 82–6 *see also* acting/actors
personification 27
Philadelphia Story, The (Cukor, George)
    147, 153

physical performance 82
pigs 116–17
Plato 47
Police Story (Chan, Jackie) 145, 149
Police Story 2 (Chan, Jackie) 145
Police Story 3: Supercop (Tong, Stanley)
    146
Prince of the Sun (Yuen Tak) 172, 175,
    177
Private Eyes (Hui, Michael) 111, 176
Prodigal Son (Hung, Sammo) 112, 118
Project A (Chan, Jackie) 112
Protector, The (Glickenhaus, James) 136

Quality Street (Stevens, George) 147
Queen's Ransom, A (*E tan qun ying hui*)
    (Ting Shan-Hsi) 75 n. 23
queer theory 152
Quinn, Anthony 192

race/racism 130, 166
    in casting 166, 174–5
Rage and Honor (Winkless, Terence H.)
    168
Raging Fire (Chan, Benny) 229, 231
Rainmaker, The (Anthony, Joseph) 147
Raw Deal (Irvin, John) 149
Rayns, Tony 101
real fighting 49–50, 52, 64
real kung fu 22–3
realism/reality 46–7, 49–51, 54, 55–6,
    114
    grotesque 115
    Lee, Bruce 120
Replacement Killers, The (Fuqua, Antoine)
    196
Revisiting Star Studies (Yu, Sabrina Qiong
    and Austin, Guy) 5
Reyes, Ernie, Sr. 169–70
Righting Wrongs (Yuen, Corey) 166, 172,
    173f, 175, 176, 177
Rigor Mortis (Mak, Juno) 78, 87–8
Road Home, The (Zhang Yimou) 197, 201
Rocky (Avildsen, John G.) 138
Rogue One: A Star Wars Story (Edwards,
    Gareth) 221
Rojek, Chris 79
Romance of the Three Kingdoms opera
    22
Romeo Must Die (Bartkowiak, Andrzej)
    192, 194, 195

Rothrock, Cynthia 163f–78, 173f
    acting skills 177
    appearance 167–8
    Badass Showdown 164
    Bala Perdida (*Lost Bullet*) 164
    biography 169–70
    Black Creek 178
    Blonde Fury, The 166, 174, 176
    Bloody Mary Killer 173
    career 164, 166–7
    casting 175–6
    China O'Brien films 167, 172, 178
    City Cops 172, 175, 176, 177
    comedy 177
    event industry 164
    as failure 167–8, 173
    fan culture 168
    Fight to Win 168
    fighting skills 170, 174
    "First Australian Tour" 164–5
    Guardian Angel 164, 168, 178
    Ho Chi-keung, Godfrey 172–3
    Hong Kong career 166
    Hong Kong recruitment and work
        170–2, 174
    Honor and Glory 164, 172, 173
    Hung, Sammo 170–1, 172
    injuries 174
    Inspector Wears Skirts, The 85, 86,
        172, 176
    as interviewer 178
    Irresistible Force 167
    "Kungfu Retrospective Live Q&A"
        164–5
    Lady Dragon 163f, 165
    Magic Crystal 172, 176, 177, 178
    Manhattan Chase 173
    as martial arts competitor 169f, 171
    Millionaires Express 172, 175, 178
    Outside the Law 168
    popularity 164, 167, 168
    Prince of the Sun 172, 175
    Rage and Honor 168
    reception 167, 168, 178
    Righting Wrongs 166, 172, 173f, 175,
        176, 177
    "Rothrock and Roll" tapes 178
    Santa's Summer House 164
    social media 164, 178
    Sword of Justice 170, 178
    Tiger Claws 168
    traits 178
    Triple Cross 164, 168
    typecasting 175
    Undefeatable 164, 172, 173, 178
    in the United States 167–8
    West Coast Demonstration Team
        169–70
    White Tiger 164
    Yes, Madam! 112, 145, 148, 149f,
        164, 166, 168, 171, 172, 174,
        175, 176
"Rothrock and Roll" tapes (Rothrock,
    Cynthia) 178
Royal Warriors (Chung, David) 146
Rush Hour (Ratner, Brett) 127f, 192
Rush Hour 2 (Ratner, Brett), 192, 197, 202

SAG (Screen Actors Guild) 129
SAMP (Stuntmen's Association of Motion
    Pictures) 129–30, 133
Sand Pebbles, The (Wise, Robert) 133–4,
    136
Santa's Summer House (DeCoteau,
    David) 164
Screen Actors Guild (SAG) 129
Security Unlimited (Hui, Michael) 176
sexism 125 n. 38, 176
*Shang-Chi and the Legend of the Ten
    Rings* (Cretton, Destin Daniel) 143,
    144
Shaolin and Wu Tang (Liu, Gordon) 103–4
Shaolin kung fu 95
Shaolin Martial Arts (Chang Cheh) 97
Shaolin Temple (Chang Hsin Yen) 27, 83,
    188–9, 191
Sharif, Omar 192
Shaw, Run Run 97, 98, 100
Shaw Brothers film studio 81, 84, 85,
    94–5, 97, 104–5, 113
    cliques 100
    Lau Gar Ban 100
    Lau Kar-leung 98, 99, 100
    Tarantino, Quentin 105
    television 104–5
    yanggang 81, 113, 114
Shek Kin 24–5
Shenbianxia (*The Knight of the Whip*) (Su
    Yi) 29
Sheng Wu Song (*A Living Hero*) 22
Sheperd, Karen 166
Shihomi Etsuko 62

shizhan (combativeness) 120
Shrine of Ultimate Bliss, The (*Tie jingang da po Ziyang guan*) (Huang Feng) 62, 68f–9, 70–1, 72
sidekicks 45–9, 50, 51–4, 56
Silver, Joel 195
Sister Street Fighter film series 62
Skinny Tiger and Fatty Dragon (Lau Kar-leung) 118
Snake in the Eagle's Shadow (Yuen Woo-ping) 98, 111
social mobility 80, 86, 90
Song of Sadness (Chiu Shu-San) 35
Soong sisters 209
Sophie's Revenge (Jin, Eva) 202
South Korea 71
special effects 212
Special I.D. (Fok, Clarence) 229
Spectacular Bodies (Tasker, Yvonne) 6
Spiritual Boxer, The (Lau Kar-leung) 98, 99
spirituality 210
SPL: Sha Po Lang (Yip, Wilson) 222, 229
Spring and Autumn Annals, The (*Chunqiu*) (Confucius) 31
Stage Door (La Cava, Gregory) 147
stage names 95
Stahelski, Chad 138–9
star studies 2, 4–5
star text 146–7
stardom 1–4, 79, 80, 90, 173–4, 205
    action stars 135
    actor action stars 135, 137
    Cavell, Stanley 146
    celebrity status 79
    cyber-based 164
    Dyer, Richard 2, 79, 94, 99, 101
    flexibility 187–8, 203
    Hong Kong 78, 79–81, 90
    Hunt, Leon 193–4
    indeterminacy 204
    kung fu stars 19
    perfect fit 99
    power of stars 67
    as product 165, 206
    stunts 128, 174
    working for 101
Stars (Dyer, Richard) 2, 94
Stars in World Cinema (Bandhauer, Andrea and Royer, Michelle) 5
starteurs 158 n. 3

Steimer, Lauren 7, 78
Stokes, Lisa Odham and Hoover, Michael
    City on Fire 222
Story of Wong Fei-hung: Part I, The (Wu Pang) 21, 22, 30, 33, 131–2
Story of Wong Fei-hung: Part II, The (Wu Pang) 23
stunt industry 128, 129–30
    Chan, Jackie 128, 129
    Hollywood 127–8, 129, 133–40
    Hong Kong 130–4, 174
    training 130, 133, 134, 140
Stunt Woman, The (Hui, Ann) 146, 157
Stuntmen's Association of Motion Pictures (SAMP) 129–30, 133
Stuntwomen's Association of Moving Pictures 130
Summertime (Lean, David) 147
Superman (Donner, Richard) 132
Sword of Justice (Maslak, Paul) 170, 178
Sylvia Scarlett (Cukor, George) 147
Szeto, Mirana May and Chen, Yun-chung 6

Tai Chi Master (Yuen Woo-ping) 146
Tarantino, Quentin 56 n. 5, 57 n. 6, 105
    Kill Bill film series 62, 95, 103, 105
    Kill Bill: Volume 1 103, 105
    Kill Bill: Volume 2 103, 105
    Once Upon a Time . . . in Hollywood. See *Once Upon a Time . . . in Hollywood*
Tasker, Yvonne
    Spectacular Bodies 6
technology 83, 203, 211, 212–13, 223
television 104–5
Teo, Stephen 103–4
Thai boxing 71–2
Thailand 71–2
Thief of Bagdad, The (Walsh, Raoul) 29
36th Chamber of Shaolin, The (Lau Kar-leung) 93f–4, 99, 100–1, 104, 145
Three Dragons, the 112
Tibet 72
Tiger Cage (Yuen Woo-ping) 221
Tiger Cage 2 (Yuen Woo-ping) 221
Tiger Claws (Makin, Kelly) 168

Tiger on the Beat (Lau Kar-leung) 104
Ting Pei 69
Tomorrow Never Dies (Spottiswoode,
    Roger) 146
Tong Kai 97
Top Gun (Scott, Tony) 178
Touch, The (Pau, Peter) 145
Touch of Zen, A (Hu, King) 110, 145
Tournament, The (*Zhong tai quantan
    sheng si zhan*) (Huang Feng) 62,
    71–2
Tracey (Li, Jun) 78, 88
Tracy, Spencer 153–4
training 52–3, 54–5, 82, 83, 100, 139
    Chan, Jackie 129, 134–5, 136
    gyms 140
    Hui, Kara 78, 83
    Hung, Sammo 64, 110
    Kwan Tak-hing 31, 96–7
    Lee, Bruce 53, 54–5, 68
    Liu, Gordon 96–7, 101
    Mao Ying, Angela 64
    stunt performers 130, 133, 134,
        140
transnationalism 6, 132–3, 165, 171,
    202–3, 212
Transporter, The (Leterrier, Louis) 195
Triple Cross (Anwari, Ackyl) 164, 168
Tsui Hark 189
    Once Upon a Time in China 27, 33,
        35, 189–90, 197
    Once Upon a Time in China II 189,
        190–1, 193, 194, 197, 220,
        221
    Once Upon a Time in China III 189,
        197
    Zu Warriors 202
Tung Wai 102
TVB television studio 104
2046 (Wong Kar-wai) 202
Twinkle, Twinkle, Lucky Stars (Hung,
    Sammo) 144
typicality 175
Tyson, Mike 227

Undefeatable (Ho Chi-keung, Godfrey)
    164, 172, 173, 178
United States *see also* Hollywood
    appropriation 225
    critique of 168
    kung fu craze 63, 70

popular culture 113
West Coast Demonstration Team
    169–70
Unleashed (Leterrier, Louis) 195

Valiant Ones, The (Hu, King) 110
Vanderschelden, Isabelle 195
Victim, The (Hung, Sammo) 111
video 173
violence 42, 112, 113, 120, 122
Visa 206
Vojković, Sasha 151–2, 154–5

Wang Yu, Jimmy 74 n. 23, 114
    Chinese Boxer, The 114
War (Atwell, Philip G.) 195
Warlords, The (Chan, Peter) 198
Warner Bros. film studio 70
Warriors Two (Hung, Sammo) 112, 117,
    118
Water Margin opera 22
Way of the Dragon, The (*Meng long guo
    jiang*) (Lee, Bruce) 44, 52, 64, 121,
    222, 227
Wayne, John 95
wen 31, 33
West Coast Demonstration Team 169–70
Wheels on Meals (Hung, Sammo) 112,
    171
When Taekwondo Strikes (*Taiquan zhen
    jiuzhou*) (Huang Feng) 62, 64, 71
whips 29–30
White, Luke 7
White Tiger (Russell, Toby) 164
Williams, Tony 188, 190
Willis, Andy and Leung Wing-Fai
    East Asian Film Stars 5
Wing Chun (martial art) 151, 208–9
Wing Chun (Yuen Woo-ping) 143*f*, 146,
    148, 150–2, 153, 154–6, 157
Wing Chun television series 118
Winners and Sinners (Hung, Sammo)
    112
Woman of the Year (Stevens, George)
    147, 153, 156
women 61–2, 65, 81, 145, 166, 203 *see
    also* Hepburn, Katharine; Hui,
    Kara; Mao Ying, Angela; Rothrock,
    Cynthia; Yeoh, Michelle; Zhang Ziyi
    blaxploitation films 70
    China Doll trope 66

Crouching Tiger, Hidden Dragon
205–7
gender 65–7
gender, combatting 147, 148–9,
150–7
Grandmaster, The 208, 209, 213
Hero 207
in Hung, Sammo films 124 n. 38
indeterminacy 203–5
obstacles 167
power of 67
stunt performers 130
taming 153
Yes, Madam! 112, 145, 149, 153–4,
166, 171
Wong Fei-hung 20, 21
films 20–2, 23, 24, 27, 30–6, 95–7,
98, 100, 101–2, 113, 131–2,
189–91
literary erudition 33
as medical practitioner 33
novels 31
Wong Kar-wai 207–8, 212, 213
Ashes of Time (Wong Kar-wai) 112,
208
beauty 209
Grandmaster, The 201f, 202, 204,
207–12, 213, 226
jianghu 208, 209
nostalgia 209
Romanticism 209–11
2046 202
Wong, Wayne 120
World Viewed, The (Cavell, Stanley) 1–2,
146
wu 31, 33
Wu Ma
Dead and the Deadly, The 112
Wu Tang Chan 104
Enter the Wu Tang (36 Chambers) 104
wuxia 21, 22, 26, 64, 110, 132, 189, 223

Xi Jinping 220
Xuejian Erliu Zhuang (*Bloodshed at the
Twin-Willow Manor*) (Lam, Tsong)
35

Yan, Cathy
Birds of Prey 128, 139–40
yanggang (staunch masculinity) 81, 113,
114

Yen, Donnie 33, 34, 121–2, 197,
219f–30
Ballistic Kiss 222
biography 221
Blade II 197
Chasing the Dragon 226, 228
as choreographer 221
"Dragon Discovered" tour 222
Drunken Tai Chi 221
Enter the Fat Dragon 223
fighting techniques 222, 224, 229
Fist of Fury television series 221,
223
Flash Point 227, 229
Hero 222
Highlander: Endgame 197
In the Line of Duty 4 221
Ip Man 222, 224–6, 228
Ip Man 2 224–6, 228
Ip Man 3 224–6, 227, 228
Ip Man 4: The Finale 219f, 220,
224–6, 228, 231
Iron Monkey 220, 222
John Wick: Chapter 4 221
Kung Fu Jungle 219–20, 229f–31
Lee, Bruce 219, 221, 222, 223, 224,
231
*Legend of the Fist: The Return of
Chen Zhen* 223, 224
Legend of the Wolf 222
Once Upon a Time in China II 197,
220, 222
politics 220, 221, 231
Raging Fire 229, 231
re-embedding 221
reception 222
Rogue One: A Star Wars Story 221
Special I.D. 229
SPL: Sha Po Lang 222, 229
Tiger Cage 221
Tiger Cage 2 221
Yuen Woo-ping 221
Yeoh, Michelle 143f–58
acting status 145–6
Ah Kam (*The Stunt Woman*) 174
Boss Level 146
career 144
Crazy Rich Asians 143, 146
Crouching Tiger, Hidden Dragon
146
dance 144

Everything Everywhere All at Once
     143, 144, 146–7, 155, 156, 157,
     212–13
fans 144
gender, combatting 147, 148–9,
     150–2, 154–7
Heroic Trio, The 146
Heroic Trio 2: Executioners 156
Hung, Sammo 144–5
Magnificent Warriors 146
Memoirs of a Geisha 146
Owl vs. Bumbo, The 144
Police Story 3: Supercop 146
Royal Warriors 146
*Shang-Chi and the Legend of the Ten
     Rings* 143, 144
star text 146–7, 148, 156, 157
Stunt Woman, The 146, 157
Tai Chi Master 146
Tomorrow Never Dies 146
Touch, The 145
Twinkle, Twinkle, Lucky Stars 144
Wing Chun 143f, 146, 148, 150–2,
     153, 154–6, 157
Yes, Madam! 145, 146, 148–50, 156,
     171
Yes, Madam! (Yuen, Corey) 112, 145,
     146, 148–50, 156, 164, 166, 168,
     171, 172, 174, 175, 176
Yim Wing Chun 209
Yip, Man-Fung 7
Young Vagabond (Lau Shut-yue) 103
Yu, Sabrina Qiong 188, 189
Yu, Sabrina Qiong and Austin, Guy
     Revisiting Star Studies 5
Yuen family 25
Yuen Biao 112
Yuen Siu-tin 25
Yuen Woo-ping 138
     *Crouching Tiger, Hidden Dragon:
     Sword of Destiny* 223
     Drunken Master 35, 98, 111, 221
     Drunken Tai Chi 221
     In the Line of Duty 4 221
     Iron Monkey 220, 222

Kung Fu Hustle 112, 224
Magnificent Butcher, The 24, 33, 111,
     117
Master Z: Ip Man Legacy 207
Snake in the Eagle's Shadow 98,
     111
Tai Chi Master 146
Tiger Cage 221
Tiger Cage 2 221
Wing Chun 143f, 146, 148, 150–2,
     153, 154–6, 157
women 151
Yen, Donnie 221

Zhang Yimou 207
     Hero 197, 202, 206–7, 213, 222
     House of Flying Daggers 202
     Road Home, The 197, 201
Zhang Ziyi 197, 201f–13
     appeal of 202
     Banquet, The 202
     Crouching Tiger, Hidden Dragon 197,
          201–2, 205–7, 210, 213
     dance 212
     Forever Enthralled 202
     Grandmaster, The 201f, 202, 204,
          210–12, 213
     Hero 202, 206–7, 213
     House of Flying Daggers 202
     indeterminacy 203–5, 213
     Memoirs of a Geisha 202
     Musa 202
     Road Home, The 197, 213
     Rush Hour 2 197, 202
     Sophie's Revenge 202
     2046 202
     Zu Warriors 202
zhenshi (authenticity) 120 see also
     authenticity
Zhu Yuzhai 31
Zu Warriors (Tsui Hark) 202
Zu Warriors from Magic Mountain (Tsui
     Hark) 132
Zuori Zhige (*Yesterday's Song*) (Sunn,
     Joseph) 29